When the Godfather of Poke/le's has been a life devoted to the game a~~~~~~~~ers the world will ever see...He spent mu~~~~~~~~~~~e looks from "respectable" people, while being robbed and cheated by disrespectable people. It is a testament to his single-minded courage that, in this more enlightened day and age, we are able to play poker in our cozy environments without risking harassment, social ostracism or eternal damnation. That's why he's number one and that's why we will forever be in his debt.

—*Bluff Magazine*

Doyle Brunson is to poker what Babe Ruth was to baseball—a larger-than-life giant of a man who not only helped revolutionize and popularize the game he loved, but set the standard for achievement and excellence by which all other players are measured. He also pioneered higher virtues as one of the first respected voices in gambling to discuss the importance of honor and trust among his peers. Brunson came to personify the notion that gambling could be a respected profession.

—*Nolan Dalla, World Series of Poker Media Director*

Doyle Brunson is a living legend in the poker world, the golf world, sports-betting world, and any other type of gambling world. He not only has played in the biggest games virtually his entire life, he wrote what most people, including me, consider 'the Bible' on poker. High-stakes gamblers love to be around him because he is a true 'action man.'

—*Mike Sexton, World Poker Tour Host and Commentator*

Doyle's victory at the World Poker Tour at the Bicycle Club Casino is the most electrifying event I've witnessed in my lifetime as a poker player. Doyle "Texas Dolly" had done it one more time, ousted one more opponent, claimed one more world championship, added one more title to the longest string of poker domination in the history of the game. Before that moment, you could argue about who really deserved to be called the best player in history. After that moment, you couldn't argue anymore. I mean, how can one man sit atop his profession for 40 years running?

—*Mike Caro, The World's Foremost Authority on Poker Strategy, Psychology, and Statistics*

There is only one man who has lived through five decades of poker with resolve, dedication to the game, and an endless passion for the purity of the competition. There is one man alone who deserves the utmost respect as a poker icon. That man is none other than Doyle Brunson, affectionately known as "Texas Dolly."

—*Allyn Jaffrey Shulman, Card Player Magazine*

THE
GODFATHER
OF POKER

THE GODFATHER OF POKER

DOYLE BRUNSON

AN AUTOBIOGRAPHY

CARDOZA PUBLISHING

The Doyleisms that lead off the chapters in this book come from all walks of life and from different folks, all the way from Will Rogers to Winston Churchill, or have been inspired by things that I have read or heard. A few are even my own.

Cardoza Publishing is the largest gaming and gambling publisher in the world with a library of more than 200 up-to-date and easy-to-read books and strategies. These authoritative works are written by the top experts in their fields and with more than 10,000,000 books in print, represent the best-selling and most popular gaming books anywhere.

First Paperback Edition

Copyright © 2009, 2012 by Doyle Brunson
— All Rights Reserved —

Library of Congress Catalog No: 2012933876
ISBN 10: 1-58042-307-8
ISBN 13: 978-1-58042-307-6
Front cover photo by Rob Gracie/GreasieWheels.com
Interior design by Sara Silberstang

Visit www.cardozabooks.com for a full list of titles.
CARDOZA PUBLISHING
P.O. Box 98115, Las Vegas, NV 89193
Toll Free Phone (800)577-WINS
email: cardozabooks@aol.com
www.cardozabooks.com

To my darling Louise:
I never would have made it without you.

THE
GODFATHER
OF POKER

Foreword

The date is November 2, 2004, and all across America voters have been streaming to the polls to choose a president to guide the nation for the next four years. Doyle Brunson and I are camped out in his office at his stylishly elegant home in the foothills outside Las Vegas. He has bet $75,000 to win $50,000 on George W. Bush's reelection. As the sun descends toward the mountains to the west, the polls on the East Coast are closing. And the exit polls have been alarming, to say the least. They indicate John Kerry is a clear-cut favorite of early voters.

Callers advise Doyle of the shifting odds, and that those odds are now, for betting purposes, suddenly 2 1/2 to 1 against Bush. A new $100,000 bet on Bush would pay $250,000. Conversely, a $250,000 bet on the new favorite would pay only $100,000—but it would more than wipe out the loss on the original bet.

Although Doyle monitors the vote on the big-screen television across from his desk, his eyes are not fixed on the set. That is because he is fielding never-ending calls on his cell phone and two home phones. A proposed poker tournament in which he is involved has encountered problems. A proposed $80 million poker duel with a Dallas entrepreneur is in the works. It's on again, off again. There are calls from fellow gamblers, agents, publicists, spokespersons, and officials for a variety of book deals, film deals, television deals, Internet poker-room deals and mergers, product endorsements, poker magazines, and poker tournament appearances. More often than not, he seems to be talking on two phones at once, maybe all three.

Louise pops in and out to see if her husband is hungry or thirsty. The dogs, Casper and Cutie, are steadfastly at his side, sprawled out on a furry white blanket atop his cluttered desk, eyeing me like I'm the neighborhood cat.

Most incredibly, I notice that amidst all this telephonic and televised bedlam, Texas Dolly is playing hold'em on Doylesroom, the Internet poker room that bears his name. I am reluctant to even ask the extent of these wagers. But despite the unsettling exit poll reports, Doyle has elected to let his original presidential bet stand: he will win $50,000 on Bush's victory or lose $75,000 if Kerry triumphs.

And so goes another day in the life of a gambler known to millions as "Texas Dolly," …a single day that explains in large part why a book begun in 2004 was not published until five years later.

No, Doyle Brunson's typical day is not like yours, mine, or anybody else's. But that shouldn't be surprising, for no mortal has left his mark on poker like Texas Dolly over the last half century. No one has played the game at a higher level for longer, or more generously shared his winning insights and techniques. No one has fought harder—often at personal peril—to protect the game's integrity. And no one has contributed more to poker's flourishing popularity as its tireless and articulate ambassador, including his early advocacy of legalizing (and taxing) Internet gambling.

Texas Dolly may blanch at the moniker often dealt his way, The Godfather of Poker, but it is one tendered by colleagues and countless fans with utmost respect and affection, and one surely earned.

✪✪✪✪✪

I first met Doyle Brunson at Hardin-Simmons University, a small West Texas Baptist college that tended to frown a bit on both of us—him because of his budding affection for poker and me because of my fast friendship with campus party animals. He was a graduate student and a genuine basketball and track star when I arrived in Abilene in 1954, but two decades would pass before I began writing about him. That was after he'd become a poker icon and I'd joined The Associated Press, where I worked for four decades. That was also after he'd survived several brushes with death on the meanest streets in Fort Worth, Texas, and sharpened his gambling skills on the back roads and in the backrooms of the Old South.

It was after he'd had a gun pointed at his head and a knife to his throat—routine bumps on a serpentine road that led to Las Vegas and widespread recognition as probably the greatest high-stakes poker player in the world.

It was also after he'd wooed and won a vivacious young woman who naively thought he was a bookkeeper—an accountant, if you will—instead of a part-time "bookmaker" and full-time gambler. Better yet, a gambler blessed, or cursed, with what his colleagues called "alligator blood," a mystic and nervy blend of relentlessness and ruthlessness at the poker table. It was also after he'd gone heads-up against the Grim Reaper, not on a poker table but on an operating table, and emerged victorious by defying the longest odds imaginable.

Doyle had become known in gambling circles across America and around the world as "Texas Dolly" just as he was becoming celebrated in the mid-seventies as one of the best and boldest—if not *the* best and boldest—no-limit, high-stakes poker players of all time. Back-to-back championships at the World Series of Poker only enhanced that image.

The Brunson story is one for the ages, a classic paradox, beginning on a hardscrabble, dry-land cotton farm in West Texas and playing out seventy years later in the glitzy casinos of Las Vegas and the flashy cardrooms across the country and around the world. It is the story of a youngster bereft of physical talent whose work ethic, resolve and stubborn perseverance enabled him to become a gifted multisport athlete—and how, after a merciless twist of fate, he transformed those competitive skills into the stamina, discipline, and recall that propelled him to the pinnacle of the poker universe.

The story of Doyle Frank Brunson constitutes many stories, some of them widely circulated as poker became TV and Internet friendly, helping extend the game's popularity beyond the gambling community and into tens of millions of American homes and countless foreign countries. Doyle's contributions included *Super/System,* the book he authored in 1978 with a handful of expert collaborators that became "the bible of the poker industry." He then upstaged his own classic with the publication in 2005 of an updated sequel, *Super System 2.*

Fifty years after we met and thirty years after I began writing about him, Doyle was still setting records and winning cherished gold bracelets at the World Series of Poker, where both he *and* his son Todd made headline news in 2005. Todd, one of the best young poker players in the world, inherited or embraced many of his father's poker skills and personal characteristics, including his wry sense of humor. In early 2005 Todd and I sat at the ESPN bar in Manhattan's Times Square and watched quietly as scores of admirers surrounded Doyle for autographs and photographs. This was the same Doyle Brunson who, because of the Bible Belt stigma attached to gambling, felt compelled years ago to tell family and friends in Texas that he was an *insurance salesman.*

"Thirty years ago people were afraid they'd be caught in a picture with my dad," Todd said with a sly smile that day in Manhattan. "Now they're standing in line."

Whether with the AP, as a senior writer for the *Fort Worth Star-Telegram* or on freelance assignment, I've had the unique opportunity to chronicle the Brunson triumphs and tragedies through these last three decades. By necessity, he often traveled the wild side of life—but always with dignity, integrity, and honesty. And he did so with that warm but crooked smile and an equally familiar and slightly warped sense of humor.

Journalistically, my greatest challenge in helping him compose this autobiography would surprise no one who knows him well. He simply is uncomfortable flaunting his many honors and achievements or even revealing his generosity and compassion—the very things that have won him countless friends and admirers and respect in and out of the gambling world. Set forth in the most basic of terms: Only reluctantly does Doyle *tooteth* his own horn. Readers will quickly realize, however, that others are not at all hesitant to toot that horn for him.

For Brunson's story is of a journey that summons the most basic of emotions, powerful and poignant, and intimately revealing. But there is one Texas Dolly story, one subplot that is less well known today, quieter, and mostly hidden from public view. It is a story of spiritual awakening, of denial and redemption that, in itself, became a consuming narrative thread in the life of this unassuming but decidedly uncommon man.

Flawed, he is. But delightfully and engagingly so.

"Used to be," he told me once, "that right after they took my photograph, they took my fingerprints."

He unflinchingly shares the bad with the good. Indeed, left totally to his own wiles, there would be more "bad" than "good" stories. But in Dolly's case, the bad is often good—good reading.

So come along on this remarkable journey with Brunson and friends, characters all. Hustle the hustlers with Titanic Thompson, gobble down a $2,000 turkey with Minnesota Fats, blow a $3 million golf match with the notorious drug dealer Jimmy Chagra. Sit in with Dolly at the original World Series of Poker about four decades ago and learn why the grand old man of poker, Johnny Moss, once fled Vegas a step or two ahead of mob henchmen. Travel the treacherous Texas Circuit and invade the Southern states with Dolly and partners Sailor Roberts and Amarillo Slim Preston as they confront bandits and bushwhackers and cavort with curvaceous blondes and archaic gambling laws en route to the Poker Hall of Fame. Laugh in disbelief at the tales and twisted logic of "Treetop" Jack Straus and fellow Texas road gamblers Junior Whited, Crandell Addington, Corky McCorquodale, T.J. Cloutier and others. Go eyeball-to-eyeball with mob enforcer Tony "the Ant" Spilotro and snuggle up in a "Binion Booth" at the famed Horseshoe Casino as World Series founder Benny Binion relates his tales of humor and horror as a Dallas gangster turned Las Vegas legend.

Along the way, relish the wit and wisdom of such poker greats as Jack Binion, Chip Reese, Bobby Baldwin, Mike Caro, Jennifer Harman, Lyle Berman, and a host of others.

Kibitz with Dolly as he drops $1.4 million in a poker game with a dying Paris billionaire and wins $1.2 million in a game for the history books billed appropriately as "The Legends of Poker." Grab a front-row seat for the biggest poker game in history, a heads-up duel at the Bellagio matching a gutsy, charismatic, and charmingly eccentric Dallas billionaire against Dolly and his professional colleagues. At this point you will know, beyond a reasonable doubt and to a moral certainty, why every gambling publication in America calls Doyle Brunson "poker's living legend" and why his autobiography is entitled *The Godfather of Poker.*

And you will rejoice to learn how a dirt-poor West Texas farm boy grew up to become an original American icon, admired not only by poker-savvy gamblers but adored by folks young and old who wouldn't know the difference between a card table and a pool table.

—Mike Cochran

Life is not a journey to the grave with the intention of arriving safely in a pretty and well preserved body, but rather to skid in broadside, thoroughly used up, totally worn out and loudly proclaiming: Wow, what a ride!

—*Anonymous quote, embraced by Doyle Brunson*

Preface

Courage doesn't necessarily mean the absence of fear.

I was terrified.

Not so much for myself but for my wife. I was accustomed to high-stakes bluffing with pots that represented all the cash I owned, and as a poker player who plied his trade in the meanest parts of the country, I'd experienced countless hijackings, killings and senseless violence—but never before did I have so much at stake.

When a man points a gun at your head, you've got to take stock of things quickly. And you have to make important decisions: ones that can abruptly change everything. If you play things wrong, everything you have could be gone, most importantly, your life.

On April 19, 1998, I was faced with such a situation. I was at the mercy of a stranger's twitch of the finger.

It's one thing when it's my life at stake, quite another when my wife is involved as well.

It all started back at the Horseshoe in downtown Las Vegas on an otherwise lovely Nevada spring night, and I was furious. It wasn't the money. It was the stupidity, a mental lapse. I'd drawn at a small straight in the wrong game at the wrong time. I had succeeded in getting myself eliminated from a preliminary tournament at the 1998 World Series of Poker and blown a chance for a cherished gold bracelet. I sat there for a moment, my grumblings drowned out by the sounds of dice games, slot machines, and roulette wheels spinning in my ears.

"How stupid!" I said to myself as I snatched up my crutch and stalked across the famous cardroom of Binion's Horseshoe Casino, the site of some of my most memorable gambling experiences.

But this night had not been one of them.

I took no consolation in the fact that just the night before I had won $90,000 and my eighth bracelet in another of the preliminary poker events.

In fact, I had totally forgotten about the money. I had stuffed the $93,000 in mostly $5,000 chips into a little leather pouch and intended to leave it in my lockbox at the Horseshoe after the game—but forgot to. To cool off a bit, I joined one of the countless cash games that sprung up around the World Series each year. But that didn't help. It was a small game and I quickly lost interest, so I picked up my stack of $500 chips and several thousand dollars in cash and shoved them in separate pockets.

I had nearly $100,000 in cash and chips when I marched out of the Horseshoe, climbed in my car, and headed to my home on the golf course at the Las Vegas Country Club. I drove through the guard gate, parked in my driveway, and walked up the steps to the front door. As I put the key in the lock I heard a noise behind me. I turned around just as two figures appeared from the darkness and rushed toward me.

One of the men was tall and thin, the other short but sturdy. They were dressed in black, wore black ski masks, and carried long, black pistols.

"Oh, no," I thought. "Not this."

Right away I recognized what was going on. As a gambler on the back roads and in the backrooms of Texas and the Old South, I'd been robbed more than a few times. But never in my own house. Such home invasions were off-limits for guys in my profession. The old-time gamblers and hijackers, even the notorious Oklahoma and Texas hijackers of yesteryear, considered a man's home his castle and seldom bothered him there. On those rare occasions when they did step across that line, the repercussions were swift and severe. But these two guys played by nobody's rules.

A miserable night had suddenly threatened to become a murderous one.

Both of the men carried bags, so I knew at once they had come for whatever money and valuables they would find inside. They would be disappointed. My wife Louise and I didn't keep much of value at home; we didn't even own a safe.

I pulled the key from the door and hurled it into the darkness—but not far enough. The tall, thin guy pointed his gun at me and held it there while his partner retrieved the key. "We're going inside," he said.

"No," I said, "we're not." I hoped I sounded braver than I felt.

"Yes, we're going inside," said the tall, menacing one.

"Do whatever you have to do, but we're not going in the house."

He slowly raised the gun up to my head.

"Then you'll die right here."

I desperately wanted to keep them from entering the house, being more fearful for Louise than myself. My mind was racing. I didn't know what to do and had seconds to come up with a plan. I recalled the story of Titanic Thompson, a legendary old gambler who spent much of his life dealing with robbers. He carried a pistol in a shoulder holster, and whenever the occasion arose, he'd fake a heart attack, topple onto the ground, and come up shooting. I'd had guns pointed at my head and knives at my throat before, but never in my own home, and never with Louise's life also at stake.

Unfortunately, I didn't have a gun, but Titanic's ruse gave me an inspiration. I grabbed my chest and collapsed at the door.

"I'm having a heart attack!" I cried. "Call the paramedics!"

That slowed them for a moment. But only a moment.

"I'm having a heart attack!" I repeated, clutching my chest.

One of them laughed sarcastically, reached over me to turn the lock and shoved open the door. They dragged me into the house, shutting the door behind them, and dropped me in a heap just inside the entryway. When the home alarm began beeping, the menacing one spun around and stuck the gun to my head.

"Give me the code," he said.

I didn't reply, but just shook my head.

"Give me the code or I'll kill you."

I mumbled some false numbers because I knew the alarm was probably my best chance, if not my only chance, to summon help. The short, stocky guy punched in the numbers I'd given him. When the beeping continued, the tall, thin guy, the one with the gun at my head, again threatened to kill me.

"I'm dying right here, right now," I said in gasps. "It won't make any difference if you shoot me or not, because I'm dying. It's my heart. Please, damn it, call the paramedics."

He didn't respond but kept the gun on me and waited. After what seemed like an eternity, the warning device quit beeping, which triggered the alarm.

The tall one became infuriated and worked me over with his pistol, hitting me again and again. He broke my glasses, cutting my eye and my head, splattering blood all over me and streaking it across the wall.

Louise came running downstairs when she heard the commotion, although I didn't realize she was there until she silenced the alarm. She had punched in the numbers from the upstairs bedroom. The guy quit beating on me for the moment and turned his attention to Louise. With my wife in this deadly mix, the stakes had accelerated enormously. While I was trying to collect my thoughts, the phone rang. The robbers knew it was the security company calling, and the short, compact guy grabbed Louise and pushed his pistol against her head. I was sprawled out on the floor moaning; there was blood everywhere, but when I looked up and saw this, I just froze.

"You go tell them everything is all right!" he said, dragging her to the phone.

I tried to get up to go with her, but the tall guy kicked me in the face and knocked me back down, again sticking his gun against my head.

I could do nothing but lie there and bleed—and think. My mind was a jumble of thoughts. I recalled all sorts of unrelated events. I thought of simpler times on a small farm in West Texas, my basketball days in high school and college, and how I once considered coaching and teaching careers. I thought about my son and my daughters and my grandchildren. I thought of the violence I'd seen and survived in Las Vegas and Texas and across the South. I couldn't help but think how ironic, after all I'd been through, that I was going to die like this.

And in my own home.

I found solace in the realization that I had lived a long, adventurous life, that I was sixty-five years old and I'd had a great run. I figured if these SOBs killed me, well, what the hell, I'd already hit life a pretty good lick.

But this was not about me now; it was about my wife.

As I lay there helplessly, if not hopelessly, the guy with the gun to my head leaned over, pulled my head up into the light, and stared at me for several seconds. I should have rolled my eyes into the back of my head, or gasped for air. Maybe he would have thought I was dying and left. But I stared right back at him. He saw the hatred in my eyes and realized I was faking the heart attack. He began roughing me up again, and as I tried to fend off the worst blows, I somehow heard Louise in the other room talking on the phone with the security company. The tall one laid off to listen as well.

"Yes, this is Mrs. Brunson," she said, her voice trembling. "Everything is all right."

The operator ignored the fear in her voice and asked for the code. Louise gave a false one, knowing an incorrect response should alert the company that something was wrong and prompt them to notify the police at once.

"That's not the right password, ma'am," the operator replied.

"Yes, I know. This is Mrs. Brunson, everything is all right."

Then Louise gave the wrong password again, and hung up. I was amazed she could remember the complex false password. Despite the pain, the blood, and the gun at my head, I marveled at how my wife was reacting to this crisis. I'd been through this countless times and wasn't prone to panic, but Louise hadn't been in the kinds of places I had and this was new to her.

The shorter man brought her back in the room and demanded to see the safe.

"No safe," I muttered. "We keep no money in the house."

The phone rang again.

The short, sullen robber picked it up and heard the operator scream, "That is an invalid code!"

In an awkward and unconvincing attempt to sound like a woman, the robber said, "Yes, I know. This is Mrs. Brunson. Everything is all right."

And then he hung up the phone.

The security operator must have finally realized that something was wrong and presumably notified police and perhaps country club security. At least, that was what I was hoping. The robbers knew their time was running out, and the short one came charging back into the hallway, cocking his gun and shouting, "I'm gonna kill you for what you've done to us here!"

I can't say my life was passing before my eyes, but I *was* experiencing some serious flashbacks. Images flew through my mind as if on a high-speed movie camera from hell. My mind was ablaze with searing thoughts—few of them good.

I knew Louise and I could die at any moment.

Book II
Texas Years

Chapter 1

I started with nothing. I still have most of it.

I was born to John and Mealia Brunson on August 10, 1933, in the West Texas town of Roby. This was ranch and cotton country, lonesome rolling prairie land roughly two hundred miles west of Fort Worth-Dallas as the crow flies. My family lived eight miles southeast of Roby in a speck of a town called Longworth, home to not quite a hundred hardy souls, one general store, a Baptist and a Methodist church, and clusters of dust devils, small whirling sandstorms dancing across the stark landscape. At its peak in the early thirties, Longworth also had a drugstore and a barbershop, and might have had a population of one hundred and fifty or two hundred people, but that was before my time.

Longworth was a friendly, tight-knit community, and everybody supported one another. If a farmer got too sick to bring in his cotton or wheat at harvest time, his neighbors pitched in to help. When someone died, friends, neighbors, and family members showed up at the front door with consoling words and a pot roast or fried chicken. Like other small West Texas towns, everybody knew everybody, and nobody was your enemy. Someone might not be a real good friend, but he was not a person you hated either. In fact, being such a small community, it seemed everyone in Longworth was in some way related.

The railroad tracks ran some fifty yards from our house, which was good news for the hoboes because my mother always had extra food to feed them. They knew the houses that fed them and always came to our door. This was during the Great Depression, in my early years, when jobs and money were hard to come by. The gypsum plant nearby provided jobs for those lucky enough to get one, but most folks near Longworth were farmers, including my family. We owned a dry-land cotton farm of one hundred and sixty acres near a community called Busby, some five miles from Longworth, and we sold milk, butter, and eggs to neighbors. Dad also managed the Busby cotton gin, so we did pretty good considering.

There were five of us in the Brunson household. Besides my mom and dad, I had an older sister and brother, Lavada and Lloyd. Lloyd was eleven years older than I was so I didn't get much of a chance to know him before he left for college at Texas Tech in Lubbock, earning a tennis scholarship. But Lavada was closer in age, just two years older. When I wasn't out with friends, we spent a lot of time playing together, so we grew up pretty close. My parents had had another son, J. T., but he died of summer sickness as an infant some sixteen or seventeen years before I was born.

We grew up in a four-room white frame home without electricity, running water, or plumbing. We drew water from a cistern on the screened-in back porch and hauled it in the house in metal jugs. There was a horse trough out there that would hold water too. A pot-bellied stove in the living room kept us warm in the winter; in summer, we raised the windows and prayed for a Southern breeze to help relieve us from the suffocating Texas heat, often sleeping on pallets spread across the floor. Air conditioning, which I take for granted now, was a foreign concept to us. We took our baths in a No. 3 washtub that was also used for laundry. That was kept outside, hanging on the side of the house. In the winter, my mother would heat the water on the stove and dump it in, which felt good in the dead of winter; that is, until you got out. Hot water was too precious to just throw away, so everybody took a bath in the same water. The last one in the tub always seemed to take a shorter bath; that usually was me, being the youngest. Inevitably, the water wasn't exactly hot by then. Now and then I'd get a treat and get to go first, but more often than not, I'd have to wait my turn.

Like all of our neighbors, we had an outhouse set apart behind the main house, a simple wooden shack with a plank seat and a hole carved out, a creaky rough-hewn door, and a metal latch to secure privacy. That shack got awfully hot in the summer, and awfully cold in the winter, but since it wasn't exactly a vacation spot, we didn't give much mind to it. We just did our business and moved on.

Our house had an underground cellar where we went many a time during tornado season. Brother, those twisters are really scary. I saw houses leveled and completely destroyed. I know that my brother-in-law swears a tornado picked up one of his cows, carried it over a mile away and sat it down unharmed.

We had an icebox to keep things cold, the milk and the butter and such. (Even today, I still call the refrigerator the icebox sometimes.) Guys brought a big block of ice to our house every day and we would chip it up and put it in the icebox.

When I was six or seven, we finally got electricity. That was an incredible luxury for us. My dad put up some lights around the house and we could read at night if we wanted to. If nothing else, it extended the evening. After a while, I couldn't imagine living without electricity. I remember when Dad bought a television for the house. It was a big event for the family; I really felt rich that day. We went up on the roof and put up a big outside antenna. I remember watching TV and thinking, boy, this is something. It's like going to a movie any time you want to. We'd sit around and watch old Westerns with the big stars like John Wayne, Gary Cooper, or Henry Fonda. To this day, I still have an affinity for those Westerns; those old gunslingers were my heroes back then.

We never did get plumbing. I didn't find out about the wonders of a shower until much later on, when I was a teen.

Like pretty much every small West Texas town, Longworth was a place where you didn't have to worry about locking your house or your car; there was no thievery to speak of. There was no serious crime either, although as youngsters we did what kids do. We bombarded the school superintendent's house with rocks one time, and now and again, we found time to steal watermelons out of a farmer's patch. Of course, if we had asked, he would have given them to us. But it was more fun to run out in the field and swipe them. Out in Longworth, with not much going on, kids had to do something. But none of our mischief was serious.

Like other kids, you had to help your family do the chores and work the fields. Someone once asked me if I might have picked cotton. I said, "What do you mean, we might have picked? We *pulled* cotton." You take the cotton and the burr, which is much easier than *picking* cotton. We sold it for a penny a pound. I started very young, about eight years old. It's just something everybody did. It's the main way we made money.

We didn't have much money, but I never gave any thought to it because we were happy. I suppose I was luckier than most because I grew up in a stable family with an encouraging mother and a supportive father. We could make do with what we had, which wasn't much, but it was better than most of our neighbors. And I had dreams and believed I could achieve those dreams. I knew I would get off the farm, go to college, get a job, make a fine living, and maybe even be somebody someday. I sure as heck didn't want to spend my life on that farm, pulling cotton, living in that lonesome little town, going nowhere. That's what life in Longworth seemed to me, and I was going to do whatever it took to get out of there.

Many young boys of my era believed that an athletic scholarship was likely their best ticket out. For me, that route didn't seem promising early on. As a kid, I was skinny and not particularly strong; worse, I was slow. I matured later than my friends, and it didn't help much that my buddies were very good athletes. It just made me feel that much more inadequate and inferior. As a youngster, when I mentioned an athletic scholarship, even Mom couldn't see that happening, despite her optimism.

"No, we couldn't be that lucky."

But I felt I could.

Like most every other kid, I had dreams, and those dreams took me far away from Longworth and those cotton fields.

Chapter 2

The mighty oak was once a nut that stood its ground.

When I say our town was small, I mean, it was *small*. There were only four kids in our class at Longworth: one girl, Mary Ann Schubert, and three boys, D.C. Andrews, Riley Cross, and myself. We all went through the first nine years of school together, and we three guys were best friends. The Three Musketeers, we called ourselves. We did everything together—worked, swam, ran, fought, and always played sports. The three of us played ball with a broom handle and a tennis ball almost every day. We'd have a pitcher, one outfielder, and a batter, and we'd play for hours. When you grew up in the country and there was nothing to do but play games, you learned to get along and to bond, as well as compete. Being less athletically gifted than Riley and D.C., I had to work harder than the other two musketeers to stay competitive, and that's how I kept up with them.

Every day we ran miles and miles to each other's homes, and many miles more to the stock tank to swim. We'd finish up with that and then shoot baskets deep into the moonlight. With all that running and swimming and playing sports, we stayed in tiptop shape.

Slowly, as I got older, my athletic skills began to improve. Our old dirt basketball court had a rim with no net, and when you shot, you had to allow for the wind. I started getting pretty good at putting the ball in the hoop, wind or no wind. And as my skills improved, it soon became obvious that I could shoot better than D.C. and Riley. It was also obvious that even though they were faster than me, I could beat them in long distances. I could just run and run and never seemed to get tired.

No matter what we did, competition was fierce. Often times we'd have fights—friendly fights for the most part, but we were considered wimps if we didn't scrap with someone. If you grew up in small-town West Texas in the 1940s, you had no choice—you had to fight. That's just what we did. Your peers would match you up with somebody that you were about equal to, and you would have to fight him. We'd go right behind the tool shed, and they'd say, "You have to fight Cornbread today." I'd say, okay, so I would fight Cornbread. We really didn't hurt each other because we never used any knives or rocks, and we would match two guys up pretty close. If it got too one-sided, we'd pull the guys apart.

I was also a Boy Scout, and we'd go camping and play "steal the flag." Once, in one of my less stellar moments, I tried to run through a barbed-wire fence and cut up my legs pretty good. I learned not to try that maneuver again. Another time I almost blew my hand off with a cherry bomb. I learned not to fool with those either. Other than those few mishaps, my childhood was pretty normal for that time and place.

Everybody in the Longworth community was religious except for one guy, D.C.'s dad, who denounced God and all things religious. He was perceived as an atheist and not well received by the community. He was the only person I knew who didn't go to church.

"I tried to go to church one time," he told me, "but you know, I just couldn't believe that stuff and I never did go again."

As far as I knew, he was one of the few guys in town that drank—and quite a bit at that—and that also made him different. That and him whizzing around Longworth in his '33 Ford, kicking up clouds of dust everywhere he went.

Every family got up and went to church on Sundays; if you didn't, you'd soon be grist for gossip. Most people attended the Baptist church; the Methodist congregation was much smaller. Community activities usually revolved around church. We had dinners on the grounds where everybody would gather and sing. Everyone loved that except the kids. But we got to play outside, so it was okay. There were always horned lizards and grass snakes to catch and terrorize the girls. That was a popular sport in those days—tormenting girls, which normally would have included the only girl in our class, Mary Ann Schubert. But D.C., Riley, and I were reduced to merely teasing Mary Ann because her daddy, Willy, was our scoutmaster.

Sweetwater, a town of ten thousand people some twelve miles from Longworth, had a Class D minor league baseball team called the Sports, and my summer highlights included going to town to watch them play. Two or three of the players got to the big leagues, including Roy McMillan, who broke into the majors as a shortstop for the Cincinnati Reds in the fifties.

Besides sports, there was not much that took our reality outside of Longworth, but on Sunday, December 7, 1941, when I was eight years old, that all changed. I learned about a faraway place called Pearl Harbor like almost everybody else—on the radio. We had come home from church and just finished Sunday lunch when Dad called the family together in the living room. Lavada and I were outside playing and came into the house.

"You need to hear this," Dad said. He sounded a lot like our preacher; I had rarely seen him this serious. "Just sit still and listen."

We had an old Philco radio with the rounded top that sat on a table next to our pot-bellied stove. Lloyd was off at Texas Tech, so our little family audience included Dad, Mom, Lavada, and me. Nobody spoke as Dad jiggled the radio knobs to improve reception. Amid the static, we listened to the news announcer explain how the Japanese had bombed our ships and army base in Hawaii and that many people were killed. Excited voices would break into the newscast with the latest reports—the damages, deaths, and the reactions from around the world.

"How could this happen?" Dad asked, as if he were talking to that radio. "How could it happen?"

After a while he looked at Lavada and me.

"Go outside and play," he said.

I didn't immediately grasp what this news meant, being so young. But I knew something was wrong, and terribly so. Mom looked like she was about to cry. The next day, as more news filtered through our Philco, we understood much more. President Roosevelt had declared war on Japan. Immediately, across America, even in our tiny town, America mobilized and prepared for battle. And that war hit home, right in our very house. Lloyd dropped out of Texas Tech and joined the Army Air Corps. He and a cousin, Jack Lytle, enlisted and trained together in San Antonio. Lloyd piloted B-24 bombers and Jack flew P-51 fighters.

Before shipping out for overseas duty, Lloyd returned home for a few days. It was an emotional time for tiny Longworth and especially for the entire Brunson family. As we said our final good-byes, Mom was in tears. No one was blind to the dangers; we knew the risks involved. And then I saw something my young eyes had never before witnessed: my dad hugged Lloyd. No crying, just a hug. I'd never seen Dad that emotional.

Like families all across America, we worried about the war and the safety of our loved ones. To keep abreast of developments, we huddled around the radio at all hours of the day and night. And we all did what we could in the war effort. Shortages of all sorts of staples were soon evident. All available materials went toward manufacturing weapons and supporting the troops overseas. There was widespread and strict rationing. I remember that meat, sugar and tires were always in short supply. Riley and D.C. and I collected scrap metal and took it to a Sweetwater depot to be melted down.

Not long after Lloyd and Jack left for overseas duty, the war came home to all of us. Jack was shot down in the South Pacific. His death colored every thought we had of Lloyd. As young as I was, I realized the most terrifying sight was the appearance of the telegram delivery boy at the doorstep. We couldn't help but worry about Lloyd. He was also a pilot and had enlisted at the same time as Jack. We were nervous enough as it was, but with Jack gone, we couldn't help but think the worst.

And then one morning it happened to us. The delivery boy came up *our* front walk. Mom turned white as a sheet; this could only mean one thing. Dad remained stoic as ever, watching the boy approach our door. He took the telegram, the paper crinkling as he unfolded it slowly. He read its message quietly and without emotion to my mother. Lloyd was "missing in action." According to the telegram, his plane had been shot down over German territory, and there was no immediate word on his fate. The disclosure sent shockwaves through the Brunson family.

The next twenty-four hours were a nightmarish blur. And then, stunningly, the delivery boy knocked on our door again the very next day. The news was better than we could have hoped for: Lloyd had made his way back to Allied lines. He was in good shape and would be back in the air again soon. By 1944, Lloyd had flown twenty-five missions behind German lines and was awarded the Silver Star. And he returned home safely as an American hero. The relief my mother felt was enormous. I could see it in everything she did. Her boy was out of danger.

At least for a while.

✿✿✿✿✿

The years flew by and it wasn't long before I grew into a teenager. Since Longworth was too small to have a high school, we spent our last three years of school at Sweetwater. Entering Sweetwater High School as a fourteen-year-old sophomore in 1947 was quite an experience. We went from a class of four to over one hundred. For Riley, D.C. and me, it was a pretty big change. Some of the more popular kids tried to make fun of us country kids, but we straightened them out pretty quick. That's when I found out that I really wasn't the wimp I thought I was.

D.C and Riley must have whipped me about a hundred times back in Longworth as kids, but compared to me they were big, strong guys, future all-American football players, and I was still only five-seven, 140 pounds, when I started Sweetwater High. I hadn't started to grow yet, so they'd just beat me all the time. But I soon found out that I could hold my own. If a fight went all the way to the end, I'd always win because of my endurance, even if my opponents were bigger and stronger. Short fights, I'd get whipped sometimes because they would break them up before I could outlast them. I avoided tangling with any big football players, but I won every fight I got in—at least every fair fight. D.C., Riley and I didn't fight each other anymore. We always fought on the same side. They were fearfully protective of me and of each other. We were a band of brothers, that's what we were.

I remember I got into an argument with this kid from shop class, and we got in a fight. The kid's name was Don Duncan. They broke it up, and afterward we went out to the tool shed and locked the door so nobody could get in and break the fight up. We just got in there and we fought like the dickens for the whole period, an hour—we would rest for a little bit, then we would fight again—and I can remember my lips were swollen, and his were too.

I wanted to play football at Sweetwater, but I was so little that my parents wouldn't let me. They thought I'd get hurt. D.C. and Riley weren't big either—five-ten or five-eleven, 165 or 170 pounds—but that was a lot bigger than me and they immediately starred on the "B" team. I was disappointed that Dad wouldn't let me play football, but they had no problems with me playing basketball. I spent all my spare time in the gym, shooting basketballs, dribbling like crazy, and improving my abilities. Like I did at home with running and competing with D.C. and Riley, and would later do in poker games, I was relentless. Shot after shot after shot, from every spot on the court, I kept shooting the ball at that hoop. Playing pro basketball was my dream and I was going to give myself every chance to succeed. If I couldn't be successful, it wouldn't be for lack of effort.

It was in the locker room of that gym that I took the first shower of my life—at age fourteen. I suspect my young buddies back then still laugh about the country bumpkin joyfully playing around in the shower like a kid visiting a candy store for the first time. Boy, was that something fantastic, a special feeling. I can still remember that water pouring down on me as though it just happened yesterday.

Despite all my practice, it was a wonder I ever became proficient at shooting a basketball. I had terrible eyesight. I first realized I had a vision problem in the one-room schoolhouse back in Longworth. When the teacher wrote stuff on the blackboard, I couldn't read it, so I would lean over and ask people what the questions were. During tests, the teacher thought I was trying to cheat. I got fitted with glasses and wore them everywhere. I even played basketball in them, so my eyebrows quickly filled with scars from getting hit. Having bad eyes wasn't the only obstacle I had to overcome on the basketball court. When the season began, I was still so little that I didn't get to play much as a sophomore on the "B" team. But in one year, I suddenly grew six or seven inches, and as a junior I was up to six-foot-one, almost six-two.

Like most towns in West Texas, large and small, Sweetwater was a football town. Everything revolved around the high school football team. Our basketball coach was a great guy, but he was primarily a football coach, and he didn't have a clue about basketball. So everything I learned, I learned by watching older players. I just emulated what they did. Another drawback to playing basketball in a football town was that the coaches put the football players on the basketball team just to keep them in shape. So even though I'd grown a lot and my talent was beginning to emerge, I played mostly on the "B" team as a junior. But I watched the "A" team play, and I thought to myself, "I know I'm better than those guys."

One of the best things to happen to me my first year was when Lavada, then a senior, was voted the Sweetwater High School Queen. That became my initial taste of recognition, my first claim to fame—the princely little brother of the school queen. She was a looker, as beautiful as Lloyd was handsome. I suddenly seemed to develop a lot more acquaintances, but my elevation to royalty somehow didn't translate into more dates or playing time on the "B" team.

I remember when Lavada started car dating, I teased her endlessly about boys, because my father always made the boy come in and sit down and talk to everybody. But her patience wasn't boundless with my teasing, and when she'd get fed up she'd haul off and slug me. For such a pretty girl, she sure packed a mean punch. Had I ever hit her back, and Lord knows I was tempted many times, Mom would have beaten me silly. Boys just didn't hit girls in those days, even if the girl was your sister.

"Better not mess with Lavada," I told my buddies. "She'll knock you cockeyed."

Meanwhile, D.C. and Riley became all-district football players as juniors. Over the years, we had become even closer, especially D.C and me. D.C. was the best looking of the musketeers, and all the girls had a crush on him.

Funny, even with our athletic successes, we were all shy. We dated girls in the class right behind us, but everybody was very conservative in those days, and we always had to get our dates home by eleven o'clock. Consequently, we were destined, or doomed, to remain sexually uninitiated throughout high school. That's just how it was in Longworth and Sweetwater in the late forties.

As a senior, I filled out a little. I was now sixteen years old and weighed about 155 or 160 pounds. I also gained strength. When basketball season finally arrived, all those endless hours shooting baskets started to pay off. Playing forward, I emerged as the best player on a very good high school team and became the district's leading scorer. The Sweetwater Mustangs had never won a basketball championship until we won our district, bi-district, and qualified for the state basketball tournament in Austin. That was my first trip to the state capital, and like the naïve country kid I was, I was mightily impressed. Austin was a big, beautiful city, and the University of Texas was awesome. I visualized playing college basketball there someday. D.C. and Riley were progressing as stars in their own right; they were both shoo-ins for all-district and all-state in football again.

In our first basketball game at the state tournament, we upset the defending champion, Texas City, 40-38. I remember one local sportswriter gushing it was the greatest, most fantastic game ever played, or at least that he'd seen. It was a good game and I scored sixteen points. More importantly, our team gained confidence with the victory. We were just a win away from the title game, and we'd already beat the reigning champion. We talked about how we were going to put Sweetwater on the map and how we would all be showered with scholarship offers.

The night before the semifinal game, a couple of school buddies staying at our hotel invited several of us over to their room for a poker game, a game I knew nothing about. I had only seen poker games in movies, probably old Westerns, and never really had any occasion to play. Poker just wasn't around any facet of my life.

They gave me a crash course on the rules, and I jumped in with the couple of dollars I had. We played seven-card stud and five-card draw ten-cent limit games that escalated to a quarter. I won two or three dollars, good money—and easy money—for a couple of hours' fun. I wanted to play all night, but mindful of our big game the next day, I reluctantly returned to my room about midnight.

We dominated the semifinal game against Corpus Christi until the closing minutes when Corpus hit a couple of quick shots to beat us, 38-

35. Again, I had sixteen points. I had seventeen points in the consolation game.

Despite the bitter disappointment, I wound up as the second leading scorer in the tournament with forty-nine points and was selected to the all-state team—the thrill of my young lifetime. My performance even earned me an invitation to play in a national all-star basketball game in Paducah, Kentucky, that summer.

On the long bus trip home from the state tournament, I wondered about what might have been had we won the championship. I thought about the homecoming revelry that would surely have greeted us if we had returned with Sweetwater's first state basketball title. So much for putting Sweetwater on the map! Like my teammates, I was crushed by our loss, but we'd done something no other Sweetwater team had done and accomplished far more than anyone expected in our football-crazed town. On the bus ride home I mostly thought about all the girls I could impress with my newly anointed all-state status.

But more than once, my thoughts returned to that first poker game. It didn't seem all that special then since sports were the most important thing. After all, poker was just another game—it could have been any game folks sat down to play. It didn't mean much except having some fun with friends. Just the same, I was intrigued, and I thought I might like to play poker again one day.

I couldn't imagine the game that night would be the forerunner of a lifelong journey into a world of gambling and a motley and often dangerous group of people. Where all roads, in one way or another, would pass through the green felt of a poker table.

Chapter 3

Don't be afraid to go out on a limb. That's where the fruit is.

After basketball season, I tried out for and made the baseball team. I was an outfielder when I was a sophomore and junior, and a first baseman as a senior. I knew I had a great arm from being an outfielder and I always wanted to pitch, but the football players got that prestigious position. Even though the coach played me in the field, I should have been a pitcher. I was miscast. I could throw really hard and had decent breaking stuff. Our baseball coach really wasn't that good. Sweetwater was a football town, and everything went back to football. I remember our football coach getting up on the stage in the school auditorium during my first year.

"Anybody who don't play football for Sweetwater High School is yellow, and you girls, you don't have anything with the boys who don't play football."

The coach was directing that message at a couple of kids he wanted on the football team but who had decided not to play. I thought that was pretty vindictive.

The one time I did get to pitch was during my senior year. We were playing the defending state champions, Abilene, and our pitcher had given up three runs in the first inning, the bases were loaded, and there were no outs. It was frustrating, and I looked over at the coach.

"Why don't you put somebody else in there?" I hollered at him.

"Who?" he said, looking at me real irritated. "I guess you think you could do better."

He was pretty upset with the way things were going and didn't appreciate my jawing at him.

"I sure can. I couldn't do any worse."

"Well, get in there, then."

I went out to the mound, warmed up with a few pitches, and faced their first guy. I walked him and then the next two batters. That made it six to nothing. I then got my pitches under control and struck out the side. I pitched the rest of the game and Abilene, the defending state champion, got only one hit from there on. It was the next to the last game of the season.

We were going to play San Angelo the last game and I was scheduled to pitch that one, but I had to go to the state track meet instead that weekend. If I had been pitching all along, I might have had a shot in professional baseball, but that was the first and last game I ever pitched. I could hit, but my main interest was basketball and I was running track, so I never pursued baseball further. When the baseball season ended, I was back at the track.

Funny enough, I got on the track team without even trying out for it. I hadn't even considered myself a runner, but apparently someone else had been scouting me out. One day at baseball practice the track coach showed up and called me over.

"Brunson," he said, "how would you like to be a runner?"

I wasn't all that excited about it, frankly.

"Oh, I guess that would be okay," I said, before I could think of a reason to say no.

"You're tall and thin and you've got long legs," he said. He'd been watching me chase down fly balls in the outfield and thought I had a good shot at being competitive on the track. "We'll make a miler out of you."

So I gave it a shot.

I joined the track team, even though I didn't go to practice. I was still playing baseball every day, and was running with the track guys only at weekend meets. The first time I ran the mile I broke five minutes, maybe a 4:50, which was pretty good. In fact, that probably would've won the district championship that year. I ran against the mile relay team that day, and even though I had no idea how to pace myself, they didn't beat me by much—and they had four guys taking turns!

I won every race I started except one, when I lost a shoe. I won district, set a record in bi-district, and qualified for state. I won most of those races by forty or fifty yards and some of them by a hundred yards. The coach thought I was a natural.

Dad didn't spend a lot of time watching my sports endeavors. But when I went to the state track meet he listened to it on the radio. I jumped out to the lead and tried to build on it—that was my running style. But the radio announcer, like most everyone, wasn't expecting me to win with the defending champion and runner-up competing, so he barely mentioned me during the race.

Dad told me later the announcer was only talking about those two guys.

"When I didn't hear your name," he said, "I just figured you got down to that big meet and got outclassed."

And that's about all he said.

Toward the end of the race, the announcer said, "Well, ladies and gentlemen, it looks like this duel was all for second place. Doyle Brunson from Sweetwater is about fifty yards out in front, and it looks like he's gonna stay there."

I won in 4:38.1 seconds.

I wondered what thoughts went through Dad's head when he heard that. He was so quiet and unemotional. Did he feel a sense of pride at that moment? Any at all?

Here I am an all-state basketball player, an all-state track runner, and an honorable mention all-district first baseman, yet my father never gave me the slightest clue about what he thought about it all. That was disappointing, but that was just Dad, and I understood. Mother more than made up for his stoicism. Dad was fifty years old when I was born, so by the time I was in high school he was kind of an elderly guy. When you get that age, you sometimes lose interest in things that excited you when you were younger. That's just the kind of man he was, and I can honestly say I was happy with Dad. He didn't get involved, but he never gave me any trouble either.

He had to be proud of me, I thought. What father wouldn't be proud?

Our high school basketball team had started five seniors: D.C., Riley, Carl Nunn, Ronald Fraley and me, all of us only sixteen years old. Having five sixteen-year-old starters was pretty unusual, and probably unheard of today, when most high school seniors are a couple of years older. It showed what an outstanding group of athletes we were, and we all got scholarship offers that spring. For me, they poured in, more than one hundred of them. My first choice was the University of Texas at Austin, the state's largest university. UT had contacted me about competing in both basketball and track, but I waited too long to make a decision. I was curious about where some of my buddies were going and kept stalling on the paperwork. When I did respond, the university had issued all its full scholarships, and there were none left for me.

It was a stupid thing to do considering that Austin was my first choice, but I suppose everything happens for a reason. It was a turn of fate that probably led me to the events that shaped my life today.

"We'll have to put you on half scholarship the first semester and you'll have to pay the other costs," I was told. That didn't work out because we didn't have the money. So I chose Hardin-Simmons University in Abilene, Texas. I liked HSU because Abilene was close to home, and because D.C., Riley, and Carl were all going there.

I also didn't go to the national all-star basketball game in Kentucky, even though I had been invited to participate. Because of my summer job at the cotton gin, I couldn't get time off to play in it—something I deeply regretted. Somewhere along the way, I started nurturing this dream about playing in the NBA. I thought I had a good shot at making it, and though I didn't play the nationals against the best high-school basketball players in the country, it was something I couldn't stop thinking about that summer. Basketball had become my shot at a better life, so I was terribly disappointed not to have played in such a big game.

But I consoled myself knowing that there would be more games in college. At summer end off I went to HSU.

At college, I wasted no time getting in a wrestling match with a big old farm boy from Abernathy, Texas. Darrell Stephens, a basketball player, weighed about 235 pounds, was six-foot-six and strong as an ox. Here I was at six-two and 170. He bounced me off the walls, throwing me around pretty good for about half an hour. Finally, though, I wore him down. I threw Darrell on the floor and sat on him. Later, I did the same thing with another varsity basketball guy. We were just playing around, but it really struck me then that I had this kind of endurance that others didn't. I wasn't as physically strong as some of those guys, but I could outlast every one of them at whatever we did. I'd just keep going. It was a characteristic that helped me both as a basketball player and runner at Hardin-Simmons. And such endurance would one day prove crucial in ways I then couldn't even comprehend.

I didn't know what to expect from college, the lifestyle and adjustments I'd have to make. Turned out, there wasn't much adjustment at all. Enrollment at Hardin-Simmons was only a little over two thousand, and most all the kids were from small West Texas towns like me. In other words, we were all as green as gourds, and commiserated about our new surroundings in familiar country-kid ways: the usual fretting about the wiles of the opposite sex, which professors were the easiest, and where the party was going to be that weekend.

At HSU, I joined the National Guard, probably because of Lloyd's wartime experience. I wanted to be part of the military. I became a little more disciplined in the National Guard, but the service battalion of the 36th Artillery Division still didn't make me like having to be an early riser, a dislike I would have throughout my life. It kept me out of the Korean War.

Besides athletics, and the fact that I didn't have to pull cotton anymore, one thing I enjoyed about college was meeting people from different places, even if those different places were mostly in Texas. Early on, I was talking with a couple of kids and we asked about one another's hometowns. One thought it was hilarious that I was from a town called Sweetwater and another was from a place called Muleshoe.

"Where you from?" I asked.

"Noodle," he confessed.

I served as co-captain of the freshman basketball team at HSU. I think I could have made varsity, but freshmen weren't allowed to play on the varsity team. So I looked forward to my sophomore year, and continued to nurture dreams of college stardom as a prelude to playing one day in the NBA. But then I sprained my ankle and missed a lot of playing time. Still, though, I played well when I did get in the games, scoring 151 points for the season, proving that I had the skills to play big-time college basketball.

I also proved I didn't have the maturity to handle my off-court activities, which brought me considerable attention. In short, I did something very stupid.

I made no excuses about the incident because I knew better and I was lucky it didn't end my athletic career right then. We'd been drinking beer much of the night and seven or eight of us jumped in our cars and headed out to a nearby lake and—always eager to spruce up our surroundings—started breaking into the cabins out there. We stole all these rugs and furniture and stuff. We took a table radio, and even a deer head off the wall. Although I might have had a little too much to drink, it was like a game and we had no concern for the consequences. I knew we'd done something terribly wrong, and I also knew it couldn't be undone.

And it bothered me even then.

We took our ill-gotten treasures back to the dormitory, which was an ex-army barracks, and decorated our rooms. A few days later, when one of the coaches spotted all this new stuff, he naturally asked where we got it. I lied. I said we had a cabin out on Lake Sweetwater, and I'd brought everything over from there. He looked at me a little suspiciously.

"That better be where it came from," he said.

One day, an Abilene High School athlete came over to our barracks and spotted something familiar.

"Hey, that's my granddad's radio," he said.

Word soon reached the athletic director, and our little group of marauders were summoned to a meeting with top school officials, as well as several stern-looking men who owned the ransacked cabins.

"The only reason I don't have you boys sent to the penitentiary is that I love Hardin-Simmons too much," one of the cabin owners said. "But y'all have to make restitution."

Hardin-Simmons administrators suspended our scholarships for a semester, which was no small deal, and banned us from the cafeteria, or "beanery" as we called it, though we could still attend school. They ordered us to apologize to everybody whose cabin we broke into and to return our bounty. This was easier said than done, because we'd thrown a bunch of our stolen treasures away when it looked like school officials might be on to us. The damages approached $8,000. That worked out to a little under $1,000 apiece, and not one of us had two nickels to rub together.

I had to go back to Longworth to face my dad, which I dreaded terribly, hoping that something could be worked out. I would have preferred a firing squad, or at least a triple whipping. Because he'd never disciplined me, or even spoken out in anger, I couldn't imagine what his reaction would be. Whatever it might be, I knew it wouldn't be good.

My father was feeding the chickens, tossing them maize, when I showed up at the farm that evening to tell him my pitiful story.

I blurted it out in bits and pieces. He never said a word.

"Dad, I know I shouldn't have done this," I continued. "Now they're going to take our scholarships away for a semester. And we've got to make restitution."

All the time I'm telling him my sad little story, he just kept throwing that feed out to the chickens, not saying anything.

When I finished, he finally spoke.

"How much?" he asked.

It was something like $890 apiece, which was a helluva lot of money.

"Don't tell Mother," he said.

Without another word, he wrote me a check. He didn't get mad or even say I shouldn't have done it. He just wrote out the check—I was stunned we even had that kind of money—and never said a thing about it again, ever.

I worked that summer at the VFW swimming pool as a lifeguard and made enough money to pay my tuition. When basketball season started, Hardin-Simmons permitted us to return to the beanery for our meals. I struggled through the semester and got back on scholarship. Not a day passed that I didn't remember seeing Dad silently throwing that maize to the chickens and then saying, "Don't tell Mother."

In college, I had only one serious girlfriend. Her name was Ann Falls and she was a wonderful girl from Ira, Texas. We discussed marriage, but the relationship didn't endure. Ann was very religious; I wasn't. I had gone to church regularly in Longworth, but didn't have the same commitment to Christianity that she did. I just couldn't see myself settling down, raising a family, and going to church and ice cream socials the rest of my life. I wasn't mentally or emotionally prepared for that. I didn't know what was going to happen in my life, but I did know that wasn't in the cards for me.

I could foresee what my life was going to be like with her, and I wasn't ready for it. I loved her dearly, but I think we both knew that breaking up when we did was better than getting married and probably getting divorced later. I think she understood that we never could have made it together—even though I had no idea back then that I was going to be a gambler. She was deeply committed to her church, which was probably the main reason for us breaking up. Ironically, the woman I would marry later, Louise, would prove to be equally religious, if not more. And my feelings toward Christianity, due to events that occurred, would take a 180-degree turn.

Still, Ann Falls was the first great love of my young life, and eventually, when we realized we had no future together, it was she who insisted on returning my ring. We abstained from sex because we were saving ourselves for marriage, which sounds strange today, but wasn't unusual in that earlier and more innocent era.

That first poker game in Austin must have caught hold of something because I started to play regularly at school—and win. For the first time in my young life, I had extra money in my pocket. Coming from my meager background, this newfound cash was like a godsend. I couldn't deny it felt good. But my school sure didn't like it very much. From the beginning, Hardin-Simmons disapproved of my poker playing, and I eventually wound up in front of the disciplinary board five times for gambling. No doubt being a star jock helped keep me in school.

But my main focus was basketball. I aspired to be a pro; that was my ticket to a better life and I felt I had a chance with my developing skills and improved athleticism.

I had waited until my sophomore year before I sat in on my first poker game at Hardin-Simmons. One night I returned to the barracks from a date, and I saw these guys with a deck of cards playing poker. So I sat down. We didn't have any money to speak of. As part of our scholarship we got $15 a month, what they called "laundry money." That was what we used to buy toothbrushes and toothpaste and tickets to the movies. I don't recall spending much on laundry, which usually laid on my closet floor in a disheveled pile, and which I occasionally raided for the least-soiled shirt, socks or underwear.

I had more important things to spend my $15 on.

In one of those early poker games, we played through the night and into the morning, which was the first time I'd stayed up all night in my life. Naturally, I cut classes that morning. As luck would have it, we had a track meet scheduled that afternoon. I knew I couldn't run that day, so about noon I went down to the pay phone at the end of the hall and called our coach, Bill Scott.

"Coach," I said, "this is Brunson. I don't feel good, I can't run today."

"Oh, what's wrong?" he asked.

"I think I'm coming down with the flu or something. I've got an upset stomach, and I feel terrible."

"Okay," he said.

I went to my room, took a hot shower, got in bed, and I was drifting off into a deep, dark sleep, the kind when you're really worn out. All of a sudden—Bang! Bang! Bang!—there was a loud knocking on my door.

"Who is it?" I said.

"It's Coach Scott, open up."

I opened the door.

"Get your clothes on," he said.

"What for, Coach?"

"I want to take you to the doctor," he said.

"I don't need to go to the doctor," I replied. "I'm not that sick. I just feel bad."

"Nah, I want to take you to the doctor."

I looked at him carefully and saw the jig was up. I was the best runner on our team, and he wasn't about to let me miss this meet.

"Okay, Coach," I said. "I'll go run."

"I thought you might. Here's your uniform," he said, handing me my running uniform. "Put it on."

It was a four-way meet: Howard Payne, Abilene Christian College (ACC), McMurry, and us. ACC and McMurry were producing very good track teams in the 1950s, ACC especially. The Wildcats recruited a great group of jumpers and runners, particularly sprinters. ACC's relay teams won many national meets. Their biggest star in the fifties was Bobby Morrow, who won three gold medals in the 1956 Olympics, the 100 and 200, and the 400-meter relay, which he anchored. Though Morrow hadn't quite arrived at ACC when I was running, any time we ran in a meet with ACC, it was a big deal. It was hard to imagine how a small religious school in the middle of nowhere—Abilene, Texas—could field such a talented squad of athletes, and on any given day beat anybody in the nation. And McMurry, an even smaller Methodist school on the south side of Abilene where the meet was held, was very nearly as good as ACC.

My event, the mile, was usually toward the end of the meet. So we jogged out onto the field, which was encircled by the track, and I went down to the end and crawled under a bench.

I was nearly asleep when one of my teammates started shaking me, saying, "Coach wants you."

I got up.

"Yeah, Coach, whatcha need?"

"Come on, Brunson," he said. "I want you to run the half-mile. We need the points."

I said, "I hardly ever…"

"I know," he said, "but we need the points. Get in there and run."

Without warming up or anything, I got over there, they fired the gun, and off I went on the half-mile. Well, I ran my best time ever, a 1:59, and won the race.

I thought it was over, so I laid back down under the bench and tried to sleep. I had just dozed off, when someone started shaking me again.

Coach was coming my way.

"Coach, what do you want?" I asked.

"They're fixin' to start the mile, get out there."

"Coach, I just won the half-mile."

"Yeah, I know," he said, "but you have to run the mile also."

I got out there and ran the mile, winning with my best time of the season again, just over 4:30. ACC had a good miler, so I had to really run hard to win. By then, I was just totally exhausted. I limped back and climbed underneath that same bench. Unbelievably, someone started shaking me again. There's not but one race left, the mile relay, and I'd never run that one.

"Coach wants you."

I was thinking the coach wanted to congratulate me on my two wins, so I went to find him. "You're going to anchor the mile relay," he said.

"Coach," I whined, pleading exhaustion, "I just got through running the half-mile and the mile."

"Yeah, I know, but I want you to anchor."

I wish I could say we won it, but we didn't. ACC had the best mile relay team in the nation, and they beat us. I did run the anchor lap—my split was 50 seconds flat, a good time, considering—but the quarter just wasn't my race.

Wee Willie Scott showed me that day what it was all about, a lesson I took to heart. You didn't fool with Coach Scott.

We won the conference basketball championship that year, and it was a big deal. People don't remember much about the Border Conference and tend to think of Hardin-Simmons as just a little old church school somewhere in West Texas. But the Border Conference, including HSU, then consisted of the University of Arizona, Arizona State at Tempe, Arizona State at Flagstaff, New Mexico State, West Texas State, Texas Tech, and Texas Western, which would become the University of Texas-El Paso. It was a major conference.

Although I had been virtually unbeatable as a high school miler, Texas Western had a guy named Javier Montes who beat me like a tied-up dog. He was probably the best miler in the nation. In my sophomore year, he won the national championship in 4:12. I was back in 4:18. He beat me race after race, year after year. I never beat him. Then again, I never wasted a lot of time training either. Because of Montes, I collected a trunk load of silver medals.

In my sophomore year, the Meet of Champions in Denton, Texas invited individual champions from most of the athletic conferences that included Texas members. It was a prestigious event, but I was excluded because I had finished second once again to Montes in the Border Conference. I was at some kind of sports function one night with my coach when the president of Hardin-Simmons came over.

"Doyle," he said, "we just got a special invitation for you to run in the Meet of Champions in Denton. This guy Javier Montes from Texas Western can't go, so you've been invited. I know you'll be going up against some great runners, but we're going to be proud of you whatever happens."

He didn't realize that I hadn't been winning any meets because I was always getting beat by Montes. Not many people knew I was among the top two or three milers in Texas, which wasn't bad for a part-time runner. I looked at my coach, and we both started laughing because we realized that finally I was going to get to run in a major track event without facing Montes. I went to Denton and won. It wasn't my best time, but I did set a meet record, and in terrible, stormy weather, clocking a 4:32.

That was the only gold medal I ever got in college, except in small meets.

Later, after Montes had graduated, I was in El Paso for a basketball game when he came out of the stands and called me over.

"You know," he said, "I've got a feeling that this is going to be your year in the mile."

"Well," I said, "maybe so—unless there's another one like you over in Mexico that I don't know about."

He grinned. "Don't worry, Brunson," he said. "Every Mexican that can run, jump, or swim the Rio Grande is already over here."

I later studied the training regime of world-class runners, and I was convinced I could have run a sub-four-minute mile or close to it had I followed a similar training schedule. When I was eighteen years old, I ran a 4:18.6—the world record then was 4:01.4—even though I never really trained or had a real coach, certainly not a full-time one. I wasn't even physically mature as a runner. My training? Twice a week I ran around an old dirt track a time or two. That was it. When I told track people this, they just shook their heads. With the right coaching over a year or so, they said, I could have drastically lowered that time given my natural ability, and very possibly broken four minutes. When I was eighteen, no one in the world had done that yet. It was not until May 6, 1954, three years later, that Roger Bannister broke four minutes in a race in Oxford, England. He ran a 3:59.4. He was the darling of the sports world that year, admired and feted by all, because he had broken one of most elusive barriers in sports.

I often wondered what could have been if I had dedicated myself full time to track. I know I had the talent. Maybe I could have made a serious run at our Olympic team, been one of the best. Maybe things could have been different if I'd had a real, full-time coach, a real track to practice on, and a real training program. For years I wondered what my potential might have been, how far and how fast I could have gone.

But at the time, I had big dreams for basketball; that's where my interests really lay and I couldn't accommodate both. I wanted to be an NBA star. And as things developed, it seemed like that possibility was not all that far-fetched. As I grew, I had bulked up and gone from being a skinny kid to nearly a two hundred-pounder in my junior year. I was known as a rebounding guard, averaging 15.9 points a game and grabbing my fair share of rebounds. I was one of the first long-range jump shooters, a new style at the time. This was when the old set shots were dominant, that is, when a shooter's feet never left the floor, making him much easier to defend against. I could also handle the ball well and direct the team; I was what later became known as a playmaker.

Being bigger and stronger was the good news. The bad news was that I couldn't carry that much weight and be a top miler. It had taken me all track season to get my weight down to around 175 pounds. Losing weight that fast cost me strength and endurance. It showed when it came time to compete. That spring, I wound up finishing second once again at the Border Conference meet. I concluded I couldn't be in top form in either sport while playing both, no matter my potential. At that point, it became clear to me where my athletic career was headed.

Meanwhile, our basketball team was in top form, and individually, I kept maturing as an impact player. Our big goal was qualifying for the NCAA basketball tournament, but to do that we had to win the Border Conference. Everyone on the basketball team was focusing in on this goal and we worked hard to achieve it. When it came to the end of the season, we ended up tied with the University of Arizona for the conference championship. It would all come down to a one-game playoff. The winner moved onto the NCAA tournament, the loser went home. I always prided myself in coming through in the clutch, showing up big when the money was on the line. Against Arizona, I didn't disappoint myself or my team. I had one of my best games ever, scoring twenty points and leading Hardin-Simmons to victory. We were overjoyed when the final bell rang and the game was over, whooping and hollering our heads off.

We were moving on to the first round of the NCAA tournament!

Chapter 4

When luck shuts the door, come in through a window.

We flew in a DC-3 to California to play Santa Clara in the finals—it was my first plane ride—and it was extra exciting because we were on our way to the most important games of my young basketball career. I liked to tell people we came within four games of winning the national championship in 1953, which was true, because there were only sixteen teams in the tournament. Unfortunately, we went nowhere in the playoffs. In the worst game of my life, I scored only nine points and we got clobbered, 81-56. I was terribly disappointed at our early exit from the tournament. I had envisioned scenarios taking us to the final game and, after a big game, me putting in the last shot at the bell and Hardin-Simmons being crowned champion.

Instead, we were sent packing.

Overall, though, my season was quite successful. I scored 428 points in twenty-eight games, and was voted the most valuable player in the conference. I figured I would be the number two guard or maybe even a small forward in the pros. I was barely nineteen years old, but I had grown up and filled out, and I could put the ball in the hole. There was little doubt that I would be drafted, but I didn't know how high or by whom. I had real long arms and could jump, and also liked to mix it up under the boards. Fred Enke, the Arizona coach, called me "the money player in the Border Conference." And it was true: I played my best in tough games, except the Santa Clara fiasco.

The Minneapolis Lakers sent an NBA scout to talk with me. The pros couldn't contact underclassmen, so they talked to my coach. The Lakers' scout told my coach I'd be their number one draft choice in the following year. He said they'd been watching me and needed a guy like me to be their shooting guard.

After my junior year, my future appeared about as golden as it gets. *Dell* magazine, one of the top sports publications at the time, picked me as one of the top ten players in the Rocky Mountain states, the Far West, and the Southwest. I was also mentioned on some All-American team picks, which was rare for anybody from the South or Southwest. Most of the All-Americans came from the big schools up East that got all the media attention. I knew I was going to get even better in basketball and that I was going to get a shot at my lifelong dream of playing in the NBA. My future looked promising, like a boy's dreams were going to come true.

That summer I got lucky. At least I thought I did. As the local celebrity jock, I got a job at the U.S. Gypsum plant in Sweetwater, even though the company normally didn't offer summer jobs. Because my co-workers knew I'd received special treatment, I always tried to do more than my share of the work to compensate. The company manufactured sheetrock, and one day we were loading it onto boxcars. The forklift would bring a big stack, and we'd load it one sheet at a time. It was a fairly routine task, and perhaps I wasn't paying as close attention as I should have been.

Suddenly, something went wrong. Terribly wrong.

This big stack of sheetrock started slipping, and foolishly, I stepped in front of the stack, trying to hold it in place. It weighed about two thousand pounds, and it caught my right leg as it came sliding down off the truck. I was slammed down onto the ground, and dust was kicked up everywhere. Looking down at my mangled leg, I saw bones sticking through my skin. Both bones had snapped and were sitting at full, ninety-degree angles. My co-workers were shocked and scrambled to help me. I didn't cry, but I sure felt like it, and not because of the excruciating pain. It wasn't just my legs that got crushed—it was my hopes, my dreams, everything I had been working for my entire young life.

I lay covered with two thousand pounds of sheet rock, dusty white sheetrock powder, and red blood. And I thought, "My God, I'll never play basketball again."

My world had crashed down around me, shattered in a most freakish manner. It was a compound fracture, but it could have been worse. I could have been killed, not that I would have cared right then. I was devastated. The irony was too strong. I felt so fortunate to have that job—a job I got only because I was a popular local athlete. And then in one life-changing second, my athletic career was abruptly altered, crushed by a truckload of sheetrock.

Somebody covered me with a blanket, like they do dead bodies. It felt appropriate. Hell, they could have buried me right there and I wouldn't have argued. I was in shock and numbed by pain. The ambulance rushed me to the hospital and a local doctor set my leg. It was smashed up so bad the nurses brought X-rays to show me what a wonderful job the doctor had done. I thought it was a good job, and I felt a dim stirring of hope. For a while, even my coach was optimistic.

"You know," he said, "you made most of your shots from the outside anyway, so you'll be able to play. You might not be able to drive in there like you used to, but you'll be able to sit out there and shoot at least."

An insurance adjuster came to see me at the hospital.

"We'll fly a top orthopedic specialist in here if you want us to," he said.

"No," I told him. "Everyone says the doctor's done a wonderful job, so I don't think that's necessary."

I had decided to sit out my senior year and play the next. That was my plan. I hobbled about campus on crutches my entire senior year, nursing a fervent hope of playing basketball again. But it became increasingly clear that the "wonderful job" the country doctor had done on my leg hadn't, in fact, turned out so wonderfully after all.

I went to an orthopedist to have my leg rebroken and undergo a bone graft. That's when I knew my basketball career—my childhood dreams of playing in the NBA, my ticket to fame—were all dashed. I can't say it came as a complete surprise. I had been on an emotional roller-coaster for a year, wondering if I was ever going to play again. This was just another dip, though a severe one.

All the while, I wondered: Why did it have to happen to me? All that athletic promise gone to waste. *My* athletic talent!

I began to look for someone to blame. First, myself. After all, when the insurance man asked if I wanted a top specialist to examine and possibly reset my leg, I'm the one who said no, the local doc had done a fine job. Afterward, I thought Dad should have stepped in and overruled me. But he had grown up in the country and, despite a year of college, wasn't really an educated man. He was accustomed to accepting the decisions of the doctors in Sweetwater, and our local physician was highly respected. All the nurses and everybody were talking about what a wonderful job he'd done. Dad probably didn't know what an orthopedic surgeon was, but I wish he had called in a specialist because it might have saved my leg. Then again, if that had happened, I wouldn't have lived the life I've lived.

Maybe, if it was a blessing in disguise—but at the time, I sure as hell I didn't see it that way.

The *Abilene Reporter-News* had christened the nucleus of our Hardin-Simmons basketball team the "3Bs"—Wade Burroughs, Tom Burks, and me—and our fate had run a cruel course. Burroughs, Burks, and Brunson were supposed to reverse the Hardin-Simmons basketball fortunes. We had been all-state players in high school. Wade's career was ruined in a freak accident one day by the swimming pool. Some of the other basketball players were swinging a broomstick at a ping-pong ball and the stick snapped in half. One piece flew across the pool and hit Wade in the face, putting an eye out. He continued to play, but was never the same. Then Tom got cancer of the kidney, which ended his dreams.

Here we were, the heart of HSU basketball, and not one of us completed his sports career successfully.

Though my athletic career cratered, I looked back with pride at what five sixteen-year-olds from Sweetwater High had accomplished—four of them at Hardin-Simmons. D.C. and Riley both made all-conference in football. In fact, D.C. made some All-American teams. Sammy Baugh called D.C. the best college end he'd ever seen, which was a pretty good compliment coming from one of the game's greatest players and most popular coaches. Carl Nunn won the national tennis championship, the NAIA, twice. I was all-conference in basketball and named the most valuable player in the conference. And the other starter on our high school team, Ronald Fraley, was an All-Southwest Conference halfback at TCU for two years. He even landed on the all-time SWC team.

So that was five kids from the small West Texas town of Sweetwater who had made a nice-sized splash in intercollegiate athletics and helped put tiny Longworth on the map.

During our bull sessions at Hardin-Simmons, with friends like Bill Neal, Scoop McPherson, Shag Henson, and others, we'd sit around and talk about what we wanted to do. Scoop wanted to be a writer. Neal was a writer, but he wanted to be a politician. I simply wanted to make a lot of money.

"How you gonna do that?" they asked.

"I don't know," I said.

But I had the drive, the inspiration. I had emerged from a poor background and wanted something better. At some point I was aware that successful gamblers had what I considered a lot of money. I wanted to be one of them. But to be safe, I had to rely on what a good education might give me. At least I thought I did.

I returned to HSU to get my master's degree in administrative education and business administration—a level of education that wasn't all that common in the 1950s—because I still wanted to live a better life than the one I'd known on the farm. Ambition compelled me to stay in school. A master's degree suggested certain values and character and it reflected on the kind of person you were or wanted to be. As an undergraduate—in fact, all my life—I had just barely gotten by grade-wise. Now, I started preparing for class and studying, and it was a new world. I began making straight As. I even taught a class on money and banking, which was kind of a hoot given my farm-boy background.

While getting my master's, I started playing poker a little more seriously, mostly because I had no money. I played in local poker games around the campus. I also had friends in many of the universities around the state—Texas A&M, the University of Texas, Texas Tech—where they always had weekend poker games in the dorms. I frequently attended those games and I won money on nearly every trip. Joe Youngblood, an all-state football player from Abilene, was down at the University of Texas, and that was generally my main place to play.

Those weekend poker games were my financial aid package, my scholarship for getting through graduate school. I was using the game as a tool to prepare for a different life. Funny, as fate would have it, it *would* be my life. The broken leg, of course, had changed everything. After I got my master's degree, I considered going into coaching. My roommate, Tom Burks, had gone to work in Anson, another little town in West Texas, coaching basketball and teaching biology for $2,400 a year. With a master's degree, I got an offer for $4,000 from Dalhart, up in the Texas Panhandle.

"Well, that doesn't make much sense," I thought, reasoning that I'd put enough effort into my education to target loftier goals. So I decided to go into the business world. I went to work for Burroughs Corporation selling adding machines and bookkeeping equipment. That was how I discovered the rowdy north side of Fort Worth, the most dangerous place I had ever seen.

In my wildest dreams, I couldn't have imagined where a job selling business equipment would lead.

Chapter 5

When you live life on the edge, you run the risk of falling over it.

My career as a Burroughs salesman was spectacular—spectacularly awful. On my very first sales call, I marched into this office in north Fort Worth and approached the owner with all the brashness of a guy with a new master's degree in business administration.

"Hello, I'm Doyle Brunson from Burroughs Corporation. I'd like to see if you have any interest in a new adding machine or cash register."

The man behind the counter, the owner, didn't say a word. He just looked at me, pointed at the door and turned around. Sufficiently demoralized, I didn't make another call that day. A short time after that humbling initiation, I was calling on a client, a pool-hall owner, when I stumbled onto a poker game going on in the back room. They were playing lowball draw and five-card stud, two of my better games. Instead of hawking my products, I sat in and cleared a month's salary in less than three hours.

"My God!" I said to myself. "What am I doing trying to sell business machines nobody wants to buy when I can sit down at a poker table and make ten times the money in a fraction of the time?"

I didn't need one of Burroughs' machines to tell me those numbers didn't add up. So I quit. Of course, my departure was hardly a staggering loss to the Burroughs folks. In the seven months of training as a salesman—at $75 a week and fifteen cents a mile in expenses—I hadn't sold a single adding machine. Or anything else, for that matter. My Burroughs experience was discouraging, but through it, I had stumbled onto something that changed my life and led to where I am today. My destiny was launched.

Who knows if I would have reached this path through some other means, if becoming a professional poker player was the master plan for my life. I can't rightly say, but once I found that backroom poker game, there was no turning back. A poker player was born.

My fledgling poker career was no different than my athletic career or anything else I did. I was addicted, obsessed. I put everything I had, all my energies, into my new vocation. Had I been married and bogged down with family, I never would have gotten into poker like I did. I couldn't have. But here I was, a single guy with no responsibilities. I knew my parents wouldn't approve of this lifestyle, but I reckon I was destined to be a gambler. It just seemed right to me at the time.

The game of poker led me to Exchange Avenue, one of the toughest, meanest streets in America. It knifed through the heart of the old Stockyards area of north Fort Worth, and was overrun with saloons and pool halls and crooks and drunks and a colorful mélange of off-the-wall characters, including cowboy types and women in tight jeans searching for good-looking cowboy types. Poker games were always going on along Exchange, the most popular games being in the back rooms of the bars and up along the hill by the old Hereford Hotel. There were probably as many craps games going on as poker games. Back in the early to mid-fifties, we played a lot of deuce-to-seven lowball, ace-to-five lowball, five-card stud, and five-card high draw—these were the main games. Hold'em wasn't played yet; at the time, no one had ever heard of the game. While gambling was illegal, the operators of the games routinely paid the street cops to leave them alone. About the only time we saw the cops was during robberies and shootings.

Exchange Avenue was my introduction to a sinister, often evil, and always dangerous element. And with the kind of crowd that frequented these games in the mid-1950s—thieves, thugs, pimps, drug dealers, killers, con men and some working guys who were the "producers" bringing money to the table—it was never boring. I saw things I'd never seen before, things I never even dreamed could happen. It was a new world and exciting, to say the least.

Over the next year on Exchange Avenue, I may never have seen the sun. I slept all day and played all night—every night. I played almost every waking hour. I didn't even watch basketball. My life was nothing but poker. Well, maybe girls too.

Two young guys about my age, Wayne Hamilton and David Vernon, were my running mates during those years. I met them in a pool hall one day and we started making the rounds together, playing poker and pool. We didn't do anything but gamble, whereas many of their associates had additional and quite dubious occupations. The good thing about running with David and Wayne was that they grew up on Fort Worth's north side and knew all the thieves, pimps, and killers, so they always vouched for me, which provided a bit more security in that treacherous environment. The three of us were accepted because we were gamblers; and while we weren't robbing or killing folks like the people we played poker with, our crooked colleagues knew we wouldn't rat them out to the law.

Most everyone was young and we were all dedicated to chasing women and partying together on the Jacksboro Highway, which was maybe a meaner street than even Exchange Avenue. Back then, it was lined with saloons and gambling dens from almost downtown Fort Worth to Lake Worth on the northwest edge of the city, an area that ran for about six or seven miles.

I read once where most of the murders out there went unsolved. I didn't need to see that in print to know that this was the case. Many of the underworld figures we ran with were immortalized in a book by Ann Arnold, *Gamblers & Gangsters: Fort Worth's Jacksboro Highway in the 1940s & 1950s.* Arnold told the *Fort Worth Star-Telegram* her literary fire was lit after reading a book called *Hell's Half Acre,* a historic account depicting Fort Worth in the latter part of the nineteenth century. That's when larger-than-life characters like Wyatt Earp, Doc Holliday, Butch Cassidy, the Sundance Kid, and others were attracted to the area dubbed by locals as "Hell's Half Acre," or more prosaically, the city's red-light district.

The forties and fifties had ushered in a new era and a new breed of gamblers, outlaws, and characters. One of the unusual ones was Elmer Sharp, who looked like a short, fat, muscular floor safe. Elmer kept a pet bear at the "private club" he ran illegally out of his garage, and if business or brawling was slow, he'd just wrestle that damn bear. They claimed the only person in town tougher than Elmer was his mama.

It was here that I played my longest session, five days and five nights without sleeping. I only stopped to eat and go to the bathroom. I didn't do drugs like some of the others, but drank tons of coffee to stay awake. After the fourth day of play, we were playing ace-to-five no-limit lowball with Virgil, an employee of the local slaughterhouse who had been playing as long as I had. The difference was he was taking pills to stay awake. Also, he was drinking heavily and smoking one cigarette after another. I didn't think that was the healthiest mixture of things he could ingest. I had known Virgil for a year or so and I had cautioned him about taking drugs and drinking at the same time.

We played a lowball hand together to the showdown and I called Virgil's all-in bet with a 7-5-4-2-A.

Virgil said: "I don't have a five in mine" and turned over A-2-3-4-7, a pretty strong hand.

I said, "That's good."

Virgil took a drink of Old Charter Whisky, reached for the pot, and dropped dead right on the spot.

That's when I found out how cold-blooded poker players can be. All of us had known Virgil and had played with him many times. After the paramedics took him away, the game resumed, and we played another twenty-four hours.

I was playing poker at this after-hours joint on the Jacksboro Highway another night when a friend of mine got drunk and out of line. He walked up to a cowboy and said, "Cowboys don't wear their hats like that; they wear them like this." And he pulled the hat down over the guy's ears and walked outside. The cowboy and his buddies followed and the inevitable brawl broke out. I had to fight one of the cowboy's sidekicks for a while, but we quickly realized my friend had cut up the cowboy pretty badly with a knife, and he was bleeding all over everything. We quit fighting to help him.

He didn't die, but my buddy went to jail, though only briefly. No charges were ever filed. That's the way it was out on Jacksboro. Violence was embedded in the fabric of Exchange Avenue and the Bloodthirsty Highway—that was another name for the road to Jacksboro in northwest Texas. That's where I played poker, and those were the kinds of people who were gambling. I knew what they did, and I knew their lifestyle. But that was their business, not mine. My business was only inside the poker room. They were personable guys, fun to party with, and we got to know one another really well. You spend that many hours jammed around a small table in a dingy smoke-filled room, day after day, you get to know people real well. But like I said, outside the cardroom, I did my thing, they did theirs. They were the players in the games and that's where I made my living.

One thing I can say about my fellow poker players, they were never dull. Nor were those poker games. You never knew what would happen, but you sure as heck knew something would. And it often wouldn't be pretty for someone. Like they say about bull riders and their injuries: It's not if, it's when.

I knew the kind of people they were and what they were capable of doing, but as long as you kept on the straight and narrow with them, you'd be accepted. And you'd stay out of trouble. For the most part. With that kind of crowd, something was always brewing, and you couldn't always get out of the kitchen before something got burnt.

The money they won or stole, or whatever they did to get it, they brought to the poker games. I was there to win that money, and they were there to win mine. That's poker. Wayne and David and I were much better players than our crooked cohorts and we regularly relieved them of their ill-gotten gains. Then they'd go steal more money, come scurrying back, and we'd break them again.

In a funny way, it seemed like we were contributing indirectly to the city's crime scene. I realized all too well that it was an unhealthy and unseemly existence, but we were young and single and it was about the most profitable game in town that I knew about. And the most exciting. I realized even back then that I craved action, something that probably went back to my athletic career when I was constantly competing, constantly in the middle of things.

Nearly all my Exchange Street pals smoked marijuana. One time they gave me a joint, so I smoked it. I just sat there and stared at the wall, totally numb. I couldn't imagine why on earth anybody would want to feel like that. It wasn't nearly as much fun as having a drink and a good time. That was my only experience with dope. To me, the greater danger was that marijuana usually progressed to heroin and cocaine and other drugs. Invariably, when guys got on drugs, it accelerated from bad to worse, causing them to do things they ordinarily wouldn't do. At least, that's the way it was with the people I knew. And I saw this kind of stuff all the time.

As a young man in that environment, I started hating all drugs, seeing what they were doing to my friends, and I began to take a perverse pleasure in getting drug dealers into our poker games and winning their money. And I did plenty of that.

Whenever the people down at Exchange Avenue got angry at one another, they didn't go out and fight like we did in college and high school—maybe have a fistfight or a wrestling match, maybe get a bloody nose or something—they just killed each other. All of these poker players carried weapons, knives or pistols, and a lot of them did drugs. It was a volatile bunch of guys, and when they weren't killing other people or each other, they were getting carted off to jail for some crime or another.

Shootings, knife fights, and fistfights happened every day down there and were actually expected.

One night we were playing poker in the back of a pool hall on Exchange. There were two tables. I was playing at one table and a guy seven or eight feet from me was playing at the other. I remember we were playing in a 50¢ ante, $2/$4 blind game, half ace-to-five lowball and half five-card draw high. About midnight, a distraught husband walked into the back room and calmly pulled a pistol, put it up to one of the poker player's heads and shot him right through the brain. He then turned and left the room. I was in the middle of a draw high pot and had just bet $20 when the shooting happened. I had aces and sevens when this occurred. I have always called this hand "Next to the Dead Man's Hand," referencing Wild Bill Hickok's famous aces-and-eights dead man's hand.

"Let's get the hell out of here!" one of the guys screamed, and we all jumped up and ran out the back door and into a creek that ran along the back of the pool hall. I splashed through that creek like a madman. I still remember how cold that water was. I also knew I wouldn't quickly forget seeing that guy get shot and killed. We fled not so much out of fear of the gunman, but out of fear of the police.

It was an illegal poker game—they all were—and we knew if we hung around we would probably get arrested, and definitely questioned. Only under extreme duress did we talk about such things with the police. There was an inviolate, if unwritten, rule that you didn't rat out people.

Another night I saw a man get stabbed in a bar. He ran out the door and down the street, and for some reason I ran along behind him. I didn't know whether I was going to try to help him or what, but I heard him calling out. I recalled that when someone thought he was about to die violently, he'd beg for help and forgiveness from the Almighty. That's what happened here.

"Oh God, please help me!" he cried, and then he fell down dead.

One day I saw what looked like an "O.K. Corral" shootout on Exchange Avenue. All the shooters were behind cars and firing away, and I saw two of them gunned down. Both died, and both were friends of mine.

And I could do nothing but stand there and watch them die. It was horrible, and I wondered again how I got caught up in such an atmosphere of violence, death, and criminal activity.

The police seemed disinclined to seriously investigate such shootings. They'd come to the crime scene and make a report, but that's about all they'd do. I never saw much of an attempt to solve the murders. Like it was open season on those underworld guys: The police seemed glad to rid themselves of that element and would just let the underworld figures kill each other off. I think it was easier for them that way. In her book, Arnold said there were sixteen unsolved gangland killings over the two-decade period of the forties and fifties, but unofficially, I knew there were many more. There were people fighting each other over crooked business transactions and drug deals gone bad, but usually, it was over a woman. And like I said, the police stayed out of it. The crime and corruption that plagued the city's north side was pretty bad, and there were a lot of rough customers that wouldn't think twice about shooting someone dead on the spot.

Occasionally, a bit of comic relief would venture into our backroom world. As a backdrop against the frequent violence, it always received special appreciation. Such was the case when the legendary Minnesota Fats came to town. It was not long after I arrived in Fort Worth. This was the late fifties, as I recall, when the all-world pool player put on an exhibition at the table that I was privileged to witness—an exhibition that showcased a singular skill as extraordinary as it was entertaining.

Forget the pool table. We're talking the dinner table.

We were playing pool in the old Texas Reaction Club in downtown Fort Worth when the subject of eating came up, which it often did when Fats was in town. Since this was Thanksgiving week, somebody suggested we settle things at an all-you-can-eat joint out on the Jacksboro Highway that no doubt would be featuring turkey on its buffet.

So off we went. When we got there, Fats and the other guy, a fellow named Harvey Fulks, ignored the buffet, and instead told a waiter to bring them each a whole turkey. Which the waiter did, whole and unsliced.

Whoever could eat the most would win $2,000.

What unfolded next was a sight only the Donner Party might fully appreciate. Harvey jerked off a leg and commenced eating, but he suddenly got distracted. It was Fats: he was thrashing through his bird like a chainsaw gone wild, devouring meat, gristle, ligament, even some of the smaller bones.

Everybody in the restaurant suddenly focused on Fats. Grown men smiled and hustled side bets. A young mother shrieked in disgust while an old woman crossed herself. Poor Harvey, he lost his concentration. Next thing we knew, nothing was left of Fats's turkey but a battered and broken carcass, picked buzzard-clean. It was shocking: Harvey had taken maybe two bites out of his turkey leg, and nearly choked.

"Waiter," Fats called out, waving his hand toward the guy. "Waiter, wouldja bring me another *boid*, please!"

With that, poor Harvey, utterly demoralized, pushed his chair back, threw $2,000 down on the table and bolted for the door.

"Wait, Harvey," I said, "where are you going?"

Without so much as a backward glance, Harvey shot back, "I'm getting outta here before this crazy son of a bitch eats me."

Fats never looked up. His second *boid* was on the way.

Life in those parts was always full of surprises, and not always good ones. One of my poker-playing acquaintances borrowed my car one night and robbed a convenience store. I didn't know it at the time, of course, but I picked up on it during a conversation at a poker game. He and his pals used my automobile as the getaway car after covering the license plates with mud.

"I'll be a sunburned son of a bitch!" I said, invoking a favorite youthful expression.

I was not too happy about being complicit in their chicanery. That night, though, I think I was more surprised than angry. I didn't loan my car out to those guys after that.

Some of my fellow players were still in their teens, and though they were young, they were highly skilled in their professional pursuits. I knew a few guys who, at eighteen or nineteen years old, were already adept at blowing up safes. These kids would take explosives out in the country and experiment with them to determine how much firepower it took to blow up a certain kind of rock. Then when they burglarized some place, they knew how much explosives they needed. It wouldn't do any good to blow open a safe if you blew up everything in it.

One of them liked to brag, "We can peel a safe like a grape."

And I reckoned he could. Even though Wayne and David and I weren't cracking safes, we felt fortunate to be in with those guys. They had money and girls around them all the time. Even though we were a little older than them—I was twenty-three or twenty-four at the time—we had lots of fun with the guys and the groupies. We were living life to its fullest and were right in the middle of the action. It was also somewhat educational for a West Texas farm boy.

In the 1950s, nobody on the north side of Fort Worth was more notorious than Tincy Eggleston. When he wasn't killing, stealing, or blackmailing, he was at least indirectly involved with some of the poker games on Exchange Avenue. He either ran them or partnered in them. He supposedly killed several guys to protect his turf or remove enemies from retaliating against him for things he'd done. Tincy was the most vicious and dangerous man on the Avenue, and that was saying something. When he got involved in drugs, things started turning real bad for Tincy, and consequently, for everyone else who came around him, including me and my buddies, Wayne and David.

Tincy started losing his edge and getting short of money. That became a problem, a big one that a lot of people were talking about. Because that made Tincy even more dangerous.

Tincy started shaking people down to get quick cash to support his habits. If you didn't give him money, he'd threaten to kill you and your family. A lot of people started getting real worried. He came to us—me, Wayne and David watched each others' backs—to see what he could shake us down for. We were together all the time, we were like brothers, and he would have had to kill all three of us if he made a move. So we told him to go screw himself. We weren't about to give him any money. I had no family so there was no one else to be concerned with. Of course, I was worried about Tincy and kept an eye on him, but I wasn't *scared* about anything. I was used to the guys in this environment and wasn't going to put my tail between my legs and crawl across the floor. If he wanted a shootout, I guess we were ready to get it on—and Tincy knew it.

It was a sign of weakness to give in to a tough guy's demands; it's something you just couldn't do. If we did something like that and gave him money, every tough guy in the area was going to come and shake us down. Tincy may have been the toughest hood in the area, but he wasn't going to get any money out of me—not unless he won it at the poker table or removed it off my dead body.

I wasn't going to have any of that.

Dealing with people like Tincy or Gene Paul Norris, another really tough guy down at Fort Worth, was always a challenge, but that's the way life was. You learned to avoid the really bad situations, and when you couldn't help it, you did the best you could and hoped it worked out. Most of the time it did, unless you were messing with the wrong people over the wrong things. It was one of the hazards of the time—constant danger. But that was part of the excitement. That type of element was there, so trouble was always in the air, just a lit match away from exploding.

What got Tincy killed was an audacious and ill-conceived attempt to blackmail some gamblers. I know the guy who killed him. I suppose I shouldn't name names, but he's dead too. I'll just call him Hiney. He became a friend of mine, and I even played golf with him. Hiney told me the whole story. He said Tincy came to him with some demands.

"You know, you're gonna have to give me 'x' amount of money," Tincy said to him, "or I'm gonna kill your family. I know it's bad, but I'm desperate. I've got to have the money. I'm gonna blackmail all the gamblers in town, and I'm gonna start with you."

"No, Tincy, you can't do that," Hiney said.

Hiney told me he had to act. After talking to other gamblers around town, he said, "Well, we gotta kill this guy." According to Hiney, they grabbed him, shot him, and buried him in a shallow grave. As they were leaving, Hiney said that Tincy's arm shot straight up out of the grave like a scene from an old horror movie. Hiney said they dug him up, shot him again, and tossed his body in an abandoned well, where it was later recovered. Not many people heard the whole story like I did, but Hiney was known to exaggerate from time to time anyway.

Back in those days, going to the police wasn't an option. You didn't go to them for anything. We just didn't handle things that way. It was either pay the blackmailer or worry about your family getting killed. If you didn't have the money or didn't want to pay it, you'd just have to kill the guy hustling you, and that's what happened. These were good guys, but what could they do?

I think everyone in Fort Worth knew who killed Tincy, but nobody held it against them. Police just didn't investigate the murders. It was almost comical; it was like they were planning to get rid of us.

What happened to Tincy happened to a lot of those guys. Bloodthirsty Highway never failed to live up to its name. There were killings and all kinds of skullduggery going on among the gangland denizens.

One of the most infamous characters at the time was a tough guy named Junior Dodd. And he was *tough*. Junior would think nothing of beating a guy to within an inch of his life or even taking that inch away and leaving him dead. And everybody knew it. One night he went into a joint called the King's X, owned by J.B. King, a friendly, personable guy who everybody just loved. Junior got into a fierce argument with J.B. and as it heated up, he pulled out his pistol and beat J.B. over the head. He bloodied him up pretty good, and it was totally uncalled for.

J.B. was not one to turn the other cheek. It was maybe a month or two later before he confronted Junior. When his quarry stepped around a corner, J.B. reportedly cut him in half with a shotgun. J.B. later got cancer, and one day he went down to the Trinity River and killed himself.

My buddy Wayne added to the danger because he was a good-looking kid and he was always going around with someone's girlfriend or messing with the pimps' girls. There were a lot of pimps around our environment and Wayne would sometimes find trouble. I wasn't involved in that because I was always after longer relationships. I was a one-woman guy. Sometimes, the inevitable fistfights would occur. They'd jump on Wayne and we'd have to intervene. But there were a couple of times it got pretty hairy with guns and things, but that was just the way of life. It was nothing to leaf through the newspaper and read that somebody we knew got killed.

One of the most dangerous toughs in town was a guy from Odessa named Curt Garret, who I knew really well. He had a run-in with a popular thug named Danny McComb at a downtown lounge, the Fortune Arms. Curt left and waited for McComb to come out, then shot and killed him. Now, Danny had a lot of unsavory friends. And Curt wasn't certain what their reaction would be to the killing. So he called a meeting of Danny's friends, and invited me to sit in. I played poker and hung out with these guys, and they trusted me. They thought I should be part of this sit-in.

Curt said, "I just want y'all to know, yeah, I killed Danny McComb. I just want to know how y'all feel about it."

I couldn't believe it. These guys, some of the toughest hoods in town, said it wasn't their concern.

"Naw, buddy, that was your business," one said.

If someone had killed one of my friends, I'd have been furious. Still, their attitude really made a mark on me. It was just the way those people were, the code they lived by. A dispute between two people, fatal or not, was nobody else's business. They didn't condone what Curt did, but they didn't condemn him either. It was the way it was.

A funny thing about Curt, he was a health nut. He didn't drink alcohol, didn't smoke, didn't do drugs. When he wasn't doing something illegal, which was most of the time, you would find him drinking orange juice and jogging. It was kind of ironic that he had a heart attack and died at about age forty-five.

There were thirty-five or forty guys about my age that hung out together on Exchange Avenue, but it became a diminishing collection of characters. It was pretty common to pick up the paper and say, "Oh, old Choc got blown up last night. He was having a beef with so-and-so." One by one, that original group of guys I played with down on Exchange were vanishing.

Not because they got tired of playing—they were either killed or sent off to jail.

Chapter 6

The only place success comes before work is in the dictionary.

I n 1957, I got one of the biggest shocks of my young life on a trip home for the holidays. I had grown up believing my father was vehemently antigambling, or at least greatly disapproved of it, but I never really knew for sure because he didn't talk about it. That part was no surprise since he didn't talk about much about anything. I knew my mother thought it was a sin, just like about everybody else in Longworth and along that long swath of America that made up the Bible Belt. So you can imagine my surprise when, after Christmas dinner, my dad, my brother, and three of my uncles suggested we play a little poker. We were playing deuce-to-seven lowball draw when my dad opened the pot for ten matches and I raised him twenty matches with a J-10-9-8-2.

My dad called and stood pat. I had no hand to draw to so I stayed pat behind him, thinking because he hadn't raised me back, I could bluff him out of the pot.

Dad checked and I bet him the rest of my matches. Dad called.

"How in the world could you call that with a 10-8-6-4-2?" I asked.

"I've been seeing plays like that for forty years," Dad said.

After getting over my astonishment that he had said that, I began questioning him how he knew anything about poker. Come to find out, Dad had put my brother and my sister through college playing poker at the Elks Club in Sweetwater.

Sure enough, the apple didn't fall far from the tree!

When I got back at the poker games on Exchange, the revelation that my father had been a poker player for my whole life would strike me now and then, and I'd just shake my head. I could hardly believe it.

Round about 1958, I first learned about a game called hold'em. There was a bootlegger that ran a poker game in Granbury, about forty miles south of Fort Worth, and we got invited to go down there to play. Red, the guy that ran the game would get drunk and lose several hundred dollars, which was a lot of money back then. Red's loose play was the main attraction in the game, and we were going to see if we could get some of that money.

We got down to Granbury and they start telling us about this game, hold'em, they liked to play. We didn't know what it was exactly, so Red and some of the others started explaining it was a variation of seven-card stud—that's what they told us. The rules weren't all that different. By the end of the hand, we'd have seven cards total like stud, only in hold'em, five of those cards were in the middle, shared by all the players. There would be one blind, a forced bet put in by the player sitting to the dealer's left (nowadays we use two blinds) and each player would put in an ante before the cards were dealt. You started with two cards and there was a round of betting. Then they dealt three cards dealt face up in the middle of the table, called the "flop." These are "community" cards, which means everybody can use them. Then comes the second round of betting, followed by another community card dealt up that is called the "turn." After a third round of betting, the last community card, the "river," is dealt up. There is a final round of betting and then the showdown, where each player makes the best five-card poker hand possible using any combination of his two hole cards and the five upcards. The best hand wins the pot.

Well, this new game sounded good to me. They started dealing the cards and we started playing right along with them. It quickly became apparent that hold'em was a fun poker variation, and it moved faster than most games. That's why it eventually became so popular. I know I enjoyed it right away.

That was the first time I played Texas hold'em or even heard of the game. I grasped the correct strategy right away—play big cards and use position as my two big weapons. Most people playing at Red's game didn't get it. They were clueless as to what the game was all about, and the key strategic concepts so I got to be the best player there very quickly. It was a lucrative game for me and I kept playing at Red's, honing my skills at this new form of poker I had learned. I also remember another thing about that game; Red's wife cooked some fine meals for us.

After a while, I started hearing more about hold'em, or "hold me darling" as most people called it back then. I suppose the game was spreading some because I started hearing of games in Waco, Corpus Christi, and other towns. I hadn't played in those places before, but I had heard the games had been deuce-to-seven lowball, plus five-card stud and draw. Some thought hold'em originated in Waco, although I've heard it said that hold'em might have begun in Corpus Christi. I've also heard that it was first played on the open prairie in the early parts of the twentieth century by wranglers who needed a game that could accommodate a lot of players, as many as twenty-one (although most games today limit a table to ten).

I'm really not sure where the game began, but given that I'd never heard of hold'em before and I was playing in games all over Texas and the South, I think the game must have started right around that time. What I do know is that it began to catch on quickly and was being played more and more.

Pretty soon, hold'em became the main game being spread.

This was also momentous year for reasons that concerned my family. In 1958, when I was twenty-five, tragedy struck at home. I lost my father, my brother Lloyd, my grandmother and two aunts on my mother's side. It was a lot to lose in one year, particularly my brother and father. I say particularly, because in both cases, I never got to know either of them as well as I would have liked.

My dad, John Frank Brunson, was born in 1883 in a small Texas town called Rising Star, and moved with his parents to a farm in Longworth when he was fourteen years old. He was the oldest of nine children, and when his father died at an early age, he became, for all practical purposes, head of the family household. He attended college at East Texas State in Commerce where he roomed at one time with Sam Rayburn, who became a legendary Speaker of the U.S. House of Representatives back in the forties and fifties. Rayburn was a close ally of fellow Texan Lyndon B. Johnson when he was Senate majority leader. Dad had some political ideas of his own, and when I was twelve years old, he ran for the state senate. Unfortunately, he ran against a popular musician-oilman-showman named Harley Sadler, who defeated him.

Dad pitched on local baseball teams and with a semipro team at nearby Rotan and spent many evenings playing poker around Longworth and at the Elks Club in Sweetwater. Although a man of modest means, he was the most successful of the Brunson litter, and the younger siblings came to him for advice and financial aid. Strangely, though, they weren't very close.

My father was the most even-tempered person I'd ever known. Nothing upset him, and I never heard him raise his voice. He could be sitting in a room reading while Mom was threatening to take us to the woodshed for a whipping, and he'd never look up from his book.

He died of a massive heart attack while mowing the yard. Although I was terribly saddened, his death didn't evoke the same kind of feelings that other deaths in my family would. He was a man of very few words, and I don't remember too many conversations with him. He didn't seem to take a real interest in my activities. I was always hoping he'd ask about what I was doing, give me a kind word about something, maybe throw a nod to my athletic accomplishments. I suppose I'd even have settled for being yelled at. I just wanted him to show some involvement. But he was aloof, in his own world. He wouldn't say anything, didn't seem to even notice. Maybe, in an indirect way, it drove me to become more proficient in my athletic pursuits, hoping one day he'd have to take notice. But whatever he was thinking, I could never quite tell, and he took those thoughts to the grave with him.

He never spent much time with me, or any of my siblings. That just wasn't him. I never once heard him say "I love you" to anyone, not even my mother. I mourned his death much like any son would mourn the loss of a father who had raised and cared for him, but it wasn't in a way I would have liked because of what I imagined other father-son relationships to be.

I couldn't help but think what a shame it was that he and I hadn't been honest with each other. Dad had played poker for years and years and helped support us with his winnings, but never talked about it until that game of matches across the kitchen table. Yet here I was playing poker professionally and lying about it because I didn't think he would approve. I kept thinking, "Just imagine the camaraderie we would have shared talking poker with each other?" I'm sure he could have given me good strategy advice after all his years of experience. More than anything, it was something in common we had that we could really talk about and I bemoaned that lost opportunity. It was a tragedy we didn't communicate about that, but his death ended any possibilities to share more of our lives with each other. And as much as I wanted to, I'd never get another chance to know him. That, more than anything else, left me terribly sad.

Lloyd was a lot older than me and left home when I was around seven years old. But what time we had together was great. In a limited way, Lloyd gave me the encouragement my father never did. I remember, especially, one of his visits home right after I had graduated from high school. He came in from an afternoon in Sweetwater and said, "I got recognized as the brother of a celebrity today." He was proud of his little brother and showed it. And that made me feel good in a way I rarely, if ever, got from my father.

I think Dad might also have been proud of my athletic accomplishments, but it was hard to know; he never said so and never showed it.

Lloyd was career military and only thirty-seven years old when doctors determined that a knot on his neck was malignant. The cancer had spread to his stomach. He went to Brooke Army Medical Center in San Antonio where they operated on him. He survived the surgery, but there were complications, and he had to go back under the knife. He died after returning to the operating table. It was a complete shock to me and a harsh lesson about the fragility of life. I went to Laredo, to Lloyd's funeral. I didn't have any money. That's when I was a young poker player and always broke. I caught a bus down there and caught a bus back. They stopped the bus down by the border, and the border patrol officers came on board. One of the officers was Don Duncan, the kid that I'd had a fight with in shop class about ten years earlier, and we had a friendly chat before the bus went on its way again.

Lloyd was full of life and everything seemed to be going his way. He was articulate, smart, and movie-star handsome. He had a lovely wife, Jonnie, and two lovely daughters, Val and Jan. Lloyd loved the military, rising rapidly within its ranks. He was already an Air Force major and was about to be promoted to lieutenant colonel.

I couldn't understand Lloyd's death that easily, not that anyone can understand death. Lloyd had been so full of vigor and was a great athlete. Just two weeks before his surgery, he had won the Air Force tennis championship. And then, like that, my brother was gone. Just as it was with my father, I barely got to know him.

It was a tragic merry-go-round that year, going back and forth to Longworth and all the family funerals. I'd see the same people on each somber occasion, as one Brunson and then another would move on, and of course, they'd ask what I was doing. Now, remember, this was the Bible Belt and gambling was frowned upon, maybe even more so than alcohol. Our small town, like other ones across West Texas, was full of God-fearing people with strong beliefs, just like my own family. Gambling was not one of those beliefs. I couldn't tell Mom's friends and neighbors that I sat down with murderers, thieves and drug dealers every day in games of poker; that these people I played with lived well outside the law. They wouldn't understand that. Nor would they understand the simple version of my lifestyle—that I played poker for a living.

I had to tell them something else, a profession that wouldn't bring great shame on the family, my mother in particular. Once, I told them I was working at the Convair aircraft plant in Dallas-Fort Worth. Most of the time, though, I just said I was selling insurance. The last thing Mom needed after losing so much—her oldest son, husband, two sisters, and mother—was to suffer the stigma of having a son that was a gambler.

Unfortunately, Lloyd's death by cancer was an ominous tiding of things to come. I didn't think much of it at the time, but later it would be impossible to ignore.

Chapter 7

If you find yourself in a hole, the first thing to do is stop digging.

After engaging in the Exchange Avenue turmoil for two or three years—this was in the late fifties—I progressed to the bigger games downtown at the old Diane Hotel. That's where the professional people played—the doctors, the lawyers, the businessmen—and where the stakes, and therefore my profits, were substantially bigger. The players weren't any better than the folks down on Exchange. Sometimes, their bad play simply astounded me. They would just ship their chips across the table.

While these games were much safer at the Diane, you just never knew what would happen.

One night I was playing ace-to-five lowball in a pot against an elderly gentleman named Red Dodson. Red said his high school date to the senior prom was Ginger Rogers, the famous dancing partner of Fred Astaire. Red was about the most conservative player I had ever seen. I kept bluffing at him, and he kept throwing his hand away. He just kept leaving me the money sitting in the middle. This went on for hours. I felt like Santa Claus had come early to visit me. I couldn't believe it, but I wasn't complaining. Finally, Red got dealt a pat hand, A-2-3-4-6, the second-best hand possible. I drew one card to an A-2-3-5 and caught a 4, giving me the best possible hand. I bet once again, expecting Red to throw his hand away as he had done all night.

To my surprise Red moved in on me. When I looked up at Red, he finally let loose his pent-up frustration.

"I know y'all have been bluffing me all night," Red yelled. "Let's see what you do now!"

I couldn't get my chips in the pot fast enough. Red spread his A-2-3-4-6 and stared at me like his troops had just marched into Rome and conquered the city.

I showed my wheel.

Red couldn't believe what he was looking at. He just stared at those cards like he'd seen a ghost. But I couldn't believe what I was seeing either. Red's face turned white, his eyes rolled back, and he started turning blue. Red fell out of his chair and was dead before he hit the floor. The doctor said he had a massive heart attack. There was nothing I could do but collect the chips and pull them into my stack. I felt bad, but that's poker and bad beats happen.

That was the second man I saw die at the table. Both were playing lowball. Maybe that's why hold'em eventually became the game of choice.

While I played plenty at the Diane, my gambling roots were on Exchange, and after seeing how much money some guys raked out of the pot for the house, I ran a small poker game out there for a while

During my years fighting the battles of Exchange Avenue, my cronies were routinely getting arrested and hustled off to jail. It was like they were on the merry-go-round from hell. They'd get out and go right back to pimping and stealing and dealing drugs, or whatever they did, as if nothing had happened. Then they'd get busted again and hauled back to jail. It was like a necessary part of their lives, going to jail. They didn't worry about it, and I couldn't understand it. After three felony convictions, which they called "the bitch," they'd go to prison for life. And when one of them got in *real* trouble, they said so-and-so "took a ride on Old Sparky." That meant the electric chair.

I laughed at them and said, "You guys are always going to jail, and obviously you've brought all this heat on yourselves. Have you ever noticed that I go in a lot of the same places y'all do and I don't get arrested?"

And then one Friday night I went to this club on the Jacksboro Highway with a group of guys and, of course, there were girls involved. Girls had absolutely no trouble luring us to the most trouble-prone bars. Well, the joint got raided, and police took everybody in the club to jail. Just about everybody but me had a criminal record, so the cops knew them. But they didn't know me, and I gave them a bogus name. They finally called me away from the others.

"It's obvious that you're not like these thieves and thugs you're running with," a policeman said. "What were you doing in there?"

"I was out there looking for women," I said. "What'd you think I was doing?"

"Well, you know this is a drug hangout," the cop said.

"I don't know about that," I said. "I don't do drugs."

But they put me back in jail anyway, and it was a lurid experience. The stench was awful and the squalor was worse. It seemed as though I was the only person in there who was sober.

"How the hell did I get into this?" I asked myself. "Women," I answered. "The pursuit of women."

I was there Friday, Saturday, Sunday and part of Monday. There was a steel bunk and no covers. Not anything, except a community commode. Finally they called me out to talk.

"You're Doyle Brunson," one of the investigators said. "We found you by your fingerprints in the National Guard records. We understand what you said, that you were out there looking for women, but that's not the place to look for women. You get on out of here and you stay out of places like that."

Now I hadn't shaved, hadn't combed my hair, my shirt was dirty, and I just looked terrible. As I was leaving, I walked right into Dean Marsh, the former dean of men at Hardin-Simmons. He had left HSU and, as I'd heard, was teaching at the Baptist seminary in Fort Worth. My mouth dropped open and I just stood there, red-faced, as he wordlessly looked me up and down.

There was nothing I could say, so I just turned around and slunk off.

Dean Marsh told someone about seeing me, "That's such a shame about ol' Doyle. At one time he was one of the most influential students on the Hardin-Simmons campus."

I vowed to do everything possible to prevent another jail experience, but that was not to be. My world was spinning out of control, although I was not really at fault for what was happening. Not directly, anyway. For instance, I was in another nightclub one evening, and the cops saw this group of guys, and they arrested all of them, me included. As we were getting into the paddy wagon, a policeman kicked me.

I turned around and belted him. In a heartbeat, it seemed like all the cops in the area jumped on me. They threw us in the wagon and took us downtown. We spent the night in jail. It was all a scam because of the bail bondsmen. They came around, and it cost us $50 to get out of jail. Street talk was they split it with the cops. No charges were filed. This time, however, while everyone else went home, they dragged me out of the wagon and took me to what they called the bullpen. They left me there for a while before finally coming to get me. They walked me around and around in front of the cops that were about to go on duty so everybody could get a good look at me.

"This big boy here, he likes to whip cops," one policeman said. "He thinks he's a tough guy."

I mean, all I'd done was hit a guy that kicked me, and they were on my case something fierce.

One of the cops sneered at me. "Yeah, big boy," he said, "you wanna try me? You think you're so tough?"

I didn't answer that question, wisely choosing to keep my mouth shut. Then they tossed me back in jail. I had to get a bondsman to bail me out. Now things were really headed south. The next week, police arrested me five times. Every time they saw me, they arrested me and threw me back in jail.

"This is no good," I told myself, overwhelmed by frustration.

I wanted to leave town, but the problem was that I had met a girl I liked, and we were spending a lot of time together. I met her on the north side, and eventually I suspected she might've once been a call girl. I knew she was the best-looking girl out there—she was gorgeous. By then, I had come, perhaps slowly, to the realization that the type of woman I was really looking for wouldn't be found in the clubs on Exchange Avenue or along Jacksboro Highway. Not that I was looking, but finding someone special was always in the back of my mind.

When I started getting busted every day, I likewise concluded that it was not just time to get the hell out of Dodge, it was way past time. My future was not promising in the current environment, and I had been reluctant to admit it. My friend Wayne Hamilton was well into drugs and David Vernon had just started taking amphetamines. So I started packing my bags for a move to Midland, a bustling West Texas city of just under a hundred thousand people, known for its oil millionaires and its poker games.

Right before I left Fort Worth, David and Wayne and I decided we needed to take what I called a farewell journey. Naturally, we chose Las Vegas. A poker-playing dope addict named Paul wanted to go with us, and we reluctantly agreed because we felt sorry for him. So the four of us jumped in my '55 Chevy and took off for Sin City. Once there, we headed straight to the gambling joints. We huddled on a corner on Fremont Street while we took our bankroll—no more than $400 or $500—and split it four ways.

"We'll meet back here in two hours and see how much money we got," I said as we headed off to different casinos.

We returned to the Fremont corner at the appointed time and everybody reported in broke. I had four or five pennies in my hand, and I said, "Well, this is what we got left." For some reason, David hit my hand, perhaps in frustration, and the pennies flew up and broke my glasses. So there we were, with even our pennies scattered all to hell, and me with a pair of shattered glasses. The only thing between our miserable little band of losers and destitution was my credit card, which I waved triumphantly over my head. "We'll take the credit card and we'll go to California to try to find Jimmy Caton," I said. Jimmy was one of the former Exchange Avenue guys, an ex-con who practiced blowing up rocks to perfect his safe-cracking skills.

"We'll go see if we can borrow some money from him."

And off we went to California, jammed in a Chevy, dead broke but for a not-quite-maxed-out credit card.

On the way to Los Angeles we stopped for gas in Barstow, California. By chance, we ran into a couple of my old pals from Fort Worth, Richard and Clarence. They weren't part of the Exchange Avenue gang, but they were like kissing cousins—they partied and schemed on the city's south side. They put us up in a motel that night, fed us the next morning, and gave us a few dollars to get to L.A. Their motive, however, leaned heavily toward something else. Clarence and Richard had stolen some cashiers' checks and wanted us to come back by Las Vegas and help cash them with their false identification cards. I had no intention of getting involved with that, but in our desperate state we briefly mulled over the offer before we declined and rolled off toward L.A. However, we were certainly grateful to them for the overnight room and board.

We did find Jimmy, and he came up with some money. With our fresh financing and Jimmy in tow, we went to Gardena in the Los Angeles area, renowned for its legal poker casinos. I held back $40 in my billfold, but didn't tell the other guys. We put all the rest of our money up, and Wayne and I won a few dollars. Our friend Paul was a very good poker player, and since we were tired, we gave him all our money to play for us. With us tagging along, he went off and found a poker game.

He was dealing no-limit lowball draw when the pivotal hand of the evening unfolded. He picked up a 6-4, which is next to the best hand you can have in the game we were playing. He and this shrill old lady raised back and forth until all our money was in the pot, probably $1,000, which was a huge amount for our group. She had an 8-5 and threw the 8 away. Paul had stood pat with what appeared to be the winning hand.

And then the oddest thing happened. For some reason, Paul flipped the top card over, which was improper. He didn't burn it; just flipped it over. I didn't know why. Neither did anybody else.

The lady started screaming and the floor supervisor rushed over.

"What's wrong?" he asked.

The lady told him what happened.

He turned to Paul. "Why did you turn the card over?"

"I don't know," Paul said.

"He's been screwin' with the deck all night anyway," the lady hollered.

He hadn't been, but he did make a horrendous mental error. The casino officials gave the woman our pot and threw us out of the club. I was as mortified as I was mad, which was a bunch.

Now we were out on the highway again, broke, and just heading out of town. Jimmy Caton's still with us when a police car pulls us over. An FBI agent, for heaven's sake, comes up to the car, calls us out one by one and searches us.

"What are you boys doing?" he asked.

"We're from Texas," I said, "and we're trying to play some poker."

"Do you know who this Jimmy Caton is?" he asked.

I said, "Yeah, we know."

"He's a thief."

"Yeah," I said, "we know that, too."

"Well, that makes us think that y'all are thieves, too," the agent said. "Get your asses back in that car and get the hell back to Texas; we've got enough thieves in California already."

We start out again, and ol' Jimmy decides he might best go back to Fort Worth with us. Now, he's broke, too.

"Well," I said, "I've got this $40 I saved back."

David, Paul, and I had decided we weren't going to get involved with the check-cashing scheme, but Wayne opted to join Richard and Clarence in Las Vegas. After we dropped him off, someone said, "Where's Villa Acuna from here?"

"That way," I said, pointing off into the darkness and the feminine pleasures that lay therein. So we took off for that Mexican border town, and promptly blew the $40. The credit card got us back to Fort Worth. I never saw Richard and Clarence again until they got mixed up in some crime and appeared one night on the television news.

Back in Fort Worth, I finally said good-bye to Exchange Avenue, Jacksboro Highway, and my crooked buddies. The multiple arrests had been a blessing in disguise. Even I finally read the handwriting on the wall: I had no future in Fort Worth. I was still pretty young, and the upcoming decade seemed to give impetus to my fresh start. I headed off to the Midland/Odessa area in West Texas and the good poker games there. I was ready to see where the next phase of my life would take me.

Chapter 8

*When you're climbing the ladder of success, be
sure it is leaning on the right building.*

One of the players at the Diane Hotel thought I was a pretty good player and began telling me about these poker games in the cities and small towns around Fort Worth and farther out in the state, what was commonly known as the "Texas Circuit" among professional poker players. These were for bigger stakes than I had been playing, and in exchange for turning me on to these games, he took 25 percent of my action for a while. This was a big step up in my poker career, an important one too, because the Circuit was where the really top-notch players were and the bigger games could be found.

The Texas Circuit consisted of thirty or forty towns around Texas and the South where poker games were held regularly. I played mostly in Texas, but I also went to Oklahoma, Louisiana, played a little in New Mexico, and sometimes traveled through Louisiana to Alabama. There were also trips to West Virginia, Kentucky, Florida, and Tennessee. Oklahoma was where most of the hijackers lived, and you had to be extra cautious when you crossed the Red River on the northern Texas border.

For the better part of ten years, beginning in 1958 when I first started trying my hand on the Circuit, I played poker almost nonstop, with breaks for eating, sleeping and once in a while, some entertainment. These were my poker years, where I devoted myself entirely to the game. I mean, I put in long hours day after day, week after week. These years went by like a blur. I'd fade the white line from town to town and game to game across the south. I was a road gambler who traveled to wherever the action could be found.

The Circuit had a nucleus of professional poker players who determined where the poker games would be held, so I'd frequently run into players in geographically different locations and got to know many of the rounders who made their way around the Circuit. There were a lot of great players on the Texas Circuit, but the one guy I kept hearing about was Johnny Moss, who was considered the best no-limit player.

I was playing in a good no-limit hold'em game in Houston when Johnny came in and sat down. I was twenty-five years old at the time and welcomed the chance to play against "the man." I was also sure that he had heard of me because everyone was always saying I was a young Johnny Moss. There was tension in the air every time Johnny and I played a pot. I had been very lucky all night and had won several big pots from him.

Moss was a big loser when this hand came up. I had the K♦ 9♦. Moss had K♣ 2♣. The flop was K♠ 9♥ 2♦. I bet. Moss raised and I reraised. Moss showed me his two-pair hand and threw it away. Pretty impressive laydown! I told him I had A-K after I threw my hand in, but I could tell he didn't believe me.

I repeatedly beat Moss every big pot the rest of the night. I really was running good. I observed how he handled the adversity and kept his cool, making the correct judgment on most every hand. I was a $35,000 winner, most of it coming from pots against Moss. He was still even at the end of the night despite all the bad luck he had against me, and I knew why he was considered to be "the man" in the poker world. Moss was country cool, if there was such a thing, and confident to the point of arrogance. But I could quickly tell his reputation was accurate. He could play. Moss was the "old-timer" of the mostly youthful group traveling the Circuit. Most of the other guys were in their twenties and thirties, but Johnny had plenty of spit and vinegar in him, and he loved to play.

While playing against Moss had given me confidence, I hadn't yet made my mark on the Texas Circuit. Nobody outside of Fort Worth knew anything about my ability as a poker player. When I started playing on the Circuit, even though I won much more than I lost, I hadn't received any real respect from the touring pros. It wasn't long after that I ran into Moss again, and this time, the meeting would take on a lot more significance to me than the first time we'd played together. In fact, it was the most important hand in my early poker career. Interestingly enough, it was one that was probably noticed by just two people—Johnny Moss and me.

One of the most popular games was in the small South Texas town of Brenham, home of the famous Blue Bell ice cream. One rainy night, after a three-day marathon poker game, it was in Brenham that I got into a hand with two opponents, one of them being Johnny Moss. Moss and me, we had an eye on each other. He was the best at the time and I think he saw in me the guy that would take his place, so he tried especially hard when we were in pots together. One thing Moss had, which was a big advantage against me, was the money. He had plenty of it and I didn't, so he could money-whip me. Well, this hand come up and I always remembered it because I considered it the turning point of my young career.

I was holding J-10 offsuit on a board of K-7-8-2-3. I had none of that board, but when Moss bet $4,000, a monstrous wager in that game, I called him with just a jack high! I was sure he was drawing to some kind of straight, and since I was drawing to the highest one possible, I felt I had to have him beat. It forced out a third player with a better hand, who I correctly figured couldn't overcall me. There was a lot of money in the pot, but I had a read on Johnny. Any hand with a queen, king, ace, or pair or better would beat me—in other words, just about any two cards. And I needed to beat *two* players. Moss showed me his 6-5, for a busted straight draw, just like I thought, and I showed him my J-10.

It was more than a call—it was a bold and brilliant move, the breakthrough that I needed. Moss looked at me, and I could see the respect in his eyes. That one hand defined the moment where I knew I was a top player, and from that point on, I was considered a world-class player by my peers.

Moss was typical of many of the players who traveled the Circuit. Poker was the means to a better life for guys who had grown up without too many other opportunities. Many of the gamblers of the thirties, forties, fifties, in those early years, and certainly the ones we played with, were uneducated. Like Moss, they had started gambling at an early age because they couldn't do anything else. They grew up dirt poor and used poker as a way out of poverty. They wanted to make a lot of money, and gambling was their way to do it. While I didn't experience their childhood hardships, that was certainly the way I felt. It was not unlike the many poverty-stricken kids from the inner cities who later wanted to use sports as their ticket to a better life.

Johnny Moss's family, poor as scattered tumbleweed, suffered one tragedy after another, and at an early age, Johnny was out there hustling for money. He often bragged that he made a living shooting dice before he was fifteen years old. I didn't doubt it. In the poker games we played, he was head and shoulders above everybody else in talent. I got to watching and studying him and developed many of my strategies that way. In fact, I learned a lot just listening to him. If I had a mentor, it was Johnny Moss. He was a dynamite player who rose above his meager background.

This is what Moss told the writer Jon Bradshaw about his early days traveling Texas:

> *It was a violent world, y'know, and I was just a fresh kid.*
> *After I got money I started to carry a gun. I used to carry*
> *a .38-Special with no hammer, so's you could get it outta*
> *your pocket in a hurry. The road was real rough in them*
> *days goin' from town to town. You always had to worry*
> *about hijackers and the Rangers. All those road gamblers*
> *and thieves and cheaters. You have to know them cheaters*
> *in advance. I got me a rundown on most of 'em. They*
> *never slipped up on the blind side of me.*
>
> *Wasn't always that way, y'understand. Used to be that*
> *gamblin' was an honorable profession, a means of holdin'*
> *your own in the world. But dope runners, pimps and*
> *hijackers, when they was picked up by the Rangers, they*
> *always said they was gamblers. They put a bad name*
> *on gamblin'. See what I'm talkin' about? They wasn't*
> *gamblers. It's because they can use that word and get*
> *away with it that put a bad name on gamblin'.*

Of course, it was the talented players that made it out of poverty, the ones who had what it took that were able to find a better life. Junior Whited, who favored the Elvis look, was one of those talented players who rose above his background. He grew up on a Texas farm picking cotton, much like me, but his family struggled to make ends meet. He didn't have shoes until he was about ten. The story Junior told is that he owned that pair just one week, losing them shooting craps with a cousin of his. They played again a few days later; that time his cousin went home naked. I don't know how that one went over with his family, but when he played his uncle craps the following year and won his grocery store, his mother didn't like that: she made him give it back. Junior said it wasn't much of a store anyway.

Freddie Ferris, "Sarge" as we all called him, was another gambler who used poker as a means to escape poverty. It was in Louisiana where I first met Sarge, one of the best deuce-to-seven players. I didn't have much money, $10,000 or so, and I had it all on the table in Shreveport playing deuce-to-seven lowball with a group of traveling pros and two or three local businessmen. I was in awe at the players in the game, guys I'd been hearing about for years. Johnny Moss, Aubrey Day from Alabama, and Broomcorn—yes, the same Broomcorn I wrote about in *Super/System.* His real name was Lawrence Herron, and he owned a lot of downtown property in Brenham—and he lost it all playing poker. Broomcorn was one of the more engaging players in those Texas Circuit days. He would have four or five Budweisers sitting in front of him at all times. I never saw anybody enjoy the game quite as much as he did. When he had money, he didn't often win. But when he got short on money, he was a tough player.

We had been playing for two or three hours when I got involved in a pot with Broomcorn and Moss. It was a big pot that Broomcorn ended up winning and it broke me. As I was getting up to quit, Sarge called me aside.

"I like the way you gamble," Sarge said. "I have $100,000 on deposit here. Use all of it or any part of it. Pay me back when you can."

That started a friendship that lasted forty years until Sarge died in 1989, the year he was enshrined in the Poker Hall of Fame. Many years after that first loan, Sarge loaned me $800,000 when I got broke betting football and I paid him back within a few months.

By 1960, I was comfortably settled deep in West Texas, in the oil-rich Midland-Odessa area and thankfully, long out of the madness of Exchange Avenue and Jacksboro Highway. A bookmaker we called Egghead Perry took me under his wing. It was rather convoluted, but we made money for each other in what amounted to a partnership. He was betting and booking and I was playing poker. It worked because I was a better player than most of the gamblers out there.

More importantly, that was where I forged a wonderful friendship with Sailor Roberts, who was not only a great friend, the most dependable and charismatic friend a person could have, but my traveling and gambling partner on the Texas Circuit. I had actually met Sailor some years earlier in the downtown games in Fort Worth at the Diane Hotel. Sailor was from San Angelo and had served in the Navy, which was how he picked up his nickname. It was in this timeframe that Sailor and I met Amarillo Slim Preston, whose nickname sprung from his hometown in the Texas Panhandle. Slim had a three thousand-acre-plus spread outside Amarillo where he raised cattle and quarter horses, and he leased several other spreads. It would, however, be a mistake to think Slim spent long days and weeks in the saddle working cattle in those years. He was a gambler like me, craving action wherever he could get it.

Sailor and I got along well with Slim and our partnership quickly grew to a pretty successful threesome. We were good friends, all of us, and it almost reminded me of my childhood buddies, D.C. Andrews and Riley Cross, the three musketeers of my youth. With guys like Sailor and Slim, dull moments didn't exist. They were two of the most colorful guys I've ever met. Everybody knew that Sailor, Slim, and I were partners. We played off the same bankroll and also shared wins, losses, and expenses. Sometimes we played in the same game, but it worked against us. Because we were partners, we had to be extra careful the way we played. Certain things were taboo, like anything that would suggest collaboration in a specific poker hand or any perception of impropriety. Our reputations for being square shooters—as opposed to some of our friends who would do anything short of mass murder to win—began to grow. The three of us played hard to win, but we did so fairly and honestly. I was convinced it was our reputation for integrity that kept us in the thick of the action. All those years, we never had a problem because we wouldn't do anything out of line.

It was nice to have someone to travel with, but for more important reasons than just the camaraderie. We watched out after each other. There was a lot of danger on the road; and with the three of us, we were more protected than if we went solo. In the Texas Circuit days of the 1950s and 1960s, many people assumed the underworld ran our games. I told them, "No, in Texas we have raccoons and possums, but we don't have any Mafias." The Mafia may have been involved in other activities in the South, I can't comment about that, but poker wasn't one of them. However, this lifestyle was every bit as exciting as my Exchange Avenue days, but not coincidentally, no less dangerous than what I left behind.

Anytime there was a lot of money involved, somebody was going to try to get it. Killers, con artists, cheats, and thieves were a fixture of the gambling landscape when Slim, Sailor, and I were traveling around Texas and the South. The foremost threat was getting hijacked, which usually meant getting robbed at gunpoint. It was funny in a way, although diabolic may be closer to the truth. You had to worry about winning the money, you had to worry about getting cheated while trying to win it, you had to worry about getting paid after you won it, and you had to worry about getting arrested before, during, and after.

And that often wasn't the worst part of it.

One night we were playing poker in a farmhouse right outside Austin. We'd had two or three games at this house—big games. Anything over a

$1,000 buy-in was considered a big game in those days. With no warning, our game was interrupted by the sounds of windows shattering and doors bursting open. Seven guys with ski masks and shotguns rushed in. Nobody had a chance to escape. The robbers herded us up against a wall and ordered us to drop our lower garments—*all* of them. We were reluctant, as we had some women friends present.

"I said *now!*" one of them shouted while drawing a bead on our backsides. We were instantly persuaded by his argument and our shyness evaporated faster than spilled water off the summer desert.

After searching everybody's pockets, one of the bandits grew impatient. "Anybody got any more money that we might overlook?" he demanded. "I haven't got time to look again, but I'm gonna take one or two of you and search you, and if I find any money on you, I'm gonna blow your kneecaps off with this shotgun."

A guy from Lubbock turned slowly toward the gunman and said, "Uh, good buddy, good buddy, there's $800 right down here that you missed," nodding toward his shirt pocket. Another one hollered out, "Don't forget this $600 right here!"

The guy grabbed the money, and then it really got scary. For some reason, robbers liked to pick on the biggest guy present, and that was usually me. I was six-foot-three and weighed about 270, and this little guy with a big shotgun turned me around and said, "Who runs this game?"

"I don't know," I answered, adhering to an unwritten rule that says you don't snitch on anybody.

He took the shotgun, hit me in the stomach with the barrel, and repeated the question. Again, I said, "Sir, I don't know."

This time he used the handle and hit me up beside the head, knocking my glasses off and breaking them. I felt some blood trickle down my cheek.

"I said, who runs this game?"

"I don't know," I said, barely getting the words out.

His shotgun was one of those old-fashioned types with hammers. He cocked both barrels, stuck the barrel right between my eyes and said, "I'm gonna ask you one last time. Who runs this game?"

I peered right down the barrel of the gun and, fortified by a burst of good sense, said, "That guy right down there in the green shirt!"

I hated to give up the guy, but I knew if they killed me the robbers would find out who ran the game anyway. It turned out okay. The owner of the farmhouse wasn't harmed. What hurt as much that night as the blows to the head and body was my pride—grown men herded against a wall, pants dropped around our ankles. After it was over, some of the women broke out laughing.

"We've never seen so many naked butts and shaking knees in our lives," one said.

I wasn't laughing. The robbers took all our money, including $6,700 from me. I remembered the exact amount because it was a hefty bankroll. Such episodes were just an occupational hazard, a way of life and death. In such instances, it could be foolhardy and sometimes fatal to fight back. Afterward, a rumor surfaced that several of the hijackers were killed in another caper, and I didn't feel a tinge of sadness.

But one night we turned the tables on a pair of hijackers. We were playing in Odessa at a popular gambling club run by a guy named Paul, whose home was actually a casino that featured craps games. High-rolling oilmen liked to play there. Two guys showed up to rob us, but Paul and another professional gambler, a comrade named Tuffy, had other ideas. Tuffy grabbed one of the hijackers, who shot Paul in the neck. Luckily, the bullet went straight through without hitting anything vital. For Paul, it wasn't much more than a minor inconvenience. He grabbed the guy and choked him, and darn near killed him. Tuffy, a fighter as his name suggested, hit the other guy three or four times. The bandits were in for a heap of trouble and, as it turned out, we had to rescue them from Tuffy and Paul; it looked like they were going to kill the guys. It was a strange turn of events since most robbers were seasoned thugs who kept their quarry under control.

Another time we were in Lubbock in a smaller game that ended with an unlikely twist. The buy-in was just two or three hundred dollars, but that didn't stop the bad guys. Wielding shotguns, a group of robbers burst in and demanded all our money. Most of us just had a few hundred dollars in our pockets, and they got all that. But one of the players, a bookmaker named Bill, had $100,000 in a satchel. When the robbers stumbled onto that, they reacted like a bunch of kids in the proverbial candy store.

"Oh, looky here," one of them said.

"Pay dirt!" chortled another.

"Merry Christmas!" whooped a third.

"Whose is this?" one of them finally asked.

"It's mine," whispered Bill.

A few minutes later, one of the hijackers said, "Okay, all you guys give us your car keys and your billfolds. We're gonna take them down the road, and we're gonna throw them out so we can't be followed."

Then one of them looked at Bill and said, "As for you, sir, we're gonna put your billfold and your car keys right by the door where you can find them. Just don't come out for a few minutes."

His $100,000 donation at least bought him preferential treatment.

Every hijacking and robbery had its own peculiar set of circumstances, and sometimes, if they didn't end too badly, we found humor in them, at least after a while. I remember we got raided one night by the cops on Fort Worth's Exchange Avenue during a Kansas City lowball game, and Sailor was in the dealer's seat.

"Just a minute," Sailor told the policemen. "I want to see if I made this hand."

The police stood there and watched as Sailor dealt the final round. And sure enough, he hit a winner.

"I haven't made a hand all night," he grumbled, "and then you guys pick this time to come barging in."

It turned out they weren't police after all, but robbers dressed as cops. They tied us up, took our money and left. At least they were thoughtful robbers, letting us finish our hand.

Odessa, where Slim, Sailor, and I were based in those early Circuit years, was the hometown of a famous Texas bootlegger named Pinkie Roden. Pinkie was never a professional poker player, but he liked to play and he was pretty darn good for an amateur. We played many times, usually at the Eagles Club in Odessa.

Pinkie owned the Inn of the Golden West, one of Odessa's best hotels. The top two floors were dedicated to a trendy nightspot, the Rooster Club, and to a very private casino-style gambling club—until the Texas Rangers, and maybe the Texas Attorney General's Office, finally put a stop to the gambling. Pinkie was also the man behind the scenes of an exceptionally popular golf tournament, the Odessa Pro-Am. The tournament routinely drew outstanding PGA Tour players like Masters Champion Charles Coody and many of the nation's top amateurs and celebrities. Rat-packer Dean Martin was there one year with actress Stella Stevens, and we had breakfast together.

Besides the golf and glamour, the Odessa Pro-Am was also known fondly for its famously illegal pari-mutuel betting operation, which permitted fans and players to bet the odds on the pro-am teams as bettors did legally at horseracing tracks across the country.

Pinkie went semi-legitimate and opened up a string of liquor stores across West Texas in areas where alcohol was legal, while his bootlegging operations supplied the many "dry" areas prevalent throughout West Texas. He became one of the city's outstanding philanthropic citizens.

"Pinkie never considered bootlegging a crime," one of his cronies told me. "He considered it a public service."

One aspect of the Pinkie Roden legend involved his souped-up fleet of back-road cars used for illicit liquor deliveries. The cars were so fast that Liquor Control Board agents and state troopers could never catch his drivers. So they did the next-best thing: when Pinkie replaced his cars with newer models, the state purchased his old ones. The irony of this always amused me.

Sailor, Slim, and I traveled everywhere on the Texas Circuit, big towns and little towns and anywhere we could find a good game. We went down to Houston, out to El Paso, back to Fort Worth and Dallas, to Austin and Waco and just about anywhere in Texas where we could find poker being spread.

I once pulled up at a game out in the country just across the state line in Oklahoma, and the guys there ordered us to identify ourselves like at an army checkpoint. I hollered back, "This is Doyle, Sailor, and Slim."

"Come on up," they said.

When we started in, I spotted a couple of guards sitting on the roof of the adobe house beside a .50-caliber machine gun. There were so many hijackers operating at the time, the Oklahomans knew the word would spread about the machine gun, and they wouldn't disrupt their games. While having a machine gunner perched atop the house was a somewhat extreme measure, all the games had guys walking around with shotguns. Oklahoma was the undisputed hijacking capital and those operators protected their games extremely well. Texas, on the other hand, was not always as wary of the dangers, and too often the hijackers would find us.

Besides Sailor, Slim, and me, there was a nucleus of professional players who went from town to town. I'm talking about old-time guys such as Martin Kramer, Jack Straus, Bob Hooks, Doc Ramsey, Pat Renfro, Ed "Junior" Whited, James "Goodie" Roy, Felton "Corky" McCorquodale, Aubrey Day, Bill Smith and Crandell Addington—all great poker players.

Crandell stood out from the crowd because he was always dressed in fancy clothing, like he was some movie star. He liked to wear expensive cowboy boots, immaculate Western outfits, and a top-line Stetson. I don't think I ever saw him play in casual clothes. He also was the rare gambler with a college degree. Along with me, he was one of the first educated poker players. Crandell was like 007 Agent James Bond. Most of us usually carried weapons on the road, but Crandell always had the sleekest, most expensive guns. He was also Hollywood handsome and had his choice of women wherever we went.

The road gamblers, as we were called, were a colorful bunch, and my traveling partner Slim was as colorful as any of them. He loved proposition bets and had a whole arsenal of tricks up his sleeve. One time he bet a guy that he could run a quarter mile in something like forty seconds. This was more than a world's record, so everybody bet him. Slim got himself a horse, grabbed hold of its tail and ran behind the horse. He'd take a step and the horse would be running, so he'd jump from here to over there in one stride. He was full of stuff like that. He beat Bobby Riggs, the ex-champion tennis player, at table tennis with the two of them playing with frying pans. He took on Minnesota Fats, betting he could beat Fats playing pool with a broomstick. Another time he took on a ping-pong champion using coke bottles for paddles and beat him too.

Slim had another trick for that Coke bottle that he made a lot of money from. He would bet that a cat could pick up a coke bottle. I've seen him do this one a lot of times. He'd take a cat, put him over that coke bottle, grab the cat by the tail and lift it off the ground. The cat would grab that coke bottle every time and pick it up. Slim was ingenious with those kinds of things.

We gambled on things other than poker, pool being one of our favorite games. At those fraternal places like the Elks Clubs, where we played a lot of poker, there were almost always pool tables, and Slim was a world-class pool player. I was good at pool, though nowhere near Slim's caliber. He would usually set up the matches because he knew all the ins and outs and nuances of pool. It was strange, but I did most of the playing because nobody could compete with Slim. They would allow him to be my coach and tell me what shot to shoot. That provided us an edge, because some pool games were kind of management games anyway. I was definitely more of a shooter than a manager.

Another guy who played the Circuit was Jack "Treetop" Straus. Next to Slim, he weaved the wildest yarns anybody could imagine and was certainly Slim's equal when it came to putting his vivid imagination into play. He was six-foot-seven, which might be why they called him "Treetop," and he was an ex-basketball player, which was why we had a lot in common. Straus was not only the most entertaining person I've ever been around, but an uncommonly creative soul, especially when it came to dodging debts. Jack compulsively bet on everything, with or without a pulse—every horse race, every ball game, every prop bet, everything he could lay a bet on—which was the reason he was broke all his life even though he won a lot of money.

Once Jack went totally overboard with this bookmaker in Houston, and didn't have nearly enough money to pay him. The bookie kept pressuring him, and Jack kept stalling, hoping to win the money to cover his debts.

That's one thing about gamblers; they love to gamble themselves out of debt. It seems it's not just a hazard of the trade, but a requirement. Usually, we find another gambler to stake us until we get back on our feet. But this time, there was no such luck for Jack. He called the bookie and told him he'd meet him downtown the next day with the money. At the appointed time, the bookie was on the street corner waiting. Here came Jack, bounding down the sidewalk carrying a sack—tall and easy to spot. He saw the bookie, waved to him and started across the street toward him. Suddenly, an unmarked car whizzed up and screeched to a halt. Two guys in suits jumped out and grabbed the paper bag. They threw Jack up against the car, shook him down, shoved him in the back seat, and sped away. Of course, the guys were Jack's friends impersonating cops and the sack was stuffed with paper.

That was typical Straus.

A couple of weeks later, Jack won the money to pay the huge debt.

"Johnny, you just won't believe what happened to me that day," he told his bookmaker when he showed up with the money.

"Don't say a word," Johnny gushed. "I saw it all!"

Few stories circulated around the Texas Circuit as good as that one, but Jack's boundless creative talents kept us entertained day after day.

One time we were playing poker in a country home in south Texas with a guy who had a small bookmaking operation. Before the game, Jack got some boot spikes and climbed up a telephone pole down the road and pulled the power switch. He left the power off for about a minute. I don't recall all the ins and outs of the intricate little scheme, but later, when we were monitoring the horse races, the bookmaker's clock was about a minute slow. Jack was picking winners like crazy. He did that for a week before the guy finally realized Jack had put one over on him.

Of course, I had my own experiences with Straus, who had a unique code of honesty. It was kind of hard to understand if you didn't know him, but Straus was an unusual guy. On one hand, he and I were so close that he refused to bet against me when I played golf or gambled on sporting events. But when it came to playing cards, he thought anything necessary to win was legitimate. He didn't rule out marked cards, sneaking a peek at my hand, or whatever other tricks he might use to relieve me of my money at the poker table—fair or foul. I knew to always keep an eye on him playing poker, because you never knew what he would be up to.

One time Jack tried to get me to go to Aruba where a friend of his owned a casino. He gave me this wild story about a drug dealer and the casino owner playing in a huge poker game. I smelled a rat and declined. It just sounded fishy. Later, I found out there was a peep at that casino, which meant they contrived a way to look at the hole cards. I confronted Straus, who didn't deny a thing. All he did was laugh about it.

So I laughed along with him. What else could I do?

We rarely had to search out a game. Almost every town had one, and the big towns like Dallas, Fort Worth, and Houston, had a lot of games. But one of our favorite places to play was over at Kramer's. When we were fixing to find a game, someone would inevitably say, "Where we gonna play next week?" The answer frequently would be, "We're gonna go to Kramer's." The action was always good, first when the game was in Brenham and later when Kramer moved to Houston. Besides, Martin Kramer and his Cajun wife fed us like royalty. Part of our nucleus, the pros, would go to Houston, where there was always a game waiting. Word would spread through Houston that our gang was coming down to play, and the local professional and business poker players gathered at Kramer's and waited for us because they wanted the challenge of playing with the best. We were past the point of playing with the milkman, the mailman, and the workingman. The affluent people played with us then, but that didn't diminish the dangers of this profession.

Hijackers raided Kramer's game one night and killed him. Luckily, I wasn't there that evening, but his death was one of the saddest episodes of my Texas Circuit experience. He was a good man and ran a good game, and we all missed him.

I survived a number of frightening and dangerous incidents in my formative gambling years on Exchange Avenue. With the exception of a few incidents, they provided little humor and were always scary. One of my most terrifying episodes involved not a gun, but a knife. It happened in Houston in the sixties. I left a poker game alone one night and a guy slipped up behind me and put a knife to my throat. I'd faced guns before, but there was something different about a knife pressed against my throat, one or two inches away from slicing it open and ending my life. It scared the hell out of me. I was simply paralyzed with that blade leaning up against my skin. I thought for an instant my heart had stopped, and maybe it did.

"Just don't move. I'm gonna empty you out," the guy said.

He reached in my pocket and took what money I had, and away he went. That didn't happen again because I became leery of certain things around poker games. I learned to avoid isolated places and strangers, and to routinely check to see if I was being followed. I became very observant. Most gamblers were instinctively alert to the dangers, especially the older ones who had experienced more robberies. It was part of self-survival.

And then there was Tooter. Tooter was a short, obese, four hundred-pound bookie who spoke with a lisp. We were playing one day in his hometown of Lubbock, "The Pearl of the Plains," and we broke Tooter, who leaped up and left in a huff.

A short time later, the door burst open and in charged a shotgun-wielding figure wearing a ski mask.

"Everybody put your *handth* up," the intruder demanded, "and put your money in *thith* bag."

We turned around and saw who it was, and a guy named Bill Smith, another bookmaker, said, "Aw, Tooter, put that silly shotgun down and come on and play."

"*Thith* isn't Tooter," Tooter said. "*Thith* is a *wobber*."

When the laughter finally subsided, Tooter reluctantly removed his mask, put down his gun, borrowed some more money, lost it all and left, once again in a huff.

Overnight, Tooter the Wobber became a legend in Texas Circuit lore.

Chapter 9

You miss 100% of the shots you never take.

S lim and Sailor and I decided in the early sixties that it was time for a trip to Las Vegas, so we wound up one evening at the Golden Nugget cardroom downtown on Fremont Street. We were looking for a little extra action and the flashing lights of the keno board on the wall caught our attention.

"How's that game work?" one of the guys asked after a keno runner making the rounds tried to hustle up some business at our table and then moved on down the floor. I was pretty curious too and wanted to play a game. We didn't know the first thing about keno, but Corky McCorquodale was there and gave us some pointers. It was the worst gamble, the worst odds in Vegas, he explained, but if the right numbers popped up on your ticket it was a hefty payoff.

"Let's put up $25 each and play and see what happens," a Vegas friend of mine suggested.

I tossed him a green chip and he got us a ticket. We filled out some numbers and handed it to the keno runner when she came around before the next game. I watched for a few minutes and concluded nothing good was going to happen. The poker game was pretty uneventful and we were, more or less, just killing time at the table. I was sitting there bored stiff when Corky came back.

"Are y'all still playing that ticket?" he asked.

"I don't know," I said. "I guess."

"Well, there's a solid eight spot up there."

I looked up at the keno board and sure enough, all eight of our numbers had come up. Though I didn't know if we still had a live ticket, my eyes lit up brighter than the flashing keno display. I looked around and saw my friend standing in line, and he was waving wildly.

We *were* still playing our ticket. And we collected $50,000.

After a killer celebration that extended deep into the night, Sailor and Slim and I took our $25,000 share back to West Texas and for the first time had some real money. With a total of some $30,000, we started booking sports bets, mostly with Egghead Perry. We could book him higher now, and anytime he got bets he didn't want, we took them. We started winning a lot of money. When we divided it, we counted out $90,000 apiece, an absolute fortune for us. I took my money and put it away, and Sailor took his money and went partying with the girls. When he wasn't losing his money, he was giving it away. Naturally, all his money was soon gone, which bothered him not at all.

Slim took his $90,000 and went back to Amarillo. It wasn't long before his money was gone, too. I took my money and bankrolled our operation again, this time taking a little bigger piece.

"There's four of us now," I said. "Slim, Sailor, me, and the money. So we each get 25 percent, and the money gets 25 percent."

That's how I got half the money and progressively grew my bankroll. Because I didn't throw my money away, I could finance whatever opportunities popped up. Once again we won a lot of money and Sailor bought big cars and partied while Slim bought more cows. I hoarded most of my winnings.

I did, however, buy me a Ford Fairlane.

The three of us—me, Sailor and Slim—continued our partnership for two or three years, still working out of Midland and playing poker all over Texas. Sometimes, it would be just be me and Slim fading the white line, going from game to game down the highway. For economic and strategic reasons, we'd get a room with two beds, and many nights we'd plop down after a game and talk poker into the wee hours, going over the different situations. We didn't have computers back then to determine the odds of winning or losing with certain hands or to help analyze all the mathematical issues associated with poker. So we did all the strategy work manually. It was tedious, but we were dedicated to becoming better players. I dealt out a hand here and another hand there and just kept doing it thousands of times. It got to where I was a lot more advanced in this game than most people. I had become a very good player through hard work and playing lots of hands and then more hands. The best way to improve your game back then was to play and play. And that's what we did.

Everybody today knows what I learned back then because it's in all the poker books. But nobody knew the right way to play before all this information got published. There were no books of any substance and not a word anywhere on hold'em, a relatively new game at the time. A lot of people don't know what a great student of the game Slim was, but he was there right along with me developing his game. Some people said Slim wasn't that great a player, but they were wrong; he was plenty good. He wasn't quite up there with Sailor and me, but he wasn't far behind either. Sailor was maybe as good as I was when he set his mind to it, but he was more interested in girls than gambling.

We had some problems we couldn't resolve with Egghead and talked of leaving town.

"What in the hell are we gonna do?" I asked Sailor.

"Well, we can't stay here with this going on," he said.

"We gotta finish the year," I said.

"No way," snorted Sailor who, in an unusual stroke of common sense, saw the writing on the wall. He packed his bags and fled to his hometown of San Angelo, a nice-sized town south of Midland and Odessa. Slim was already back in Amarillo.

I should have left, but I stuck around, although I was increasingly uncomfortable with the Egghead situation. I guess it was the greed factor; I knew I was going to have a big year. And I wasn't the only one who was uncomfortable. So was another member of our Midland gambling group, a Fort Worth bookie named James Winningham, nicknamed "Puny." Egg and I together were staking Puny, so he got half of what he won and we got the other half. Puny had good customers all around the state, not always big players but good solid people. A very prominent newspaperman and pillar of the community from Fort Worth was one of them, and he really enjoyed betting on college football games.

Puny and I finished out the year without incident. Even though we owed Egghead a debt of gratitude, there was no way to continue our association under those circumstances.

So we took our money and split.

It was the early sixties. Slim was still in Amarillo, Puny returned to Fort Worth, and I headed down to San Angelo and joined up with Sailor, who wasn't playing much poker but was booking sports bets. Pretty soon we were doing the same things we had done back in Fort Worth, gambling and partying with the girls, but with fewer mishaps. The girls were plentiful and I was going out with a different girl almost every night of the week. Monday night was little June Bug, and then Paula, Linda, and so forth. I could hardly keep track of all their names. It was a lot of fun, and arguably the most enjoyable fringe benefit of the gambler's lifestyle.

Everybody in San Angelo, as well as the police, knew me as Paul Waner, a name I only used in gambling circles. I borrowed the name from one of the great baseball players some years earlier—a pretty colorful character in his own right. Lloyd and Paul Waner were Hall of Fame baseball players from the 1920s to the 1940s. Paul was a legendary drinker who maintained that a fellow needed to be relaxed at the plate, and drinking was the best way to relax. If he arrived for a game a little wobbly, he developed a unique way of sobering up—he did back flips across the field. Paul would have fit right in on Exchange Avenue, and I think I would have enjoyed knowing him.

When my friends asked why I took that name, I gave them a somewhat more sober answer, "He had a brother named Lloyd, and I had a brother named Lloyd."

However, the real reason I chose another name in the first place was because San Angelo was less than a hundred miles from Sweetwater where I was still well known for my athletic accomplishments. I didn't want word to get back to my hometown that Doyle Brunson was gambling in San Angelo.

One night, some of us descended on a honky tonk called the Dixie Club where a party was in progress. The entire staff of a San Angelo pharmacy was there, celebrating and dancing to Country & Western music.

And that's when I first saw *her*. If ever there was such a thing as falling in love at first sight, that's what happened to me. Her name was Louise Carter. She was dark-haired, cute, personable, and vivacious. Louise was a pharmacist at Perkins Drugs, and she was there at this joint only because all her co-workers were there for a party. She didn't ordinarily go to places like that, I quickly learned. I knew one of the girls who worked at the pharmacy and she introduced Louise to Sailor and me. Louise danced with me and listened to my spiel, but she was not at all impressed. She thought I was married and Sailor was single. It was the reverse; Sailor was married, though separated, and I was single. Many good-times relationships, yes; marriage, no. Louise had married as a young girl and was divorced and was the mother of a beautiful daughter named Cheryl.

I was totally infatuated.

Once I'd danced with her, I sensed that she was the girl I had been looking for all those years. I loved her smile, her laugh, her bubbly personality. I invited her out for coffee after we left the nightclub, but she wouldn't go. I invited her to dinner. No luck. The next day I went by the drugstore and watched her working. I concluded that she was the most efficient person I'd ever seen. She had a phone to each ear; she was talking to two or three different people, filling prescriptions, and still her lively, effervescent personality was so magnetic.

It depressed me that this girl of my dreams was so elusive. Finally, I persuaded her to have a cup of coffee with me on her break, and I tried to get a date with her.

"No," she said firmly, a rejection that all but shattered me. It had been said that country boys were usually pretty shy and never took rejection well, whatever the circumstances. I discovered there was a nugget of truth in that.

At least once or twice a day I'd go into the drugstore under the pretense of looking for something. She sold me toys, vitamins, multivitamins, aspirin, everything in the store. I bought every contraption she recommended. It didn't fool anyone, particularly Louise. I couldn't get a date with her, but I persisted.

"No, no, no, no," she would say.

After two or three weeks of rejections, I quit coming by. But I hadn't given up completely.

It wasn't long before Sailor and I convinced ourselves it was time for another trip to Las Vegas; we were ready to crash the Big Time again. We got hold of Slim and he was ready to go as well. I think I had $100,000 or so and Slim had a little money. Sailor had none, as usual. But we always shared what we had. I always carried Sailor when he was broke, and a few times he carried me. We were like brothers.

The Big Time was not to be. Again, Vegas just about broke us. It's not that we played poker badly, we were just very unlucky. Devastated, Sailor and I returned to San Angelo and Slim headed back to Amarillo. We didn't have much money, but I continued to get by playing poker.

One day Sailor and I went out to the municipal golf course in San Angelo and as usual we were gambling. Not high, just $100 or $200 matches. After nine holes, I had him $800 down, so we played an "emergency nine," golf jargon for an extra and previously unscheduled nine holes.

After eighteen holes, he owed me $1,900.

"I ain't got it," Sailor whined.

"If you can't pay up," I said, "I'll take your dog. He likes me better than you anyway."

Flirty was a beautiful German shepherd, and he really did like me better. Sailor squawked about it like crazy, but he didn't have a bunch of options.

"If you don't pay me, Flirty is mine," I said.

"Okay, dammit, he's yours," Sailor finally conceded.

I knew it was kinda cruel to take Sailor's dog, but I did give him visiting privileges.

That Sailor had no money wasn't unusual. He had a lifelong habit of just giving his money away. One time he rented a car at the Las Vegas airport and the attendant told him he couldn't let him have a car without a credit card, which he didn't own.

Sailor said, "I'll put up a cash deposit."

The attendant scoffed and said sarcastically, "It would take $20,000 to get this car."

Sailor said, "Okay," reached in his pocket, pulled out four $5,000 packets of money and handed them to the attendant, who nearly fainted.

Sailor never paused to sweat the small stuff. Or the big stuff, for that matter. He confronted life with an amusing nonchalance. Once he was sick as could be, and I was deeply concerned and insisted he see a doctor. When the diagnosis indicated he was okay, Sailor was disappointed.

"I was hoping the report was bad," he said, because I was gonna drink a chocolate milkshake every thirty minutes until I died."

In San Angelo, everybody congregated around midnight at Sam's Chicken House after most places closed. They came there to eat after they'd been to the movies, the nightclubs, the beer joints, the poker games, or wherever. Sailor showed up sometimes with the most gorgeous women imaginable. But with Sailor, looks, size, shape, age, or color made no difference. He was an equal-opportunity lover, and treated every one of them like his own little princess. She could be a local beauty queen or a local heiress, or maybe just the cheapest hooker in town. It mattered not. No man ever appreciated women like Sailor Roberts. Indeed, nobody looked at women, money, life, poker, or anything else quite like Sailor.

I always enjoyed seeing what surprise Sailor would bring to Sam's; you just never knew what the plate of the day was. But I had my own female ideas, and that was somehow to get to Louise. Not much was working, but while plotting a new strategy to win over Louise, fate intervened. A beautician named Maybelle had run into a Hardin-Simmons graduate who told her all about me, and Maybelle approached Louise on my behalf.

"Louise," she said, "I told you Doyle Brunson was the man for you. He's not married, he's never been married, he has a master's degree from Hardin-Simmons, and he was a star athlete there."

But even then, I don't think Louise was much concerned because I had stopped coming by the pharmacy. She just wasn't interested at the time, so nothing developed. But I do think a seed was planted, and it just needed some time to grow.

A couple of months later, Sailor and I were having dinner at a steakhouse, and I saw Louise with some clown who looked like a prison-camp refugee. That gave me new hope, because I knew I was better looking than he was. When she saw me, I winked at her and she smiled and waved.

"Well," I said to Sailor, "maybe I've still got a shot."

The next day I went to the drugstore. Everything had changed. She was very friendly, and even receptive to going out. We started dating, and it was, as I thought it could be, a match made in heaven or someplace awfully close. I mean, I was in love! It probably took her a bit longer, but she reciprocated pretty fast. She asked me what I did, and for some reason I told her I was a bookmaker. I really wasn't, but I was living with Sailor, and he was still booking sports bets. I was probably trying to impress her.

I sure never 'fessed up to being a gambler or even a poker player. I guess I thought that a bookmaker sounded less onerous than a poker player, and sure enough, she said, "Oh, that's nice."

And I said to myself, "Yeah, this gal's a girl after my own heart."

In reality she thought I was a *bookkeeper*, an accountant. We dated for a month or so and really hit it off, and started talking marriage. She knew I played poker, but she didn't know quite how serious a pursuit it was for me. Not yet anyway.

But there was trouble brewing.

One day her boss at the pharmacy came running in. "Where's Doyle?" he asked.

"I think he's at the house," she said.

"We gotta get to him! I just got word that they're fixing to get raided."

"What do you mean, raided?"

"My God, Louise, don't you know what Doyle does?"

"Yes, he's a bookmaker," she replied.

He looked at her and started laughing. "Louise, do you know what a bookmaker is?"

"Yeah, he keeps books for people."

Her boss was incredulous. "Do you know what a bookie is?"

She looked at him with this stunned look on her lovely face and said, "Oh, my goodness!"

Louise was not dumb, just remarkably naïve. She had spent most of her life in school, working her way through the University of Kentucky and then through the pharmacy college at the University of Georgia. This was her first job out of school, and she was good at it—she became the number-one pharmacist at a chain of 150 drugstores. But to put it ever so mildly, worldly she wasn't.

But she proved herself a real trooper. She and her boss rushed over to warn me that a federal raiding party was on our tail. They tried to block off the street with their cars, but it was too late. The feds had already arrived and were busting down our door.

What happened was that one of our friends, a big-time bookie named Duck Mallard, had visited San Angelo over the weekend and booked his bets on our home phone. The Texas Rangers or the FBI picked up our number through wiretaps on phones that people were using to call Duck. Unfortunately, investigators concluded we were running a major bookmaking operation. Sailor had a few customers because he knew all the sports bettors in town, but his bookmaking operation was amateurish by comparison. Sailor wasn't there though; he was out playing golf or running after some girl.

Duck's the reason we got busted. I wasn't pleased with him over that caper, but with a marvelous name like Duck Mallard, I couldn't stay mad at him for long. His associates swore that was his real name, and maybe it was.

Meanwhile, the German shepherd I won from Sailor was throwing a fit. He was as harmless as a kitten, but he could *act* vicious.

"Get that dog under control or we're gonna shoot it," one belligerent agent said.

That "killer dog" was nothing but a big old friendly hound that was barking his head off because somebody kicked the door down and invaded his turf. What would anyone expect a dog to do? I got him quieted, but surprisingly, that incident, would come back to haunt me in later years.

After the raid, they tossed me in jail. They took me down and threw me in the drunk tank. The place was full, and the feds left me in there to stew for a while. They were having a tough time figuring out who I was because I was still using the name Paul Waner, which made it difficult for them to gather evidence about me. Gamblers could honestly say, "No, we don't know any Doyle Brunson."

Finally the sheriff, not the feds, confronted me with an ultimatum scripted straight out of a John Wayne movie.

"Son," he growled, "don't let the sun set on your ass in San Angelo. Get outta here or I'll throw you under the jail," meaning he would lock me up and pretty much throw away the key.

I got.

A friend had wrecked my car a short time before the raid, so I borrowed one of Louise's two cars, an old Nash. I packed up my meager belongings, borrowed some money, loaded up Flirty in the back seat of the car, and hit the road back to Fort Worth. I told Louise I was going to play poker. Even though she still didn't approve, she had come to understand my gambling; that's just what I did. She stayed on in San Angelo and was summoned to appear before a grand jury investigating the raid. I couldn't believe it, but she stonewalled the prosecutors repeatedly, even taking the Fifth Amendment a few times.

If possible, I loved her even more.

She was a stand-up girl, even though it would have been fine if she had told them everything she knew about my gambling activities. Fact is, she didn't know anything, and there really wasn't much to know. The case was eventually dismissed, but I stayed out of San Angelo, carefully heeding the sheriff's advice. I didn't want to get arrested every time I left my home; I'd already been through that.

Louise and I corresponded until finally she quit her job and moved to Fort Worth, despite opposition from her friends and mother. They weren't too keen on her quitting her respectable job to marry a gambler.

On August 19, 1962, a couple of years after we met, we were married in a funeral home in La Marque, Texas, where my sister Lavada's husband worked. That's right, a funeral home. But it was brand new and the chapel was lovely. It was a small, beautiful wedding with a Baptist minister performing the ceremony and mostly family members attending.

Of course, there may have been a few minor complications to the matter. Because I was tied up in a poker game, I had sent Sailor to take Louise to get the marriage license and he had to identify himself as Doyle Brunson. I know this was unusual, but it was a good game; I couldn't pass up the opportunity. And we needed the money. I could imagine the look on Louise's face when Sailor showed up at the courthouse instead of me! She was also fretting over the fact that our marriage might be annulled if anyone found out about Sailor's masquerade.

"I never heard of anything so bizarre in my life," she said of the whole affair. I think Louise was getting the idea that life with a gambler might turn out to be a bit unusual.

We spent our honeymoon at the Jack Tar Hotel on the beach in Galveston, and everything was coming up roses.

I assured Louise when we got married that I would stop gambling; I would find a legitimate profession. I think I meant it too. I liked the idea of owning a sporting goods store and had some aspirations in that direction. By then, I was already twenty-nine years old and considering a real job that would allow us to live like regular 9-to-5 folks. Having a normal profession had a certain appeal, that is, until I really started thinking about it. I told Louise that I'd keep playing poker only until I found something suitable. Her expectations were that I would do so and it would happen in the sooner, rather than the later, timeframe.

Despite my promises, we were living in Fort Worth. That's where I knew people, and I figured the heat from the cops had cooled off. Sailor and Slim and I were still partners, still a gambling team. We were traveling around the country and making enough money to live on.

Then Sailor shot himself.

We were out somewhere in Fort Worth, the poker game had broken up, and we had gone to have a beer at a nightclub owned by one of the big-time players. All of a sudden, this knockout gal from Houston came bounding up to our buddy Wayne, who was a handsome guy—about six-foot-four, black wavy hair, a great smile and personality. The girl threw her arms around him.

"Boy, you're the best-looking guy I ever saw. Will you buy me a drink?"

"Sure," Wayne said, winking at me.

"Wow, nothing like that ever happened to ol' Doyle," I was thinking.

We had a beer and then drove out to a Western joint, the Stagecoach. There were five or six of us, and some of the group decided to go across the street to a saloon where many of Fort Worth's tough hoodlums hung out.

"I don't want to go," I said. "There's nothing over there but trouble."

But they ignored my warning and went anyway. Right away, a rough character named Bubba Rainwater started dancing with Wayne's new admirer. Wayne saw what was happening, but he didn't want trouble over some girl he'd just met. He left the girl and one of our friends at the saloon and rejoined us across the street.

Then the friend came over to the Western place and said, "That girl is over there saying Wayne Hamilton is nothing but a punk for abandoning her."

"Well, I can't have that," Wayne said. "I guess we'd better go over there and get her."

"Okay, we'll go with you," I said.

Anticipating trouble, one of the guys in our group said, "Wait a minute, I've got a gun in the car."

When the guy returned, Sailor, now sufficiently over-served, said, "Let me have that gun." He shoved it in his pants and we walked across the street.

Sailor looked like Dean Martin as John Wayne's gunslinger sidekick in the movie *Rio Bravo*. I recognized a lot of guys from Exchange Avenue, and several of them greeted me. Wayne's girl was on the dance floor. "You know, Gerald," Wayne said to the bartender, "I don't want any trouble. I've just come to get my girl, and then we're gonna leave."

"She's out there with Bubba," said Gerald.

"I know," Wayne said, "but she came with me. I want to leave with her. Then he can have her if he wants her, I don't care."

I looked around, and Sailor was over there twirling the gun like some old-time gunslinger. All of a sudden, bam! Everybody hit the floor, because these guys were used to people getting shot and killed in Fort Worth.

Here came Bubba to confront Sailor, who'd just shot himself. The bullet had gone down through his knee and out the back of his calf but somehow missed bones and ligaments. Sailor had the pistol in his hand and a dazed look on his face.

"What's going on?" Bubba demanded.

"I just shot myself, you goofy son of a bitch," Sailor moaned.

Bubba grabbed the gun out of Sailor's hand and fired a shot on each side of Sailor's head. They stood there, silently staring at each other. I thought surely somebody was going to get killed.

"Let's get out of here," I said.

One of the thugs sitting at a table, Chew Tobacco Bill Anderson they called him, said, "Yeah. Y'all git your goat-smellin' asses outta here."

We got.

"Man, that was close," I said. "Where's Sailor?"

"Sailor's still in there."

"Come on," I said, "we gotta go get him."

"We're not going back in there," somebody said.

"I'm gonna go back and get him," I said, "or at least try to."

As I approached the door, Bubba had a gun jabbed in the Houston girl's ribs, and he was backing out of the place with her. I backed off while he marched her to his car, hopped in, and drove away. I never saw either one of them again.

With that gun and Bubba out of range, I ran back in to check on Sailor, who was standing there, kind of in shock, blood running down his leg.

"Come on, Sailor," I said, "we gotta get you out of here. We gotta take you to the hospital."

I took him by the arm and led him out, all the time hearing the squish, squish of the blood collected in his shoe. We spent the night at the hospital.

When I got home, Louise was more than casually curious about how something as innocent as going out for a beer could lead to a nearly disastrous confrontation with guns, kidnapping, blood and an emergency trip to the hospital—and how I happened to be in the middle of it.

"Beats me," I told her.

Chapter 10

People think a rabbit's foot is lucky.
It wasn't very lucky for the rabbit.

E xploring the back roads and back rooms of Texas with Slim and Sailor took an unexpected and near fatal turn toward the end of 1962. Several weeks after Louise and I married, she got pregnant, which thrilled us both. But three months later in December, I awoke one morning to find an ugly little knot on my neck. That would have been no big deal, except it was the exact same symptom my brother Lloyd had discovered four years earlier before cancer killed him. It was a terrible jolt, like a runaway truck bearing down on me that I couldn't escape from. Even when my doctor dismissed the discovery as probably inconsequential, I was still shaken. He prescribed antibiotics, but a week later the knot not only hadn't disappeared, it had grown slightly larger.

"I don't think it's anything to worry about," the doctor said, "but we better operate and take it out."

I felt an ominous cloud hanging over me.

I entered the hospital in Fort Worth assured of no more than a thirty-minute surgery. When the doctors opened up my neck, they exposed a melanoma that stemmed from a black mole doctors had removed a year earlier in San Angelo. In the months after the removal, I had played a lot of golf and the sun had apparently activated melanoma cells that still lurked in my neck. The Fort Worth surgeon began removing those cells at once, worried that the cancer would attack my brain and plunge me into a coma. Then when they opened my chest, they found the melanoma cancer had spread through my body like wildfire. Alarmed, the surgeon called in several more specialists. They worked closely with pathologists during the surgery, sending tissue samples back and forth. The melanoma didn't respond to radiation or chemotherapy, only to surgery. And they said it was too widespread to even consider further surgery.

In the end, they agreed unanimously that nothing more could be done, explaining to Louise that there was no case history of anyone with such an affliction living longer than three or four months. Within a number of weeks, they said, the cancer would reach my brain and I would lapse into a coma. They advised Louise to return me to the hospital when that happened, but forewarned her that I would remain in a vegetative state the last few weeks of my life. Despite the shock, Louise handled the crisis remarkably well. Her inner strength emerged when the going got really tough.

Nobody told me immediately about the deadly diagnosis. In fact, they let me rest a couple of days before even informing me of the malignancy, and they decided against giving me any hint that it was life-threatening.

Before they sewed me back up and sent me home to die, I asked the doctor, "Did you get it all?"

"Nah, we didn't have time," he explained, "but melanoma is like a black corruption. You can see it with your naked eye, and we could see it all through your body when we opened up your neck and shoulder and your chest cavity."

He didn't say much more than that, but I'd heard enough to know that something was terribly wrong. I also sensed that there was something he wasn't telling me.

After informing Louise that there was no chance I would live to see our baby born, the doctors sent me home to await the inevitable. But Louise found their verdict unacceptable, and she told them so. They conceded that some cancer hospitals might have an experimental drug that could temporarily prolong my life, but they were not encouraging. They said my body couldn't endure more surgery at the time and that any such attempt would probably be fatal.

I was resting at home when Louise made an appointment at M.D. Anderson Cancer Center in Houston, considered by many the best cancer hospital in the world. It was a trying time. We had just gotten married, we'd put a deposit on a house, and my financial situation was less robust than even I was. But Louise insisted on taking me to Houston.

She was determined that I live to see our first child born.

Meanwhile, people began dropping by our house in Fort Worth, even some of the old poker players who weren't close friends. A couple hundred folks came by, and their reactions would have awakened a dead man, which I kind of was. Wayne Hamilton broke down and cried. Even Johnny Moss dropped by, and though he expressed no emotion, I knew he wasn't making a routine social call. I'd played poker long enough with Moss to know that a lot of my chips were in this pot.

All of them.

It was soon obvious that everybody was showing up to say good-bye. Finally, I zeroed in on the gravity of the situation.

I might die.

Word spread about my illness. All across West Texas and elsewhere, people held prayer sessions for me. One little girl, a Catholic, encouraged her whole school to pray for me. And she kept reassuring Louise, "Don't worry. I know he's going to be okay!"

I developed an ambivalent attitude. I wasn't 100 percent convinced I was going to die. I'd spent most of my life overcoming adversity, and I held out hope that I might do it again. Still, the message rang clear: the odds were stacked against me.

Two weeks later, Louise and Sailor took me down to Houston for another round of surgery, not to save my life, just to prolong it a few months. I was in the operating room fifteen hours, from 7:30 a.m. until 10:30 p.m. They did some radical head and neck surgery, removing a lot of flesh where the mole was. They took out all the lymph nodes on the right side of my face and my head. Several doctors worried that I might die on the operating table. It turned out—miracle of miracles—they found not a trace of cancer.

Nothing. It had just disappeared.

When I came to, they told me the stunning news. Although physically I felt terrible, I was overcome with relief emotionally. All I managed to say was, "Obviously, the doctors made a mistake in Fort Worth. It wasn't really cancer, but something else."

My main doctor said, "No, the frozen slides indicated otherwise. The mole that was removed in San Angelo was even marginally malignant at that point."

He said the San Angelo doctors hadn't removed enough tissue around the mole to contain the cancer, and when I got back in the sun, it spread. The frozen sections confirmed that it was some kind of high-grade melanoma. But it had just vanished.

"We don't have any explanation for this," the doctor said.

He called it a spontaneous remission, and said he and his colleagues had seen such an occurrence only a few times. I could only speculate whether the "spontaneous remission" would or wouldn't have occurred if

Louise hadn't insisted on the surgery. I suppose it probably wouldn't have, and I most assuredly would have died.

Throughout my two- or three-week convalescence in Houston, Louise hardly left my side, even though she was well into her pregnancy. We couldn't afford a special nurse, so she and Sailor, posing as Mr. and Mrs. Roberts, took a small hotel room near the hospital. They then switched off, one remaining at the hospital with me while the other got a few hours' rest. Though my prognosis in Houston was good, my doctor warned me about becoming too optimistic.

"Melanoma is like a deadly rattlesnake that can lay dormant in the bloodstream for ten or fifteen years, then strike again at any time or place," he told me. "I don't want you to think you're completely out of the woods."

With those cryptic words of caution ricocheting around in my head, I soon left Houston, recuperated quickly and continued my quest for green-felt riches, periodically returning to the hospital for checkups. But lo and behold, my rattlesnake appeared fangless.

I grew up in a Christian household, but no one ever accused me of being a religious person. Far from it. After my recovery, it should have dawned on me that this was more than a miraculous healing. It didn't. I was caught up in myself—in my pride and ego, determined to be rich if not famous. I just gratefully accepted the fact that my cancer was gone, but I didn't wake up one morning and say, "Thank you, God." It wasn't that I didn't believe this was a miraculous healing that God sent forth. I believed God intervened for some reason, though for what reason I had no idea. I didn't give God any credit. I just walked out of the hospital thankful that I had survived cancer. I was young and alive, and like many young people I thought I was bulletproof, that I had beat cancer and was going to live forever.

But significantly, though quietly, I had changed. I was beginning to appreciate the beauty of life and the wonders of the world around me. The sky never appeared so blue or the grass so green. I'd hardly noticed the flowers at the hospital, but overnight I realized their quiet, reassuring beauty. I walked out of that hospital with a fresh outlook. I appreciated Louise even more, recognizing the depth of her love, faith, courage and support throughout that nightmare. I realized also what a good, faithful, even loving friend Sailor had become.

While I rejoiced in my newfound lease on life, there was a flip side for Louise. I had promised her I would find a so-called legitimate occupation after we married. But I knew now life was short and unpredictable, and that it would be a mistake to live it doing something I neither enjoyed nor could commit to. I wanted to be a poker player, a high-stakes poker player. I wanted to make a lot of money. And truth be told, I knew I wasn't really home free. The chief surgeon at M.D. Anderson cautioned me about becoming too optimistic.

The doctor's message kept rattling around in my head: *Melanoma is like a deadly rattlesnake that can lay dormant...*

I didn't know if anyone ever ranked sins, but I imagined my obsession with making money was probably right up there near the top. I figured the affliction, if that's what it was, stemmed from my meager financial background and my athletic competitiveness. Moreover, I loved to gamble. I didn't know what else to do. No way was I going to coach or teach. While I admired those professions, I thought those who dedicated themselves to such jobs were the most underpaid people I knew.

I wanted more.

I possessed no business skills, as I proved so vividly in my first job out of college and later through so many misguided ventures. The only thing I was truly successful at was poker, and it stood to reason that gambling would be my vocation. Putting all my doubts and misgivings aside, I decided I wouldn't continue to worry about what my friends and others thought about my choice of a career. I was a gambler; it's what I wanted and that's just the way it was.

I knew I faced a problem with Louise because, bless her heart, she was just square as an apple box. She never knew anything about my business, never knew whether I won or lost. We never talked about gambling around the house because I knew it upset her. I told her my decision, and though she didn't agree with it, she accepted the inevitable. As I said, she could cope splendidly with the monumental decisions.

I thought to myself, "Doyle, you are one lucky SOB."

Times were tough for a spell after my brush with death. There wasn't a lot of money around the Brunson household, and Louise was four months pregnant. I had no insurance, and couldn't pay the immense hospital bills in Houston. Because I was a resident of Texas, I was fortunate that M.D. Anderson had accepted me as a patient. I may not have gotten royal treatment like the insured patients, but I got treatment.

Five months after my surgery, our first child, a daughter, was born. We named her Doyla, a namesake decision linked to my bout with cancer. She was a beautiful baby who looked just like her mother.

Her birth, however, presented an immediate and significant challenge: I had to spring her and her mother from the hospital, which required money I didn't have. I was playing poker around the clock, just trying to win enough money to pay the bills so the hospital would release them. We were huddled over a table in the back room of a pool hall on Main Street in downtown Fort Worth. I was a few dollars ahead, but not enough to get them out.

So I devised a plan. I would send Sailor to the hospital.

"Identify yourself as me, and sign the necessary release papers," I told him. "Stall 'em until I win some money and I'll come get y'all."

Sailor was hardly giddy about my brilliant scheme. "If your brain was as big as your balls, you could fly to the moon," he allowed, but he took off just the same.

When he got to the hospital, Louise predictably grilled him about his presence—and my absence. Even while the poker game was going on, I thought about Sailor's mission of desperation, and how he might squirm out of his predicament. But mostly I just laughed to myself as I pictured him trying to placate Louise. I didn't laugh too hard, though—my newborn baby and my wife were in the hospital and I had no money to pay the bills. I'd played in some high-stakes games before, but this one generated a new and different kind of pressure.

We were playing deuce-to-seven lowball when the key hand was dealt. I had an 8-6 and I bet it. A man in a bowling shirt across the table immediately raised me. Sweat was beading across my brow, and I didn't think it was the room temperature. I actually felt my stomach churning. It was a big pot and there was a lot riding on that money in the middle. With time running out, I called the bet.

And won!

"I'm outta here, boys!" I announced.

I scooped up the money and raced to the hospital to pick up Louise, the baby and Sailor. The look on Sailor's face when I showed up was grand relief, but he also let me know he didn't like the duties I'd assigned him.

Pulling me aside, he said, "You ain't near as smart as you think you are, especially when it comes to women."

I argued a minute or two, but he was right. Neither of us knew what we would have done if I'd lost.

Thankfully, I didn't have to think on that one too hard.

Chapter 11

In the valley of the blind, the one-eyed man is king.

L ouise was a rock during this time, mid-1963. I was still recovering, we had a new baby in the house, and Louise's mother had come to live with us while undergoing treatment for the cancer that was slowly killing her. There was a lot of pressure on our family, most of it on Louise. One day after visiting her mother in the hospital, she came running to me all flustered, almost in tears.

I thought her mom had taken a turn for the worse.

"What's wrong?" I asked.

"I was walking downstairs," she began, clearly agitated, "and as I was coming in the door, this guy in a raincoat, he just walked by, and he opened his raincoat and he didn't have any clothes on under it."

"Well," I said, "he's a flasher. What happened?"

"He opened that raincoat," she blurted, "and he grabbed a-hold of himself with both hands, and he started swinging that thing at me like it was a snake."

"Louise," I said, more than mildly impressed, "he took hold of it with *both* hands?"

"Yes, that's right."

"And you let that guy get away?"

If looks could kill, I was a dead man. To me, a run-in with a two-fisted flasher seemed unusually funny.

Louise, somehow, didn't find the humor in that.

After recovering from the cancer scare, I returned to the tables with a fresh appreciation for being alive. It's amazing what a new lease on life will do for a man. I got back into my game, along with Sailor and Slim, but it was different than before. Some latent abilities surfaced that I didn't know I had and I started playing better, more instinctively, than I ever had. I read my competitors more accurately and discovered a self-assurance I'd never known. Incredibly, I won fifty-four times in a row. At some point in some games, I would be losing, but I stayed until I won and the streak kept going. Or the games didn't break up while I was behind. It was so uncanny it got to be a joke. The regular players would say, "Well, here comes Doyle, there goes our money. He don't ever lose." I just got better and better. I couldn't begin to explain what happened. Perhaps it was simply that I had finally dispelled any doubts about my profession. It was possible also that the brush with death unleashed some dormant ability. I knew only that for fifty-four straight games, I couldn't lose. I also knew I had made enough money to clear up medical bills and other debts.

I was on my way.

When I finally did lose, at a game in Oklahoma, it was no big deal. It wasn't a major loss or particularly shocking. I never really paid much attention to the winning streak other than to have some fun talking about it, although I didn't quickly forget the last hand of the night in that Oklahoma game.

No-limit hold'em had become the game of choice and that's what we were playing. I held a 10-9 and my opponent a J-8. The flop had come 7-9-10, giving me top two pair, tens and nines, and my opponent a straight. I didn't make my full house, and his straight won a big, big pot. The game broke up right after that, and while I was a loser for the first time in fifty-five games, it wasn't traumatic. Sailor, Slim, and I talked about it when it was over, about the streak, and how I could forget about it and start a new one.

As we barnstormed across Texas, the three of us continued to benefit from our reputations as stand-up, honest gamblers. We weren't alone in this regard, but it seemed sometimes we were in the minority. We always had to be alert to the gamblers we played with, as many were unscrupulous and tried to get the money any way they could. We took our hits here and there, but over time we became experts in the many methods cheats used against us and, for the most part, were able to protect ourselves. On Exchange Avenue and the Texas Circuit, just about anything went in those days, as long as a gambler could get away with it. For professional poker players, it wasn't particularly unethical to take advantage any way possible, which sometimes included blatant, downright cheating. One only had to remember the types of guys we were playing with. I never got involved in their cheating scams because I almost always won without having to resort to dubious methods.

If I hadn't won, would I have cheated? I thought not, but considering that poker was my livelihood and my family might go hungry if I didn't win, the temptation would have been strong.

While a man's word in the gambling world was his bond, honor among gamblers got slightly warped at times. Nothing illustrated this better than an experience I had in Mississippi. A friend of mine we called Captain John, who was kind of a burglar, invited me to Vicksburg to play a wealthy bar owner known as Barney. He liked heads-up hold'em, which sounded pretty good, since I didn't mind going head-to-head with anyone. So I flew down to Mississippi and managed first off to get lost in the Civil War Memorial Park, a huge, scary place. I finally got out of the park and found the bar, and while Barney was ready to play, I was a little winded after the long trip.

"I'm really kind of tired" I told Captain John. "I'd like to rest tonight and play tomorrow."

"Okay," he said, "but I'm gonna play tonight. Why don't you take a piece of my action?"

Now the object of inviting me down there was to take my money, one way or another and not necessarily honestly. But I said okay, and foolishly took 50 percent of his action. I went to bed fully aware that I had given them the perfect opportunity to rip me off. But the next morning, Captain John told me he had gone head-to-head with Barney and beat him rather handily.

"Here's your part of it," he said, handing me several thousand dollars.

It was an honor thing. The code held that you didn't betray the confidence of a friend by losing his money intentionally. You didn't do that to friends. You could cheat them or have them cheated, but you didn't betray them. There's a fine line between doing something underhanded to somebody—like breaking your word—and pushing the rules a little in a game where it's almost expected.

Still, like I said, Captain John was kind of a bandit who flirted with honesty but seldom romanced it, and he and Barney were sure they would win the money back anyway.

And Barney did his damnedest.

Right away I realized he was cheating, that he was playing what we call a "light." That meant he had a tiny mirror, and when he dealt, he could see the cards. But I'd been exposed to that, so I could spot it pretty easily. He wasn't that good a player, so I was beating him anyway. When he dealt,

I got out. When I dealt, I played. It didn't take him too long to realize that I'd caught on to him.

And he quit.

More times than not, it was just Slim and me on the road, because chasing women became Sailor's primary goal. But Slim felt like I did. We took our poker seriously and tried to maximize our efforts in winning. At the same time, we had to watch our backs and stay alert to the many dangers of playing poker.

Unlike Tooter, the tongue-tied "wobber," most of the gunmen I encountered were accomplished killers. Some guys I knew were playing poker in Alabama one time with a good friend I called H.O. I wasn't there, but the hijackers burst in and blew my friend's head off with a shotgun while robbing the game. I was certain it was a personal-grudge shooting, because they targeted him for no apparent reason. Unlike a lot of the guys caught up in such violence, H.O. was not an unsavory character, but a real nice Southern boy from Alabama. It might have just been a dispute over a woman.

Poker took me to some strange places and landed me in some tight spots. One of the scariest occurred in the sixties when I was a young pro and open to interesting propositions. A known hoodlum and poker cheat named Bill Douglas wanted me to take on a moonshiner in the hills of West Virginia.

"Why don't you go play him?" I asked.

"Because he knows my reputation as a cheat and he won't play me," he said. "He's heard of you, and he wants to play you."

"Yeah, I'll go play him," I said.

"I'll put up half the money, and you put up half the money, and we'll split the win," Bill said. We immediately made flight reservations. I had met Bill on a trip to Las Vegas, and he just took a liking to me for some reason. He was one of the first of the so-called 21 counters to show up in Vegas and beat the blackjack games with extraordinary recall and card counting. He got himself barred from most of the casinos, although he served as a consultant for the Binions for several years.

After we landed in West Virginia, we drove a couple of hours up into the mountains where this guy had all his moonshine stills. Think of the movie *Deliverance* and that's what it was like.

When we found this guy, he said, "You want to play?"

"Yeah, that's what I came to do," I replied.

The guy wasn't a very good player, and I soon got him thousands of dollars down. I was feeling quite pleased with myself when suddenly he pulled out a pistol and laid it on the table. That got my wholehearted attention real fast, and he said in a quiet, threatening voice, "Son, you better not win any more of my money."

I had been in some unsettling spots before, but nothing quite like this—stuck in the remote hills of West Virginia with an angry and armed moonshiner who was a vastly inferior poker player, but tired of losing. I didn't know what to do. Or say. I was just staring at him and pondering my dilemma when Bill walked over.

"Well, he's probably gonna win more money, and after he wins it, he's gonna turn around and hand it to me," Bill told the moonshiner. "Then it'll be up to you and me."

I'm sitting there, watching and listening and not knowing what the hell is going to happen next. But I'm thinking, "Damn it, Doyle, you went to college, got a master's; you know better than to get in a fix like this!"

"Fine," the moonshiner shrugged.

He dealt and we continued to play, and sure enough I finally broke the guy—about forty-something thousand dollars. Bill walked over, and I handed him the money. The moonshiner grabbed his pistol, and out of nowhere Bill came up with his gun at the same moment.

Like something out of a movie, Bill said, "Now, you can put that gun down, and we'll both live. Or you can pull the trigger, and we'll both die."

His voice didn't tremble, his hand didn't shake. I'm thinking that even in the movies I'd never seen anything like it. Mainly, I thought, "No good can come from this—none at all."

"This gun's got a hair trigger," Bill continued. "It'll go off when you shoot. You call it."

The old moonshiner stared at him for what seemed an awfully long time, then put his gun down. In one swift motion, Bill whacked him aside the head. The guy dropped to the floor and lay there in a pool of blood.

"Come on, let's go," Bill commanded.

We hurried out the door, scrambled into the car, drove out of those hills and caught a plane back home.

I thought I'd been around tough people, after Exchange Avenue and the Jacksboro Highway, but this guy Bill had nerves of steel. I didn't know much about cheating, and he showed me ways to keep people from cheating me. He would take a small percentage of my games when I went to Vegas, and I made him some money. I didn't, however, go on any more excursions with him, which I suppose validated my formal education.

Bill got involved in a similar prearranged country poker deal, this time in a trailer in Memphis, Tennessee, when robbers hijacked the game. They shot him with a small .22 caliber, and the bullet hit a vital area and killed him. It was hardly a staggering loss to the world, but Bill had his good points. He was a gutsy guy and I respected him. He was only about forty-five when he was killed.

Another time in the late sixties, I was out drinking beer in Midland with a friend named Johnny Wheeler, and we went over to what was commonly known as "colored town." Most every place in Texas had colored towns, where many of the blacks lived and where most of the businesses were black-owned and operated. Like the white section of town, they too had their gambling joints. That night, we were in a nightclub playing small stakes poker in a game in the back with mostly blacks and I won all their money, about four or five hundred dollars. We were doing a little drinking and as I got up, I was laughing and joking around with the players. I was bragging and acting kind of foolish and decided to give them their money back.

"Here, guys," I said, "I'm one of the best players in the world. Y'all didn't have a chance."

I'd collected a $15,000 gambling debt earlier in the day and I was feeling generous. When I handed them their money, they whooped a bit, thanked me and walked Johnny and me to the door. We had started to the car when this big, husky guy stopped Johnny, who was drinking heavily and probably not thinking too clearly.

"You got a light?" the guy asked.

I noticed for the first time that Johnny was wearing a diamond stickpin, and I sensed at once that something bad was brewing.

"Come on, Johnny, let's go," I said.

But he reached into his pocket. "Yeah, I got one," he said.

The guy hit him and shattered his jaw, grabbed the stickpin and went after the $400 in Johnny's pocket.

I had a pistol in my car and started running down the dirt road to get it. Without warning, a group of black guys converged on me. These were not the ones we'd played poker with. This was a gang of thugs, total strangers, who had been lurking outside waiting for us. They tripped me, knocked me down in the dirt and started kicking me in the head and body. I tried to get up and they hit me and knocked me down again.

I was thinking, "Quit kicking and hitting me, and I'll give you the damn money." But they seemed determined to knock me out.

I'd been hit some awful licks in my life, but I'd never been knocked unconscious. I grabbed handfuls of dirt and hurled it in their faces, and finally got to my feet and hit the big guy, knocking him flat. When he went down, all his cohorts fled. Then the big guy struggled up and he took off too.

I figured they were afraid the police might show up.

It was a wonder I didn't get knifed or shot, or injured even worse. They did break some ribs and my nose, scratched me up pretty badly and tore one of my ears loose. I was covered in blood. They didn't know I had that $15,000 on me. If they'd done it right, I'd have given it to them without a struggle. But they wouldn't stop fighting.

Afterward, I got some information on the guys that attacked us and telephoned one of my well-connected friends named George McGann. George loved poker but was deeply involved with the Dixie Mafia, whose criminal activity—murder was a specialty—stretched from Kentucky through the South to West Texas. He lived just east of Midland in Big Spring, a town whose only brush with fame was in the late sixties when portions of the Academy Award–winning movie *Midnight Cowboy* were filmed there. George knew all the hoods and underworld players in this area of West Texas, and I told him what had happened.

"I'll come over there and help you," he said. "What were their names?"

I told him what I knew.

"Oh, man, those are Chuck's boys."

"Who's Chuck?" I said.

He told me about some guy he knew there. "I'll see what I can do," he said. "Call me back in an hour or so."

When I called back, George said, "Yeah, I talked to Chuck. He said the guys that jumped you didn't know who you were and they're sorry they did it."

"I just want that one guy," I said, "the ringleader who was kicking me in the head. I want to know who he is and I want to find him."

George laughed and said, "That wouldn't do you any good; he'd whip you again. He was cut from the San Francisco 49ers last week."

"Okay," I said, "we can forget that."

The next day Chuck came by my house. He was a glorified pimp with a gang of thugs and a notorious reputation as a killer, among other things.

"They're sorry they did that to you, and they understand if you feel you have to do something about it."

"Just tell them to give Johnny back his diamond stickpin and his $400," I said.

"Oh," he said, "they've already blown that."

I told him Johnny's jaw was broken and all wired up, and said, "Johnny says he's gonna go to the police, and I can't talk him out of it."

Chuck wasn't fazed. He just put me in touch with a well-known hood in Dallas named Creepers, so-called because he had a special fondness for getting up behind his victims and killing them. Creepers made it perfectly clear that going to the police was not among Johnny's options.

We decided to blow the whole thing off.

Chuck did have a parting question for me. "Just out of curiosity," he asked, "how much money did you have on you?"

"Fifteen thousand dollars," I said.

That left him speechless.

George McGann led a colorful life and a series of later revelations proved interesting. He had married a singer-showgirl-actress named Beverly Oliver, who emerged as a mysterious figure in the investigation of the Kennedy assassination. She also authored a book entitled *Nightmare in Dallas*. In 1963, Beverly was a seventeen-year-old performer at Six Flags Over Texas, the amusement park in nearby Arlington, and later appeared at Abe Weinstein's nightclub in Dallas. She maintained she was in Dealey Plaza when President Kennedy was slain and that she had inadvertently filmed the assassination with an experimental camera. She said two men identifying themselves as federal agents later accosted her and confiscated her film, which she said was never returned. Beverly went on to star in several forgettable films such as *Hot-Blooded Woman*.

She and McGann married in 1966. His best man was a reputed Dallas underworld figure and a known acquaintance of Jack Ruby, the Dallas strip-club owner who gunned down Lee Harvey Oswald two days after Oswald allegedly killed the president. Four years after Beverly and George married, McGann was murdered in a gangland slaying in Lubbock. I often thought about all this and recalled what one of my old gambling cronies named Buddy used to say. He insisted that normal people routinely enhance and exaggerate their stories, while gamblers had to tone down their yarns.

That was because the gambling tales were always so outrageous to begin with.

✪✪✪✪✪

There was something about Las Vegas, an allure of some kind, that always seemed to draw us back, me, Sailor, and Slim. Vegas was the big-time gambling capital, and given that we believed we were really good at poker, we thought it might be a profitable idea to try our skills against the Vegas players and perhaps relieve them of their poker-playing bankroll.

At least, that was our plan.

It was around 1970 when we decided to give Vegas another shot. By then, many of the original mobsters who had started operating in Las Vegas, guys like Bugsy Siegel and Meyer Lansky, had died out and a new breed of casino operators had arrived in town, bringing with them more sophisticated gambling operations and, consequently, better games. We were delighted to discover that the Vegas gamblers had started to play no-limit Texas hold'em, which had been our main game for quite some time. Once the game was introduced, all the Vegas players, along with the hotel owners, loved no-limit so much it replaced almost all of the other poker games. In fact, it was myself and other Texans, guys like Crandell Addington, Corky McCorquodale, Sailor, Slim, Johnny Moss, and Jack Straus who had introduced the Vegas players to no-limit Texas hold'em in the late sixties, and it was catching on.

We took more than $100,000 with us, which wasn't a bad bankroll since we all were adept at no-limit hold'em. We had this big plan we discussed on the way there, and the way we figured it, it sounded pretty profitable.

We got ourselves down to the cardroom in good spirits, but that high didn't last too long. Puggy Pearson, the poker kingpin at the time, was on a tremendous hot streak, and he beat us like a borrowed mule. Most of the players in Vegas, including Puggy, didn't have any idea what they were doing at Texas hold'em. But while we were immensely superior players at that game, we experienced a terrible run of luck.

"Gambling isn't the money, you know," Puggy liked to say. "It's the competition. It's layin' your ability on the line and invitin' challenge. That's what I take pride in—being a winner."

His thoughts might have been illuminating, but they were less than inspirational to us. Seemed like he beat us every pot.

We left town not only broke, but dead broke. My pride wouldn't permit me to borrow any money. While I didn't have a nickel, I did have a plane ticket. I knew I was spending too much time away from my family, but deep down, I knew I was a better-than-average gambler with an uncanny knack for coping with the pressures of the profession.

That loss was a devastating blow to us, essentially dissolving our gambling partnership, and I spent a lot of time reflecting on the long plane ride home. We lost our entire bankroll, and believe me, there is nothing more cantankerous than three broke gamblers. But it was a good, amicable separation. It had been great fun teaming with Sailor and Slim, a wonderful experience, but now it was over. It was just time to go our own ways.

The Brunson family had been growing during the Circuit years, and with that, my responsibilities. Pam was born September 4, 1964, fourteen months after her sister. We planned Pam knowing my cancer could, according to the doctors, recur at any time. Louise had very much wanted another child to raise with Doyla. As a little girl, Pam quickly bonded with Doyla, which thrilled both Louise and me. And then on August 7, 1969, Todd was born. Getting broke, like I seemed to do so often, took on an entirely different meaning after our family started expanding. I had a lot more mouths to feed, so the stakes were higher.

Well, here I was, broke once more.

I was good at making comebacks from being broke, then getting broke again and coming back again, but Louise never quite understood my way of thinking. I suppose she appreciated the luxuries of knowing we had enough food to put dinner on the table each night and, given my track record, I couldn't blame her. Louise had become a serious investor and was doing quite well. She had inherited several thousand dollars when her mother died and was adamant about keeping her investments separate from mine for fear I'd gamble everything away. Maybe she felt that way because I was so good at getting broke, but of course I couldn't blame Louise. After working her way through two universities, it was no mystery why she was so cost conscious. Her daddy had gone broke in the Great Depression and never made a comeback, so she had grown up poor and didn't want to relive those hard days, her poker-playing husband notwithstanding.

After the Las Vegas fiasco, I was so broke when we landed at the airport back home, I had to call Louise to come get me because I didn't have money for a cab. Bless her heart, she was employed full time for a pharmacy chain, working long hours, and seldom complaining. She was none too happy, but she came and picked me up.

It was an awfully quiet ride from the airport.

Chapter 12

You never test the depth of the water with both feet.

I never knew anyone like the Binions—Benny, a legendary Texas gangster and Las Vegas casino owner, and his sons Jack and Ted, and their sister Becky. Jack and Benny and I had become good friends from an earlier meeting in 1969. A guy named Tom Moore, a Texan from San Antonio and part owner of the Holiday Casino, and another fellow, Vic Vickrey, were hosting a "Texas Gamblers Reunion" up in Reno. They invited a bunch of the players from the Texas Circuit to play some high-stakes cash games, trying to drum up business during a slow part of the year for them. They also invited some *producers*, players with big bankrolls who overestimated their abilities.

Of course, I couldn't pass up an opportunity like that.

Nor could a bunch of other players: Jimmy "The Greek" Snyder and Minnesota Fats were there, along with Jack and Benny Binion, Amarillo Slim, Corky McCorquodale, Aubrey Day, Sailor Roberts, Jack Straus, Jimmy Casella, James "Longgoodie" Roy, Crandell Addington, Sid Wyman, Bill Boyd, Johnny Moss, Charles Harrelson, Puggy Pearson, and some others. It was quite a gathering of great players.

Little did I know that these games in Reno would not only affect my life but also change the course of poker forever.

The event, which lasted one week, featured five live games: Texas hold'em, Kansas City lowball draw, razz, stud, and ace-to-five lowball draw. Players could rebuy chips if they went broke, just like in regular cash games. We played a lot of poker and had a lot of fun. Crandell won a trophy for the best "outside" gambler, that is, a road gambler with no "inside" affiliations, as opposed to someone who worked for a casino or cardroom.

Moore found out to his dismay that pretty much all we wanted to do was play poker, so he didn't get enough action at his more profitable games like blackjack and craps, the reason he had invited us there in the first place. So when Jack asked Moore if he was holding the convention the following year, Moore figured it wasn't worth the trouble.

Jack and Benny figured it different. When Moore sold his business, the Binions used that tournament as a springboard for what they thought was a grand idea: A World Series of Poker that would be played at their casino in downtown Las Vegas. They were looking to get publicity for the Horseshoe and attract players.

They could not possibly imagine how successful that idea would be and what kind of tree would grow from that little seed. I don't think anyone could have.

The very next year, in 1970, Jack and Benny Binion invited all the Texas Circuit players to Las Vegas, and hosted the first World Series of Poker at the Horseshoe casino. That inaugural year, there was no tournament format, just five different poker variations that a bunch of us played for cash. There were about thirty different players competing in the various games and when we were done playing, we awarded each other trophies. A lot of the great players were there—Moss, Puggy, Slim, Sailor, Straus; even Titanic Thompson, the famous hustler, came to play, though he was pretty old at the time. Benny asked everybody to vote for the best player, but he couldn't determine a winner that way—we all voted for ourselves! Then Benny got around this deadlock by asking us to vote for the *second-best* player. We all thought Johnny Moss was that candidate and awarded him a trophy as the "best all-around player," what we later called the first world champion. It wasn't a tournament like we play today, just a bunch of cash games. You kept what you won.

That would all change the following year.

Meanwhile, I spent more time with the Binions and got to know them real well. Jack and I had bonded right off the bat, and I considered him the coolest-headed guy I'd ever met. We'd been in some pretty tight spots and I'd never seen him get ruffled or flustered, which undoubtedly contributed to his success in the business world. I even made money in some of Jack's real estate deals, which were about the only times I ever made money in anything other than gambling. Jack and I played a lot of golf together, and he had a smooth, beautiful swing. He'd hit a tee shot and we'd say, "Wow!" But his golf game went downhill from the tee box. He couldn't chip and he couldn't putt, but he could hit those tee shots like a scratch golfer.

Jack ran the casino, but in a real crunch he turned to Benny for help or advice. Jack told me something once that sounded as though it might have come from Benny.

"I'm not very smart," he said, "but I recognize talent. I try to surround myself with smart people." Of course, that's what really smart people do, and Jack was very smart. I took that advice to heart.

I had heard countless stories about Benny even before I got to know him. During his Texas regime, gangster types fought for control of the town they lived in. Benny was no different. At least two of Benny's competitors died violently, one of them in a shootout on a Dallas street. The shootout was similar in a way to the shootings on Exchange Avenue in Fort Worth in that the police really didn't investigate them too seriously because they deemed it good riddance of the undesirable elements involved. Benny's other competitor got blown up, and it was common knowledge who did it. But Benny was never convicted of killing anyone, and he sure as hell admitted nothing.

When questioned about his checkered past, Benny would say, "Well, boy, tough times make tough people."

Benny did go to the joint for a stretch. Beginning in 1953, he served almost three-and-a-half years in Leavenworth for tax evasion. The feds got him like they got a lot of the mobsters, people like Al Capone. They couldn't get them on the big charges, like murder, extortion, or whatever they were after them for. There either weren't any witnesses that stepped forward, or who were alive long enough to talk. So they sent the tax people in. The Internal Revenue Service brought a case against Benny for $875,000, and he was one of the few people I'd ever heard about who paid the full amount plus interest and *still* got sent to jail. Everyone I knew speculated that the feds prosecuted him because they felt he had gotten away with so many other things.

Benny "sold" his ownership interest in the Horseshoe to a friend, Joe W. Brown, then bought it back when he got out of prison in 1957.

Every small town had a boss gambler—the guy that ran the games— and the bigger towns had several. But the big-city mobs were always leery of Texas, particularly Dallas, because Benny Binion, a Texas legend even then, wouldn't permit a mob presence to intrude on his activities. He controlled Dallas with an iron fist.

"Tell me, Benny," I once asked. "Did the mobsters ever come down there when you were doing all this high rolling in Dallas?"

He flashed me a bemused smile and said, "Yeah, they came, but they didn't leave."

I was told that there had been numerous attempts on Benny's life. Some insisted that Benny crossed the line when he gunned down some guy on a Dallas street. It started getting real hot for him in Big D. In the end, authorities concluded it was best he leave town.

"I had to get out," he said. "My sheriff got beat in the election that year."

In 1946, Benny packed up $2 million in cash in a big suitcase and traveled across the country to Las Vegas. Benny told me he never let that suitcase out of his sight. He told me how, on the long drive to Nevada, he'd stop in hotels on the way to Vegas and have a bellhop take it to his room.

One porter said, "Man, this is heavy. What's in it?"

Benny laughed and told him, "That's full of hundred dollar bills." And the bellhop laughed, too, unaware that his hotel guest wasn't joking.

When Benny moved to Vegas, it was still a pretty small town, about eighteen thousand people, with only two casinos on the Strip at the time, the El Rancho and the Last Frontier, along with a bunch of sawdust casinos—so called because they spread sawdust on the wooden floors instead of carpeting them—downtown along Fremont Street.

Benny was a partner in a club after he got to Vegas, but soon he came up with the idea of opening a real gambling joint. To Benny, that meant gambling Texas style. You bet what you wanted and he'd take the action. His rule was that the customer's first bet set the limit. He couldn't compete with the upscale places on the Strip on their level, nor did he want to, but he could sure as heck make a better place for real gamblers.

"I'm going to open this town up to real high gambling," he said. "I'm going to give the players better odds. I'm going to let them bet whatever they want to bet. I'm going to have the highest limits in town. I'm going to have the best food and the cheapest drinks."

And that's what he did. In 1951, he bought a downtown Las Vegas casino that was originally opened in 1937 as the El Dorado Club, which he renamed the Horseshoe. This was five years after Bugsy Siegel had opened up the flashy Flamingo over on the Strip, the model that would set the stage for the extravagant casinos to come. The El Dorado had a big tax loss, around $870,000, which Benny found pretty attractive as well. In short order, the big-time gamblers began pouring into the Horseshoe. He covered all their bets. While Las Vegas casinos capped their customers at

$50 per bet, Benny took $500 and he gave them better odds. It was well known that Benny would book any bet.

One famous story about Benny's willingness to take any bet took place in 1980. A man named William Bergstrom came to the Horseshoe with $777,000 in cash stuffed into a suitcase. He brought another suitcase with him, an identical match, but this one was empty. Benny welcomed the man's action and the cage gave him $777,000 in chips. The fella walked over to the craps table and put it all down on the "don't pass" line. Three rolls later he won, went back to the cage, and filled up both suitcases with the cash, $777,000 in each, and went back home. I didn't hear anything further about that story for a while, but I didn't need to. I know how gamblers are. I also knew Benny wasn't worried about the loss. He knew that money would make it back to the Horseshoe's cage. Gamblers are gamblers. Sure enough, Bergstrom came back in 1984, and made it $1 million, again on the "don't pass" line, the largest recorded bet at that time in Las Vegas history. This time the money stayed behind. It took just one roll.

There came a time when Binion's Horseshoe made more money than some of the bigger, fancier casinos on the Strip. It was just a down-home, no-frills casino with square food, a place where you could feel comfortable. A gambler's place. You felt that as soon as you walked in. You got fair odds, could bet as much as you liked, and gamble without any of the pretensions of the fancier places on the Strip.

The professional poker players liked to play there when the World Series rolled around. With the tournament events and the great ring games going during the spring when it was held, the Horseshoe was a poker paradise.

Our friendship flourished, Benny's and mine. I knew people wondered how or why an honest, educated Texas farm boy would befriend a known gangster and suspected killer whose victims included the King's English. I could only tell them he was probably the most engaging guy I'd ever known. He had unbelievable charisma, one of the more obvious reasons he was so successful. People were just drawn to him. Benny was personable, innovative and a compelling storyteller. I spent quite a bit of time with Benny at his private booth in the coffee shop at the Horseshoe, where he held court every day. His table, which was always reserved for him, overlooked the action on the casino floor and there was a phone behind it so he could take his calls. Benny always wore Western-style clothing including a cowboy hat, but he was famous for the solid gold coins he used for buttons on his shirts.

He was my mentor in some tough times, mostly off the table, a friendship that really came in handy through some difficult spots.

He knew that Jack and I were best friends, and he opened up to me. I often sat at the "Binion Booth" in the Sombrero and listened for hours and hours to stories from the old Texas days, and a few from Las Vegas, that just curled my hair. Benny was one tough hombre and anyone that stepped on his toes soon lived—or didn't live—to regret it.

He had a bunch of observations that I thought were pretty enlightening.

- Never follow an empty wagon.
- Courage is a fine thing, but if the shooting starts, get down on the floor.
- Every man is honest—as long as he can afford it.
- Trust everyone, but always cut the cards.
- Don't ever tell a lie—unless you have to.
- Believe in justice. But spell it "Just Us"
- The only bad luck in life is bad health. Everything else is an inconvenience. Benny had that one printed on the old Horseshoe matchbooks.

His best though, and one of my favorites, was Benny's own Golden Rule, which he had posted in his office: "He who has the most gold, makes the rules."

That one said a lot about Benny.

Besides recognizing the potential of the World Series of Poker and getting it started in 1970 along with his son Jack, Benny made another lasting mark on the game. He arranged one of the most famous poker games ever, a 1949 match between Johnny Moss and Nick the Greek Dandalos. The Greek was popularly known as the top poker player in the world—though not in Texas, the heartland of the greatest players—and one of the most famous gamblers of all time, an acclaim he reveled in with gusto. "Gambling fame is usually followed by a jail sentence," he often said. He was still a dashing figure at sixty-six years old, a dapper dresser, and enjoyed nothing more than high-stakes action. He wanted to play high-stakes heads-up no-limit poker and asked Benny to find him an opponent.

Benny persuaded Johnny Moss, his childhood friend and the best poker player in Texas—probably the best poker player anywhere at the time—to come out to Las Vegas and play Nick at his casino.

"They got a fellow out here calls himself Nick the Greek. Thinks he can play stud poker," Benny said when he phoned him. "Johnny, I think you should come out here and have some fun."

Moss had been a road gambler for many years, and Benny had often staked him, so he knew how good Johnny was. So did the professionals who played the Texas Circuit, where he was a legend. Moss, then forty-two, made arrangements right away to get from Dallas to Vegas. The conditions were that Moss and The Greek would play the game in public so that spectators could watch them. Benny wanted to take advantage of all the publicity this match could bring to his new casino. His guys set up a table and room to accommodate spectators, and the two famous gamblers got it on.

I like Jon Bradshaw's description, in *Fast Company*, where he relates Moss's account of the famous game:

> *When I come into town that Sunday night, well, we set right down to play. No point in puttin' it off when there's money to be made. We played five-card stud from Sunday straight through till Thursday. On Thursday night, I told him I was wore out and was agoin' to bed. 'What's the matter?' that ole Greek says to me, 'can't you take the pressure?' Well, I slept for about twenty hours and y'know the Greek didn't even go to bed. Seventy years old and he just sat around playin' craps awaitin' for me to come back to the table. And I did and we played through till Sunday night again and I went back to sleep...*

> *The entire game must've lasted four months, maybe five. And then, when the end comes, that old Greek smiled, got up from the table—we was playin' ace-to-the-five, I remember, and I had him against the cold nuts—and he says to me, 'Well, I guess I got to let you go, Mr. Moss.' I had broke him, y'unnerstand...He just got up and he smiled and he set off to bed.*

The Greek's concession comment became one of the most famous lines in poker lore, ranking with another that became part of the Greek's legacy. In his later years, he was almost broke and playing $5/$10 draw poker in Gardena, California, when a stranger walked up to him.

"Aren't you Nick the Greek?" this stranger asked.

"Yeah," Greek replied.

"Aren't you embarrassed to be playing over here in this cheap game?"

The Greek gave him a withering look and uttered one of the most memorable lines in poker, "Action is action."

Nick died shortly thereafter.

I had heard plenty about the Greek, but I only got to play with him once, in the early seventies, at the Dunes Hotel. The Dunes was sitting where the Bellagio is today. We were playing no-limit hold'em and I knew Nick's reputation as a very strong, aggressive player. I knew he was going to try to push me around. As I watched him splash chips around the table, I marveled at his total disregard for money and, even though he was at the end of his career, Nick was still a force to be reckoned with.

I remember this one hand where I had 4♠ 4♣ and Nick had raised the pot. I called him. The flop was K♦ 7♦ 2♣. I was first so I checked. Nick made a large bet. I figured he was trying to push me out of the pot, possibly with a flush draw. I felt sure my fours were good, so I called. The fourth card was the 3♠, which looked harmless. I checked. Nick bet again and I called. The last card was the 8♦, which would complete a flush if someone had been drawing at it.

I was watching Nick closely and he actually slumped in his chair when the last card hit. That made me think Nick thought I was drawing at the flush. I figured he had nothing and checked expecting him to bluff. After I checked, Nick must have felt I didn't have the flush and he moved in on me. I called him and he got up and quit the game without showing his cards. I broke him.

If I hadn't been alert I wouldn't have won that pot. This was the one and only time I ever got to play with Nick the Greek Dandalos, the most famous gambler in the world at that time.

Nick left Las Vegas shortly after that.

Johnny was hardly reluctant to discuss that marathon game with The Greek, but he never claimed to have won $4 million as some accounts have reported. I always suspected it was substantially less than that, but I never learned the specific amount. Some people claimed that the game never happened, but they are wrong. I asked Jack Binion about it one time and he told me they did play, and Moss did make Nick quit, though the stories might be exaggerated.

There was a hidden twist to the Dandolos-Moss game that illustrated just how cunning Benny Binion could be. Not unlike the Greek, Johnny was a notorious craps shooter. After the match ran its course, Moss went over to the dice table and dropped most, if not all, of the money he won from the Greek.

You can bet Benny was in the background smiling. As it turns out, he was the real winner of that marathon poker game. The scenario had played out exactly as he'd intended. He got all the publicity and on top of that, most of the money too.

Benny Binion might have been a Texas gangster, known killer, and ex-con, but at the same time, he was widely respected in Las Vegas, and not just because he founded the Horseshoe and the World Series of Poker. There is a little-known fact about him: if the cops ran out of cash and needed a bundle of money on short notice for a drug sting operation, they could get it from Benny's casino cage. On the other hand, Benny never asked for help if he caught a cheat or pickpocket on the premises. Pretty much everyone knew that those kinds of infractions were handled in-house by burly security guards. They made an impression on the perpetrators— even after they got out of the hospital.

No one in his right mind messed with Benny Binion.

The thing I liked about Benny was his humility. Here was someone that even the toughest hoods and mobsters didn't fool with, and he could laugh at himself being the weak guy in a story. He was so self-assured, so self-confident, that he often was the butt of his own jokes and stories. I always said it takes a pretty confident man to make himself the joker in the stories, and that certainly was Benny. He told me once about going to Hot Springs, Arkansas, to party and gamble on the horses. He took the toughest guy in Dallas with him. They got to drinking and raising hell in their hotel room, and this one-armed hotel security guard came up and told them to hold it down.

"Okay," Benny said.

But they didn't, and in a few minutes the security officer was back.

"I told y'all to be quiet," he growled.

Benny kind of shoved the house dick, and the guy hauled off and slugged him.

"He knocked me over a couch and flat on the floor," Benny said. "I was lying there waiting for my 'toughest guy in Dallas' to step in. When I finally heard them fighting, I raised up and looked over the couch and this security guy had my guy's head under this stub of an arm and was beating him with a blackjack.

"I just went 'arghh' and fell back on the floor like I was hurt. I wasn't about to get up and fight that one-armed gorilla."

That was Benny. He knew what he was and who he was, and he never felt it necessary to put on phony airs.

During the World Series one night, a known hijacker wandered in to watch the games. That made us all nervous, so someone told Jack and he told Benny. Benny walked over and sat down at a table with the guy.

"You know," Benny said to the man, "you're makin' a lot of my customers uneasy."

"Oh, really?" the guy said somewhat indifferently,

"Yeah, really. I want you gone and I don't want you comin' around here anymore."

"Well, this is a free country," the guy said. "I ain't doing nothin' wrong."

"Look," Benny said without raising his voice, "you're a young man, and you think you're tough. I'm an old man, and I know I'm tough. If you think not, let's just go out in the parking garage right now."

The guy looked at Benny's dead-serious expression. He got up and left without another word.

From what I knew about Benny, that hijacker made the right decision.

Chapter 13

The secret of success is to start from scratch and keep on scratching.

In 1971, the Binions changed the format of the World Series of Poker to a freezeout, the same format we use today, where all the competitors play until one player remains—the champion. Benny decided there needed to be a real tournament with a real winner for the World Series to attract media interest, and ultimately more players, to the Horseshoe. Benny realized that without the real competition like other sports had, the tournament had little chance to get the widespread publicity he was looking for. It would lack the drama and public interest necessary for success. The idea for the freezeout had come from *Los Angeles Times* journalist Ted Thackrey, who suggested to Benny a winner-take-all, no-limit Texas hold'em elimination tournament. Thackrey told Benny that he and Jimmy "The Greek" Snyder—the other Greek—could get nationwide publicity if the event were an elimination.

Benny immediately saw the wisdom of this advice.

This 1971 World Series of Poker marked the first poker tournament ever played as a freezeout. It was decided that the entry fee would be $5,000—winner take all. I was pretty excited to try this new concept and, being a friend of the Binions, I was eager to participate. There were only six players for this first tournament: me, Johnny Moss, Puggy Pearson, Sailor Roberts, Jack Straus, and Jimmy Casella. Casella was reputed to be connected to one of the New York crime families. All of us were Texans, except for Puggy and Casella. Fittingly, Moss, who we all thought was the best no-limit player at the time, won the tournament and the $30,000 prize.

Interestingly enough, the Horseshoe didn't even have a poker room in 1971. The very profitable table games and slot machines were too valuable in the limited space the Horseshoe had to spread for the less profitable poker games. They just cleared an area and set up poker tables. After the Series, they would drag back the slot machines and table games and carry on as usual. When they bought the neighboring Mint Casino in 1988, they opened a poker room.

It would have stretched my imagination to believe that this modest tournament, the first ever, played by just six players in its inaugural year—with no publicity, fanfare or press contingent—would later turn into an internationally televised event featuring tens of thousands of players, fifty plus events, and a combined prize pool that would exceed $100 million. I don't think anyone could have seen that coming.

In 1972, the Binions raised the buy-in to $10,000, and we had the same six players from the year before, plus Slim and a man named Roger Van Ausdall. Actually, there were twelve players signed up, but with the cash games so good, only eight of us played. The Series that year got the interest of national television and that changed everything. For me, in particular, that really changed things.

Slim won the tournament, which was the best thing that could have happened to poker. But there's a story behind the story.

I probably could have won the World Series that year, but given the circumstances of my life, it was not something I wanted to do. When we got three-handed—with me, Puggy and Slim the last players left—I was presented with a problem I didn't want to face: the media. All of a sudden, here came these TV cameras and reporters to cover the world championship and the results would be splashed over newspapers and media everywhere. I got real uncomfortable about that. Media coverage was great for the World Series and for poker, but it was the last thing I needed. People back in Longworth, particularly my mom and the family, didn't know what I did for a living. I was afraid of the publicity that winning this event would bring, and the terrible shame it would bring to my family. They didn't know I was a gambler back in Texas where I lived at that time. I had concocted all these stories that I was an insurance salesman, or I was in the oil business, and so forth.

When we stopped and took a break, I pulled Puggy and Slim aside and said, "I don't want to win this thing because I don't want all the publicity."

"I don't want it either," Puggy said. But Slim, who loved attention, said, "I do."

That's when we said, "Let's just let Slim win it."

We came right out and started playing crazy so we could let Slim win. Slim, a natural showman, got to where he was putting on a big show, hamming it up and showing his cards to the crowd. He was playing to the audience and clowning around, rather than just playing his cards and getting on with the game. With all Slim's showboating and entertaining, the TV cameras ate it up. I got really irritated with Slim's antics, but I wasn't the only one. Jimmy the Greek and Jack Binion were watching, us and they got pretty agitated too.

Finally, they stopped the game and told us to come back to the office. They closed the door, and Jack got right to it.

"It's obvious what you guys are doing. You're going to cause a big scandal here. You just can't do this."

"But Jack," I said, "I just don't want the publicity."

I kept thinking about all the shame this would bring on my family if all those TV cameras and media started showing me as a participant in a Las Vegas poker tournament, particularly if I won it. We talked it over a bit and Jack saw where I was coming from. Jack was a fellow Texan, so he had a pretty good understanding of the Bible Belt and what I was talking about.

"Okay, Doyle, we'll let you withdraw and you can keep the money you have now."

Slim and Puggy were agreeable. By this point, we had lost enough chips to Slim where he was up close to us, so the three of us made a deal. I withdrew from the tournament, citing stomach problems, and left the Horseshoe, leaving Puggy and Slim to play it out. Then they played on the square once I withdrew. Slim ended up beating Puggy as we had hoped. He became the 1972 WSOP champion.

Slim was the perfect spokesman, and his victory probably changed the course of poker. He hit the talk-show circuit and gave the game a boost of legitimacy, taking the game out of smoky backrooms and into America's living rooms. Suddenly, the Horseshoe and the World Series of Poker were on the map. And everything took off from there. Over the years, Slim ended up with eleven appearances on the *Johnny Carson Show*, and three more on *60 Minutes*. I believe that without Slim's victory, the World Series would never have advanced to the popularity it has reached today and likely would have faded away over the years. He really started people talking about poker. I could never be Amarillo Slim Preston and make all the outrageous claims and be on the TV shows and do what he did. The first TV show I was on, I was sacred to death, but Slim just loved all that attention.

The Binions, of course, also had a lot to do with the eventual success of poker tournaments, as did the group of us who decided to play the original

WSOP. They organized and ran the tournaments in the first place, giving impetus to the history that would follow.

Afterward, I told my family about how I withdrew from the tournament and they said if I had consulted them, they would have been happy if I had won. Louise, Cheryl and Doyla knew I was playing, but the neighbors didn't. In hindsight, I would have liked to be the winner back in 1972—that would have given me three world championships—but I never really look back on it with regret because Slim did so much for poker. Back then, we didn't attach much importance to the World Series, because it was still in its infancy. It didn't mean a whole lot to me or Puggy, certainly not what that championship means today.

"Well, don't worry," I said. "They're going to have it every year and I'll win one of them."

I really felt like I was a tier above everybody at that point and wasn't worried about it.

In the 1973 World Series of Poker, Puggy Pearson defeated twelve other players to win the championship and the winner-take-all prize of $130,000. I didn't get very far that year, but while I was impressed with ol' Puggy, I wasn't surprised either. Not only did Puggy win the tournament, he did it convincingly. He broke most of the players himself. It was a terrific tribute to Puggy's ability that he won the championship playing no-limit hold'em because, like the other players in Vegas at the time, he wasn't adept at no-limit. He was a limit player.

However, I knew the real story: Puggy was simply a tremendous card player, highly competitive, and he had a great feel for the game. Like a tiger in the jungle, he was blessed with natural instincts. Here was a guy who had a sixth-grade education, had two illiterate parents, grew up dirt poor, and didn't know odds and probabilities, yet he had this terrific instinct that made him great. He didn't know why he did some of the things he did, but they would be the right things to do.

Puggy was the best poker player in town when I arrived in Las Vegas—all the big games were built around him—but he was not skilled at no-limit Texas hold'em, the main game. So while he had a good run at the WSOP, I liked playing with him in the no-limit side games. Away from my table, Puggy was on a different level than his competitors. He just ate them up. His explanation for why there were so few good poker players compared to him was pure Pugese: "Poker has a language all its own, but you don't expect most folks to understand it, any more than you expect 'em to understand Egyptian."

Jimmy "The Greek" Snyder, Binion's spokesman and PR Director for the World Series of Poker, was absolutely amazed at Puggy's performance in the Main Event. "The man's a machine," The Greek said. Snyder, widely known later as an analyst on a CBS sports program, *The N.F.L. Today*, did a great job for Benny. He was able to promote the coverage of the Series nationwide, a feat that was greatly helped by Slim's year-long stint promoting the WSOP after he won the title in 1972.

Actually, it was Snyder who was responsible for my nickname, Texas Dolly, at least indirectly. When he was writing a column in the *Las Vegas Sun* about the World Series of Poker, he always identified me as "Texas Doyle." At the time, I was trying to avoid publicity because of the stigma attached to gambling back in Texas. Jimmy and I became pretty good friends and I asked him not to use my last name. He agreed, saying Texas Doyle would work fine. When we were together, Jimmy called me Doylee. Another writer overheard "Doylee" and thought he was saying Dolly, and started referring to me as Texas Dolly. The name caught on, and when *The Associated Press* picked it up, it more or less became official.

I would be Texas Dolly from that point on.

★

Chapter 14

I've learned in poker, there is a fine line between genius and insanity.

I n my early gambling days I often heard about a renowned gambler, pool hustler and con artist named Titanic Thompson, who had an even flashier reputation than Minnesota Fats. I'd heard all sorts of colorful stories about Titanic and his exploits and couldn't wait to meet him. Titanic was hardly a role model—unless you were an aspiring con artist—but he certainly was a legend. A Dallas writer friend named Carlton Stowers, who wrote a classic book about him, *The Unsinkable Titanic Thompson,* told me that not only was Ti a world-class con man, he was an expert at most everything he undertook: golf, pool, dice, pistols, rifles, even pitching pennies. He was also a national skeet-shooting champion, a world champion horseshoe pitcher, and a sensational bowler. As a sports professional, had he devoted himself, he could have been in several halls of fame.

Ti could do more things better that anybody I've ever known. I don't pretend to vouch for the veracity of every Titanic Thompson story—Ti's life was surrounded by an aura of legend and myth—but I know many of them were true. They say he played Ben Hogan right-handed and beat him, then played Byron Nelson left-handed and beat him. Think about that. No bigger golf legends than those two. I never said he could beat Hogan and Nelson all the time, but he was equally good right- or left-handed, which was better than rare. It was unique.

If he hadn't made so much money and had so much fun hustling, he would have been one of the leading professionals on the PGA Tour.

Stowers marveled at Ti's athletic ability. He said, and he was right, that Ti could have made a world of money legitimately, but he preferred hustling. Stowers joked that it was plastic playing cards that put a lot of gamblers out of business. The old Bicycle cards were cardboard and could be easily marked. You could rough up an edge or scratch them with your fingernail, for instance. That was Ti; nothing he ever did was on the square. Ti sashayed in and out of Texas, but was not a Texan. He rarely used his real name, Alvin Clarence Thomas, perhaps because he never really knew his father. The elder Thomas, a farmer of sorts in Arkansas, preferred gambling to farming and disappeared before Ti was a year old.

You can't tell stories about gamblers without including Titanic Thompson. When I was a young gambler, he was still dazzling us all with his creative, gimmicky bets. Ti was the absolute master of the cunning proposition, and he had an endless string of tricks he would use to separate gamblers from their money.

One of my favorite Ti stories was about the time he met Nick the Greek Dandolos. It was at an airport, and they recognized one another right off and shook hands.

They were standing there talking and Ti said, "I hear you got a lot of gamble in you, Nick."

"Yeah, I think I got as much gamble as anybody who ever lived," Nick countered.

Ti reached in his pocket, pulled out a $15,000 bundle of cash, tossed it on the floor, and said, "I'll flip you for this."

Nick just smiled, pulled out his bankroll, counted out $15,000 and pitched it down beside Ti's.

"You're on."

Ti plucked a two-headed coin from his pocket and flipped it.

"Call it."

"Heads," said Nick.

Ti reached up, grabbed the coin on the way down, stuck it in his pocket and, gushing with mock admiration, said, "Damn, Nick, you will gamble, won't you?"

Of course, if Nick had called "tails," Ti would have let the two-headed coin fall to the ground and snatch up the $30,000.

Different versions of that story and another, the watermelon story, are still going around. It was in Hot Springs, Arkansas, that Ti supposedly pulled off his famous watermelon scam, maybe for the first time. He was staying with a bunch of other gamblers at one of those old hotels where folks gathered on the porch in the late afternoon. Early one day Ti drove out in the country and found a farmer with a truckload of watermelons. He offered the guy $100 or so to count the watermelons, give him the exact number, and then at a designated time drive into town with the truckload of melons intact.

Ti went back to the hotel, plopped down in a rocking chair on the front porch, and was shooting the bull with his cronies when the watermelon truck came rolling down the street.

"How many watermelons you reckon are on that truck?" Ti asked innocently.

His pals were notorious for making bets like that, and they quickly took the bait. Everybody put up $1,000 and guessed at the number of melons, the closest winning the entire pot. They stopped the guy, then bought and counted the melons. Naturally, Ti won.

The only person happier than Ti was the watermelon farmer.

Once Ti bet a buddy he could throw a dime atop a multistory building. Impossible, the guy said, backing up his belief with a $500 bet. Ti walked across the street, bought an orange, poked the dime into it, hurled the orange atop the building, and scooped up the $500.

It was in Chicago one winter, according to another story, that he bet a bundle he could drive a golf ball five hundred yards. He covered all the bets, loaded up his clubs, drove to a nearby beach, and hit a golf ball that was last seen skidding across frozen Lake Michigan.

Another story I loved about him involved a West Texas road sign on the Big Spring highway alerting motorists that it was eight miles to Midland. He drove out in the middle of the night, dug up the sign and moved it two miles closer to town. He and his gambler friends were driving along the road the next day and Ti purposely avoided glancing at the sign.

"How far you think it is to the Midland city limits?" he wondered aloud.

His buddies, who had just spotted the sign, proposed a $1,000 bet on who could guess closest. They said eight miles. Ti said six, and of course, he won that bet too. I'm told Ti also pulled off the same bet near Evansville, Indiana.

When talking about guys like Titanic, you had to wonder where fact ended and fiction began. He was up in years when I first met him back in Texas, but I'd heard about him all my life. He was a daring and dangerous person who had reputedly, on separate occasions, killed five men when they tried to rob him. Like most gamblers, he had a disregard for his own life. When someone approached him with a gun drawn, like during a robbery attempt, he would grab his heart and tumble to the ground, fake a heart attack, and reach for a pistol he carried in a shoulder holster.

Then he'd come up shooting.

I never dreamed how much that story would help me one terrifying night many years later.

I finally met Ti in the sixties, and something Stowers told me proved dead on. "Had he been an actor," he said, "he would have received an Oscar award." Ti was always up to something, but you could never tell by the way he proposed bets, or suggested ideas that nearby gamblers took him up on. Like with the watermelons or the signs, Ti had the situation set up from the get-go. He always had a plan, all the angles worked out. In one respect, Ti was no different from the celebrities he hustled—he had an ego as big as the ingenious con games he invented. "He won millions of dollars in schemes that would stagger the imagination," Stowers said.

Ti didn't always get the best of it, as witnessed by one of the clever golf wagers that backfired on him. In the sixties, Ti and a well-known Dallas gambler named Ace Darnell took pro golfer Ray Floyd, then a young unknown, to El Paso to play a gambler named Gene Fisher, one of the best amateurs in the state at that time. Floyd would soon become a major force on the PGA Tour, and one day a member of the World Golf Hall of Fame.

The El Paso guys acted unimpressed with the young Floyd and told Ti and Ace, "We got a Mexican kid out there on the course driving that tractor that can beat your guy, if you'll give our kid a couple of shots a side."

Winking at his pal, Ti accepted the bet. Well, the "Mexican kid" was Lee Trevino. Early on, Floyd was not playing at the top of his game, and Trevino beat him handily. After two days, Ti and Ace were $18,000 losers and they were now playing even. They demanded another game. Rising to the challenge, Floyd shot a sixty-five and beat Trevino by two strokes. Ti got half his money back, but that was it.

The disgruntled Dallas hustlers stuck around for a few days playing the locals $100 and $200 a hole, and only recovered some of their losses.

Back in the sixties, robbing gamblers was an everyday occurrence, and Ti wasn't immune to those threats. However, a hijacker took his life in his hands when he went up against Ti. One night a bandit caught him without his pistol and took his bankroll. The next day, there was a knock at his door. To Ti's amazement, there stood the robber. The guy said he hadn't realized just who it was that he'd robbed.

He'd come to apologize and return the money.

I played golf with Ti toward the end, when he was in his seventies, and I really got to know him well. He couldn't hit the ball more than a couple hundred yards, but he still had that magical touch around the greens. I couldn't believe his chipping ability. He tried to teach me how he did it, but it was a futile effort.

"You're good enough," he finally said and gave up on me.

A few years before he died, I finally accepted his invitation to go out to his house in Fort Worth to visit. Ti was going to teach me some of the math on hand match-ups. He said I could take the knowledge to Las Vegas, win a lot of money, and give him a percentage of the profits. Turned out I had done all the math before and already knew everything he showed me.

While a genius in many respects, he was not a great poker player, at least when compared with the top professionals. He cheated at poker sometimes, but we let him do it to keep him playing. Why? Because he was entertaining on the one hand and often a loser on the other.

Shortly before his death, Ti was living in a rest home north of Fort Worth. When the weather was good and he was feeling okay, he'd get the male nurses to take him over to a nearby pitch-and-putt course where he'd hustle anybody he could find for a couple of bucks.

After beating his pitch-and-putters handily, he'd announce, "Young fella, you've just been hustled by the king himself, Titanic Thompson."

In his book, Stowers recounted a story about Ti at the time of his death—a story that said worlds about this guy and his reputation. Word of his passing spread quickly across the Tennison municipal course in Dallas where for years he had perfected many of his golf scams and fleeced countless people with his gimmicky propositions. A teenage caddy came racing out in a golf cart to report the news to a foursome of gamblers at a green on the back nine. The players paused to remove their hats and caps and pay their respects.

"What a shame. We've lost the greatest and craziest hustler that ever lived," one of the old-timers said.

Another sidled over to the young caddy and said, "You ever know Titanic Thompson, son?"

"No, sir, can't say that I did."

"But you say he's dead?"

"That's what I was told."

"Well, son, let me say this to you: I knew ol' Ti for a lot of years. Likely he *is* dead. But take my advice and don't go bettin' any of your money on it."

I hadn't been in Vegas but about a year when Titanic died. It was 1974 and he was eighty-two years old, scamming to the very end. Losing a gambling legend like Ti made gambling a little less fun—and a lot less entertaining.

There was just nobody like him.

Book III
Las Vegas

★
Chapter 15

A successful job is when you don't know if you are working or playing.

I n 1973 the pressure of trying to make a living playing poker in Texas became too great. I knew I was one of the best players on the Circuit, but the games had dried up and it was difficult to find action. The government had imposed laws making it illegal to cross state lines to gamble. You could even go to jail for possessing a deck of cards. That made it risky to go to Alabama or even Oklahoma to play poker.

"I've gotta make a living, and it's getting harder and harder here," I told Louise.

I'd been going to Las Vegas regularly, and I felt it was time to make it permanent so we decided to make the move. The Horseshoe had already hosted four World Series tournaments—all of which I played in—and I had also played plenty at the Golden Nugget and the Dunes, where the big action was, so I was hardly a stranger to the town. After undergraduate schooling on Exchange Avenue and graduate college on the Texas Circuit, it really was time for post-graduate poker studies at the gambling capital of the world.

We had a motor home and a car, and we packed all our belongings and kids and headed west in the dead of summer. Todd celebrated his fourth birthday on the road. We passed through Amarillo and spent a memorable night with Amarillo Slim on his ranch, where Doyla got bit by one of his pet horses.

Louise was not overjoyed with the move, but she didn't say much. She was certainly smart enough to see the problems with staying in Texas. And while she hated to leave our home, she was excited about finding a nice house in Vegas. With three kids, we needed lots of space, and so we settled in a beautiful 5,500-square foot home on the east side. Most of the neighborhood children were soon hanging out there, and Louise "adopted" a couple of them because their living conditions were deplorable. She quickly became known as the "mother" of the neighborhood.

At the time, all the poker games were played at the Golden Nugget in downtown Las Vegas and I did most of my playing there. I was familiar with the Nugget because, in the late sixties when I used to come out to Las Vegas and play, that's where I went. Actually, in the early years, it was the only legal poker room in Nevada. It was a sawdust joint, just like you see in the old Westerns, with red wallpaper, sawdust on the floor, and a bunch of old-time gamblers playing cards. Bill Boyd ran the poker room at the Nugget from 1946, when it opened, to 1982, when he retired (and was replaced by Eric Drache). Bill always ran a good game. I think his salary was 18 percent of the profit the cardroom made, so he really promoted poker. He hasn't gotten enough credit for being one of the main contributors to poker; however, he's largely responsible for keeping honest poker going in Las Vegas back in the early days before the WSOP. He made the rake reasonable so the poker players would get a fair shake.

Though there was cheating in other cardrooms when more began to open in Las Vegas, Bill didn't put up with much foolishness. He was old school. In fact, he shot a guy, Nick Simpson, who controlled the cheating around town, mostly in the casino games. At the time, there wasn't any mob presence in the poker rooms. Nick tried to move in on Bill's poker games, but Bill Boyd ordered him to stay out of his cardroom. Nick didn't do it, they argued, and Bill got a gun and shot him outside in the alley; he got him right in the rear end. I don't know if that's where he was aiming, but I reckon Nick got off easy. Bill probably wasn't prosecuted back in those days. Like Texas, many things were handled between people without too much outside interference.

I was an outsider in 1973 and didn't exactly know how to handle the blatant cheating that was going on. But eventually, after I had lost a lot of money trying to overcome the problem, I learned to work around it. While Bill Boyd kept the Nugget pretty clean, it was impossible to stop all of it, so you had to protect yourself, especially in the other cardrooms where cheating was more open. If there was cheating going on, you could feel pretty quickly that things were out of the ordinary. You could just tell. When real big money is involved, you know somebody is going to try to get it by any means they can. It's just human nature. I learned that a long time ago and I always stayed alert to the danger signals. I learned about different ways people mark cards, hold cards out, collude with each other, put peeps in the ceiling, run out cold decks, and all kinds of different cheating methods. I had to keep the lines of communication open with certain people to learn about stuff like that; if you didn't keep up to date with what the cheaters were doing, you'd be at a big disadvantage and be more prone to getting cheated. Some guys showed me things out of friendship, or I paid them for the information. You just needed to be aware of what was going on if you had any kind of big money at stake.

Despite the problems with cheating, the games were easy, and I was playing and winning just about every day. After playing against all the tough no-limit players in the Texas games, I could hardly believe how easy the games were in Las Vegas. I was so much better at no-limit poker than anybody in Vegas, it was like picking strawberries. I mean, there were some good card players—like Sid Wyman, Puggy Pearson, Red Wynn, Joe Bernstein, Bill Boyd, and "Nigger" Nate Lanett (he was half-black and he didn't take offense to it; it's just what people called him). They were all really top notch, but they didn't understand how to play no-limit. They were limit players, and there's a world of difference between no-limit and limit. In limit poker, betting was structured and you could only bet what was allowed for the game. But when it came to no-limit where you could bet as much money as you had on the table, they didn't understand the nuances required to be a top player.

I didn't play limit games back then; there was no reason to. If there wasn't a no-limit game being spread, I'd just go out and play some golf, or go home.

While I played a lot at the Golden Nugget, it didn't attract the high rollers like the Strip casinos did, so eventually, when poker games were introduced to the Dunes, we played there frequently. I remember Sarge Ferris saying that when he started up his car every day, it just went straight to the Dunes. It drove itself. That's where the biggest poker games were held. The "change-ins," what we call buy-ins today, ranged from $10,000 up to $100,000, depending upon the players. That was big money back then, equivalent to five times as much today. These high-stakes games were spread at the Dunes because the principle owners of the hotel were poker players and they wanted to attract the high action to the games. Wyman was one of the players, along with Bob Rice, Charlie Rich, Todd Durlocker and Major Riddle, the majority shareholder of the Dunes until he lost his stake in the hotel playing poker. Riddle was a really bad player, what we called a "producer." He'd just hand his money away at the table.

One guy that did know how to play no-limit was my friend Crandell Addington, and we tangled pretty good one night in a game that neither one of us will ever forget. I had just moved to Vegas from Texas and was trying to promote hold'em because the local pros hadn't played the game much and weren't very good at it. Johnny Moss had also moved to Vegas and was running the cardroom at the Aladdin Hotel and Casino.

I walked into the cardroom one day and saw a six-handed hold'em game going on with some of the biggest high rollers in town. Lots of money was on the table, so I took a seat to get my share of it. This game kept going for forty-five days. All the hold'em players in the South had heard about it and were flocking to Vegas to play. After several days, Crandell and I were the two big winners. We had all our money on the table when I got dealt two sevens. Crandell had two kings. He raised and I called. The flop was K♣ 4♥ 2♦. Crandell bet and I raised him, hoping to push him out of the pot. He just called, hoping to beat me in a big pot. The fourth card was a 7, giving me a set of sevens. Crandell bet again. I raised him, confidently believing my three sevens were good. Crandell called. The river card was the last 7 in the deck! Crandell checked, I bet, and he moved in. I had the nuts and busted him, sending my toughest opponent back to Texas.

There was almost a million dollars in that pot and the old-timers told me it was the biggest pot in Las Vegas history at that point.

There was another great thing about playing in Las Vegas: it was relatively safe. The atmosphere in a controlled gambling environment was appealing after all I'd been through in Texas. I didn't have to worry so much about being hijacked, robbed, or hassled by cops—it was unbelievable. I didn't need to carry a gun anymore, and when I won money, I knew that I could walk out the door with it. And unlike Texas, where the cops could raid the game at any time or hijackers could come in with shotguns, the cops in Las Vegas actually *protected* the games. Now, that was a feeling of security I'd never experienced before. Every day I played, I almost had to pinch myself to get reminded that this was for real.

If I had known how much easier it was to be a professional poker player in Las Vegas than on the Texas Circuit, I would have moved a lot sooner than I did. But I didn't. And it was all because of Johnny Moss and an incident that had occurred some twenty-five years earlier. I knew Moss had spent some time in Vegas and I would ask him about the poker games.

"You guys don't want to go out there with all the bad people and everything," Moss used to tell me, Sailor and Slim when the subject came up. He painted pictures of us getting killed within a few months, if we were lucky to survive that long. Shaking his head side to side, he allowed as to how he was lucky to survive himself in the treacherous Las Vegas environment.

Well, that wasn't the whole story, not by any means. Later, we found out what really happened, and it had to do with a less than wholesome habit of Johnny's.

Mobsters ran Johnny out of Vegas after they caught him cheating in the late 1940s. I'm surprised they didn't kill him, and they probably would have if he hadn't been rescued. The episode occurred shortly after the notorious gangster Bugsy Siegel was killed on June 20, 1947. A Chicago mobster named Gus Greenbaum was sent into Vegas to take over the Flamingo Hotel and Casino. He later became associated with the Tropicana and the Riviera as well. Greenbaum was a poker player, and the Flamingo hosted a big poker game where Johnny was a regular. Despite our age difference, about twenty-five years, Johnny and I became friends later in Texas, but the one thing I didn't like about him was his tendency to cheat. In those earlier days, in the forties and fifties, it was almost acceptable. Everybody was looking for an edge, and honesty often got trampled in the process.

Even in Greenbaum's game, a guy you wouldn't want to mess around with, Johnny was not one to give honesty an edge. In what amounted to an outlandish scheme, Johnny posted a couple of cronies in a room above the table with a sophisticated mirror device to read his opponents' cards and relay that information back to him. Moss won millions before they got suspicious and finally nailed him. Apparently, Greenbaum's henchmen caught Johnny's guys hiding in the ceiling. Once exposed, Johnny took the blame.

"Listen, these guys work for me; it was my deal," Moss said. "They were just doing what I told them to do. Just turn them loose."

Greenbaum took the bait and released everyone but Johnny, who they presumably had different plans for. That most likely wouldn't have been too good for Johnny's future survival. But once freed, Johnny's guys went straight to their car for shotguns, and then they returned and threw down on everybody. They backed Greenbaum and his guys away from the table and escorted Johnny to safety.

He got away, but the word was out: "Don't ever come back to this town."

Mob influence was still strong in those days and Johnny's exploits were not quickly forgotten, so he stayed out of Vegas for another decade or so to keep from getting killed. Greenbaum was not one to forgive and forget and Moss knew it. But neither were the mob bosses if they felt things weren't right. In a fate similar to Bugsy Siegel, who had run afoul of his mob bosses back East, Greenbaum and his wife were murdered at their home in Phoenix in 1958, their throats cut, reportedly because Gus had been stealing mob money that had been skimmed from the proceeds of Vegas casinos.

Years later, when Moss decided to give Vegas another shot, many of the original mobsters like Greenbaum and his cronies had long since died out and he felt it was safe to return. I wasn't surprised when I learned about Moss's exploits in Las Vegas, and especially not when I learned that the devious old fox had been knocking Las Vegas because he wanted us to stay in Texas where we could keep the games going.

When I wasn't playing poker in the cardrooms around Las Vegas, I was often out at the golf course trying to win money. Just like at the poker tables, people would try to get your money any way they could, fair or foul. Soon after I arrived in Las Vegas, a couple of "mentors" privileged me with a lesson—a quite valuable if extremely expensive one. Willing student that I was, I learned that golf wasn't always the gentlemanly sport it was reputed to be.

I dubbed my tutorial the $300,000 Milkshake Caper.

I was playing a guy named Billy at the old Sahara golf course, and he was a slightly better golfer than I was. He was spotting me a stroke and a half each nine holes and I beat him on the front nine. He put a double press on me on the back, and I accepted it. As we made the turn, Billy's friend Elmo disappeared for a few minutes and reappeared with a chocolate milkshake for me. I was even par at that point, and birdied the first two holes on the back side. Billy wanted to press again, which I thought was a little strange, since I hadn't used any of my stroke holes yet.

My first stroke hole was in fact the twelfth, a long par-four, which I hit in regulation. As I lined up my birdie putt, I started getting dizzy. I four-putted the hole, then proceeded to bogey or double bogey the remaining six holes. It didn't take me long to figure out what had happened. I never learned what they put in that milkshake, but I knew they had spiked it with something and that it cost me more than $300,000.

At least I learned my lesson. Never again did I drink anything on the golf course that I didn't bring with me or know the source from which it sprung.

Meanwhile, the World Series had been growing steadily and getting more publicity around the country. Slim was doing his thing on the talk show circuit and as magazines and newspapers were covering the event, people started following the game. By now, thousands of newspapers across the country, big and small, printed pieces on the World Series of

Poker. It was a good thing for poker, because it brought players, but it was also a good thing for me, because it made poker more respectable in the eyes of the public. I became less self-conscious about being a gambler, at least as far as folks back home were concerned. That laid the groundwork for me making a more serious run at the championship.

I played again in 1974 and 1975, but didn't get as far as I would have liked. But that was to be expected in a tournament. One bad run of cards or one unlucky draw and your tournament is over. It isn't like cash games, where you can reach into your pocket and keep playing.

Moss won in 1974 for his third championship and Sailor won in 1975. I took special notice of Sailor's victory because it now meant two-thirds of my old road partners, Slim and Sailor, had won the championship. I started looking at the World Series differently; it took on a different meaning to me. I felt I was the best no-limit player, yet I hadn't won the championship and the recognition that went with it. With Sailor now winning the title, that reality struck home to me.

What I really liked about the World Series though—as did other top players—were the side games, where high-rolling gamblers and poker players would come to play with us. The cash would get distributed pretty good around that time of the year and I got my share of it—I kept winning steadily and building my bankroll.

But in the cash games, away from the World Series, there was a different side of poker unfolding, and it wasn't necessarily so pretty. This was away from the TV cameras and the media coverage and the public eye. Las Vegas was still a mob town, and you had to be careful how you navigated the waters. In particular, I'm talking about one of the most dangerous men I've ever met.

Maybe *the* most dangerous.

Chapter 16

The only difference between a rut and a grave is the depth.

I t took me precious little time to learn that Vegas, like the Texas Circuit, had its dark and dangerous side. Unexpected and disruptive outside influences soon descended on us in the form of a Chicago mobster named Tony "The Ant" Spilotro.

Anybody who's seen the movie *Casino* knows about Spilotro. Joe Pesci portrayed him—it's amazing how much Pesci resembles him; in fact, I'd say he's the spitting image of Spilotro. In the movie as in real life, Tony could be personable and even likable in a twisted way. But it was a really twisted way. You just had to block some things from your consciousness to see that charm. Like the fact that he was a stone-cold ruthless killer that the FBI said may have been involved in as many as twenty-two murders, most of them committed slowly, cruelly, and very painfully. Those were only the ones they suspected. Mobsters routinely got somebody to do their dirty work for them, but Tony reputedly did it himself because he enjoyed it.

Spilotro was the most dangerous person I'd ever known and easily the scariest. He was evil—you could just feel it. According to a story making the rounds, he shot a guy right outside a casino sports book, then ran his car over him several times. Most of the things about him in the movie *Casino* were true. They say he did put a guy's head in a vise and tightened it until the guy's eyeball popped out. He hung another guy on a meat hook two or three days before killing him. Spilotro was the real McCoy, a sadistic monster who enjoyed delivering death. It was no secret that if you got on the wrong side of it with Tony, you were in a heap of trouble.

Spilotro was probably the first mobster that tried to organize the poker-room cheating. Tony, a snake named Shoeshine Nick, and a third guy called Mike the Hammer formed cheating rings in the limit games. It made it virtually impossible to play and win unless you were a member of the group. I didn't realize the strength of those team partnerships in the early stages, and consequently I got cheated a lot.

I wasn't familiar with real mobsters. We didn't have any organized mob stuff in Texas like they did up East in the big cities, or I probably would not have been as bold as I was about confronting Spilotro. I always seemed to get in his way. He tried to draw me into cheating rings at the poker games, but I refused. Tony kept badgering me to join his partnerships and I kept refusing, telling him no, no, no. He wasn't pleased, and it got to be sticky. He didn't like me much, at least in the beginning, but he respected me, begrudgingly. I'd been dealing with dangerous guys my whole adult life and wasn't about to be ordered to cheat players when I didn't need to or want to. Naively, I stood up to Tony several times and he didn't like it one bit. He was used to being feared and totally unaccustomed to anyone telling him no. I was too dumb or too stubborn to give in. I didn't fully grasp at once what a powerful and dangerous figure he was. For a while, Spilotro kind of tolerated the situation.

But only for a while.

My friend Billy Baxter from Georgia and I finally had a serious run-in with Tony involving a kid out of New York named Stu Ungar. It was bound to happen given the close circles we ran in, and sure enough, that time came. Stuey was a great gin rummy player and high-stakes poker player, destined to become one of the greatest names in the World Series of Poker. Stuey was short and skinny and had such a baby face, you'd have thought he was a high school kid more suited to flipping pennies. But looks were deceiving. Billy and I were gambling with Stuey for very high stakes. We also partnered up for some golf games, and were making a lot of sports bets and playing some gin rummy with Stuey as well. Spilotro got wind of it and summoned Billy to a meeting. Of course, Billy was scared to go—and scared not to—but he did meet Tony at the Tropicana.

"What's this about?" Billy asked, acting as nonchalant as possible looking into Spilotro's reptilian eyes.

Inside, Billy was shaking, but he tried to look calm on the outside.

"I want to tell you something," Spilotro said. "I know you and Doyle Brunson are booking, and I'm telling you that when you book another bet, I've got 25 percent of it. I'm gonna be your partner from now on."

"Well, Tony, you know we've already got some partners," Billy replied.

"You listen to what I'm telling you," Spilotro said. "Don't book another bet in this town unless I got 25 percent."

Billy courageously told him he was certain that I wouldn't much like this proposed new arrangement.

"I'll tell you what you do," Tony snarled. "You go tell that big, fat partner of yours that if y'all ever book another bet in this town, a bet that I ain't got 25 percent of, I'm gonna take twelve ice picks and stick them right in that big, fat hustle-gut of his. Now you go tell him what I said."

Billy tracked me down as quickly as he could.

"Doyle, we gotta talk. I met with Spilotro last night."

"Yeah, what did he say?"

"He said he's taking 25 percent of us from now on."

"I don't know about that," I said, feeling uncommonly brave. "What else did he say?"

"He told me to tell you if we got caught booking any more bets in this town without his 25 percent, he's gonna stick twelve ice picks in that big fat belly of yours."

I looked at Billy. "What's wrong with *your* belly?"

Billy didn't think that was very funny. He was getting scared, a quality I soon was going to understand real good. I went and met with Tony, and he said flatly that nobody could do anything in Vegas any longer unless he had a piece of the action.

"If you guys are going to make football bets, I have a piece of it. If you and Baxter gamble with Stu Ungar, I've got 25 percent of whatever you do with him."

When I asked him why we should do that, he went nuclear.

"All I hear about is Doyle, Doyle, Doyle!" he shouted. "I'm sick and tired of hearing about Doyle. If you don't like it, I'll stick twelve ice picks in that big fat gut of yours!"

At least I knew that Billy got the story straight. Before I could think of a good response, Tony brought up Benny Binion, who he knew was a friend of mine.

"As far as that old man downtown goes, tell him he better stay downtown," Tony warned.

I looked into those snake eyes and said, "I'm not a messenger boy, but I sure would like to see you tell him that."

That was the end of the conversation, but he had gotten his point across. To make sure, he had me followed for a while, and then he sent one of his henchmen named Herbie to tell me he didn't want any more trouble out of me, to stay the hell out of his way.

He did take 25 percent of anything Billy and I did with Stu Ungar, and Baxter and I did beat Stuey out of some big money. That was the only "business" dealings I ever had with Tony, although we did some other gambling. I felt that if we'd lost, he would have paid his 25 percent, but I wasn't certain. You could only guess at such money matters with Spilotro.

Tony threatened to kill anybody that crossed him. And he wasn't a guy known for making idle threats.

"You can't kill everybody," I told him once.

He just got that evil grin on his face and replied, "No, I won't have to kill everybody. Just the first one."

This was the same Tony "The Ant" who once gave a nun $15,000 just for the hell of it.

I later told Benny about that meeting with Tony, that he was shaking down people all over Vegas. Quite a few paid him off to avoid a confrontation. I heard rumors that Tony had considered Benny one of his potential targets.

"What would you have done if he had come down here to the Horseshoe and tried to shake you down?" I wondered.

"The only reason I wouldn't shoot him on the spot was that I might have hit somebody standing behind him," Benny replied without a moment's hesitation.

Nobody intimidated Benny Binion. The "Texas Cowboy" wouldn't put up with any nonsense, and most everybody *alive* in Vegas knew it.

Even Tony.

Benny was my go-to guy when I had problems that I couldn't take anywhere else. Like Spilotro. Once, when Tony was making threatening noises, which got me a little concerned, I went to Benny for advice.

"This guy is for real," Benny said of Spilotro. "You know he'll kill you. You better go kill him."

I thought about that, but I was a poker player, not a killer, even though taking out Spilotro may have been the prudent thing to do—at least if I looked at things like Benny did. Of course, I didn't adhere to that advice, but I didn't fault Benny's foresight and logic. With Tony, it was like Hotel Hell: Once you checked in, you couldn't check out. Like the Texas Circuit, gambling in Vegas sometimes involved taking the ultimate risk, especially with a guy like Spilotro. If you made the wrong wager, you could be betting your life.

I was convinced it was my close friendship with Jack and Benny that kept me alive. Benny had my back. Without that protection, I have no doubt that Spilotro would have killed me, and probably my new, young friend Chip Reese as well.

It was in the Flamingo Hotel and Casino in 1975 when I first saw David "Chip" Reese at a poker table. Like the other local pros, I was licking my chops over his bankroll. We were accustomed to seeing bright young "hometown champions" show up in Vegas and we quickly separated them from their money. Little did I know that I was looking at one of the two finest young all-around poker players in the world, Bobby Baldwin being the other. We soon found out that he could play with the best of us.

One night we were playing seven-card stud high-low split no-declare; that is, seven-card stud high-low, and the best cards at the river would win—you didn't have to announce whether you were going high or low, as you did in "declaration" or what we called "cards speak." Johnny Moss, Puggy Pearson, Nick Vachicano, Jimmy Cassella, and I were at the table and nobody, including me, was playing very well. I had played enough high-low split games in college to know the concept of playing for the low side of the pot and letting the high fall where it would. A young, baby-faced, blond-headed kid was watching us play and then he sat down in our $400/$800 eight-handed high-low with his entire bankroll of $8,000. Well, this hometown champion beat us up pretty good, relieving us of a lot of money. He won real big, and I could see that it wasn't luck. This new kid was for real. Chip told me later he couldn't believe how bad we played high-low.

At Dartmouth, the cardroom at Chip's Beta Theta Pi fraternity house was immortalized as the *David E. Reese Memorial Cardroom* when he graduated. He was on his way to Stanford with his economics degree when he decided to pull into Vegas and see what the town was all about. Chip had been there for a month playing in the $5/$10 and $10/$20 stud games, and had built his $400 bankroll into the $8,000 that he used to sit in our game. His early successes at the seven-card stud cash games put a halt to his legal career before he even set foot into Stanford. Chip immediately realized where he belonged and what he was going to do. He neglected to tell his parents about his little detour, and it wasn't until almost a year later that they realized their son wasn't on his way to being a respected professional. Instead, he was a gambler.

I can only imagine their reaction.

Chip was the most natural poker player I had ever seen, probably the only guy ever to hit town and become an immediate success. He could win at all the games, and while we quickly learned how good Chip was, he just as quickly learned that Vegas wasn't Dartmouth. For one thing, Dartmouth didn't have a Tony Spilotro to deal with. Chip was only twenty-two or twenty-three and fresh out of college when he arrived in Vegas. Naively, he got lured into Spilotro's web. But as soon as Chip realized what he had gotten involved in, he broke it off, which was seldom successfully done with those mob guys. Spilotro ordered him to do something crooked.

"I can't do that," Chip told him.

"There is no 'can't.' There is only 'won't.'"

But Chip held his ground, winning my admiration for standing up to Tony.

I had one particularly vivid face-to-face confrontation with Spilotro. He was reneging on a golf bet, and we got in a shouting match in the parking lot. I protested, maybe a little bit too much. He got right in my face and stared at me. Spilotro's eyes never closed, never blinked. They were dark and frightening, like a snake's eyes. It was the scariest moment I'd ever had, except when that robber stuck his knife to my throat back in Houston. Flashes of what this man was capable of doing passed through my brain. Finally, I just walked away, but I had nightmares later.

When you look at the face of death, it's something you don't easily forget.

My confrontation with Tony in the parking lot had to do with him backing out on a golf bet in a game Chip was involved in. Chip knew that if Spilotro hadn't disrupted the golf match, Chip would have lost $90,000 to me. When he heard about Tony reneging, Chip tracked me down and handed me a brown paper bag containing $90,000. It was a class act, so typical of Chip.

I was repulsed by the things Spilotro did and the things he stood for—which occasionally involved cheating, extortion, torture, and murder. However, he'd hang out with us at the golf course because he liked to bet on golf matches—he didn't play golf himself—and football games, and he gambled high, which I did like. He lost most of the time, which I also liked. I guess he respected me enough that he never tried to muscle me on the bets we made. He didn't pay some of the other people, but he always paid me, maybe because he liked the challenge of betting against me.

Before a game one day at the Desert Inn course, Jack Binion and I got a tip that our group was going to be hijacked on the first hole, where a nearby gate would permit anyone to drive right up to the green. We routinely carried large sums of money with us on the golf course, because we bet heavy and paid off right after the matches were over. I guess someone was looking to take that from us. Such a scheme was not all that far-fetched, so we relayed the information to Benny. He ordered us to load our golf bags with shotguns and pistols and even an automatic rifle or two.

"When the shooting starts, y'all get down on the ground," he instructed.

I suppose a different group of people might have called off their game that day or left the money home, but we weren't about to let a little complication like that get in the way of our golf match. When we walked up to the first green that day, we were eyeing the gate and ready for anything. The guns were loaded and we all knew what we were going to do. We were poised to open fire when the hijackers showed up. Fortunately, they didn't. I suspect they got cold feet or heard we'd been tipped off.

Spilotro was with us that day, and he wasn't at all happy about the situation; we hadn't told him about the hijacking tip. Afterward, when we filled him in, he said, "Why the hell wouldn't y'all tell me? Were y'all going to leave me out there barefooted?" By barefooted, he meant without a gun.

"Well, Tony," I said, "we were going to take care of it if anything happened."

That's the way we thought in those days. You try to take care of your own business.

We called those golf outings the "Spilotro Days," as Tony often was out there with us. He also sat in sometimes as a spectator in our poker games, and while I'm not as superstitious as some, I decided one day he was making me unlucky. Without considering the potential consequences, I told him to move. He glared at me with those dead eyes and kind of growled, but he moved.

Spilotro told us stories about growing up in the Chicago mob, which I found captivating. I forced myself to overlook the cheating and treachery in his stories and his present-day activities—for the most part, anyway. One time in particular, though, it was difficult to do. We were at the Desert Inn and a super golfer named Jim was in from Louisiana. Jim was a friend of Slim's that I'd golfed with before in Fort Worth, and he was one of the best amateurs I'd ever played with. I brought in Jim and a guy named Ken to play with me as partners against a Las Vegas team Tony had assembled to bet against us.

Jack Binion was with me, and so was Slim, and we were betting fairly big—a $100,000 Nassau with presses. The result was we might be playing for hundreds of thousands of dollars by the end of the day. It was the three of us against two of the top players in Vegas. Because I'd played with Jim before, I thought this was a cinch. He would have been on the PGA Tour except for a felony conviction as a youngster. I saw him shoot sixty, sixty-one and sixty-three at the Las Vegas Country Club on three consecutive days—about the best golf I'd ever seen.

So there we were at the Desert Inn playing from the tips, the championship tees, and right away I noticed that Jim wasn't performing as I'd seen him before. Fortunately, the Las Vegas opponents weren't playing their best either, and I shot what was one of the best rounds of my life, a sixty-nine, from the tips. My partners may have helped me on one hole, but in effect I'd beat Tony's guys by myself and we collected the money. Afterward, I pulled Jim aside for a little heart-to-heart.

"Were you stalling out there?" I asked. "You damn sure weren't playing your best."

"No," he insisted. "I had no idea you were that good. I can kind of stall around and play when I need to, but I'll open up tomorrow."

Like a total fool, I made another bet for the next day. I shot my customary eighty and my partners played lousy again and the Las Vegas guys beat us out of all the bets. Come to find out, Tony had indeed gotten to Jim and Ken. My guys had agreed to dump off and not play well so Tony could win. But they did get to feeling a little guilty or remorseful or something and had tried to skip town the night before our second match. Tony caught them at the airport, took them back to the hotel, locked them in their room, and wouldn't let them out until we resumed the match the next day.

That was the kind of guy Tony Spilotro was. It's hard to imagine that I could say I liked somebody like him. But he was interesting and entertaining, and at those rare moments, I did almost like him. Of course, I had to put the worst of Tony out of my mind temporarily.

Which wasn't so easy sometimes.

Chapter 17

Blessed is he who expects nothing, for he shall never be disappointed.

J ack Binion and I flew to Florida once—it was the mid-1970s—for a rendezvous with a prominent millionaire businessman and high-stakes Vegas gambler we'll call Sam. Sam had won $168,000 from some of my colleagues in Las Vegas, and we were delivering the money for them. Actually, we were going to Florida to gamble with Sam himself, to try to win the $168,000 back—and bundles more. Sam loved action, the higher the better, and we welcomed the opportunity to oblige.

"He plays golf," Jack said. "Maybe you could play some golf with him."

When we got to Florida, Sam was at the course with some apparent golf vultures and a touring PGA pro, Al Besselink. I walked up and introduced myself.

"I'm with Jack, we brought you the money," I said. "I hear you play golf."

"Yeah," he said. "We're fixing to tee off right now. What's your handicap?"

"Thirteen."

"Well," he said, "that's what I am. We'll play."

I didn't think he could be lying any more than I was. He asked me what I wanted to play for, and I knew he was a high player, so I said, "I'll play you a $5,000 Nassau," which was a lot of money.

"I don't play that cheap," he said.

"What do you want to play for?" I asked.

"I'll play $7,500 five ways, two-down press."

"Okay," I said, aware that the bet could escalate to $50,000 or so.

We teed off, and I beat him fairly easily. He started screaming that I had misrepresented myself, but I came to find out he had been the No. 2 man on a college golf team that included a future touring pro. In reality, I was probably a 75-76 shooter, and he was probably a 74-75 shooter. Real close.

Jack was there with me as my betting partner, enjoying all the action. He'd put up half the money for the wagers, and although he was a multimillionaire, and later a billionaire, he wanted to win as badly as I did. As I stood over the ball for a crucial shot on a pivotal hole, I happened to glance over at Jack. He had his fist clenched tight and an anguished look on his face, and I couldn't help laughing. I backed off a few moments and said, "Relax, Jack, I'm the one who's got to hit this shot." I hit a good one, and we won the money.

But talk about strange sights: I had hurt my back, and the guy who owned the Horseshoe Casino was carrying my clubs to protect the bet!

We played the next day and when Sam beat me, he said, "Maybe you were telling the truth about your handicap."

So full of bull, this guy. Afterward, he invited us to his Florida home.

"You want to play some pool?"

"Yeah," I said. "I play pool."

"You want to play eight ball for $10,000?"

And I'm thinking that while I was not a great pool player, I was well above average. After all, I had been one of the best players in Sweetwater.

We played a few $10,000 games and it was pretty even. Next thing I knew, we were pitching horseshoes real high, about $5,000 or $10,000. I had never pitched horseshoes, but we were about the same.

"You want to go shoot some baskets?"

"Yeah," I said, "I'll shoot some baskets with you."

I had a little shoulder trouble and hadn't touched a basketball in a long time. He would average eight out of ten free throws, and I would make seven or eight. We were real close at everything we did, even gin rummy. He might have been just a shade better than I was at gin, except that my ability to concentrate for long periods would wear him down. In a long session I usually beat him.

Sam had tremendous energy at everything he did. I thought I had a lot of stamina, but I was heavy and my leg was bad. We'd spend all day gambling on golf from seven o'clock in the morning until dark. We'd eat dinner, then play gin rummy until two or three o'clock in the morning. The next day we'd start the whole procedure over again, and damned if he wasn't wearing *me* out.

He was a couple hundred thousand winner when one day, out of the blue, he said, "Do you play poker?"

"Yes, I do," I said. "I'm one of the best players in the world."

"Oh, really? I'm pretty good, too," he said, giving me a skeptical look. "Let's play."

That was the end of him. Sam was an exceptional amateur poker player, but was completely outclassed—after all, I played for a living. I beat him rather handily. After two weeks, Jack and I returned to Vegas and all we could talk about was my Florida gambling experience.

What a thrill! I'd never gambled that high before. It was the damnedest two weeks gambling that you could imagine.

Over the next bunch of years, Sam and I became not only very good friends, but well-seasoned gambling rivals. He liked to gamble high; I liked to gamble high. It was a perfect match. I traveled many times to Sam's home, paying or collecting six-figure sports bets and using those occasions for high-stakes golf and card games. Of course, money didn't mean all that much to Sam, as he had plenty of it. On all my trips to his homes, Sam proved not only to be one terrific gamer, whether at the poker table, the tennis court or the golf course, but a generous and good-time host as well. We played many, many rounds of golf, a lot of gin rummy, and a whole lot of poker. We gained a lot of respect for one another. Over the years, I beat him out of a lot of money, though it never affected our friendship.

When I first met Sam, we attended a game between the Kentucky Colonels and the New York Nets of the old American Basketball Association. It was one of my more memorable experiences. After all, basketball had consumed much of my life, dating back to my schoolboy days when my dream had been to someday play professionally. Yet on the night the Colonels and Nets played, I realized I hadn't seen a basketball game in at least ten, maybe fifteen years. And I was in for a shock. I'd never seen black players on the court. Back when I was in college, the NBA was an all-white league; they didn't allow blacks to play.

Before I even had time to acclimate myself to the "modern" game, this tall, Afro-haired black guy came racing down the right sideline with the ball. In one fluid motion he wheeled toward the basket, took two steps, and just dunked it.

My mouth fell open—kind of like a West Texas farm boy seeing a Vegas floor show for the first time. That was my introduction to Dr. J, the All-Pro Julius Erving. I couldn't believe just how much basketball had progressed since my heyday, and I was amazed at the remarkable agility of these guys, Dr. J in particular. He was unstoppable that night and contributed mightily as the Nets captured a last-second victory. I later met Dr. J, who had a terrific personality, and told him about my experience.

"If I ever felt like a white guy who couldn't jump, that was it," I said, and I meant it, having witnessed the performance of such stunning athletes that night.

Dr. J broke up laughing.

✪✪✪✪✪

It wasn't long afterward that my spirits came crashing back to earth with the news that Doyla, my firstborn, was suffering from a terrible affliction. This was 1975. Doyla was flowering into a beautiful twelve-year-old, effervescent and kind-hearted, and she was a budding piano talent. Doctors discovered she had a debilitating spinal disorder known as idiopathic scoliosis. The malady caused severe curvature of the spine. Specialists recommended radical procedures, including the implantation of a steel rod in her spine or placing her in a body brace for a year.

Louise intervened. The body brace wouldn't be an option.

Following my miraculous recovery from cancer and Doyla's birth, Louise had become an even more devout Christian, and she went right to work implementing her beliefs. She organized marathon prayer sessions for Doyla that included taking her to Los Angeles to see Katherine Kuhlman, the famous faith healer. Louise also had several churches and groups praying for Doyla's healing. Within three months, my daughter's spine had straightened 100 percent. The severe curvature was gone. I saw the X-rays with my own eyes. Medical specialists acknowledged that hers was one of only three known cases of such an occurrence without surgical assistance or the use of body braces.

Doyla's recovery came on the heels of a second medical miracle in our family. Not long after my recuperation from the cancer surgery, Louise developed a uterine tumor, which normally required extensive surgery and removal of the female organs. Not unlike my melanoma, her tumor disappeared before doctors could operate. After our "miracles," Louise got involved with foreign missions and continued to spend countless, joyful hours as a servant of the Lord.

"It's so exciting to be a Christian," she told me. "Such an exciting part of living."

I wasn't listening. Or at least not hearing.

After those last two miracles, it did began to dawn on me that perhaps God was indeed revealing Himself to me. He had done so repeatedly, but I had refused to acknowledge Him. It would seem that three miracles would be enough to convince even the most skeptical person that God not only existed, but that for some reason, His hand was on our family.

I continued to struggle with that realization, but it was too deep for me. I finally quit trying to figure it out. There simply wasn't room—or the desire—in my life to initiate a full-court press on Christianity.

I was too obsessed with my life in the gambling world.

Chapter 18

You can't send a duck to eagle school.

Sometimes your mind slows things down and you see events playing out like a movie up on the big screen. The 1976 World Series of Poker was one of those times. I'd already watched my poker-playing buddies—Johnny, Slim, Sailor, and Puggy—take down the championship and I really wanted to win this thing. I was sure I was the best player at the time, but I needed that title for validation, not just for myself, but among my peers. I also wanted to prove my abilities to Louise. Although she never once expressed a desire to watch me play, and in fact, never once saw me play a hand—Louise had no idea about gambling and poker—I knew she was proud of my accomplishments at the table.

Being the World Champion might accomplish that.

The Main Event, the most prestigious event of the year in poker, was a gathering of the greatest no-limit hold'em players in the world. The field comprised twenty-two players, headed by former champions Puggy, Slim, and Sailor, along with three-time winner Johnny Moss. Only one of those championships went to a non-Texan, Puggy, but he had played with us a lot.

For the first time, I wasn't afraid of the publicity that winning would generate—not that I wanted the public notoriety, because I didn't—but the WSOP had received so much press over the previous few years that the stigma of being a professional gambler was diminished. And by now, my competitive instincts overrode everything.

After six appearances and no world championships, I was anxious for the 1976 Main Event to begin. I'd had a good start to the Series, winning the deuce-to-seven draw preliminary event, but the $10,000 buy-in Main Event was the one I really wanted to win. Me and every other poker player.

While there was good money to be won in the tournaments, it wasn't just the Main Event that was the attraction—it was the big side games, where amateurs and hometown pros would mix it up with us, trying to take on the best players in the world. Those adventurous players weren't used to our level of competition and made a big mistake you often see at the poker tables: they overestimated their abilities. Which was perfectly fine with me. Between the tournaments and the cash games, there was little time to sleep. It was money-making time for us with all the easy action in town. This was not the time of year to take your vacation.

The Main Event got under way with a lot of excitement in the air and a lot of ribbing back and forth at the tables. Slim and Sailor were in full form, playing to the crowd and the increasing media frenzy that now accompanied the World Series.

"Hey, things are looking up," Sailor announced. "Last night, Slim and I were betting on what time the six o'clock movie came on. He liked six-thirty. I won that one."

Slim would come back with one of his favorites: "Got half a mind to slip a rattlesnake in his pocket and ask him for a match."

Underneath the jabs, we were plenty focused, and it wasn't long before everybody got pretty serious. We lost two great players right out of the gate. Johnny Moss was eliminated in the first two hours, followed in quick order by Jack Straus. I'd like to say that the field got easier, but it was an all-star lineup of the greatest no-limit players competing. But at least I was two tough players closer.

I was playing great poker. I felt I had a real opportunity to win if I maintained my concentration and stayed on my game, which meant being aggressive, aggressive, and more aggressive.

At the end of the first day, I was in good chip shape and the field had narrowed. We were down to eight players when Bobby Baldwin got eliminated. He was a great young player who would go on to win the championship just two years later—but this wasn't his year. Puggy went next, along with Bert Rice, a Texan. Crandell had taken out both Puggy and Bert on one hand with trip fives and proceeded to break Sailor next with three queens. That got us four-handed: Crandell, Jesse Alto, Hufnagel, and me.

Crandell took great pride in how he presented himself—he was always the flashiest dresser in the game—and for the tournament, favored a three-piece suit with a matching flawless Stetson, a lustrous silk tie and top-of-the-line cowboy boots. Crandell's claim to fame was that he never loosened his tie at the poker table. I had run up against him many times around the Texas Circuit and felt he would give me the most problems in the tournament. He knew how to play and, like me, he was aggressive, throwing a lot of bets at the pot. He'd bluff with nothing and just as easily trap an opponent with a monster.

Crandell confidently exhaled blue rings of smoke above the table, but his confidence wasn't quite enough to carry him all the way. Holding a pair of jacks, he thought he'd caught me bluffing. I wasn't. I sent him and his cigar to the rail with three nines. With Crandell gone, I had one less landmine to dodge. Playing three-handed with my toughest opponent out of the way, I liked my chances. I figured I could outmaneuver and outthink these two relative newcomers to the game. With his youth, talent and flashy style, Hufnagel had earned his nickname of "Fast Eddie" from the movie *Hustler* starring Paul Newman and had already put in an impressive performance. I would have liked his chances if I hadn't been at the table.

But I was—that championship title would have to run through me. Finally, I broke him when he went all-in with a pair of eights against my pair of jacks.

The championship came down to me and Jesse Alto. Jesse, who ran the largest poker game in Houston, was a good player with a great record—he eventually made six Main Event final tables—but he didn't have my expertise at that time. I was picking my opportunities to wear him down and found a good one after I beat him in a big pot. I had played with him plenty and knew he was a notorious "steamer," meaning that he had a tendency to play recklessly after losing a big pot. And I had him steaming pretty good.

I was in solid chip position, holding twice as many chips as Jesse. "If I can win the next hand, I might break him," I told myself. We had played all night, and it wouldn't be much more time before dawn. I thought I could beat him out of his chips before long.

On the next deal, I drew the 10♠ 2♠, not quality pocket cards and a hand I wouldn't ordinarily play, but I was playing out my hunch. Jesse was in the small blind and tentatively raised the pot. I called him since I had so many chips and had position on him. The flop came A-J-10, giving me a pair of tens. Jesse bet and I called him. While my bottom pair of tens with a worthless kicker wasn't strong, I didn't put Jesse on much of a hand either.

A deuce fell on the turn, giving me two pair. Jesse was first and led into the pot with a small bet. I figured to have the best hand and moved in on him. He took a hard look at me, trying to gauge where I was at. We still had another card coming, and it would cost Jesse the rest of his chips to see that card. If I won, it would all be over. If I lost, he would win a big pot and be right back in the game.

I could see that Jesse was feeling the effects of our marathon session. We'd been going at it for thirty-two hours straight, something I'd done countless times in my career, but never before with so much prestige on the line. Jesse's eyes had dark shadows underneath them, and they were hooded with weariness. He was drinking coffee to stay alert, and his head drooped slightly so that he observed me from a lower angle, resting his chin more and more on his hand. The stubble on his beard was a full day past a five o'clock shadow and he looked like a man who needed some serious sleep. I don't imagine I looked a whole lot better, certainly not with all the cigarette smoke making my eyes bleary. But none of this detracted from my concentration or Jesse's; neither one of us was going to hand the championship to the other just because of a little sleep deprivation.

Jesse didn't deliberate as long as I expected before he called my all-in bet. That wasn't a good sign. All of Jesse's chips slid right into the pot.

I thought my two pair was good and he'd need a lucky river card to win the pot. But I was wrong about who would need it.

"What've you got?" I asked.

My heart sank when Jesse showed the A♥ J♥. The board cards were A-J-10-2, giving Jesse aces and jacks—better than my tens and deuces. He was a prohibitive favorite to win this pot. Of course, I didn't know that until we got all the chips in the middle and turned over our cards. Because he was steaming, I just knew he was going to play this hand regardless of what he had, and it was simply bad luck for me that he had happened to wake up with a quality hand. Many times before I had called him without a pair, with just ace-high, and it was good. More than any other player, when Jesse Alto was steamed, he just shot his money off. That's the main reason I played that 10-2. But this time, he had picked up a big hand.

"You've got me beat," I said turning over my 10-2.

But I knew if I lost the pot, I would still have about one-third of the chips and could easily come back. There would be plenty of play left, and I was confident I could take back the lead. Also, there was one more card to play, the river, and I had four "outs," cards that would make my hand the winner. If either of the two remaining tens or deuces got dealt, I'd make a full house and have the winning hand. I was an 11 to 1 underdog to get one of those outs, but even if that card didn't help me, I was still in this game.

When people take a quick look at a hold'em hand, it seems like the game sometimes comes down to one lucky card, and they write it off as that. But poker is not played in one hand; it's a long series of hands and if you make the right decisions, the chips will come to you. A lot of trapping and setting up of plays occurs way before a pivotal hand comes down. The top players play their opponents, not their cards. That's what separates them from the merely good players, who don't fully understand that concept.

The tension in the room was heavy as everyone waited to see the final card. As the railbirds leaned in over the table, the dealer hesitated ever so slightly, waiting for the go-ahead nod from Jack before dealing. I'd never experienced such a significant moment at a poker table.

If I got my card here, it would be over.

I felt the weight of all those hours of play as the dealer slid the card off the top of the deck and turned it over. Wow! Was it really the ten of diamonds? The noise rising from the spectators jammed up around the table and the TV cameras undeniably confirmed it. I'd made a full house, tens over twos to beat Jesse's two pair.

I was the new World Champion of Poker!

I got up from my seat with a smile that must have been wider than my Stetson hat. Everybody was screaming their congratulations, jumping up and down and clapping their hands and each others' backs. Their jubilation was contagious, finally spilling over on me:

I'd been waiting for this moment a long time.

In some ways, this victory was the greatest thrill of my poker career, but in other ways, my elation was tempered. It was as though winning the championship was my due. In 1972, okay, I didn't win it, I gave it to Slim. In 1973, Puggy won it outright. Then in 1974, it was Moss again followed by Sailor in 1975. But now it was my time. I felt like I was supposed to win so I wasn't particularly surprised. It wasn't so much the money that really struck me, a big pile of it in stacks of $100 bills that Jack Binion pushed over to me. I had picked up $220,000 for the victory, which was a lot of money at the time and the most ever won in a tournament, but the championship meant more than the money. It validated my standing among the great no-limit players that I regularly competed against in cash games.

I had played world-class poker to win that match and felt, deep down, that the title belonged in my hands. It was also gratifying that Slim, Sailor, and I had completed the championship triangle from our partnership days.

When that last card crowned me champion, I felt like I had just climbed Mount Rushmore. I was mentally and physically exhausted. I was glad it was over. The truth was I wanted to get into one of the side games, which were always particularly good during the Main Event.

For one year at the minimum, I would hold the crown as the World Champion of Poker. As a poker player, there isn't a better feeling in the world.

Chapter 19

When you're in deep water, it's a good time to keep your mouth shut.

After I won the championship, Louise thought I might quit playing poker and find a "legitimate" job. She was always secretly hoping that I would find a more accepted means of making a living, but I was at the height of my abilities and playing as good as ever. And now, with the world championship being mine, I was even more committed to the game. Not that "retiring" had even crossed my mind.

When a reporter asked me about that, I told him that such a move was unlikely, but also how proud I was of my six-year-old son. He had made his first bet on the golf course a few days previous, betting twenty cents on me and getting back a dollar.

Over the next year I killed the cash games, playing even more confidently than before. But at the same time, I was anxious for the next World Series of Poker to get started, waiting for the chance to defend my title. Soon enough, the months clicked off the calendar and here it came around again. The field numbered thirty-four in the 1977 World Series of Poker, up by nearly a third, and was again attended by the top no-limit poker players, mostly Texans. I knew my old traveling buddies, Slim and Sailor, wanted to win that title as much as I did, and so did the other thirty-one players.

I'd gone into the Series feeling confident, like no one could slow me down. I'd already had a good run in the preliminary events, winning one of the two seven-card stud high-low split tournaments. That was my third gold bracelet and I was figuring to get myself one more.

In addition to all the top players, a couple of eccentric amateurs were competing with us for the title. There was Milo Jacobson, a tall, heavyset, retired nightclub owner whose poker adventures had been largely confined to the Elks Club back home. I wasn't sure he had what it took to win the poker championship, but if we were competing for a booze title, Milo would have won that one hands down. He was knocking down 86-proof shots of Canadian Club like he'd just come in off the desert and had been handed a jug of water. For a sheer display of drinking endurance, I'd never seen anything like it. Another amateur testing the waters, Cadillac Jack Grimm, was sponsoring an expedition to the mountains of Washington, Oregon and western Canada to hunt for Big Foot, the huge, hairy cousin of the Abominable Snowman. Grimm also had hired a photographer to find and photograph Scotland's Loch Ness Monster, and had put up a $5,000 reward for the capture of Big Bird.

Slim, like usual, was in fine form, playing up to the media and the crowd. He was pretty entertaining for people that were new to him, but I'd heard his lines for so many years, it kind of got like when you've been married forty or fifty years. You tune things out. That's what I did with Slim. I knew what he was going to say almost always before he said it. Slim got all fixed up for the big event, sporting a canary yellow cowboy suit, gold boots, and a big, satiny hat. In between hustling side bets, he was spinning tall tales and one-liners, and had most everybody laughing. Slim grabbed hold of one group of folks by the rail, and shot them one of his favorite lines.

"I'm from this town called Amarillo. It don't ever git no bigger. Ever' time a woman gits pregnant, a man leaves town."

Soon enough, all the jabbering stopped, the tournament started, and we got down to the business of playing some poker. I started mixing it up from the beginning, playing aggressive poker and winning pots. Right away, chips started coming my way, and they got to accumulating in my stack. This tournament was the only time I ever jumped out in front and got way ahead to start with. I became the chip leader early in the first day and kept growing my chips as one player after another one was eliminated and the field narrowed. By the end of the first day, I think I had about half the chips in the tournament.

I don't know what Cadillac Jack was hunting for in this tournament—I didn't see any signs of Big Bird or Big Foot—but Grimm took his exit on the second day. The other amateur had an entirely different story line going. Milo was astounding us all, drinking steadily but playing good poker.

"I don't know much about poker," which was a bit of an understatement, "but I can beat these coffee drinkers!" Milo boldly confessed.

And for three days he did.

We were astonished at Milo's performance. I mean, the drinking part of it. He was downing shots of rye at a greater rate than I could fathom, and at the same time, outlasting all the seasoned pros in the tournament. Slim got busted, as did Straus. Crandell got broke too, and even Moss took an exit, but Milo kept going strong. I guess that hard alcohol, like they say, is a strong preservative. Jimmy the Greek had originally called Milo a 100 to 1 shot and conceded that even those were generous odds. I think if Greek had factored in the rye, he would have stretched those odds out a bit.

Milo was still around when we got down to the final table of six—and unbelievably, he was still drinking. The other four players included Sailor and Junior Whited along with Buck Buchanan, twenty-seven-year-old Gary "Bones" Berland, and myself. The first two victims were Buck and Junior. Sailor was next to go. He tried to run Milo out of the game, but Sailor's wired eights were second-best to Milo's kings, and he was gone. But when Bones made an 8-high straight against Milo's trip fours, it was over for the former nightclub owner.

"That was fun," said Milo, as he staggered off to find a fresh rye and water.

Now it was Bones and me heads-up, but I thought Bones never really had a chance. While he was a promising young pro, he didn't have my experience at the game, nor did he have the momentum. I had made all the right decisions during the tournament and had 80 percent of the chips when it got down to the two of us. I had held the chip lead continuously since the first day, never even coming close to surrendering my chip dominance.

We played a bunch of small pots before the key hand came up. I was dealt a 10-2 offsuit in the big blind. Bones didn't raise, so I got to see the flop for free. It came 10♦ 8♣ 5♥, giving me a pair of tens. Bones had 8-5 in the pocket and flopped two pair. I checked, and Bones, trying to trap me, also checked. The fourth card was the 2♣, giving me the bigger two-pair hand. I bet, trying to get more chips out of Bones. Not realizing his two pair weren't any good, Bones moved in on me. I beat him into the pot, calling his bet. The fifth card was another 10 making my full house, tens over twos, and giving me the championship.

I didn't need that last 10 to win the pot, but it was ironic that I had won the championship two years in a row with 10-2, making a full house each time. For some reason, I wasn't as excited as the first time I won.

The 10-2 pocket cards instantly became known in hold'em as the "Doyle Brunson." I didn't particularly like the ten-deuce being immortalized in my name because it isn't a quality hand. But I couldn't prevent it any more than I could prevent being nicknamed "Texas Dolly," which wouldn't have been my choice either. The ten-deuce were just two cards that popped up at the right time under peculiar circumstances and twice won the championship. And that's why it was so unusual.

What most people don't know is that the 10-2 almost won a third WSOP Championship. In 1981 Perry Green and Stu Ungar got heads-up for the championship. Perry had more chips than Stuey and they got it all in. The flop came J♦ 9♣ 8♣. Perry had the 10♣ 2♣, and Stuey had the better hand with A♣ J♣ for top pair and the nut flush draw. Perry had an open-ended straight and a flush draw. The fourth card was a 6 and the last one was a blank. If a queen or 7 had come that wasn't a club, Perry would have won the tournament with a straight and it would have been the third time a 10-2 had won it—and the hand would have become even more famous.

Jack Binion counted out my winnings, $340,000 in $100 bills, and pushed them over to me. The prize set a record for the most money ever won in a tournament. All those piles of hundred-dollar bills wrapped up neatly in thick stacks were a pretty sight to see, but the money was secondary. Being the champion, that's what really mattered.

With two consecutive World Series of Poker championships, I knew I had achieved something special.

Chapter 20

Sometimes opportunity knocks; at other times you have to pursue it.

About a year after my second World Series of Poker victory, I got this strange idea in my head. I don't know what got into me, but I started to write an advanced book on beating the game of poker, something that hadn't been done before. There wasn't a credible poker book out there. *According to Hoyle* was about the only poker book that even made sense. It wasn't good, but I think it was the best one. I wanted to create something different, something I could be proud of. My financial situation might have had something to do with it, because for the first time in my career, I had made enough money not to look back. Besides the money I won at the World Series, I was cleaning up in the cash games and my bankroll was as flush as it had ever been.

I think the book had become a new challenge for me. It was something I could try to achieve outside of playing poker.

One of the first people I turned to for help with this project was Mike Caro, whose reputation as the best draw poker player in the world made him a perfect fit for the book. I originally met Mike when I invited him over to my house back in 1975. When he rang the doorbell, I looked out the window and couldn't believe what I saw. Here's this guy with a scraggly beard and messed up hair that made him look like Charles Manson. His nickname was "Crazy Mike," and he lived up to that name with his wild looks and even wilder antics at the table. It took me no time at all to realize that Mike was an unusual person, something I couldn't help but get reminded of every time I saw him. I soon learned that Caro was a heck of a writer too, who would prove indispensable to the book.

To coordinate the project, I hired a sportswriter named Alan Goldberg to help me put the book together. I had never read anything about poker that made sense to me, but I liked what Goldberg had written. I read some of his columns and he did know poker. Goldberg recorded my words on tape and then put what I had said into writing.

I assembled the best players in the world, the experts in each game, and collaborated with them on their specialties. They included Bobby Baldwin, limit hold'em; Chip Reese, seven-card stud; Mike Caro, draw poker, statistics and poker odds; David Sklansky, high-low seven-card split; and Joey Hawthorne, limit lowball. Caro also helped me immensely with the lowball section. My chapter on no-limit hold'em was the centerpiece of the book and the most pages were devoted to its coverage. All the contributors worked really hard on their sections. They'd come over every day and we'd concentrate on getting it done. Everyone really wanted to make his section as good as possible. Joey Hawthorne, however, was hard to collar. He was really talented, but we couldn't get him over to do the writing; he'd just flake out on us. Mike stepped forward and actually wrote the lowball section in the book, while Joey just approved it and made a couple of changes. The truth is that it should be Mike's section too.

I took about a year off from the tables on this project, and barely played any poker. I was consumed with this book project and devoted all my energies to it. I had a lot of ideas about poker, but I'd never before put them into writing. It wasn't like sitting down at a card table, which I was used to—writing and putting the book together was the hardest work I'd ever done.

After we got all that writing done and I'd gone over the strategies with my contributors, we had to go about putting the whole thing into a finished book. My first thought was to get my book published by one of the major New York publishers. I approached some of them to see what could be done. The meetings didn't turn out too good. I was looking for a partnership and they were looking for an author. Publishing companies gave me offers, and maybe they were good, but I knew very little about royalties, marketing, and distribution. I had heard horror stories about people writing books and not getting paid their royalties.

"How do I know how many books you really sell?" I asked.

"We keep records," they told me.

"Yeah," I said, "but I don't have access to them. Why don't you let me print the books, I'll sell them to you, and then you can distribute them?"

They wouldn't do that.

"Okay," I said, "I'll just do it myself."

And that's why I decided to print the book myself. I formed my own company to publish the book: B & G Publishing, for Brunson and Goldberg. I was impressed with Goldberg's early work and made him an equal partner. I spent $400,000 buying equipment and hiring people. As a rule, poker players are terrible businessmen, and my venture hardly made me an exception. Normally, you just hire somebody to typeset a book and prepare it for the printer, but no, I had to *buy* the equipment.

When it came time to name the book, I gave it a catchy title: *How I Made Over $1,000,000 Playing Poker*. After too many complications and problems to mention, we got the book off the press in 1978 and started selling it, all 600-plus pages of it, at $100 a copy. It was a tidy sum in those days, but for serious players, it was well worth the price. The book's publication was seen as a landmark event for poker players. And I suppose it was. It was the first time the deep secrets of poker had been put into print, and I had gathered some of the top minds in poker to contribute to it. The book covered a lot of aspects and strategies that no other book had ever discussed. I focused on the psychological warfare of poker, and went into depth about how to play specific hands, explaining how and why you did certain things—again, something no previous book had done.

Immediately, the book caused a stir among professional players. I gave up a lot of secrets and all the pros wanted to know why. Sure, lots of players learned some things, but more than anything, the notoriety received by the book brought many more players to the game. I also think more people played the big-limit games because of *How I Made Over $1,000,000 Playing Poker* than any other factor. It made good players out of mediocre ones and really good ones out of good ones. And the good ones that had money, they would come play with me. But few could really master the system I described because it's too aggressive for almost any player. I've known only three high-stakes players who tried to play exactly how I recommend in my book. Two were successful and one went broke.

The style of play is not for everyone and you need years of experience to understand the nuances. The idea is for players to take the concepts and strategies in my no-limit section and adapt them to the style that suits them best. When I talk about *style*, I'm talking about the range between playing tight or playing loose. That range can be huge and can get players into trouble if they're playing out of their comfort zone.

I printed five thousand copies of the book in a brownish-red colored hardcover and slowly started selling copies. In another fit of madness, I bought classified ads in every major newspaper in the country with a circulation exceeding 100,000. Orders started coming in, but not enough to pay the costs. Problem was, there wasn't much of a market for $100 books. On top of all my other expenditures, I was getting eaten alive by overhead. The result of all the equipment, staff, office space and the rest of the costs, including a few other books we published—*Bobby Baldwin's Winning Poker Secrets*, one on blackjack, maybe one or two others—was that I was going broke from this business.

After the first edition sold out, I changed the title to *Super/System*—the name it still goes by—and reduced the retail price from $100 down to $50 to generate more sales.

If I had to do it again, knowing all the problems I'd have, I might not have written *Super/System*. But then again, maybe I would have. I compare it to having a difficult child. Even though the kid may give you trouble, once you have him, you don't throw him back in the ocean like a fish you don't want. You keep him. The problems you deal with, the rest of the package, you're real proud of. That's kind of the way I felt about the book when it was being written and all the trouble we had with the business aspects of the project.

Then Goldberg and I had a disagreement; I bought him out after the book was published and dismantled the company.

I placed a young woman in charge of the remaining business. Left for a year without supervision, something happened that both surprised and disappointed me. The young woman developed a slot machine habit, a pretty expensive one that ate up all her money. When her income wouldn't sustain her, she began to "borrow" money from my company while struggling to keep the records credible. When I found out about it, I was stunned and disappointed in her as well. I had trusted her and now she was taking all the money. I got hot under the collar and summoned her to my office. After a minute or two of yelling, I calmed down a little and started to feel real bad.

"I know you didn't mean to do it," I said, perhaps subconsciously recalling some of my past foibles, "so I guess it won't do me any good to holler. Sometimes people do things without really knowing why. Deep down, you're still an honest person."

We drove over to the Sahara Hotel, and because she was broke, I handed her a $100 bill.

"When you get your head straight, come on back and I'll write you a recommendation for a new job," I told her.

Well, Caro was beside himself when he found out about this. He'd put a lot of work into helping me get the book completed and had become a real good friend during this time. I think he probably wanted the young woman prosecuted, if not condemned to a desert firing squad. But he finally mellowed out and penned a line later that simply floored me. "Doyle, a former athlete, is very tall and heavy," he said. "But it wasn't until then that I truly understood the size of this man."

I decided there was hope for my wild-haired friend after all.

There were a few interesting asides to this project. One day a guy walked into my publishing office and asked if I remembered him. I didn't. His name was Dick Turnbull, the safety engineer who had covered me with a blanket at the gypsum plant when my leg, along with my youthful dreams, had gotten shattered. Years later, by chance, fate, or whatever, Dick became Mike Caro's mentor in a book-discussions program.

The marketing manager I had, Bruce McClanahan, ended up owning one of the biggest mail order companies in the world. He even had his own zip code, he got so big. He came to me and wanted $5,000 to start up his mail order company. I said, "No, I'll loan you the $5,000, but I don't want to get involved in that." Bruce ended up a multimillionaire. He did pay it back, but I could have had a piece of his company for the same amount of money.

That was just one in a long line of bad business decisions I would make.

Chapter 21

If you don't prepare to win, be prepared to lose.

W hen I wasn't playing poker, you'd usually find me out on the golf course. I was working on *How I Won Over $1,000,000 Playing Poker* and hitting the golf course now and then to keep from going stir crazy. Also, when a good opportunity would come along to win money at golf, I couldn't pass it up. Well, these opportunities to hustle my fellow poker gamblers often turned into opportunities for the other fellas. I'd lost plenty of money on the greens and it got to be a joke among my friends that the companion guide to *How I Won Over $1,000,000 Playing Poker* should be called, *How I Lost Over $1,000,000 Playing Golf.*

I didn't think that title was too funny, especially after a long day in the hot desert sun with my fellow golfers reminding me of their bright idea while collecting my money.

I didn't really start playing golf in Fort Worth seriously until I was thirty, and I became almost as obsessed with it as I was with poker. Even though my leg was bad, I still had good coordination and athletic reflexes. I got pretty good pretty fast, but never as good as I could have been because I was too heavy to develop a proper swing. I had to alter my swing because my belly was so big I couldn't get it out of the way to get through the ball the way I should. The weight that I started gaining afterward was a spin-off from my leg injury. I smoked back then, and every time I quit, it seemed that I gained twenty pounds. I went from about two hundred and twenty pounds when I got married to over three hundred pounds in about three years.

My awkward swing did have an upside, though, because I never hooked the ball; I always faded it. The Texas golfing whiz Lee Trevino told me that was good because I usually knew which way the ball was going. So I was at least consistent.

When I was still in Fort Worth, I got into a group of golfers that played every day. There was a little jeweler named Curtis Skinner over in Arlington and two other guys, James Clements and Mozelle Neeper. James was a radio disc jockey and Mozelle grabbed the numbers out on the north side in the black community. They were both great guys and my first real close black friends. We played the municipal courses because of them. We couldn't go to the country clubs because blacks weren't allowed, which we joked about constantly.

"I'm going to Great Southwest Golf Club tomorrow because the only black guys you see out there will be shining shoes," I'd tell them. They always laughed and gave me hell about being a honky. "A fat honky," they called me.

We played a popular municipal course named Meadowbrook a lot, and we gambled kind of high. We played up to a $300 Nassau, which is actually three separate bets; one on the front nine holes, one on the back nine holes, and a third on all eighteen holes. Whoever won the most holes would win that bet. There would also be at least one automatic press—it started a new $300 match—when either side got two holes down. We could lose a thousand dollars or more if we weren't careful.

One tragic incident marred what was, for the most part, a wonderful time. Mozelle was about my age and had a daughter who was twelve or thirteen years old. Some guy was trying to get his daughter to go somewhere with him one night and Mozelle went to his car to stop him. The guy shot and killed Mozelle. I thought I'd grown immune to all the violence, but that was a shocker.

It seems like I've spent my whole adult life chasing poker games and golf games. Golf gave me the athletic outlet I no longer could get with basketball, and besides, it was a great gambling game. Some of my best adventures came on the golf course, and of course, high-stakes gambling was always part of those matches. I've won a lot of money on the greens, and lost a lot as well. But golf games always kept life interesting. I loved betting on golf and so did my buddies. In fact, all the poker players I knew loved betting on golf, either on our own games or the others.

We figured, why not set up a big tournament where we could all compete? Some of the players weren't very good golfers and we'd give them a proper handicap so they could compete against the ones that were pretty good. Then the match would come down to who played clutch with money on the line and who didn't. Everybody liked that concept.

So in 1977 I got together with Jack Binion to form a high-stakes golf tournament we called the Professional Gamblers Invitational (PGI), which no one in his right mind would confuse with the PGA. For one, these weren't the top golfers in the world, though we did have some pretty good ones. For another, there was probably more money bet in this tournament than the top pros earned in a year on the PGA tour. It was a spin-off of sorts of the World Series of Poker, although Jack had gotten the idea a couple of years earlier after watching a group of about fifteen or twenty gamblers knock heads on a Fort Worth course.

Jack's concept was to invite gamblers from around the country to Las Vegas for what essentially was a high-rolling gamblers' golf tournament. Jack was pretty selective with his invitations because we didn't want cheaters and sandbaggers. It was impossible to weed them all out, but we had a good idea about the caliber of golf those guys played before they were invited. We got all the high-playing golfers from across the country coming and playing in the PGI. I made matches with lots of guys who knew they should win, though they didn't, usually because of the pressure, the choke factor. There were some good golfers: Freddie Barnes, a gambler from Mobile, was one of them and Sam Simms, who ran the numbers in Nashville—they both loved to play golf and gamble and they had plenty of money. Jimmy Johnson, a bookmaker from St. Louis, also played.

With Jack's guidance, I put together the games, making bets that ranged between $500 to $10,000. In the beginning, $500 matches for each nine holes were mandatory, and Jack did the handicapping. I was the "bell cow," a good farm-boy term meaning that I initiated the wagering, and I bet with everybody. I made games with all the players, and if somebody didn't do well, I'd make him a better game. Jack and I gave good bets to keep the games going. Obviously, you can't break a guy and continue playing.

We'd make all the bets in the morning before we played, and I'd write them down on a paper placemat I'd picked up from a coffee shop where we'd eaten breakfast. Once, as our foursome rolled down the third fairway, I pulled out that placemat and went down the list. I'd made a total of $276,000 in bets, which, with the "press" wagers, could have totaled over one million dollars. After I added up those numbers, I felt like a beer cooler had exploded in my chest. At the time, it was the most money I had ever played for in a single round. But I stayed calm and it turned out pretty good—I won most of those bets.

I overmatched myself many times. That was my philosophy in golf as well as in poker. But that was part of the reason people wanted to gamble with me. I couldn't stress it enough: "You gotta give action to get action." Somebody once told me they'd probably carve that on my tombstone. I still felt I had an edge when I overmatched myself because I had confidence in pressure situations. I knew I could perform in the clutch. I made games that favored my opponents because I would shoot my way out when the press bets started rolling in toward the end—and they would choke. Usually, when you take people out of their comfort zone, make them play over a level they're used to, they get nervous and don't perform so well.

There were others in the tournaments with similar talents for performing under pressure, and I lost a lot of money finding out who those guys were. After a series of painful lessons, I christened certain players the "Magnificent Seven." Those were seven guys who seldom, if ever, choked; they were the real money players. I learned that I couldn't give them an advantage and still win. They'd beat me to death.

My Magnificent Seven consisted of Billy Walters from Munfordville, Kentucky, one of Vegas's largest sports bettors; Lefty Bennett of Nashville; Jerry Erwin of Indianapolis; Jamie Thompson of Wichita, Kansas; Roland Othick of Albuquerque; Tommy Fisher of St. Louis; and Dewey Tomko of Winterhaven, Florida (who partnered with Chip Reese and me in the Line Movers, our Las Vegas tout service). Others played well under pressure, but none like these guys. They won enough money from me to prove it.

Our games grew bigger and bigger. One day at the Desert Inn course I shot my best round of the year and won well over a million dollars. *Sports Illustrated* sent down one of its finest writers, Bud Shrake, to cover one of our events and they wrote a piece on it in their August 15, 1977, issue:

> *Using money as the measure of size, they played the biggest golf tournament in the world in Las Vegas last week. You could take the purses from a dozen Greater Open Classics and still be barely within range of the amount of cash that 58 guys teed up for in the third Professional Gamblers Invitational at the Sahara Nevada Country Club.*

Although not a golfer, even Amarillo Slim showed up to gamble at the PGI. One year he was betting a $9,500 Cadillac per hole and another time he won $5,000 in a footrace with a football player, running from one of Jack Binion's tee shots to the green.

Word got out about how much money was changing hands at the PGI, and some of the players slipped into the tournaments with false handicaps. That ended the high-stakes wagering because even we weren't foolhardy enough to play for big money with guys we didn't know. Before it ended, though, I developed great rapport with men like Freddie Barnes, Sam Simms, Jimmy Johnson, Jerry Erwin, and of course, Dewey Tomko. And there was always my high-rolling Florida friend, Sam.

Each summer, between tournaments, I traveled my own little golf circuit to play with them, starting in Mobile or Dallas and swinging through Oklahoma City and Nashville and several towns in Kentucky and California. We were all good friends, and remained so. I won a lot of money on my little tour.

The PGI had been so successful and so much fun that we decided to start another golf tournament in Las Vegas, but this time rather than a bunch of degenerate gamblers whooping it up, we'd invite the top players on the PGA Tour. The idea was a winner-take-all, match-play tournament. A couple of my friends and I floated the concept among the leading players on the pro tour. They loved it—Jack Nicklaus, Arnold Palmer, all the great ones. We settled on a $5,000 entry fee, and the winner would take the whole pot. Nobody else would get a dime.

We offered to find sponsors for any of the golfers who were reluctant to ante up the $5,000 entry fee, with the sponsor taking half the money if they won the tournament. Most of the guys we talked to said no; they were pretty gutsy and preferred to put up their own money. There was so much interest among the players we approached that we decided to move forward with the idea. We selected the golf course and began working out the details.

But it got shot down before we could get it off the ground.

This was the seventies, and Deane Beman, the commissioner of the PGA, didn't like the idea of the PGA getting involved with a gambler, namely me. He sent letters to all the players threatening to ban them from the PGA Tour if they participated in our tournament. And that killed it. The hypocrisy really got me. Most golfers make bets, even if it's a dollar or two. So what's the difference if we were betting more?

I wasn't about to give up. So I ran the idea by the mini-tour players and the non-touring club professionals, who were exceptionally good golfers. Both groups were all for it, so we moved ahead with that plan.

Then Beman threatened to shoot that one down, too.

That's when I called Joe Ed Black, an old college friend at Hardin-Simmons who had become the head of the PGA. (Beman was the head of the PGA Tour). Joe had been a member of HSU's national championship golf team when I was in college, and besides being an exceptional golfer, he was just a good, bright person. He went to his colleagues and said, "Look, I know this guy Brunson. He's all right. Let them have their tournament." We got sanctioned.

The event was a successful, entertaining tournament from the beginning. Like our original concept, it was a winner-take-all tournament. We cut the entry fee to $2,500, and the winner got somewhere between $75,000 and $100,000. The players loved it. It got so popular, it became known around the country as "The Dolly." We never made any money off the tournament itself, but we had a swell time watching the golfers—only the club pros and mini-tour players were allowed to play—and betting on the matches. Some of the young players eventually qualified for the regular PGA Tour. The tournament ran for seven years, until the Dunes course was closed. We couldn't find another course that would accommodate us like the folks at the Dunes, so we discontinued the event.

Golf was a game where you don't often see tempers get out of hand. But one time, in a game my friend Bill Baxter called "the damnedest golf match ever," a match nearly ended in a fistfight between me and a big ex-football player.

And a tough one at that.

Billy and I were betting against a real high-roller from Myrtle Beach, a guy named Tyson Leonard, and a borderline pro that Tyson brought with him. Billy was betting, but not playing. I was "scrambling" off my ball, that is, hitting two shots each time and taking the best one for my shot. We had some big bucks on the line coming up to number sixteen at the Las Vegas Country Club course. We were two up on one match, even on another. The sixteenth was the No. 1 handicap hole, a par four, and I hit my second shot, a five-iron, three inches from the hole for a pickup birdie.

Billy walked on up towards the green and I hung back in the fairway to watch Tyson's buddy, a scratch golfer, hit his second shot. And he hit a good one.

"Where did it go?" I shouted to Billy.

"It looked like it went in the hole!" he hollered.

I just laughed, knowing how unlikely that was. But it did go in the hole for an eagle two. Then things went from bad to worse. This guy chips in from off the green to halve me with a birdie at the seventeenth hole. At eighteen, I pitch up to the hole for a gimme birdie, and Tyson's guy holes one from off the green again for another eagle.

We ended up losing $80,000 after I had birdied the final three holes!

We agreed to play another nine, and lightning struck again. I was on the green in two at the par-5 first hole, and damned if this guy didn't chip it in again for an eagle to win. We halved the next eight holes, lost the match and wound up dropping a total of $160,000 on the day. On that one four-hole stretch, he had gone eagle, birdie, eagle, eagle, which I'll bet had never been done before.

But that wasn't the end of the story.

We all showed up at the course the next day, and I was ready to get it on again. More than ready—I was eager. You expect to play the same game the next day if you lose—if you want to. That was customary. But Tyson and his pal jumped in a cart and drove off with two players we had been gambling with before we interrupted the game to play the high-stakes match with them. I knew Tyson and his pal would be there and I got mad when they ignored me and teed off with the guys I usually played with.

"What are y'all doing?" I asked.

"We're gonna play golf," Tyson's guy said.

"What about us?" I said.

"Pal, that game's too tough for me. I'm done with that."

"You don't come to my country club, sign my name, then run off with my customers," I said. The "customers" were the two gamblers I knew we could beat.

"If you're looking for trouble, you're in the right spot," the Clemson ex-football player said.

"Well, I'm looking for it," I yelled.

Billy maintained that I went crazy and said he'd never seen me so angry. I was madder about the guys refusing to play us again than I was about losing the $160,000. Both sides backed off, so there was no bloodshed. Which was a pretty good thing, since it most likely would have been my blood that was shed.

Another time, I was playing in Miami with a wealthy Florida businessman on a course we'd gotten on because of Don Shula, then coach of the NFL's Miami Dolphins. It was a very tight match and, on the ninth hole, I had hit my chip shot about nine feet past the hole with a big right-to-left break in the putt coming back. A fellow in our group that I'll call Al, spotted my ball and threw it back to me. When it came my turn to putt,

I put my ball down by the mark and discovered I now had only a six-foot putt with no break. I looked at Al and he winked at me.

I was so rattled I didn't even hit the hole with my putt.

"You'll play a lot luckier if you let me mark your ball. All I want is 25 percent of the action," Al said as we headed to the back nine.

"No thanks," I said.

That would have been dishonest, to begin with, and on top of that I didn't want to jeopardize my relationship with the wealthy businessman.

Later, Al showed me a magnet on the bottom of his putter. If you marked your ball with a 1941 steel penny, you could pick your ball up and easily move it with little risk of detection. After learning how it worked, it was almost comical watching Al in action. And though I never used that gimmick myself, it saved me a lot of money because it was a common ploy adopted by golf hustlers. Thanks to Al, I could spot that scam immediately.

I was always looking for a *legitimate* extra edge on the golf course, whether it was putting my opponents at a disadvantage because of the size of the bets, outplaying them under pressure, performing better than they expected because of my bad leg, or obtaining better clubs.

I was playing one day with a guy from Corpus Christi named David Baxter, and I really took an interest in his equipment. He made golf clubs, extra long ones with limber shafts that added a little bit of a whip to them. I hit them a few times on the driving range and realized that with these clubs, I could hit ten or fifteen yards longer per club than with my own set. My leg was getting more problematic as I got older, and I couldn't hit the ball very far anymore. So I was always looking for more distance and these clubs seemed as though they would really help me out.

I offered to buy them.

"No, they're not for sale," he said.

I was playing high-stakes golf all the time, so I offered him $1,000. Those clubs of his would really give me an edge and could be worth many times that amount.

"Nope."

"I'll give you $2,000."

"No."

"Well, I'll give you $4,000."

He thought and thought and he finally said, "You know, it took me so long to get these clubs like I wanted them, to get them weighted right. I'm just not going to sell them."

"I'll give you $8,000 for them."

"Sold!"

It did turn out to be a good purchase, but somehow I lost track of those clubs. I quit playing for a short time and misplaced them. I looked everywhere for those blasted clubs and never did find them.

Here's one of my favorite golf stories from the early days. My friend Jo-Jo from Corpus Christi was a fairly good golfer and a prince of a fellow, but at about five-foot-ten and four-hundred pounds he resembled a dumpster. He had a shaggy beard and unkempt hair, which gave him a raggedy kind of look. I knew Jo-Jo was a small-stakes gambler who didn't have much money, but despite his protests, I made him play a $1,000 Nassau one day. He probably only had a couple of thousand dollars to his name, and he totally choked under all that pressure.

He was $7,000 down after nine holes.

I told him he had to bet it all on the back side, and he was frantic. His hair was standing straight up and his beard was all gnarled and tangled by the wind, an ugly, miserable sight. Here I am out there on the course with this guy who looks like he's just escaped from a mental institution, when this lazy old dog comes ambling by. He's walking real slow, like he can hardly move.

The hound glances over at Jo-Jo, then freezes. He starts growling, barking, and frothing at the mouth. And then he charged. Jo-Jo took off like a sprinter, not a four-hundred-pound dumpster. He managed to escape unharmed, but the sight of that decrepit old dog giving chase to an equally pathetic-looking Jo-Jo was like a scene from a Three Stooges movie. I couldn't help myself and just stood there laughing uncontrollably.

Jo-Jo couldn't buy a break that day, but I was financially flush at the time so I let him win the back side to get even. I'm glad I did because he passed away several years later.

I still laugh when I think of Jo-Jo racing off down the fairway chased by that mangy old dog.

Chapter 22

Experience may be the best teacher, but it's also the most expensive.

I 'd been away from the tables for nigh on nine months while working on *Super/System* and I guess the layoff took its toll. I was hoping to win three in a row, something that had never been done and would likely never be done again, but I played too aggressively in the wrong spots and never got my game going.

Ironically, Bobby Baldwin won it, proving what we all knew, that he was one of the best young poker players in the world. He'd won two bracelets the year before, so it wasn't surprising that he picked up this third. Bobby was thrilled about winning the championship, but I did rib him pretty good about missing out on a last longer bet with me. He was a sharp guy, and later went on to be the President and CEO of the $9 billion dollar City Center project in Las Vegas.

I've only made two royal flushes in my career and ironically both times were against Bobby. The first one occurred at the Golden Nugget in downtown Las Vegas in 1981. The second one, in 1993 at the Bicycle Club in Los Angeles, really showed what a great player Bobby is. We were playing $3,000/$6,000 limit hold'em. In a raised pot, I held the J♦ 10♦ and Bobby held two black aces. The flop was A♦ K♦ 4♥. Bobby bet. I raised, he reraised, and I called. The turn was the Q♦, completing my royal flush. Bobby bet. I raised, and he called. The river was the 4♣ giving Bobby aces full.

After three bets and raises, Bobby made the most unbelievable laydown I have ever seen. He told me later that he thought I had to have the royal flush to make the last raise. He must have remembered that royal I had made twelve years before. Even so, I think he should have called. To this day, I tell him I had kings full.

Overall the Series wasn't too bad for me. The cash games were great and I picked up another gold bracelet, winning first place in the seven-card stud high event. That tied me with Moss for the most gold bracelets at five, which meant a great deal to me since I considered Johnny to be one of the greatest poker players I'd ever seen. The Series that year was notable in that a California nightclub owner named Barbara Freer became the first woman ever to play in the Main Event. Barbara didn't win, but she lasted a lot longer than I did.

An episode at the Las Vegas Hilton one day concerning Bobby revealed some of the complications that bettors run into. I was playing in a tournament, but the really huge action was unfolding on the side. Celebrities and hometown champions were in town trying their hand against the top players. I had my eye on a big-time bookie from Texas who was famous for losing large amounts of money playing poker. He was taking a beating from Bobby while I sat at a nearby table waiting for my turn, watching and drinking coffee. Then, for no discernible reason, I got to feeling a little funny. I went to the keno lounge to stretch out and relax for a couple of minutes.

I woke up ten hours later.

When I got back to the table, still groggy, Bobby was just polishing off the bookie to the tune of $600,000. I'd missed my shot at him. I'm not sure what happened, but I would bet a bundle that someone spiked the coffee I'd been drinking. I never suspected Bobby, who was a good friend of mine, but he had a gambler backing him in that game. I figured the gambler did it, or paid someone to do it, to keep the bookmaker playing and losing to Bobby.

Just another hazard of the business.

I always stayed clear of drugs myself—that is, when my food or drink wasn't getting spiked—and tried to steer my friends away from them or help where I could, so I agreed to be an expert witness at a friend's criminal drug trial in Montana. I'd left little doubt about my feelings toward drugs, and all my friends knew it, but Danny Jones was a good friend and so was his lawyer, David Chesnoff. I don't know if Danny was guilty of the drug charges he was on trial for, but I like to think he wasn't.

I showed up to testify wearing my big Texas hat. People in Montana are a lot like Texans; they like their hats, and obviously I wanted to fit in. Chesnoff took me through the routine direct questioning, establishing my qualifications as an expert witness.

The prosecuting attorney grew visibly weary, but that didn't slow Chesnoff down. Finally, he got to the salient point.

"Mr. Brunson, you've seen Mr. Jones playing a lot of poker?"

DOYLE BRUNSON

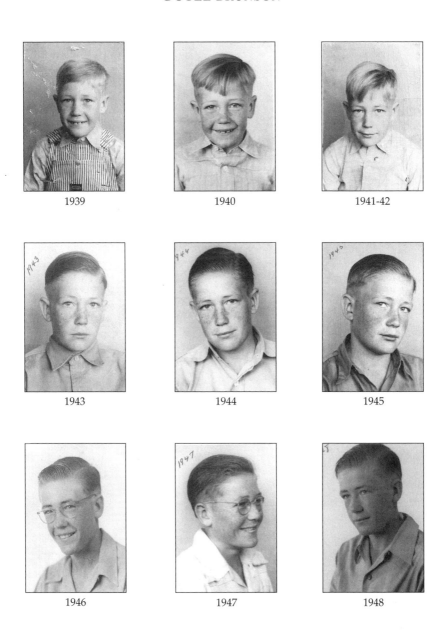

These are my early school years in West Texas, starting from 1939 when I was six years old, through 1948.

Brunson Sets Mile Record; C. Nunn Wins

LUBBOCK, April 22—Doyle Brunson of Sweetwater High School set a new record as he outclassed the whole field in the mile run at the regional meet here Saturday, winning the one-mile event in 4:45.3.

He finished the race 45 yards ahead of second place Stuart Dowlin of Amarillo. John Thompson of Brownfield was third and Gillespie of Plainview, fourth.

It was one of the few events in the meet where a competitor showed so much winning power over his opponents. Brunson will enter the state meet at Austin next.

Carl Nunn of Sweetwater copped the boys' singles title for the right to go to the state meet, May 5-6, also.

In the first round Friday, Sweetwater's Nunn beat Miller of Plainview—5-7,6-4 and 6-1. In the finals Saturday, Carl beat his old foe, Gene Fisher of Odessa, 6-2, 7-9, 6-0.

Nunn and Brunson will be entering a state meet for the second time this year. The two boys were on the Sweetwater High School basketball team that went to the state tournament in March, coming out fourth best of the eight teams entered. Brunson was chosen on the _____

Some clips from my budding athletic career.

Top: I'm on the right.

Bottom: The Hardin-Simmons University basketball team. I'm number 22 on the lower right.

Opposite page, bottom right: In August 2008, more than 50 years later, the HSU team got together for a reunion at my Montana home for three days of laughs and memories.

DOYLE BRUNSON

DOYLE BRUNSON
All Border Conference
First Team and
Most Valuable
Player

Officials Choose Former Mustang Most Valuable

Sweetwater's Doyle Brunson, now of Hardin-Simmons University, has been selected all conference and most valuable by the coaches and athletic directors in a poll conducted by the Arizona Daily Star.

As a weakling Doyle received his first basketball at Longworth while in grade school. He was in the Roby school one year before entering Sweetwater High School for three years where he failed to letter his first year in basketball.

Playing part time with the B team and part time with the A team he lettered his junior year. After baseball and track in his junior year Doyle entered in the fall heavier and taller. Playing in several tournaments was selected on the all star team each time. The 6-2 forward was high scorer in the district going with the Mustangs to the state meet where he was selected on the all state team.

Doyle, who is a junior has earned two letters with the Cowboys and has scored 205 points in conference games for a total of 413 points for the season.

Brunson does not confine his athletics just to basketball as he is a outstanding track man in the distance races, winning the state in the mile run his senior year in high school.

He also lettered in baseball at first base while in high school. Doyle is a standout on the H-SU track team.

Doyle Brunson
. . . all conference
. . . most valuable

A couple of history making young men on the Forty Acres in 1952-53 were "Honk" Green and Doyle Brunson, who helped bring "big time" basketball to the campus of Hardin-Simmons University for the first time in history.

Green rewrote all H-SU annals in scoring 496 points and Brunson scored enough to rank right behind him with 412 points.

Green, who never played High School basketball, began his basketball career at Hardin-Simmons. Brunson was named on the All-Border Conference second team. Brunson was named on the first team of the league and also had the honor of being

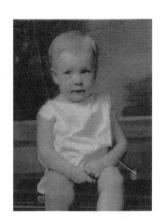

Top: My parents with J.T., a brother I never met.

Top right: I'm just getting started in life. Lots of adventures to come.

Right: My brother Lloyd was as handsome as he was smart.

Bottom right: My mom.

Bottom: When my sister Lavada was crowned High School Queen, my status went up in Sweetwater.

Louise and I were younger back then.

Louise and I tie the knot on
August 19, 1962.

Left: Louise was a pharmacist when I met her. I knew she was the one.

Bottom: Louise and I at a dinner party.

More recent picture of me and Louise.

Top: In 1977, I won my second consecutive championship against second-place finisher Gary "Bones" Berland.

Right: This is the original invitation to the World Series of Poker in 1970.

Bottom: After one of my championship wins.

MR. BENNY BINION

cordially invites you to join him

in the anything goes

World Series of Poker

APRIL 13 Thru 17, 1970

Complimentary room, food and beverage will be provided by

Binion's

HORSESHOE HOTEL
& CASINO

LAS VEGAS

Left: My original book, *How I Made Over $1,000,000 Playing Poker.* I've since changed the title to *Super/System.*

Right: My induction into the World Poker Tour's Poker Walk of Fame outside the Commerce Casino in the LA area.

Bottom: My paycheck from the Burroughs Corporation. It was my one and only "real" job.

A vintage shot of me in old Las Vegas.

The famous Casper card protector.

I'm all in here and feeling pretty confident about the situation.

best friends

Top: The three musketeers: DC (left), Riley, and me.

Right: Bob Tremaine, a basketball star at HSU and a minister who helped me through the tough times when my daughter Doyla died.

Bottom: The three musketeers in their later years. That's D.C. on the left and Riley on the right. We're up in Alaska, fishing.

Tincy Eggleston plays solitaire as he awaits start of his trial on gambling indictment in Fort Worth, TX; the case was later dropped because of the missing witnesses. 10/22/1951.

Top: A classic shot of Puggy Pearson, one of the all-time great poker players.

Left: A young Chip Rease. We soon found out that he was no "hometown" champion —he could play.

Top: Benny Binion (left), owner of the Horseshoe Casino in Las Vegas and founder of the World Series of Poker, with actor Chill Wills (center), and master hustler, Titanic Thompson (right).

Right: My great friend and traveling buddy, Brian "Sailor" Roberts with, appropriately, a girl looking over his shoulder.

Bottom: Johnny Moss and Jack Straus at the poker table. James "Puny" Winningham, a friend and bookie dating back to my days in Fort Worth, is standing on the left.

Top: A classic shot: left to right, Amarillo Slim, Johnny Moss, and Benny Binion.

Left: At a tournament in the Amarillo Slim Super Bowl of Poker in Reno, I came in first and won a matching pair of silver-plated shotguns and a Chevrolet Blazer. The $265,000 that came with them wasn't too bad either.

Top: Me and Sailor Roberts.

Middle: I'm with my best friend Jack Binion.

Left: Wayne Hamilton, my old running buddy in the mean streets of Exchange Avenue and the Bloodthirsty Highway in Fort Worth. He was another guy who met his demise due to drugs.

Top: Joey Hawthorne was an original contributor to *Super/System*, but tragically, he died from a drug overdose while he was in his forties.

Left: Jimmy "The Greek" Snyder, Binion's spokesman and PR Director for the World Series of Poker, was widely known later as an analyst on a CBS sports program, *The N.F.L. Today*. He was responsible for my nickname, Texas Dolly.

Left: When there's a lot of money on the table, I'm always looking to get my share.

Middle: Mike Caro and I filming video how-to segments on poker strategy. The Mad Genious and I have worked together on various projects over three decades. He was instrumental in the publication of both *Super/System and Super System 2*.

Bottom: After a match with millions on the table, Andy Beal (sitting) made us pose for this picture. We were bleeding inside and we had to look happy for him. Also in the picture, left to right, is a doctor named Keon, Ted Forrest, Jennifer Harman, and me.

"Yes," I said. "I have seen him playing many, many times." I told the jury he often played in games where he could win or lose $20,000 or $30,000.

Then Chesnoff asked me, "How would you classify Mr. Jones as a gambler?"

"He's a smart gambler," I said.

"What do you mean, 'He's a smart gambler?'"

"Because he stays out of my games."

The jurors started laughing so hard that Chesnoff decided not to call any more witnesses, and they promptly voted to acquit. I can't say for sure my clever response helped Danny's case, but at least it didn't hurt it.

Another time, my testimony in a case also got the jurors laughing, but this time, with a less successful result. This case wasn't about drugs, it was about the IRS. In the late seventies, I flew to Dallas-Fort Worth to help an old friend, Byron "Cowboy" Wolford. Cowboy, who hailed from East Texas near Tyler, was a champion calf roper, an old-time road gambler, and an accomplished poker player. He was also a character with a big heart, which could prove exasperating at times. More than anything, he was a good friend, and that's why I appeared in federal court one day in Fort Worth.

Cowboy, who never hid the fact that he and the law sometimes got crossways, had gotten himself arrested in an undercover sting operation. The undercover agents were posing as Internal Revenue Service employees who claimed they could fix IRS tax returns, and some of the gamblers had fallen for the ruse and given them money.

But Cowboy said he had repeatedly refused the offer.

"I ain't got no trouble with the IRS and I don't need your help," he told the guy.

The guy persisted, Cowboy said, until Cowboy finally gave the man $500 just to go away. And that's how Cowboy said he got busted for bribery. At the trial, the defense was trying to establish that Cowboy was indeed a guy who tossed money around freely and would give somebody money just to get rid of them.

"Yes, that's his nature," I said. "He's a very generous guy and he does throw money around carelessly."

I told the court about the time Cowboy and I partnered up for a poker game in Waco, back during the Texas Circuit years. We combined our bankrolls and lost about everything we had. We got back to Fort Worth with $52, and I was thinking about buying food and milk for my family.

We stopped for a cup of coffee, and Cowboy tipped the waitress $50. "That poor lil' gal was a single mom tryin' to raise two kids by herself," he explained. That's the kind of person he was.

"If I'd had a gun that night," I told the jury, "you wouldn't have had to worry about this trial because I would have shot him right on the spot."

That got a big laugh, but the jurors weren't in a jovial mood. They convicted Cowboy, who spent a year in prison. I thought it was terribly unjust.

I also thought the troubles I had when I tried to open my own poker room with Eric Drache in 1979 were unfair. Eric and I had applied to get licenses at the old Silverbird, and that's when the trouble started with the Gaming Control Board. The board began by questioning us about some old, innocuous incidents that had no bearing on our ability to run honest card games. Some of the questions they asked flirted with the incredibly stupid. They brought up the fact that Eric had been arrested as a teenager for running money for New Jersey bookmakers. And they quizzed me about my arrest years ago in San Angelo. I guess these were reasonable questions, but it went downhill from there.

They checked my records and said, "I see here where you got arrested by the FBI, and you had a killer dog."

Flirty, the dog I won from Sailor, would probably have been flattered, but I had to explain that he was harmless, just kicking up a fuss because the strangers were making hostile noises, like any dog would do. But he didn't attack anyone. They wanted to know more about my police record, all the details, but I couldn't help them much there. I told them I'd been arrested many times and why, but I couldn't prove when or where because the police had destroyed the records.

There was one clown whose favorite expression was, "This is just the tip of Pandora's Box." He couldn't even get his metaphors straight. Once he said, "I see in your rulebook that you allow check-raising. I've seen some bad things from check-raising."

"I've been playing poker since I was twenty years old," I said, staring at him in disbelief. "I've never ever played in a game that didn't allow check-raising. I don't know what you're talking about."

Another time, he said ominously, "I see you're going to have a telephone in the poker room. How can we allow you to have a telephone in the poker room when you might pick it up and call Chicago to see what the line is?"

I informed the gaming board member that the line was made in Las Vegas, not Chicago. After dealing with this foolishness for way too long, I unloaded on the three-man board.

"I don't need non-gamblers to tell me anything about gambling!" I couldn't understand why people who didn't understand gambling were on the control board. They were professional and business people and hadn't a clue about anything.

The board decided to get the criminal investigation squad of the Internal Revenue Service involved in our case. IRS agents followed me around for about a month, though I didn't know about the surveillance until later. Then I learned that the agents were laughing about the fact that I wore out the whole team single-handedly, that they couldn't keep up with me. They said I was sleeping only about three or four hours a day and playing poker the rest of the time.

They turned up nothing. After it was over, I blew up at an agent.

"Why are you picking on me when I pay my taxes, and there are all those guys out there that don't pay their taxes, and you're not hounding them?"

That outburst came back to haunt me in a ludicrous, but damaging manner. This same criminal agent called me up later that year and said, "I see you're going for licensing."

"Yes sir, that's right. I am."

"I wonder, when we were talking, you were telling me about some people that didn't pay their taxes," he said. "Now, can you tell me who they were?"

"No, I can't tell you who they were," I replied. "To start with, I said that in the heat of the moment. I have trouble keeping up with my own records, much less somebody else's records. That was just an expression, even though there are probably people who don't pay their taxes out there."

"Well," he said smugly, "you know we either write favorable or unfavorable reports to the Gaming Control Board."

"In other words, you're telling me that you're gonna write an unfavorable report unless I tell you who those people are?"

"Essentially, yes."

"If my becoming an informant determines whether I'm licensed or not, I'll just have to not be licensed," I said, struggling to control my anger. "because, to start with, I don't know who didn't pay their taxes. And if I did know, I wouldn't tell you. That's the end of this conversation."

He wrote an unfavorable report to the board, and a member said to me, "You won't cooperate with the IRS. How can we license you?"

"I cooperated with the IRS in every manner about my own affairs," I told him. "The agent wanted me to inform on people that I knew nothing about—and I wouldn't."

The Gaming Control Board sent an agent to the house demanding to look at all our financial records. They thought there was some inappropriate activity and set up an investigation to look deeper into my taxes. They may have had their investigators as weapons, but I had mine too: Louise. I felt pretty good about my chances in this battle.

"Well, you know, my wife takes care of most of that stuff," I told him. "I'll have her show you whatever you like. How long is this gonna take?"

"Uhhhh," he said, "it could take two or three weeks."

I told him that was okay, that I was going to play golf and that I'd be back in four or five hours. "Louise will show you everything you want to see," I said, escorting Louise into the kitchen.

Understand that Louise keeps immaculate records of everything we do. I mean everything; every nail she buys, ever repair she makes, every dime she spends—everything. And she never passes up an opportunity to brag on her rental houses in Texas and her pets and her kids and grandkids and everything you can think of.

Dropping my voice to a whisper, I told her, "I want you to bring out the pictures and show him everything and everybody. And brag all you want."

So I left to play golf. When I returned many hours later, Louise was sitting there smiling and this poor guy was standing up at the table and shoving all his stuff in his briefcase. In her own inimitable and charming way, my secret weapon had worked perfectly when I really needed it.

"How you coming?" I asked innocently.

"Well," he replied wearily, "I think we're just about through here."

He left and never came back.

Good ol' Louise! I knew I could count on her.

After all these problems, plus a few other indignities, the Gaming Control Board denied our license by a two to one vote.

That wasn't the end of it either. The owner of the Silverbird, Major Riddle, was a pretty influential man about town. Riddle was the biggest percentage owner of the Dunes—until he got to playing poker. He loved the game, but was such a bad player that he lost most of his holdings in that casino, then went north on the Strip and opened the Silverbird, where he continued to lose almost all the fortune he had accumulated. When Riddle was at the table, I was playing night and day to be sure I got my part of his money.

He went to the Gaming Commission on our behalf to appeal the Gaming Control Board's ruling. The commission consisted of five members and their vote had to be unanimous to overturn a board decision. Harry Reid, a prominent local lawyer and the Nevada lieutenant governor in the early 1970s, had been appointed to the Gaming Commission in 1977. He later was elected a U.S. Senator and became the Senate Majority Leader in 2007. Reid was, in fact, the commission chairman when we appeared before the body, and the commission voted unanimously in our favor. That is how we got our licenses to operate the Silverbird cardroom.

The poker room was an immediate success. We lured gamblers away from all the other casinos and the games were prospering.

We'd been at the Silverbird little more than a year when Major Riddle died. Other management came in and took a look at our salaries and branded them exorbitant. They were too shortsighted to see that we were earning our keep. We had increased business in the cardroom, and on top of that, the poker players gravitated to the casino tables and games. Successful cardrooms, as most casinos know nowadays, were good for business, although some owner/operators couldn't see the forest for the trees. So after all this roller-coaster craziness, we got ousted a year or so after we'd begun our cardroom operation.

Here we could stand up to the Tony Spilotro types and prosper in the mob-connected world of poker, but we couldn't overcome the "legitimate" casinos who shot themselves in the foot because of their ignorance.

Funny how things work.

Chapter 23

When you wallow with pigs, expect to get dirty.

J immy Chagra had his bad side: drug smuggling, drug dealing, bribery, strong-arming and complicity in murder. But he had a good side too, at least as far as I was concerned—he liked to gamble high. In fact, when Chagra flew into Las Vegas from El Paso, casinos rolled out the red carpet to cater to his every whim. He was reputed to be the highest of the high rollers, what we call a "whale" in Vegas. In those terms, Chagra was Moby Dick. He didn't play for hundreds or sometimes thousands of dollars, like they did back on Exchange Avenue. Chagra played for hundreds of thousands of dollars. He might even lose millions in a single night. He hung out with celebrities and threw money around like it was rice at a wedding—I suppose business was going real good for him. Eventually he bought a house and lived in Las Vegas—that is, before changing his address courtesy of the U.S. penal system.

In the mid-seventies when I met him, it was also said that Chagra was one of the biggest drug dealers in the country, a kingpin of a drug empire that smuggled massive amounts of heroin, cocaine, and marijuana into the country. I couldn't speak for that, but I do know his money moved around real good. He would come to Vegas with footlockers full of cash, ready for action of all kinds. He loved craps and blackjack mostly, but one day he discovered the poker tables. That's the year when Christmas came early for the Las Vegas poker pros. Despite his well-earned credentials as a dangerous man, Jimmy Chagra was always a welcome visitor to our games. We liked the way he recklessly tossed his cash around, like it was Monopoly money. I suppose it was that way with successful drug dealers; it came in fast and they had to do something with all that money. The U.S. government certainly wasn't getting its share.

But we were.

Chagra reminded me of the folks I had played with on Exchange Avenue. He made fast money, he could be a lot of fun at the table, and he could be extremely dangerous if you crossed him. But there was one big difference between the underworld guys on Exchange and Chagra: Jimmy was big time. Big enough that the feds took a special interest in his activities and later, because of a murder he had orchestrated, spent more money in the investigation of that crime than they had ever done before.

Jimmy's most endearing qualities were threefold: he insisted that we play for huge stakes; he wasn't nearly as good at poker or golf as he thought he was; and except for a couple of notable occasions when he threatened to kill me, losing didn't seem to bother him much, which was also okay by me. I admired those gambling traits. Except, of course, that little part about him threatening to kill me.

For me, it's always been the same when it comes to gambling: The higher the action, the better the game. That's what particularly excited me about playing with Jimmy Chagra, especially because he nearly always lost.

But not always.

One day at the Las Vegas Country Club, where we frequently played, we gathered for a golf game and he demanded a $250,000 bet with everybody—everybody being Puggy Pearson, Jerry Erwin, and me. Pug was a scratch golfer, and Jerry was also very good, but they didn't want to play that high. So I volunteered to stake them, which meant I would furnish the money if we lost. If they won, they got half of it and I would get the other half. What that boiled down to was that we started off playing three $250,000 matches with automatic two-down presses. If anybody got two holes down, another $250,000 match would kick in for the remaining holes. We could win or lose five ways, equaling $1,250,000 on each match, or a total of $3,750,000 for all three matches. That was a mind-boggling amount of money, especially in the seventies.

Jimmy's game was worse than ever, and the three of us beat him the first two holes, automatically jump-starting three new $250,000 bets. On the third hole, Jimmy knocked his third shot into a bunker. Pug and Jerry and I were on the green in two, and a blind man could see we were better golfers. I knew we were going to beat him all five ways that day, winning a whole lot of money. After giving Pug and Jerry their share, I was going to pocket more than a couple million dollars.

Now Puggy had some unusual habits that earned him a dubious reputation on the golf course. He was inclined to move his ball around from time to time, teeing it up in the rough, that sort of thing. I had cautioned him to be careful, to treat Chagra with kid gloves.

But evidently he wasn't listening.

We got up to the green and Pug's ball was about thirty feet from the cup. All he had to do was two-putt to win the hole. Chagra was in the sand trap, so Pug could even three-putt and probably win it. There was a little sunspot in front of Pug's ball, and for some strange reason—it was absolutely no advantage—he reached down and relocated his ball a few inches around the sunspot. He didn't accomplish anything, just Pug being Pug. As always, Jimmy had his bodyguard out there with him, and the guard saw Puggy move the ball.

"Jimmy," he blurted, "Pug moved his ball!"

The timing was terrible for several reasons, number one being that Jimmy was under intense pressure because federal agents were closing in on his operations, even to the point of monitoring our golf games from atop nearby buildings and from small aircraft.

Jimmy flew into a rage. He came barreling out of the bunker shouting obscenities and dire warnings at us.

"You blankety blank sons-of-bitches, I ought to blow all of you away!" he screamed.

He pronounced the game over, jumped in his golf cart, and sped away, my $2 million dollars-plus disappearing with him like dew off the morning grass. I was furious with my golfing partner and vowed to never ever let Pug live that down.

A subsequent outing with Chagra, but without Pug, fared no better. I played Jimmy a nine-hole match for $375,000, again with automatic and unlimited two-down presses. I'd developed a back problem and wasn't playing as well as I normally could, but I knew I could still beat him. I started off with a bang, a par and a birdie, and he pressed. I won the next two holes, starting another new match and hiking the stakes to $1 million-plus. Jimmy was playing awful, and I knew I couldn't lose. But I got to thinking that beating him really bad might not be too smart. I didn't know his financial status, although I was reasonably certain he had a million dollars in the cage down at the Horseshoe. I was thinking that if I kept beating him and he kept pressing, there was no telling how much he would want to play for on the last hole. I hated to do it, but I started "throwing off." I deliberately wouldn't win a hole because if I won too much I didn't know if I could get paid. That's not as unscrupulous as it might sound, just part of the gambling business. I purposely lost a hole or two and after six holes, I'm up on two matches and even on a third with three holes to play.

I'm saying to myself, "That's good. I want to win two bets. I want to win my seven or eight hundred thousand because I'm sure he's got that much."

That was my thinking, anyway.

Well, we came up behind this fivesome on a par three hole, and they wouldn't let our twosome play through, which was the usual custom. We had to sit there and wait. My back had begun to bother me and, suddenly, it just froze up. It was almost too painful to even swing the club. I could barely hit the ball, but Jimmy wouldn't let me quit. He won two of the last three holes and got even for the day.

So Pug cost me a couple of million in one game, and that stupid fivesome and my aching back got me for a million in the second outing. But I played Jimmy several more times, and without Puggy or a bum back, I beat him out of a lot of money.

Anything you ever did with Jimmy and brother Lee—golf, poker, pool, or whatever we were gambling on—was always a long, treacherous walk on the wild side. Chagra didn't really care about the money, and it was nice that he lost consistently. But strange things invariably happened when you got mixed up with people as dangerous as Jimmy. And they could get combustible when an individual dangerous ingredient, one by the name of Chagra, got mixed with an even more dangerous ingredient, a character by the name of Tony Spilotro.

In a small town like Vegas, they were bound to meet, and one night that's exactly what occurred at a nightclub in an incident that could have turned real ugly, real fast. The way I heard it—at least this was Jimmy's version—was that this little guy came into the club and told him to get the hell out of his booth. Neither man knew the other, and Chagra wasn't about to give way to some punk barely five-and-a-half feet tall.

"I don't see the name 'Midget' printed on a reservation card on this table," Chagra said, staring Spilotro down. He told Spilotro to go get his own booth and probably a few other things too. Knowing Spilotro, I could only imagine what was going through his head. Trouble was averted temporarily, probably because Spilotro was outnumbered, but Tony was not one to forgive and forget. Not that Jimmy was one to fool with, but a confrontation like that with Tony was sure to end in a heap of trouble. Spilotro left the club, but word of that meeting got around to people who not only knew both parties but also what the implications of that kind of confrontation could mean.

One of those people was Oscar Goodman, the lawyer for both Spilotro and Chagra, and he wasted no time trying to defuse this powder keg.

Early the next morning, Chagra got a morning phone call from his attorney demanding that he immediately get into his office for an emergency meeting. These dangerous men were at odds, and Goodman was trying to resolve it peacefully before a war broke out. Chagra told me that when he got into Goodman's office, "that midget" was there again. His attorney insisted they shake hands and that they make up and get along.

I also heard Oscar's version of that meeting, which included a comical side note. There was a lot of tension in the room between these two powerful men, both megalomaniacs. Goodman probably figured, and correctly I imagine, that Spilotro was already devising imaginative plans for his new foe when there was the sudden sound of an explosion. Goodman, the high-profile mob lawyer and dynamic future mayor of Las Vegas, immediately dove under the desk, thinking there was some kind of mob shooting, and bullets and blood would be splattered all over his office. After a few seconds, when nothing further happened, he sheepishly crawled back out, and red-faced, looked at the bemused smiles of Chagra and Spilotro seated comfortably in their chairs.

An exploding light bulb had caused the noise; it also defused the anger and animosity in the room. Years later, Goodman, a good friend of mine and the "cool, collected big-time attorney," was still embarrassed about his panicked scramble under the desk in front of these two men.

Gamblers and drug dealers have one thing in common: we both like to protect our investments. Sometimes, that can have an ironic and mutually beneficial twist to it, especially when it concerns the same situation. One time, Chagra got involved in a serious dispute with another drug dealer called "Junkyard" Johnny and whisked him away for some private discussions. Junkyard owed Jimmy a bundle of money, some $50,000, and he couldn't pay it—that was because he'd lost all his money gambling with me and my professional colleagues.

When we got wind of that, we decided to get involved—we couldn't let anything happen to Junkyard. We didn't want to lose one of our favorite customers, so a bunch of us pooled our money and paid off Junkyard's debt. Freed from Chagra's clutches, Junkyard resumed his ways and continued tossing his money away playing poker and golf with us. Junkyard was fortunate we felt so highly of him as a friend—and especially lucky we wanted to protect our investments.

Chagra always overrated his abilities—I guess he thought his success in his business activities extended to everything else he did—and that usually worked out pretty good for me. After a monstrous game at the Silverbird one late spring night in 1979, Jimmy got to bragging about his pool game.

"I'm a great player," Chagra said. "I can beat anybody at 9-ball." A friend named Billy said, "Let's go try him."

Billy was a good pool player, but not a great one, and I expressed my doubts.

"We might not be able to beat him, but we can always quit," Billy insisted. "We might make a big score."

I knew Jimmy overrated his golf game, so I said okay, and we headed over to Chagra's house. Jimmy's house was pretty impressive, a place where you might expect a drug dealer to live. It looked like a castle in a horror movie, complete with giant gates and big, tall fences. Guards were walking around with machine guns day and night. We started playing and it quickly became obvious that Billy was the superior pool player. He was beating Jimmy handily. At the time, I was battling an enlarged lymph node that blocked air intake into my lungs, causing me to drift off without warning. Billy would come shake me awake, and each time, Jimmy looked a little angrier.

Chagra was about to stand trial before a San Antonio judge nicknamed Maximum John, because of the full sentences he gave convicted drug dealers, and it didn't put him in the best of spirits. By the time we left that night, Jimmy was furious at the drubbing Billy had given him.

"I'm gonna take you pool hustlers out in the desert and break your fingers," he warned.

Billy was justifiably frightened, but I laughed and said, "See you tomorrow, Jim."

"Yeah," he snapped, "I'll see you."

The next day a hood named George, an ex-con with a reputation as an accomplished arsonist, approached Billy and me. "I hear y'all have a beef with Chagra and he's not going to pay you. Give me 50 percent of the bet, and I'll collect the money for you."

"George," I said, "I'm not giving up anything. All we did was gamble and win."

The following day, George was back, offering to collect the money for 25 percent. I declined.

"This is a very dangerous man," George warned.

I paid George no mind and dismissed him.

Billy was worried enough to hire two bodyguards, so I promised him I'd go talk to Jimmy. "I know Jimmy from my Texas days," I told Billy, "so don't worry, I'll take care of things."

Then I went over to Chagra's house to talk with him. "What's the problem?" I asked Chagra. "This guy George says you're mad and intend to hurt us. He wants a commission to collect our money."

"Are you crazy?" Jimmy said, "I've got a lot of problems, but I'm not worried about a little dab of money."

He left the room and returned with a trunk on wheels. He opened it up and counted out the $300,000 he owed us. I glanced in the trunk, and there must have been $5 million there, maybe more. I'd never seen that much cash before.

A month or so later, on May 29, 1979, the day Chagra was set to go on trial for drug-smuggling, Judge John "Maximum John" Woods, who would be presiding over the case, was killed. A guy named Charles Harrelson, father of the actor Woody Harrelson, was prosecuted and convicted of murdering the judge and sent away for life. Though he was acquitted of the murder charges in the judge's slaying, Chagra was sentenced to thirty years for his drug activities. In February 1980, after being a fugitive for about six months, Chagra was arrested in Las Vegas and sent away to Leavenworth, the tough federal penitentiary in Kansas. Leavenworth was the former home of the likes of Al Capone, Machine Gun Kelly and Robert Stroud, the famous "Birdman of Alcatraz, who served twenty-eight years there before being transferred to the San Francisco Bay prison.

The FBI later caught Chagra on tape during visits to Leavenworth in 1980 telling his brother Joe, who was his lawyer, that he had hired Harrelson and used his wife to deliver the hit money. He also implicated Joe in these discussions. The FBI was after Chagra and anyone associated with him for the murder of Judge Woods, so they worked around the attorney-client privilege by claiming the two were talking as brother to brother, not as attorney to client. Joe got ten years for complicity in the murder, and Joe's wife got thirty years for bringing $250,000 as payment to Harrelson. Chagra also earned ten years for obstruction of justice in the murder of Judge Woods and, in a separate trial, a life sentence for the attempted murder of a federal prosecutor.

I wouldn't see Chagra again for almost thirty years.

Chapter 24

Great moments are born from great opportunities.

The World Series of Poker had become an annual ritual, the biggest event of the year for poker players. Every spring when it came around, pretty much all the best poker players made it to the Horseshoe in downtown Las Vegas to play and say howdy to people they hadn't seen since the previous year. As usual, I focused on the side games, where the real money was, but of course, the tournaments were always important to me as well. This particular year, 1979, marked the tenth annual running of the Series.

Sensing the importance of the occasion, the Binions celebrated the history of the World Series of Poker by founding the Poker Hall of Fame. Jack Binion, Eric Drache and some players formed a committee and elected seven charter members: Johnny Moss, three time Main Event champion; Wild Bill Hickok, the famous gunslinger who died at the poker table holding aces and eights; Felton "Corky" McCorquodale, an old-timer I played plenty with on the Texas Circuit and who helped bring Texas hold'em to Las Vegas; Red Wynn, a great old-time poker player from Fort Worth who was good at all the games, particularly stud and any no-limit game (and a close friend of mine); Sid Wyman, a high-stakes player who owned pieces of the Dunes, Sands, and Riviera; Nick "The Greek" Dandalos, the country's most famous gambler in his day, the man that Moss broke in that legendary game back at Binion's in 1949; and Edmond Hoyle, an expert who wrote about game rules in the 1700s. That last one was an odd choice, considering Hoyle had died some one hundred years before poker was invented.

Moss and I were tied at five gold bracelets apiece heading into the preliminary events, so we both were angling to take the lead. I struck early, winning in the mixed doubles event, but Moss won one as well, keeping us tied at six. Bones Berland, who finished second to me in 1977, picked up two bracelets, so he was right behind us with five. I didn't get very far in the Main Event, and would have to settle for another year of waiting.

There were two notable events in the World Series that year. Barbara Freer, the first women to enter the Main Event the year before, won the women's seven-card stud, becoming the first women's bracelet winner. And the Main Event was won by an amateur, Hal Fowler, who beat Bobby Hoff heads-up. Bobby is one of the premier hold'em players in the world. It was the biggest upset in the history of the World Series. Fowler was not only the first amateur to win the championship, but the first one to win any money at all. It was a fluke, but we figured it would encourage other recreational players to fork over the $10,000 entry fee and take a shot at the pros. Baldwin got to the final table again as did Moss and Addington, but nobody was able to overcome Fowler.

The Horseshoe was buzzing with excitement as the 1980 WSOP rolled around and, as usual, the contingent of Texans made up the majority of the field. No-limit Texas hold'em was our game, and it was a matter of pride that a Texan should take home the championship.

I was primed to be that individual.

The World Series had expanded to twelve preliminary tournaments—including Omaha high-low, razz, seven-card stud, and five-card draw—plus the Main Event. I'd already missed out on two gold bracelets during the preliminaries, coming in second both times, and I was hoping the third time would be the charm. The Main Event had grown to seventy-three players and the winner's share would be $385,000. That was a hefty growth from 1979, where fifty-four players competed and first place had been $270,000.

It was a hot spring day when the tournament kicked off at Binion's. I can remember looking around the room and seeing all those great players. One of them was a diminutive kid fresh from New York named Stu Ungar. Stuey, only twenty-six years old but well known around the poker room, was a newcomer to the Series. He had only minimal experience at no-limit poker and virtually none in tournament play, but he was a great card player and a natural in no-limit hold'em, where aggression and fearlessness are two of the most important qualities of success. Stuey had those in spades. If possible, he was even more aggressive than I was, a style that can lead to a quick exit in tournament competition, but can also get you a pile of chips if the cards fall your way.

Stuey was already a gin rummy legend on the East Coast when he came to Vegas in 1976. He beat every top player in Vegas too, and after a while, not one gambler in town would sit down with him for a game of gin. He was too good; in fact, he was far and away the best gin rummy player who ever lived. No one had a chance against him. In gin, he possessed a special something, and whatever it was, he took it to the grave with him. But no-limit hold'em was a different story. It was a game he was barely familiar with; maybe he played one or two times before. It's not that he was a beginner at tournaments—I mean, he had *never* played a poker tournament before. He had no concept of no-limit hold'em strategy, but somehow managed to stumble through. Stuey was simply a genius with cards. I started watching this newcomer to the WSOP, interested to see how he would do. He learned as he was going along, and by the end of the first day of play, he was still around competing for the title.

Meanwhile, experienced players were getting eliminated, and the field was getting smaller.

I'd been playing good poker and survived along with Stuey to see the second day. You can't get too excited that early in a tournament because there are still a lot of cards to be dealt. Until you get to the last few players, you just worry about picking up chips and marching toward that final table. We still had a long row to hoe.

For three days, I buckled down and advanced deeper into the tournament. And every time I'd look around, that young man from New York was still there. It's not easy to survive in this game. You have to tiptoe around a lot of land mines to make it through a no-limit tournament. At any time, an opponent can set you in for all your chips, or you can make a move on a man and get in trouble. If you've read him wrong or get an unlucky card with all your chips in the middle, all that patience and tough play won't mean anything. You'll be walking away from the table, shaking your head.

By the time we'd reached the fourth day, only five of us were left, the final table. I'd survived a stretch where my chips had gone down to $44,000 real late in the tournament, but I'd made a run to get right back into the mix. And it was amazing—Stuey was one of them. His aggression, coupled with good cards, had gotten him through the early stages of the tournament and he was a surprising survivor at the final table. The others players included Johnny Moss and a couple of lesser-known but respected pros, Jay Heimowitz and Charles Dunwoody. (It wasn't until the following year, 1981, that nine places were paid.)

Finally, after a lot of hands had been played, it came down to me and Stuey. While I could see that Stuey had tremendous raw talent, he was new to the game, which gave me a big edge. I felt pretty confident I would beat him because of my experience. All that stood between me and my third championship was this brash young kid out of New York. I really wanted to tie Moss by winning that third title.

When we got two-handed, he had the chip lead almost 2 to 1. But I whittled him down to where he held only a slight advantage, about $400,000 in chips to my $300,000. Despite the chip differential, a bookmaker set the line making me a 6 to 5 favorite. During a break, Stuey wanted to bet someone $50,000 on himself, but I told him I'd take that bet myself.

A big hand came up where I made two mistakes, one of the worst hands I've ever played. I brought it in for a raise and Stuey called, making around $17,000 in the pot. I had A-7 and the flop had come A-7-2, giving me two pair. A lot of times in this situation I would put a big bet out there to throw off my opponent, but instead, I underbet the pot, trying to suck Stuey in. That was my first mistake: It gave him a chance to make his hand cheaply—as opposed to me forcing him out with a big bet and taking the pot down right there. The turn card—the fourth open card on the table—was a 3. I figured I had the winning hand, so when Stuey bet $30,000 or so, I made my second mistake—a critical one—and went all-in with $274,500. I was surprised when Stuey called. He was holding 5-4 and had hit an inside straight, ace to five! The fifth card was no help and Stuey won his first championship.

His victory was one of the most unbelievable feats in World Series history, an amazing accomplishment considering that just four days before, he had rarely even played the game. But as future events would show, Stuey was no ordinary player and his victory was no fluke. Despite a desperate battle with a multitude of personal demons, he'd turn out to be the greatest tournament player ever.

I was terribly disappointed. There's no worse feeling for a poker player than getting eliminated out of the Main Event. And the closer you get to winning it, the more it hurts. Finishing second is about the worst feeling in the world; at least it felt that way at the time. I knew that if someone had broken Stuey the first day, I would have won my third title. He actually got better and more confident as the tournament progressed. In all the years I'd played poker, I didn't think I'd ever seen another player that actually improved as a tournament went along. He used the World Series and all of us as a training ground, all the way through to his final championship hand with me.

But it wouldn't be the last time Stuey and I mixed it up, and not just at the poker table.

✪✪✪✪✪

After the World Series, it became all too clear that poker had changed. In fact, you'd have to be a blind man to not see what was happening—no-limit cash games were drying up, at least for me. I had won so consistently, the Vegas players got to where they didn't want to play no-limit when I was around. I broke up games just by sitting down in them. People didn't want to play with me, so they'd just pick up their chips and leave. I had some theories that were ahead of their time and had become so dominant in no-limit Texas hold'em that all the cheats thought I was cheating because I won all the time. For seven years, from 1973 on, I don't remember ever losing in a no-limit poker game where the predominant chip on the table was a black chip ($100 value). There weren't that many of those games, but when they came around, I'd just clean up.

The Texans would flock into town from time to time, and when they did, we would start a no-limit hold'em game. There was a game at the Aladdin that didn't break up for six weeks. Never broke up! We played with a $25 ante and one $100 forced blind, which was big for those days. That's ten times the money it is now, and the Texans just destroyed all the local players and the Californians who played with us. We'd also see top players from different parts of the country, all the hometown champions, and they got a real quick lesson at our table—fact was, they didn't have a chance against the old-time, no-limit Texas hold'em players.

No-limit poker isn't for the timid. You can bet as much as you want any time it's your turn to act, including pushing it all in. The danger is that somebody with more chips than you have might call your bet and send you to the rail. As my longtime Texas buddy Crandell Addington contends, "Limit poker is a science, but no-limit poker is an art. In limit, you are shooting at a target. In no-limit, the target comes alive and shoots back."

Eventually, I came to the realization that as a poker player, I'd have to play limit poker to get any action, which I started to do. I also played games I'd never played before—razz and stud eight-or-better—which cut into my earnings.

Limit hold'em was a different game altogether, primarily because it minimizes the bluff factor. I had played no-limit my entire life until I moved to Las Vegas—and the change in focus from the big bets in no-limit to the methodical betting of limit was hard to adjust to. Like the limit players had trouble adjusting to the big bets and bluffing of no-limit, I had trouble adjusting to the more mathematical approach of limit. In no-limit, you're programmed to throw your hand away when you think you have the worst hand; in limit, you sometimes call, even when you might be a big dog to win, if you think you have the pot odds. If it costs you one bet when there are twenty bets out there, you call because you only need to be right one out of twenty-one times. In no-limit, that call could cost you all twenty-one bets because your opponent often bets the size of the pot, so, you're programmed to throw your weak hands away. I occasionally threw hands away in limit games that, because of the math, I should have played. I'd catch myself after the hand was over and ask, "What did I do?"

I took some lumps in the beginning because I not only had to adapt to the limit games but to the cheating as well. If there was cheating in the no-limit games, I could overcome it, but in the limit games, it was a problem.

Sometimes, the cheating actually had a comical side to it. I can think of no better example of how we tolerated our colleagues' ethical lapses than Joe Bernstein, who was an uncommonly likable and entertaining fellow, if something of a compulsive card cheat. Like many road gamblers of his time, Bernstein wasn't above a little "innocent" cheating, but he was not sneaky about it, which I figured only a fellow gambler could appreciate. A big-time gambler named Nate Raymond once staked Joe to a poker game while Nate played gin at another table. Out of the corner of his eye, Nate saw Joe slip a chip into his pocket. He pulled out his knife, moved up behind Joe, put the blade to his throat and told him he'd seen what he did.

"Aw, Nate, I've been stealing for forty years," Joe said. "I can't stop now!"

Stunned by that convoluted logic, Nate shrugged, put his razor away and calmly returned to his game.

Another time, Bernstein and Sid Wyman, a future poker hall-of-famer, were playing gin, and on no fewer than three occasions, Wyman caught Bernstein with an extra card in his hand. After the third time, Wyman jumped up, threw down his cards, took his glasses off like he was gonna hit him and said, "Joe, I told you, you can't do that."

Joe got all pouty, and said, "If I can't do that, then I'm not gonna play anymore."

At the Stardust one time, the IRS rushed in and broke up our game, scooping all of Joe's chips off the table—about $4,000—because he hadn't paid his taxes. Bernstein began cursing the agents, and then chased them out the door, shaking a single $25 chip and shouting, "You didn't get this one! You didn't get this one!"

With a character like Joe, a little cheating was tolerable.

While I preferred no-limit poker, playing limit games was the new reality for me in Las Vegas. I learned new poker games and new skills, eventually learning to beat the limit games. Like all poker, and life itself, you just need to adjust to changing circumstances.

Brother, did that thought come home to me in a terrifying manner.

Chapter 25

The meaning of life can't be told. It's gotta be lived.

Sometimes, happiness has a way of lulling you into thinking that life is a permanent ride in a convertible on a smooth country road with the wind tossing your hair around. All the while you're forgetting that life has some detours. Just ahead around a blind bend in the road, you're gonna have to apply the brakes awful hard while you watch all that happiness suddenly get yanked away from you.

It was just that way for me in the summer of 1980. I took stock of my situation and was pretty happy where everything sat. My poker career was going strong, my golf game was pretty good, and I had lots of good friends around me. Even more importantly, my family was happy. There was my wonderful wife, Louise, as lovely and charming as ever, three remarkable children, daughters Doyla, Pam, and son Todd, and a lovely and very special stepdaughter, Cheryl, Louise's daughter from a teenage marriage that didn't work out. She was twelve years old when Louise and I got married, and I've come to think of her as my own.

By any measure, we were a happy clan with the normal ups and downs, a close-knit family with everything going well.

But then life slammed its brakes on me. Fate struck with cruel irony.

Not too long after her miraculous recovery from the spinal disorder, Doyla became bulimic, regurgitating food to prevent gaining weight. On the surface, it sounds like a simple Twiggy-type thing or a desire to look like a willowy fashion model. But it was much more complex than that. When Doyla was first diagnosed in 1979, the affliction was prevalent among weight-conscious teenage girls and young women. Several celebrities have suffered from it: Paula Abdul, Princess Diana, and Pat Boone's daughter, for instance. And singer Karen Carpenter died from it.

Every member of my family had struggled with a tendency to gain weight, so the affliction must have been rooted in the Brunson genes. Doyla inherited my compulsiveness. Anything she did, she did to excess.

Doctors would later learn much more about bulimia and find treatment for it, but that wasn't the case in the late seventies and early eighties. Louise was experiencing some frightening premonitions, and we did everything in our power to help Doyla. We took her to psychologists and doctors at UCLA and to an internist at St. Francis Hospital in Honolulu. But it was a disease, a sickness, for which there was no real help at the time. Even the doctors didn't understand bulimia or anorexia, though both were practically an epidemic.

We reached out for help that eluded us.

Doyla would insist she was doing better, but the sickness always came back, and her condition worsened. It was compounded by a heart-valve problem called mitral valve prolapse, which was not considered life threatening. If the electrolytes that controlled her heart got out of balance, they could cause a short circuit to the heart. It was a disorder treated with potassium. Doyla was under the care of one of the best cardiologists in Southern California. She also was seeing a highly recommended psychologist who taught at the University of Nevada-Las Vegas. Still, she remained sweet and reassuring during much of this ordeal in the early 1980s.

She entered UNLV in 1981, the local university in Las Vegas, and appeared finally to be doing better. Always devoted to helping other people, she was studying to be a Christian psychologist. Doyla confided to me that she was happier than she'd ever been, that she realized the seriousness of the problem and was over her sickness. She said she was doing well in school and making new friends. She was back to her bubbly self, like her mother, and playing the piano beautifully.

Because she appeared to be doing so well, Louise even accompanied me to Reno for the Super Bowl of Poker in 1982. We were at a show in a hotel one night when I realized Louise was crying.

"What are you crying about?" I asked.

"I'm just thinking of Doyla," she said.

I wondered if she was having another of her premonitions, which surfaced from time to time and often proved accurate.

Louise herself suffered from severe, even life-threatening allergies, and a few days after we returned to Vegas, she flew at her doctor's insistence to Hawaii for a week to recuperate. While there, she received a phone call from Doyla late one night. Doyla had been out on a date and had just gotten back to her apartment at UNLV.

Mother and daughter chatted about the usual things—her studies, her friends and one another's health problems. Doyla said she felt fine, just tired, and ended the conversation that night as she always did.

"I love you, Mom," she said.

The next morning two men wearing coats and ties rang my doorbell. They were from the university, two somber administration officials. Without explanation, they asked to come in. I'm wondering, "What's Doyla done now?"

"What do you want to do with the remains?" one of them said.

"What are you talking about?" I asked.

"Didn't anybody call you from the university?"

"No," I said.

"Oh, we're so sorry. We didn't mean to break the news this way. Your daughter died during the night."

Your daughter died during the night.

I felt as though someone had struck me over the head with a club. I was stunned beyond comprehension. I stared at the men, dumbstruck, my mouth open like a bass that had just lost its last breath.

The two men from UNLV blanched at my reaction, one immediately fixing his eyes on the floor.

"We're, we... we're, er, awfully sorry, Mr. Brunson," one of them said.

I just couldn't grasp what was happening. How in God's name could my daughter be dead? She had been fine just the night before, had even talked with her mother by phone a few hours earlier, assuring her everything was all right, and extending her affectionate and cheerful good-bye. *I love you, Mom.*

I stood there, shattered. What had happened to my firstborn child?

The embarrassed visitors from UNLV did their best, gently, nervously, to explain what they knew, which wasn't much. Whatever they told me, it could just as well have been in Chinese anyway. I couldn't comprehend anything they were saying except *Your daughter died during the night.* I would have to piece together the full story of my daughter's death later, with help from others: Not long after Doyla had gone to bed, the house mother awakened her and asked her to drive another of the girls to a hospital emergency room for treatment of an eye injury. Doyla stayed at her friend's side at the hospital most of the night, then returned to the campus that morning. Apparently, the last person to see her alive was her friend at the hospital. People there said she appeared well and had not complained of feeling ill, though she did tell someone she felt tired. After arriving back at the dorm, Doyla lay down. She apparently suffered a relapse of her heart condition. She died in her sleep. Her heart stopped. It was March 16, 1982.

She was eighteen years old.

Although Louise was recuperating from her asthma in Hawaii, I was not alone, thank God. My daughter Pam was with me and almost eerily, my mother, my sister and her husband were visiting. It was uncanny that the three of them were there at this tragic moment, because they had never been together in our new Las Vegas home.

Even one of my college roommates and very good friend Ray Hibler was there.

Pam heard me cry out and came running. I told her Doyla was dead. We clung to one another in sheer desperation and wept uncontrollably. It was the only time I had cried since I was a kid. It was a crushing blow to learn of her death, especially in that manner. At first, I was angry at UNLV, but it wasn't the university's fault. It was just a miscommunication on somebody's part. I almost felt sorry for the two men from the college. They were embarrassed at breaking the news the way they did. Before leaving, they asked if they could lead our family in prayer. I said, yes, of course, even though I was not a praying type of guy. It was a kind gesture on their part, and I particularly appreciated their attempts to comfort me and my family. After the prayer was done, they quickly excused themselves, apologizing yet again. I thought fleetingly how awkward and unsettling this duty had been for them.

I knew I couldn't easily cope with this tragedy, that I needed strength. And fate had intervened to help me find it. Just a short time before Doyla's death, I had run across an old friend from Hardin-Simmons in Reno. His name was Bob Tremaine who had been a basketball superstar at HSU. We had been friends since my junior year at HSU when he was a freshman on the Border Conference championship basketball team. Bob entered the ministry after graduation and was in Reno for a Baptist gathering. Talking with him for the first time in nearly thirty years, I learned he had lost a teenage daughter. He told me all about her and shared the terrible feeling of loss that he had experienced.

I now telephoned Bob in Texas and told him about Doyla.

"Bob," I said, "I need you to go with me to Hawaii to tell Louise."

He didn't hesitate. "I'll be on the next flight," he said.

As expected, he was a tremendous source of comfort on the long flight across the Pacific. He talked to me about his daughter's death, and how a parent must try to cope with the saddest of tragedies. Short answer: *You can't.* There is little comfort anyone can provide who hasn't suffered a similar crisis.

"Well, we understand," they say. And though they're well-meaning, they *don't* understand, because unless they've been through it, they don't know the pain and the agony of losing a child.

I was heartbroken and deeply worried about how to tell Louise, as she had been quite sick when she left Las Vegas a few days earlier. The entire flight I was thinking, "How do I tell her?" I thought the news might be too much for her. It certainly was for me.

Once there, I stopped at a phone down the hall at our condominium to call ahead.

"I'm here," I said.

"Is it bad news?" she asked at once.

"Yes," I said. "Bob Tremaine's with me."

When she opened the door and saw me, she knew. With a stricken look on her face, she said, "It's Doyla, isn't it?"

"Yes."

Louise collapsed on the couch, crying softly for several minutes. Then she stood up and said, "Well, I know Doyla's with the Lord."

Once again, I had underestimated Louise's strength and character, her faith. I had come to comfort her, and she wound up comforting me. Louise's faith in the Lord was what sustained her. "If I hadn't been a Christian, I don't know what I would have done," she said. "I know the Lord will help get me through this."

Bob was an enormous help, sharing those terrible moments with both of us. I felt helplessly small and inconsequential.

Just empty and lost.

"I know what you're feeling," he said, and we knew he did. He assured us the Lord cared, would watch out for us, give us strength, and we would one day smile and laugh again. To be honest, we didn't feel as confident as he did about what our future held, but his words offered hope and comfort. I knew I'd always be indebted to Bob Tremaine.

We immediately returned to Las Vegas to make funeral arrangements, and then I took Doyla back to where I grew up, back to Longworth. We buried her in Palava Cemetery, up the road a few miles toward Sweetwater, in the Brunson family plot secured with a little fence and a large inscribed headstone: The dead in Christ shall rise first.

And I thought: *One of these days, I'll be back. This will be my resting place here beside you, my firstborn, on this wind-whipped and lonesome West Texas land that I'll always call home, especially now.*

I returned to Las Vegas, heartbroken, distraught, and without a clue what to do. Doyla's passing had knocked the wind out of me. Somehow, air got in and out of me, but even that didn't seem easy. I wasn't the only one badly affected: Pam became an emotional wreck and started acting up, giving us all sorts of problems. She and Doyla had been very close. Now, suddenly, Pam had a huge void in her life. Like so many teenagers, she didn't know how to handle sudden emotional turmoil, especially a loss this devastating.

In my condition, I couldn't see through it on my own. My reservoir of strength had been drained.

"We've got to do something," I told Louise.

"I know, Doyle," she agreed. "We just have to get Pam some help. We can't do it ourselves."

We decided the best thing would be to send her to a renowned church school, Oral Roberts University in Tulsa, Oklahoma. Not unexpectedly, Pam was less than enthusiastic about the idea. But it didn't matter. I ordered her to get on an airplane for the trip to Tulsa. She stayed there for two years, and it worked. She got her life back in order, for which I was enormously grateful to the university.

By this time, Louise had become an even more devout Christian. She started attending the Assembly of God church because she liked its emphasis on teaching, and she wanted to learn more about the Bible and Christianity. After Doyla's death, she insisted I attend her church because she wanted me to hear things she thought would be enlightening or comforting. Pastor Mel Stuart knew my story, and that I thought Doyla's death might somehow be punishment for my lifestyle. I couldn't explain why, but I thought I should quit gambling. I didn't know the rationale for that thinking because I never saw anything wrong with gambling. I was just so distraught and confused I couldn't think clearly.

Stuart counseled me many times, and his support proved invaluable. "You don't have to do anything different," he said. "Take your time. You don't have to change anything. God accepts you as you are but He may open other doors later. Just pray and seek His will for your life."

He continued to counsel me for months—what I should do and how I should react to things. I also talked constantly with Bob Tremaine.

In addition to these two caring men, I was blessed with a compassionate and caring support group, but the main person who helped me through my daughter's death was Louise, the strongest person and the most dedicated Christian I'd ever known. She has what I called "holy boldness." She could talk about Christianity and pray with anybody. Little things would upset Louise, but her character surfaced when the going got really tough, like after Doyla's death. She was a source of strength and inspiration when I needed it most.

I was a lost, hurting soul, and I couldn't shake my sense of guilt. What's more, I couldn't find the answers I needed. I had started wondering, "What is life's meaning? Why are we here? Why would a loving God let Doyla die?" The words of the actor Marlon Brando came to mind. Among his last words before he died, he said, in effect: "What in the world is life all about?"

I was in a terrible quandary. I tried to play in the World Series of Poker that spring, thinking it might help get my mind off things. But it was too painful. I finally just got up in the middle of the tournament and walked out. I couldn't sit there any longer. I didn't even know if I wanted to continue gambling. I went home and continued searching for answers to the questions that have been plaguing folks since the beginning of time, especially those who have been blessed with the joy of a child only to have that joy taken away in cruel and inexplicable ways.

Why did God heal my little girl and then allow her to die?

Of all the people in the world, couldn't He have chosen someone else to accompany Him in heaven? What kind of cruel joke did He play on me, on Louise, on everyone who loved Doyla that He would take a precious child full of all the promise of life for His own purposes? All my life I had heard people talk about the loving and kind God who cares for us all, but at that time all I could do was mourn for my child and repudiate the selfish omnipresence who took her from me.

I was nowhere close to God, even though I had become friends with Pastor Stuart, who had conducted Doyla's service.

I told very few people this, but I even considered suicide. The pain was so great that I didn't care whether I lived or died. That's how utterly devastated I was. Doyla's death was like a big hole in me that I couldn't fill. I didn't really want to kill myself, but it was a way to end my pain and loss and I thought on that for a while. I wanted to think I was too strong to go through with it, and I might have considered it more seriously, except that I knew how it would hurt the remaining members of my family. But still the thoughts were in my mind.

"Had you gone so far that you knew what means you would use to kill yourself?" a friend with whom I shared these feelings once asked me.

"It really didn't get that far," I told him. "But I'm sure I would have used a gun since I was pretty adept at guns, comfortable with them." Growing up in the country, I've always handled guns well and I was a marksman in the National Guard. "At the time, I didn't carry a gun," I added. "Probably a good thing."

Suicide was just for weak people, I had always thought, and I considered myself a strong person. But Doyla's death broke my heart and spirit. Yet from the depths of that barren and painful existence would come a new beginning. It would come by the grace of a God that I neither knew nor understood at that time, and through the support of my family and friends, including some of my poker-playing colleagues.

In the end, it was a beginning, and I decided to confront the issue head on, and find out for myself what Christianity was all about. Many times, usually at Louise's urging, I had tried to read the Bible. I could never understand it. It seemed like it was written in a foreign language, and I wondered if it was just me or if others had the same difficulty.

And then suddenly everything changed.

I began to understand what I was reading. I discovered also that while I was reading, I didn't hurt. And because it took the hurt away, I read every day. I read and read. For days, weeks, months, I read the Bible. I read it from cover to cover. I read back through it again and marked passages that really touched me. I came to feel that there was much more to Christianity than I had ever realized. I began reading Christian literature in addition to the Bible. Louise, along with Bob and Mel, recommended much of my reading material.

One day I was reading *The Living Bible,* which I readily embraced because it was written in laymen's terms, unlike many other translations including the King James version, beautiful as many of its passages are. In the book of Matthew, I came across a verse that just jumped off the page at me. It was chapter 6, verse 34. I read it and reread it, struggling to decide what to do with my life. It said, in effect, "Don't worry about tomorrow. Tomorrow will take care of itself. Live one day at a time."

I was not a guy who'd seen angels or had heard the voice of God speaking to me, but that verse jumped out and grabbed me by my lapels.

The more I read, the more I came to understand the basic concept of Christianity. I discussed this with some of my friends, Chip Reese in particular. He was so articulate and incisive, I thought he might turn out to be a preacher. We were already neighbors and good friends, but we became even better friends. He knew how I was hurting, so he would read the things I was reading and we'd talk about them.

Pastors Bob and Mel suggested that I host Bible study sessions for my friends, and said they'd contribute their time and expertise. I wholeheartedly took them up on this. Pastor Stuart also assigned one of his associate pastors to the studies. Hayseed Stephens—his real name was Harold, but everyone called him Hayseed—was another evangelist who came to our gatherings. Hayseed had been an All-Border Conference quarterback at Hardin-Simmons and was drafted number one by the New York Titans, who became the Jets of the old American Football League. Hayseed was the first Jet quarterback.

All these guys jumped at the chance to come out to Las Vegas and conduct our Bible studies.

Tremaine, in particular, was unbelievable. He would go down to the poker rooms and sit for hours, talking to guys and listening to their problems. His newfound congregation included a few drug addicts and others who didn't have the first idea about Christianity. But Bob was so patient, so effective. He offered good common sense to people's problems—no pressure, no fire, no brimstone. He became a familiar figure in the poker rooms around Vegas, well-known and respected. And many of the casinos and their executives were most supportive of our study sessions and Bob's outreach efforts, especially the Golden Nugget and Steve Wynn.

My colleagues besieged Bob for counseling and guidance, and they got it. In the early stages, only a few showed up at my home, but attendance grew steadily. Louise cooked these grand meals and everyone sat around and listened to whoever was conducting the Bible studies. It was like starting a new church. I tried talking about Christianity myself, but I wasn't good at it. I sensed it was not my calling to tell people about God. I had just found God myself, and was still searching for answers. I couldn't explain things. I left that to Bob and Mel and Hayseed, who was pretty forceful, and like Bob, got some tremendous results.

I had been reading the books about prophecy and they just blew me away. By that time, I had more than a rudimentary knowledge of the Bible. I knew who to call on when I had questions. It was incredibly exciting. I had satellite TV and I tuned in to Bible studies all around the country.

In particular, I started watching the Trinity Broadcasting Network, which showcased some of the greatest preachers in the world: Dwight Thompson, E.V. Hill. You name 'em, Trinity had 'em.

For a year, I concentrated on television, the books, and the Bible studies. To enhance our own studies, I brought in speakers I'd seen on TV, and such celebrity Christian athletes as Rosie Greer, the all-pro tackle from the Los Angeles Rams, and Meadowlark Lemon, the Harlem Globetrotter star. I got the singer Roger McDuff and some of the local pastors to come as well.

The poker players loved it.

"Come on, it's time to go to Bible study," they'd say, sometimes walking away from poker games with a million dollars on the table.

The sessions lasted about eighteen months, during which some really marvelous things happened. I saw dozens of guys quit alcohol and drugs cold turkey, and never go back to them because their exposure to Christianity had changed their lives. Following the sessions, they would seek out the preachers for whatever help they needed.

And they always got it.

★ Chapter 26

Luck may bring you riches, but it will never bring you wisdom.

I hadn't played poker in the year since Doyla died. I was dizzy, fatigued, and felt physically ill. Sometimes I felt I was going to die. It might have been withdrawals from gambling, the death of my daughter, or just plain hypochondria. It was a pattern that repeated itself throughout my entire life—every time I stopped playing, I'd go into these doldrums.

While thrashing about over my own poker career, a gambler from El Paso called me in 1983 and said he'd struck gold in the mountains out there.

"We can start a mining company and give the proceeds to various religious groups," he said. "You can determine the recipients."

It sounded good. While I might not have been ready for poker, I couldn't resist action, even if it was foolhardy. Doyla's passing had devastated me and I needed a change of scenery.

What better than a foray into gold mining?

Thus ended the Bible classes and started a new adventure chasing gold; or as it might have been in my case, chasing fool's gold. I went down to El Paso, bought a house, and invested several hundred thousand dollars in this mine. It was another one of my crazy schemes and another loser, but it got me out of Las Vegas for a while, which I needed.

What I didn't need was for the FBI to raid my home in El Paso.

I never contended that I was faultless during my intermittent brushes with the law, but this time I was Mr. Clean. It was the mid-eighties, and the FBI was conducting a massive raid all across America, targeting most everyone with a record of involvement in betting or booking sporting events. I was in regular contact with many bookmakers and bettors, so I learned early that morning what was coming down. While I did bet, the federal agents were more interested in the bookmakers, so I wasn't too worried.

But about one o'clock that afternoon, the doorbell rang. I opened the door to find three carloads of agents on my doorstep and outside my house. I asked the agent-in-charge what was up, and he explained what I already knew. I told him I wasn't booking, and if he didn't know it, he should know it.

"No," he said, "I don't know it, and I want to look through your house."

"Do you have a search warrant?" I asked.

"No, but I'll go get one if you don't let me in," he said.

I knew he was bluffing, because if he could have gotten one, he would have had it with him.

"You're not coming into my house without a warrant," I said.

"Look, asshole, if I have to go get one, I'll do it." He called me off to the side and said, "And I'll come back and tear your floors up, your walls down, and your house apart."

If it was a bluff, it was a good one. I still didn't believe he could get a search warrant, but I had nothing to hide.

"Sure, come right on in!" I said.

He walked through the house, found nothing irregular or illegal and realized I was not one of the bad guys, not one of the targets he was looking for. His tone changed dramatically. He became extremely courteous and apologized for bothering me.

In turn and in time, I developed a lot of respect for those guys. They were just doing their jobs. But back then, I wasn't all that thrilled with having my house gone through by a bunch of strangers, particularly the FBI.

It was a brief interlude in a tough year, marked mostly by me searching for any kinds of answers that would see me through. My hope, and my solace, remained with the teachings of Christianity. I continued to study Christian literature and prophecies, but while I didn't consciously try to change things in my life, things did begin to change. I routinely had taken God's name in vain; G-damn this and G-damn that. Suddenly, it sent cold chills over me when I heard that, even though I still uttered profanities sometimes. I thought most of those profanities were more jargon than cursing anyway. I didn't want to be fanatic about such things, and I knew I couldn't force my values on my friends.

I tried talking to Puggy, a dedicated atheist.

"You think there's some big so-and-so sitting on a throne pointing down at us, telling us what's going to happen?" he said. "Let me ask you a question: Who made Him? If you say He made us, who made Him?"

I didn't have the answer.

I believed there might have been a time dimension we didn't know about. Eternity? I didn't know. I did know that a certain amount of faith was essential. I recognized that it was the prophecies and the Christian literature that were important to me. I sought and found answers to questions I'd always wondered about, many of them in the books of an author named Josh McDowell, whose writings explained Christianity simply and clearly. When people asked, I wholeheartedly recommended his books at Christian bookstores.

I knew what I now believed, but I wasn't going to try to cram it down anyone's throat. Everyone was entitled to his or her own beliefs. If I had argued with anybody, which I didn't, I would have pointed out that I believed in Jesus, and I'm going to die. The nonbeliever is also going to die. If the nonbelievers are right, I'm no worse off than they are. However, if I'm right, they are going to be much worse off than I am. I was not fanatic about my beliefs. I lived in the real world, which was not easy to deal with sometimes, especially in my environment. I did the wrong things many times, but now I was trying to do right.

I greatly admired the wise person who said, "Christians aren't perfect; they're only forgiven." That's the way I went about handling life, all the time believing very strongly in Christianity.

The death of Doyla contributed enormously to my conversion. By extension, there also were probably two to three hundred nonbelieving poker players who came to believe, people who probably never would have believed if she hadn't died. Some of them, besotted by abusing alcohol and drugs, probably owe their lives to Doyla.

I found comfort in that. And in the big picture, if one could see it that way, Doyla lived on.

It was during this time that I reached out to my gambling friend, Stu Ungar, who was in really bad shape. Stuey had gotten in over his heads with drugs, and Louise and I became really concerned about his well-being. I thought a change of venue might do him some good so we flew Stuey into El Paso and picked him up at the airport. We took him into our home for two or three weeks to try and rehabilitate him. He got lots of good home cooking and spiritual inspiration, along with all the love my family could supply. Unfortunately, our efforts were unsuccessful and when Stuey returned to Vegas, he got back into his old ways.

Coping with Doyla's death as I did gave me a strength I'd never had before. After spending so long meditating about my poker career and my lifestyle, as well as the concept of Christianity, I concluded that the answers I'd been seeking were hardly clear-cut. But I found the answers I thought best for me. I came to understand that life is short, that we all go sooner or later. My meditations also confirmed my feeling that we should do what we enjoy doing, within reason.

I decided I had been right all along. There was nothing sinful about my poker career. And I embraced it with fresh enthusiasm.

We moved to San Clemente, California, and I started playing at the Bicycle Club in Gardena outside Los Angeles. The California climate was good for Louise's lungs, and Californians had just legalized hold'em in their cardrooms. Plus, I needed the change from El Paso. My gold-mining investment had turned predictably disastrous, and my ex-partner had converted that investment into a fleet of trucks and a gravel-hauling enterprise. Not surprisingly, I didn't profit in that venture either.

After my prolonged sabbatical from poker and my soul searching in El Paso, I found the Southern Californian action pleasantly soft, and I won quite a bit of money in a very short time. Bringing in money again and competing at a game I loved did wonders for me and, by extension, my family.

Finally, I returned to the green-felt jungle. It was time to go back to Vegas, the center of everything for me. Like a magnet attracting metal, it beckoned me home.

Las Vegas, that's where I belonged.

Chapter 27

Make failure your teacher, not your undertaker.

S
ome successful gamblers believe they're God's gift to the world of business and finance, that everything they touch is golden, that they're gonna make money by the truckload. I'm not one of them. A lot of my business ventures have headed south faster than a gaggle of geese. Even today, I laugh—or shudder—at some of the schemes I've come up with or pursued.

I just couldn't help myself.

Once, Chip and I bought a big stable of racehorses, but our nags got stuck in the starting gate and we never cashed out a dime. Then we came up with the "fan camera" idea, a camera that had an image of a celebrity built into it. When you snapped your own picture, the photograph showed you sitting beside the celebrity. We were on the verge of signing a contract with Time Warner when we got shot down by the greed factor. Behind our backs, one of the partners went to McDonald's with the idea and when Time Warner found out, the deal got killed. It's noteworthy, however, that Polaroid eventually came out with a similar product, even though we had patented our idea.

Even that didn't curb our appetite for investment schemes. We blew a bunch of money on an African emerald mine. Then there was "Cadillac" Jack Grimm, a poker player from Abilene who had also attended Hardin-Simmons. Jack was a pretty good player, but not good enough for our games, and he lost a lot of money in a short time. After he got to know me, he campaigned vigorously to get me inducted into the HSU Hall of Fame. He failed due to my association with gambling, but I always appreciated his trying.

Jack was a true entrepreneur, and he lured Chip and me into a number of ventures, including a couple of oil schemes that went belly up. Two bigger suckers than Chip and me never existed, so we bought into a couple of his most bizarre schemes. Jack told us he was trying to raise the Titanic and had spent a lot of money on a sea voyage the previous year. He was going back, and needed new investors. Naturally, we signed on. He invited us to go along, but at the time, the poker games were too good to leave.

"Just take some photos and send them to us," I said.

He set sail and actually located the very spot where the Titanic had sunk. He sent us pictures and, indeed, it was exciting. But he ran out of money again and the expedition was canceled. I think the crew that finally found the sunken ship used much of Jack's information. Because of that, he said we would get our money back. We never did.

But Cadillac Jack wasn't through with us quite yet.

He came back to Vegas with pictures of what appeared to be a boat jutting out of the summit of ice-covered Mount Ararat in Turkey. I don't know if the photos were authentic, but they appeared to be.

Was this Noah's Ark?

We salivated at the opportunity to invest in what would be the discovery of the ages, rationalizing that we were investing with Jack's money because we had won it playing poker. As I recall, the expedition reached the purported site, but climbers were forced to abandon the mission due to bad weather. The Turkish government subsequently closed its borders to climbers, and some twenty years would pass after Jack's second Titanic voyage, a U.S. archeological research organization was granted permission to survey the mountain. Its findings were inconclusive, but the organization hoped to return. I learned later by chance that a member of my sister Lavada's Sweetwater class of '48 had actually headed up that expedition. Bartell LaRue was his name and we had played baseball together in high school.

In the early nineties, Chip, Dewey Tomko, and I had some good years with Line Movers, our tout service that offered sports advice and bets over a 900 number. It was Chip who best described the Line Movers philosophy: "Years ago, sports betting was a battle of hunches. Today, it's a battle between those with the right information and those with mere hunches. Believe me, the right information always wins."

One year we were a phenomenal 70 percent successful picking winners. We combined the knowledge of computer analysts, statistics and insights from other big-time sports bettors, along with our own individual methods, to end up with the finest sports picks in the nation. Fact is, we had one truly spectacular year. It was a fickle business. We'd have a bad week and the bettors quit calling. When the government began regulating

900 calls, that didn't help the tout service, either. Finally, unable to sustain profits, we closed down the business.

Another deal involved orange groves in Florida, something I did with Jack Binion and Dewey. We had almost five hundred thousand orange trees, and I think I had 15 percent of that deal, so I must have had fifty to seventy thousand trees. Dewey got me into that one. It wasn't one of my horror stories because the orange trees were a great tax write off, saving me tons of money depreciating them. The groves were right outside Orlando and when some abnormal weather conditions came in there, they froze. We either had to plant new trees, which would take several years to start bearing fruit or do something else with the land. It was in a pretty good area right next to Orlando Disney World, so we decided to build a golf course. We named it Southern Dunes. It was voted in the top 100 golf courses in America, but the competition was so tough with golf courses in that area, it wasn't a success. We finally sold it. We got some money out of the deal, so it wasn't too big a failure.

If Jack Binion was involved I usually did okay; he had a good head on his shoulder for business, something I lacked entirely. We did some deals with property out in California that we made some money on, and with some riverboats in the middle of the country that worked out real good—I had a small piece of that too.

But when it came to disastrous investments, nothing rivaled my television caper of the mid-1980s. Emeralds, gold-mining, cameras, racehorses, arks and everything else paled in comparison. Ironically, this financial fiasco was based on the noblest intentions: We thought we could serve the Lord—and make a little money on the side.

Or maybe it was the other way around.

Through the associate pastor who helped me through the tough times after Doyla's passing, Harold "Hayseed" Stephens, Chip, Dewey, and I met this preacher from Kentucky, an ex-drug addict, ex-alcoholic, and ex-half-ass gambler—which is what I called him. The preacher—we called him Slick—had reformed and wanted to start a Christian television network. He explained that you could get construction permits through the Federal Communications Commission to build television stations and later sell the stations for a lot of money. I was familiar with the Trinity Broadcasting Network, which was the most successful Christian network around. Our new preacher friend had the FCC permit for a city in one of the southern states.

"Let's do it," I said. We signed some contracts with Slick, but in reality, our handshake was our bond. We trusted the guy because he was a gambler who had turned religious, and that was good enough for us. We had a lot of cash, and we poured buckets of money, and I do mean *buckets*, into building a studio and a tower with a great signal, the best in the area. Slick was to be the soul of the station—telling his story and offering Bible teachings, along with other programming—and we planned to bring in celebrity guests, big-time Christians, and even provide housing for our guests.

It was a wonderful scenario—for disaster, that is.

We turned the operation over to Slick and waited for the money to roll in. Instead, I started getting calls from bill collectors, and then their lawyers. It didn't take a sophisticated businessman to figure out that we had a problem. A serious one. I was filled with anxiety when I hopped on a plane to Mobile, Alabama, where we had built the tower. After making a few inquiries at the station, I confronted Slick. He had about as much a grip on reality as a man on the moon.

"Dammit, Slick," I said. "I hear you haven't been paying our bills. You've just been throwing 'em in the trash."

I got right up in his face and let him have it, almost screaming. "You've gotta pay these people, Slick. This is no damn way to run a business!"

Slick didn't appear to be particularly fazed by the dire nature of our situation—like our electricity getting cut off and strange guys coming in and carting off our furniture and office equipment.

Personally, I thought it was hard to make a go of a television station when your electricity got repossessed.

"It don't make any difference," Slick said. "I don't have the money to pay them anyway."

Lucky for me—hell, lucky for Slick—I didn't carry a gun back then.

I was so distraught about this fiasco that I stopped playing poker. Meanwhile, Chip, Dewey, and I borrowed another $2 million from a bank, meaning I now had to come up with $20,000 a month in payments. We managed to keep the station going, barely, but it was losing another $10,000 to $20,000 a month on top of the $20,000 in payments. I had 60 percent of the station, and Chip and Dewey 20 percent each.

We tried to stop the hemorrhaging, but there was no controlling it, and we kept sinking deeper into debt. I was now spending all my time flying back and forth, trying to get things straightened out. Dewey ran out of money, so then I was stuck with a $40,000 to $50,000 deficit every month.

Chip was paying his 20 percent, but I was paying 80 percent. The debts continued to mount, and I had to borrow $2 million from Jack Binion. So now I owed the bank $2 million and Jack $2 million. I was getting more and more frantic and was about tapped out.

Then along came Fox TV, which was just starting up, and the Fox people offered us something like $15 million, mostly because we had this great signal. Somehow, though, Slick legally owned 51 percent of the station. He could do what he wanted, which didn't include selling out to Fox. Finally, in sheer desperation, I found a guy in New Orleans named John Marshall who ran a successful radio station. He agreed to come run the television station. He wanted to switch from religious to secular programming to increase revenues enough to pay the bills.

I met Slick at a coffee shop and told him, "I'm taking over the station. You're not doing your job, and I'm going broke."

He puffed up and took offense, and refused to surrender control.

"You told me I could take it anytime I wanted," I reminded him.

"Yeah," he said, "but I've put too much time and effort in it."

That's when I took a cup of hot coffee off the table and dumped it in his lap. I turned the table over right on top of him, right in front of everybody, and he went crashing to the floor. I walked out and went back to the TV station.

Slick had already hauled off most of the good equipment, but eventually I got rid of him and avoided a trial by giving him $70,000, plus all the equipment he had made off with. But that was after I'd gone through nearly a dozen lawyers, and after John Marshall had gotten the station to a point where we were at least breaking even.

Later, the Home Shopping Network offered me $5 million for the station. That would have bailed me out, but everything was in such a mess I foolishly didn't take it. I thought it was worth more. I simply didn't know how to extricate myself from the financial nightmare, though I knew the property was valuable, and kept making bad decisions. With the help of two lawyer friends—they didn't charge me a cent—I later, and finally, got rid of the station, selling it for $2 million to a guy affiliated with Trinity Broadcasting. I paid the bank back. Dewey had made some money and he paid me back. I started playing poker again, and I won enough to pay off the loan from Jack. In fact, Chip, Dewey, and I recovered everything we'd squandered, clearing our entire indebtedness the way we always did: We returned to poker.

Afterward, while that pain was still fresh, someone had the nerve to ask me if the television venture was the business nightmare of my life. If I'd had the power, my stare would have turned him to stone. There was an odd side story to this television ordeal. The attorney we had helping us with the FCC papers, a pilot named Tom Root, tried to commit suicide. I don't know what he was depressed about, but he decided to take his life. He got into his single-engine plane and just flew it straight out over the ocean until he wouldn't have enough gas to get back to land. He evidently had a change of heart just before he crashed, and he sent out an SOS. The Coast Guard came and picked him up.

That was an unusual way to attempt to end your life. I believe I could certainly find a better way than that if I was going to commit suicide. In fact, a guy I knew did have a better way.

Well, at least a more interesting idea about it.

On April 16, 1989, one of our gambling friends from Texas, John Jenkins, whom we nicknamed "Austin Squatty," died a death about as bizarre as I'd ever heard of. And very possibly the cause was money problems. We called him Austin Squatty because he was short and squat, and he walked with a waddle. He was a big-time antique book and documents dealer in Austin, one of the nation's largest, and a well-known Texas historian. He also published over three hundred titles through his company, Jenkins Publishing Group, several of which he wrote. But over the years, he spent more and more of his time and money in Las Vegas playing poker.

While Squatty wasn't an exceptional player, he participated in the satellite games—one-table tournaments where you can win enough for an entry into a bigger event—during the World Series of Poker and won good money. Near the end of the mini-tournament, he would usually make a deal to split the prize with whoever was left. Or he would suggest a tradeoff: "I'll let you win it, and I'll take a piece of you in the big tournament."

Squatty allegedly got into financial trouble that led to vague, though never proven, suspicions that he had torched his warehouse in 1987 to collect the insurance. In fact, while he was never charged with arson, authorities did rule that arson was the cause of the fire. Curiously it was the third fire that had occurred at the Jenkins Company premises. In the 1970s, a lot of folks suspected less than noble intentions when he sold a large collection of Texas Revolution letters that later proved to be forgeries, though Squatty maintained his innocence.

Some say he decided to kill himself, but wanted to make it appear like he was murdered so his family would benefit from his life insurance. According to the story, he blew up a big balloon and tied a pistol to it. He drove down to a shallow portion of the Colorado River outside Austin and waded out in the swift current. He put the pistol to the back of his head and pulled the trigger.

He toppled over dead and, as the story goes, the current carried the balloon and the pistol downstream. They found Squatty's body near a public boat ramp in Bastrop County, Texas. The gun was never recovered. The local sheriff believed it was suicide. The justice of peace ruled it a homicide, but no arrests were made.

Squatty was a nice guy, quiet and mild-mannered. I've still got some kind of cartoon book that he offered me $25 for. Every time I see it, I think about him.

Chapter 28

Anyone can hold the helm when the sea is calm.

When Tony Spilotro got whacked in 1986, Las Vegas went straight. It was no coincidence. Spilotro had caused so much havoc in Vegas and upset so many law enforcement agencies that the mob honchos back in Chicago summoned him home for a meeting. Oblivious to the ruckus he was causing, Tony believed he was about to be rewarded with a top job in Chicago since he'd run such a ruthlessly efficient operation in Vegas. The mob bosses saw things a little differently and their meeting didn't end on a high note. The severely beaten bodies of Tony, who was forty-eight, and his forty-one-year-old brother, Michael, were found buried in an Indiana cornfield.

They had been buried alive.

Some say Spilotro was executed because he'd been running afoul of the mob bosses back in Chicago; others believe it was because he'd been having an affair with the wife of his boyhood pal, Frank "Lefty" Rosenthal. Lefty was another piece of work. Before he got to Las Vegas, his pedigree included convictions for sports fixing and bribery, and he was suspected of bookmaking, racketeering, bombings and procuring explosives for known gangsters. The Chicago mob put Rosenthal in charge of four casinos— the Stardust, Hacienda, Fremont, and Marina—even though the Gaming Commission had denied him a gaming license. Rosenthal ran the casinos with an iron fist, much to the chagrin of the Gaming Commission, and to the surprise of Alan Glick and his Argent Corporation. Glick was the man who had bought the four casinos, and thought that *he* had the privilege to run them.

He shortly learned different.

Glick purchased the Stardust in 1974 with the help of a $62.7 million loan from the Teamster's Union pension fund. But that money, as he was soon to find out, came with obligations. And it also came with Lefty Rosenthal, who was running things for the mob.

In the movie, *Casino*, Lefty's character was portrayed pretty accurately by Robert De Niro, right down to the scene where a suspected cheater was shocked right off his chair with an electric cattle prod and brought to the back room where the man's hand was worked over pretty good by a mallet. That was this guy's first warning. Word on the street was out—for cheats, there might not be such a "friendly" warning the next time. I'd heard about that, and many others did too. It became pretty common knowledge: You didn't want to run afoul of Lefty or his good pal Spilotro. While a heated meeting with Lefty wouldn't be too pleasant, it would be far better than a similar one with Spilotro.

Lefty actually ran a first-rate casino operation, and was a great innovator who made his mark on Las Vegas. He was the first to introduce sports betting in a casino, the Stardust, and the first to hire female blackjack dealers. Lefty's new ideas brought a lot of money into his casinos and, presumably, to the mob back in Chicago where the skimmed money was being sent.

I met Lefty at the Stardust when I played there one time, and later appeared on his TV show, *The Lefty Rosenthal Show*, with James Caan and Frankie Avalon. He raised a lot of eyebrows with his show, both good and bad. He had interesting guests—the premiere show featured Frank Sinatra, who I heard had made his first-ever TV talk-show appearance on Lefty's show—but he also irked the gaming commission and perhaps the mob, who may not have liked his high-profile and sometimes inflammatory appearances.

I enjoyed Lefty's show, but I can't say I was friendly with Rosenthal. He was pretty aloof, and quite an egomaniac, one of the few people I'd met who acted like a big shot and really was a big shot. Lefty was a great sports bettor, actually he was a genius at it, maybe the best I'd ever met. But he wasn't a poker player. At least I never saw him play. When he was running the Stardust, he came around the poker games occasionally and would watch the game for a while, and I'd often see him walking around the sportsbook or the casino on his rounds. But otherwise, I didn't have much interaction with him. While Lefty kept his casino games free from cheats, I can't say the same about his poker room. All the cheaters were there, so I didn't play in the Stardust much. I heard the guy he had hired was running the cheating, but I can't say if Lefty was involved with that or not.

Later they tried to blow up Lefty in his car in Tony Roma's parking lot, but he miraculously survived. He then moved to Florida where, presumably, it was a bit safer—and not just for him. Things were already changing even before we learned of Spilotro's demise. I can't say that there weren't many people who rejoiced at the news, especially the poker community, which was now free from his control over the games. Spilotro's slaying, the death of Shoeshine Nick from cancer, and the departure of Mike the Hammer—the organized crime trio that had a stranglehold on the casino poker action—had enabled the honest gamblers to get a toehold in the poker rooms and put an end to the cheating cartel that hovered over all the games. With Spilotro and his two henchmen gone, there was no organized resistance to our move to clean up the card games. It helped that we had good support from the casinos, of course, because this was a big effort and took a serious commitment. Cheating had been rampant, that's just the way it was.

The only ones who didn't support what we were trying to do were the cheaters themselves, and their days were numbered.

The principals of this cleanup effort were Chip Reese, Bobby Baldwin, Eric Drache, and me. It was Eric who originally questioned the unwritten rule that you don't rat out somebody caught cheating or stealing, whether in a poker room or elsewhere. Time and again he'd shake his head and challenge the status quo.

"Who do you think made that rule, an honest man or a crooked man?" Eric asked. "Let's break that rule, and if we see anything wrong in our poker games, instead of being quiet about it, let's speak up and get this business cleaned up."

It was in 1986, after Spilotro's death, that we actively started cleaning up the Vegas poker scene. The Dunes was a symbolic choice for our strategy session because of its role in the colorful history of Las Vegas. Cary Grant and Lucille Ball were among the legions of big names who had performed there, along with a couple of my favorites, Telly Savalas and Phyllis Diller. Now, with Spilotro out of the mix, the danger appeared over. There was a vacuum of power and we aimed to fill it. It seemed like a good time for honest players to set new ground rules before somebody showed up and tried to take Spilotro's place.

People had done all kinds of things around the poker tables that adversely affected the game. They weren't always cheating exactly, but they were being unfair. And we stopped all that. We called people down right at the table when they did something improper. When a player in our game cheated, we told him at once, "You can't do that here. You'd better go play somewhere else." If players sneaked a card off the table or shorted the pot, we challenged them on the spot. Vegas poker had been corrupt for years, and we were the vigilantes who cleaned it up. Our campaign succeeded because we were the best players, and the majority of our colleagues agreed with us. We simply refused to tolerate cheating, major or minor.

And we stopped it.

✪✪✪✪✪

In 1989 my mother died at the age of eighty-eight from a blood disorder. She was one of the most instrumental people in shaping my life and her passing was a blow to me. I felt like some big heavyweight boxer had knocked me upside the head. I was seeing stars. Through the years, my mother encouraged me, taught me, laughed with me, cried with me, and sometimes—when I deserved it, though not often enough—gave me hell.

My mother was born in Arkansas to Dutch-Irish parents and moved to Texas in a covered wagon as a six-year-old. She remembered seeing Indians, probably as they traveled through Oklahoma. Her parents settled in Longworth and eventually had twelve kids, two of whom died at birth. She met and married my dad in 1918 when she was seventeen. My father was thirty-three and, because of the age difference, they were never that compatible. Their interests weren't the same. Daddy would just up and go, he never liked to stay home, but Mom was always happy to have her kids around her. She cared little for material things and wasn't very worldly. Instead, Mom focused completely on the family. She was very loving and protective, and wanted everybody close and under her watch. With a smile, she often said, "I want to be able to eyeball my family."

She was a volatile, outspoken type who got mad in an instant, then dismissed her anger just as quickly. What spankings we got, we got from her.

"I don't like doing this," she would say as she prepared to administer punishment, "but you deserve it—move your hands."

I remember when I was about twelve years old, my mother wanted to spank me for something I did. When you get that old, your mother can't hurt you anymore. It struck me as funny and I started laughing at her.

"Come over here—you come over here!" she ordered.

I looked at her like I wasn't going to move, but she wasn't having any of that. Then she picked up a board!

"Mother, you're going to hurt me if you hit me with that board," I said. "I'm not going to come over and let you hit me with that thing. You can spank me, but not with that board; you'll break something."

She laid that board down and never tried to spank me again. Mother was the one I went to with my troubles, not my father. She was the strength of the family. I could talk to mother about most anything—but poker was one subject I never mentioned. Nor did I talk about poker with my father. Whether it was listening to my problems, counseling me on difficulties, or meting out due justice for infractions I committed, my mother was always there, always involved, always nurturing. She was my Rock of Gibraltar, and I missed her greatly and will miss her until my very last breath.

When my dad had died some thirty years earlier, at a time when I was full of myself and absorbed in a rollicking gambling career, I was not so moved. I was sad, of course, but Dad was a distant, aloof figure, an unemotional, stoic presence from whom I inherited my poker face. In many ways, I hardly knew him. I'd always remember that time at the farm after my escapade raiding those cabins with my teammates, when I had to confront my father.

He just passed out that maize to the chickens, listening, not saying a word. My dad wouldn't say anything; you could hardly get him to talk.

Benny Binion died the same year as my mother, and he was another big loss in my life. He developed heart problems in the mid-eighties and at one point was hospitalized and given only a few days to live. But Benny took an experimental drug and recovered enough that he returned one evening to the Horseshoe. I remember Jack pushing his father into the steakhouse in a wheelchair, and Benny looking at Jack with tears in his eyes. I could really relate to the gratitude he felt at being spared because I had experienced almost the same thing twenty-six years earlier.

As I watched Benny, a flood of memories washed over me. I recalled the many times I had sat in the Binion booth with him. He had told me stories about the old days in Dallas that I doubt anyone outside his immediate family ever heard. The sign on his desk up in Jack's office said a lot about him: "My enemies can do no right and my friends can do no wrong."

Benny wasn't the smartest man I ever knew, but he was the wisest. He counseled me about the pitfalls of a gambler and gave me invaluable advice about life in general. One story Benny liked to tell was about a man who got hysterical losing $1,000 at the craps table. Benny called him over to his table and asked about the problem. The man explained that he was a Baptist minister back east and wasn't sure if he should repent before his congregation.

"Listen here," Benny said, "I'm going to give you back $1,000, but you better not tell about this incident. The Lord will forgive you, but the congregation won't."

Some time later, Benny said, the minister sent him a note of thanks and a check for $1,000.

The miracle drug couldn't last forever, and toward the end of 1989, Benny went back in the hospital and everyone, including Benny, knew he wasn't coming home this time. I went up to see him in late December and he wasn't doing well. Besides being almost family, Benny and I shared another bond. Benny had lost his first-born daughter, Barbara, and I had lost mine, Doyla. He knew how I had withdrawn and searched for answers after Doyla's death, and he asked me how I felt about death and the hereafter. I shared my Christian beliefs, and was shocked when he told me he also believed. Here was this tough old cowboy with a reputation as a dangerous killer telling me he believed in God. He admitted he'd done a lot of bad things, but at the same time, he maintained that he had tried to live an honorable life.

Benny was eighty-five when he died on Christmas Day, 1989. His death marked the symbolic end of a transitional era in Las Vegas that began years earlier, punctuated by the slaying of Tony Spilotro in 1986.

Benny was the last of a special breed that had died out, sold out, or been sent off to prison. He had a big impact not only on poker but on Las Vegas itself. Benny understood customer service better than just about anyone and tried to make his players feel special. He was charismatic and personable and he could talk to people on any level. He was always interacting with his customers on an eyeball-to-eyeball basis. That's why he knew them so well and was so successful making them feel that his casino was their home away from home. If you wanted to talk to Benny, you just went over to his booth. No introductions were needed and you didn't have to get past any security guards or secretaries. Usually, he'd take the time for people, and the special ones, often those wearing cowboy hats, would get to sit down and share a bowl of chili with him.

"If you want to get rich, make little people feel big," Benny used to tell me.

And Benny is responsible for so much that poker players take for granted today. Along with his Jack, he started the World Series of Poker in 1970, but introduced the first freezeout poker tournament ever played in 1971. Benny also started the Poker Hall of Fame, which resided in the Horseshoe for many years. Through the years, there were many men who had the pleasure of meeting Benny Binion and were better off for it, including me, and I reckon there may have been an unfortunate few who would have been better off if they hadn't.

Benny's death more or less underscored the passing of the most colorful era in Vegas history. Sin City was cleaning up its gambling act and gangster and mob image, and was going corporate.

The transition to corporate ownership in the casino industry actually started with the arrival of Howard Hughes in 1966. When Hughes moved to Las Vegas, the city had a reputation as a mob stronghold, and the Kennedys—President John F. Kennedy and his brother, Attorney General Bobby Kennedy—were applying heat from Washington to clean out mob ties. But as Hughes, a national figure and listed as the richest man in America by *Fortune* magazine, started buying up hotels, beginning with the Desert Inn in early 1967, perceptions started to change. For Hughes, purchasing casinos came with great tax benefits. For Las Vegas, having the prominent businessman and one of the country's largest defense contractors put his stamp of approval on the town sure beat the mob. It was a PR breakthrough for the city at a time when big metropolitan papers were running exposes of mob skimming.

"How many of these toys are available?" Hughes asked his right hand man, Robert Maheu, after picking up the Desert Inn. "Let's buy 'em all."

Hughes followed up his purchase of the DI by buying the Sands, Castaways, Silver Slipper, Frontier, and Landmark casinos. After his spending spree, he became the largest employer in Nevada and his seven casinos accounted for 16 percent of the state's income. One of Frank Sinatra's jokes in his show summed up Hughes's influence on the town: "You're wondering why I don't have a drink in my hand? Howard Hughes bought it!"

Hughes left town about four years after he arrived, when his purchase of the Stardust was thwarted by U.S. Attorney General Ramsey Clark for fear of a Hughes monopoly in the casino industry. But his influence stayed; he'd paved the way for corporate investment, which had previously been blocked because regulators had no way of knowing who the investors were. After Hughes, the city looked at things differently and big public corporations like the Hilton, Ramada, and Del Webb (which also owned the New York Yankees) started coming in.

I never did meet Hughes, but then neither did anyone else. He locked himself up in the DI for four years, taking over the entire top floor. Hughes bought the property after the first few months when the hotel would no longer rent him rooms. Only his nurses would visit him. But I sure wish he had come down and played. Fortunately, there were other casino owners who did, men like Major Riddle and Sid Wyman, and I'd get the chance to lock horns with them.

Most people are not aware that Hughes also bought a large tract of land on the west side of Vegas, originally to house Hughes Aircraft. But when his key employees refused to move to the desert, the 25,000-acre parcel lay vacant. This tract later became known as Summerlin, one of the city's most fashionable residential areas, named after Hughes's grandmother, Jean Amelia Summerlin.

Once guys like Spilotro and Rosenthal were gone, the transition from mob-based joints with liberal skimming operations and muscle-enforced policies to corporate casinos with procedural methods really began to take hold.

Personally, I liked the old Las Vegas better when everybody knew everybody. But with all the old-timers gone, it couldn't be helped.

Progress has a way of changing things.

Chapter 29

Sometimes you get, sometimes you get got.

One of the most remarkable poker games I ever played in was with a Frenchman who, while courageously battling cancer, arranged a game that cost me well over $1 million dollars—and darn near my marriage.

A handsome, flamboyant French billionaire named Francis Gross first came to Las Vegas in the early 1970s. He and his brother owned shops up and down the Champs-Èlysées. They were also involved in the media business, both newspapers and television. Francis started playing in the smaller poker games and moved up to the bigger games over the years. He didn't much care whether he won or lost. Although he usually lost, he could be tough when he put his mind to it. He just enjoyed playing, and he was fun to be around.

Francis was only about fifty or fifty-five when he developed pancreatic cancer. He would call and say he was still looking forward to coming to Vegas and playing with us again, that our games were the most enjoyable times of his life. But we knew from reports that he was getting worse and worse and wouldn't be able to make it.

So in 1992 seven or eight of us just packed up—Chip, Bobby, and Johnny Chan included—and took the poker game to him. Jack Binion went too, but not to play, just out of respect for Francis, a good friend of his. Francis had a $30 million estate in the middle of Paris and it was filled with Picassos and Renoirs and the works of other famous painters. His collection was reputedly valued at $100 million. One painting that looked like a fat lady sitting on a commode was said to be worth $30 million.

Francis was delighted to see us and treated us like visiting royalty. He had the most famous chef in Paris prepare meals for us each day: French food, Italian food, steaks, seafood, everything. They laid out wonderful pastries and rare French wines. They even tried to fix Texas-style barbecue, but that didn't work out too well.

We started playing each morning about ten o'clock and broke for lunch at about one. We played a couple more hours until his strength gave out—he was taking morphine to ease the pain—and he'd have go back to bed. But first, he made arrangements for us to go out to the best places in town that evening. Francis dressed up for every game; it was the last fling of his life and he wanted to enjoy it in style.

We stayed for a couple of weeks and it was an unforgettable experience and a great game, even though I was in the midst of a terrible run of luck and lost $1.4 million. But it was a great action game, probably as good as any I'd played. We were playing $3,000/$6,000 limit and the no-limit games had a $100,000 cap. But it was a big game and the pots would frequently get capped. Oddly enough, Francis was the big winner. It reminded me of that old story about gamblers who have an amazing run of luck right before they die. Most assuredly, Francis had that run of luck, and he was, without a doubt, dying.

When we said our good-byes after our last day, Francis told us he'd see us in Las Vegas in a few months. We went along with the charade, hugged him, wished him luck and left. I knew a thing or two about cancer and I admired the courage and buoyant spirit he displayed. We knew we'd never see him again, and I believe he knew that also.

"See you in Vegas soon, my friends," he assured us, over and over. "Yes, I will see you soon."

From time to time over the next few weeks I thought about Francis and that Paris poker game. I wondered about his pain, if he was still lucid enough to recognize his family, and if, indeed, he still believed we'd all get together again in Las Vegas soon. I even wondered if there might be a leftover miracle somewhere for Francis.

Three, four months passed, and we never heard from him. Then one day word came that our genial and gracious friend wouldn't be seeing us again soon in Vegas. Or ever. Later, a friend of his told me that Francis had asked him to put a fax machine in the coffin so we could keep him up to date on what was going on. I believe that our last poker game in Paris brought him genuine happiness. And I hope it left him knowing that he had indeed hit life a good lick, had gone out a winner and had humbled some of the very best poker players in the world along his courageous and spirited final journey.

It was the best money I ever lost.

But the story of the Paris poker game didn't end in Paris. Back home, I was talking with Chip Reese on the phone about the $1.4 million loss, not realizing that Louise had overheard the conversation.

"You lost what?" she screamed.

I was just glad she didn't have a sharp object in her hand. I'd had million-dollar winners and losers many times in my career, but Louise didn't know or understand that. She didn't know anything about poker and couldn't tell a straight from a flush. After hearing of my Paris loss, she told me I had to quit gambling, that I was going to lose all our money.

"Louise," I said, "that's just another day at the office."

To label Louise "conservative" didn't do the word justice. She'd always had a different take on money and finances than me. For instance, one night in a game I lost $350,000. When I got home, of course, I didn't mention anything about it to Louise. I was pretty irritated about the loss, however, and it was weighing on me. I got up the next morning and, probably out of guilt, invited her to breakfast at a nearby IHOP. I got an omelet, and we split it. I couldn't eat very much because of recent surgery. She also asked the waitress for a half order of cheese blintzes. We were both fairly full, so we didn't eat but a few bites of them.

As we were leaving, Louise said, "That was a *big* half order. I wonder how big a full order is."

I looked at the check and said, "No, that must be a full order."

"How much was it?"

"It was $7.95."

She complained all the way home.

"I know you think I'm tight and old-fashioned," she steamed, "but I'm just not going to pay $7.95 for something when I eat just a few bites. I'm not going to do it."

I couldn't believe it. I'm sitting there listening to Louise complain about a $7.95 breakfast, while I'm silently fuming about a $350,000 loss the night before.

So it was inevitable that our different perspectives over money would one day clash head-on, which they did over the $1.4 million loss in Paris. She was not to be mollified. She kicked around my rationale of "just another day at the office" for a while, but no amount of explanations would pacify her. True to her conservative nature, she eventually issued me an ultimatum.

"Either you retire or I'm going to get a divorce," she demanded.

Now that was a stunner. Not that I was sleeping, but that sure as heck woke me up.

"I'm at the peak of my game and I'm not about to retire," I argued, convinced by my keen gambling instincts that she was simply bluffing. Next thing I knew, she hired a lawyer and filed for divorce.

So much for my keen gambling instincts.

She insisted on dividing up the community property, but I told her no. I didn't want anything but my poker bankroll, my car, my clothes, and the dogs. Most everything we owned was in her name anyway, and I wanted her to have it all. I didn't even hire an attorney.

Hell, I loved her!

Her attorney looked over my proposed arrangement, shook his head in disbelief, and said to Louise, "Are you sure you want this divorce, Mrs. Brunson?"

The lawyer looked at me, and I told him I just needed enough money to bankroll my poker games. Like I'd always said, money has no real value until you run out of it. However, stealing a line from Benny Binion, I'd also been known to say, "I've been rich and I've been broke. I prefer rich."

Louise left because of money. She was afraid she could lose her money someday because of *my* gambling. She had her savings and her business investments, which represented a lot of money. And even though I didn't have access to it, she thought she might be liable in case I had any indebtedness. She may have been right. In the settlement arrangements, I somehow wound up with the house we were living in, and Louise moved into an apartment.

I was a lost soul. I couldn't sleep and I could hardly eat, which for a three hundred-pound man was like ordering a super-sized portion of misery. Two very long weeks crawled by. Then one morning, the doorbell rang and I opened the door. There Louise stood, looking every bit as forlorn as I felt.

"It looks like we made a mistake," she sighed. "I'm coming back."

And I can say now with a mixture of pride and deep relief that we've been inseparable ever since.

Thankfully, I got my appetite back as well, and not just for food, but for the game I loved, poker. I kept at the cash games, earning back my big losses from the game in France, and winning more on top of that.

✪✪✪✪✪

A couple of years later, in 1994, I participated in what I considered the toughest final four in any tournament anytime and anywhere. It was at the Four Queens in downtown Las Vegas, and after three days of grueling play, we got down to the final four players: Chip Reese, T.J. Cloutier, Erik Seidel, and me. We had just eliminated two other really tough players, Jack Fox and Berry Johnston, the 1986 Main Event champion.

You've got to expect that a weak player or maybe two will be around at the end. But this time you couldn't pick four guys who have been on a higher level in tournament play than the four of us. I knew it was the best players I had ever seen who had made it through a large field—Chip, who I consider the greatest poker player ever; T.J., who's won more major tournaments than anyone alive; and Erik, who would have eight gold bracelets by 2008, more of them than anyone in the world besides Phil Hellmuth Jr., Johnny Chan, and me. I knew these were the best players I had ever seen make it through such a large field.

The defining moment in the tournament came when I moved in before the flop with the 9♦ 2♦, the hand known as the "Montana Banana," a hand so weak that "bananas will grow in Montana before it wins anything." But global warming might have changed a few things, at least judging by what unfolded next. Eric had been running roughshod over the game for a while, pushing me and T.J. around, and forcing us out of pots. I was trying to stop him. Nobody can make me keep throwing my hand away for too long, and it was time to turn the momentum back in my favor. T.J. folded the small blind, but Eric, who had raised from the button, thought long and hard. Finally, he called me and turned over an offsuit A-J. I showed him my 9-2. Eric was about a 3 to 1 favorite. But the flop gave me a flush draw and I turned a flush, sealing Eric's fate. I was on my way to winning the championship.

That shows how much luck is involved in winning a major tournament. Of course, you've usually got to play well to get down to final heads-up play to even have that chance, but along the way some luck helps.

Despite the euphoria of my victory, a pall had shrouded my week. And once again, it had to do with drugs.

I've always hated recreational drugs because I've seen what they do to people. Time after time in my life, people I knew, family of people I knew, and even good friends have died from abusing something that they told me was supposed to be fun. Maybe using illegal drugs was fun for a while, but things always seemed to end the same way: being fatal, not fun.

My anti-drug feelings reached new heights during my early years in Vegas because I saw so many people ruining their lives, including David Vernon. Along with Wayne Hamilton, David was my friend back in Fort Worth. David didn't get involved in so-called hard drugs, but he became something of a pill-head, popping things they called redbirds, yellow jackets, and bennies. David came to Las Vegas about the same time I did in 1973, but he lacked the talent to become an exceptional poker player. He was good enough to make a living, but the pills were getting to him. One night after he'd taken pills of some sort he dozed off in his apartment with a cigarette in his hand. The mattress caught fire and he died in the blaze.

Drugs got the better of another guy close to me, my good friend and old traveling buddy, Sailor. And it just about tore me up. Sailor had come to watch me play, but we hardly engaged in our usual poker banter or laughter about old times on the road. Moreover, I barely recognized him. He was wasting away. Drugs had ravaged his life with a vengeance. I wanted to help him; I wanted to visit the old Sailor I knew and cared so much about, but he slipped away, avoiding me. Sailor's plight left me heartsick, because he had been a friend like no other. He was with me when I met Louise and he was there for both of us during my long bout with cancer. We traveled together, gambled together, partied together, lived together, and shared many wonderful experiences and grand adventures through the years. Sailor really had a heart of gold and was a genuinely colorful character—kind, caring, gentle, and generous to a fault. He was the kind of man that would borrow money so that he could lend it to some stranger with a hard-luck story—or give it to some woman. He was always giving money away to somebody.

Like many of the gamblers I knew, Sailor accumulated a lot of money, probably about a dozen times. And each time, he went broke.

And then Sailor got on drugs. As in most cases when gamblers got involved with drugs, it was a much younger woman who introduced Sailor to cocaine. Later, he escalated to crack. It wasn't a gradual change to his life as it is with a lot of addicts. Almost immediately, the Sailor I knew was gone. I've never seen such a dramatic transformation in an individual's personality before or since. He became moody and desperate. Previously, his friends could hang their hats on what Sailor told them. He had always been such an honorable and personable guy. But after the drugs kicked in, he would lie, cheat, steal, beg, or borrow to feed his ever-increasing habit and that of his girlfriend. He was not selective; he abused cocaine, morphine, and heroin. He even began popping pills and smoking crack through a pipe.

"Sailor took to drugs like a kid takes to candy," a friend once said. Many of his friends tried to help me get him off the stuff. His response to my pleas made my blood run cold.

"Doyle, I like what drugs do for me."

After awhile, I just didn't know what to say to that. "How could it have come to this?" I wondered. I just kept thinking of the Sailor I'd always known and couldn't reconcile the fact of what he had become. As Sailor's health began to deteriorate, he became emaciated. It broke my heart to see him waste away before my eyes, but I could do nothing to help him. I gave him money several times, but he used it to support his habit. Then he contracted hepatitis C, which all but destroyed what was left of his liver. As his condition worsened, Sailor moved in with a mutual friend named Bobby Hoff, an ex-drug addict who also had contracted the disease, but had enough self-discipline to curb it with diet, exercise and vitamins. Every time I saw Bobby at a poker tournament I gave him several thousand dollars to cover the costs of Sailor's upkeep. But each time, I was terribly saddened by what had happened to one of my dearest friends.

The last time I saw Sailor, at that Four Queens tournament I won in 1994, he showed up looking so gaunt and ghastly no one wanted to sit beside him. He was like a walking dead man. Not long after, he got deathly ill and entered a hospital in Los Angeles. I was in Montana when Bobby called me. He told me that if I wanted to see Sailor again I better get to L.A. in a hurry. I flew to California at once, but it was too late; he was gone before I got there.

I don't know if it was luck, fate, or what, but Louise happened to be in California attending to some of her investments. She hurried to the hospital right away and was holding his hand when he died—thank God.

Then there was this talented young kid from Texas who came to Vegas shortly after we did. He was about twenty-five years old, very quiet, and a real Southern gentleman. I can't remember his real name, but everyone that knew him called him "Waterhole." When I asked why, they told me his money was so hard to get, it was like taking it out of a hole in the ground filled with water. After playing with him in several side games, I had to agree. Waterhole knew how to play. He'd come to Vegas to play and always took more money back to Texas than he had brought with him. This boy had a lot of talent.

Waterhole showed up for the main event in 1973, and when we got down to twelve players, the two of us got into a pot. I flopped two pair, and got him all in with aces. The river card paired the board, giving him the higher two pair and busting me. I remember that hand well because it was the last time I saw him. He got eliminated later that day and headed back to Texas. He stopped in Phoenix and went into a hotel coffee shop to eat. When Waterhole went to pay his bill, he pulled his roll out of his pocket, flashing several thousand dollars while he searched for small bills to settle the check.

"You better put that money up, son," the cashier said.

"I don't have any place to put it," he said.

"I wish I had that problem," she joked.

He just handed her the roll of money and said, "Here, now you've got that problem."

He walked out of the coffee shop, rode the elevator to the top of the hotel, and jumped to his death.

Nobody knew why. He just did it. I've often wondered what could have been the cause. No one said it was drugs, but if I was a betting man...

My other gambling buddy from those Exchange Avenue days, Wayne, also met his demise courtesy of drugs back when I lived in Fort Worth. He had been coming by my house to borrow money, which I gave him. Soon, though, I realized I was just compounding his drug problems because the money was going to support his habit.

I finally told him, "No, Wayne, you're strung out on drugs, and I'm not giving you any more money."

The next thing I knew, he was arrested for passing counterfeit money, convicted, and sent to the penitentiary where he promptly got in an argument with a fellow inmate over dope. The guy snuck up in the middle of the night and stabbed him in the heart. In a scene reminiscent of the saloon stabbing I witnessed on Exchange Avenue, I was told that Wayne jumped up and chased the inmate down the hallway, then suddenly toppled over and died.

But Wayne wasn't the first in his family to die from the curse of drugs. Some years earlier, his stepson hanged himself with a belt in the closet, just a year after his mother and Wayne married way back in 1960. Stuey's stepson also hanged himself when he was barely a teenager. He committed suicide in the parking lot of the Hilton Hotel where he used a cord off his mother's television. And I could only guess at the reason.

Still another suicide that affected me personally was Jimmy Casella, a gambler from New York who killed himself in 1973 after getting on drugs. He called me collect the day he died, but I didn't accept the call because I thought he just wanted to borrow more money to buy more drugs. The word on the street was that he had married a young woman who was running around on him. I've always regretted not taking his call, although the odds were not good that I could have helped him.

I can't name all my friends and colleagues who were destroyed by drugs, and more often than not, a woman was involved. God bless 'em, I do love women. Still, as a rule, women, drugs, and the middle-aged male crisis added up to a volatile mix. The forty- and fifty-somethings would get mixed up with these young girls, and they'd go out partying. Maybe the girls could handle it, but the poker players with addictive personalities were vulnerable. Many times the girls would be doing recreational drugs, and to prove how young and hip they were, the guys would jump in feet first, consuming pill, powder and whatever like there was no tomorrow.

And sometimes there wasn't.

Chapter 30

*The essence of courage is not that your heart doesn't quake,
but that no one knows it when it does.*

"I'm gonna kill you for what you've done to us here!"

The tall, menacing guy was standing over me with a long black pistol pointed at my head. It looked like he meant business and had had enough of our stalling. I was totally at his mercy, useless, unable to help Louise. When I heard those words, I thought Louise and I had bought the farm, and I don't mean the one I grew up chopping cotton on. The two men in black who invaded our home in 1998 held guns to our heads most of the time. They were outraged because we had no safe, no valuables in the house. They beat me bloody and threatened repeatedly to kill us both.

Then they got really mad, because the security company had finally realized Louise had given them an invalid code, a signal that there was trouble in the house.

And here I was sprawled on the floor, beaten nearly senseless, ninety-something-thousand dollars in my pocket I'd won the day before at the World Series of Poker—money I'd forgotten about. Likely, I could have just given it to the robbers and they would have left happy.

I'm gonna kill you for what you've done to us here!

The words chilled me, but my concern was mostly for Louise. In the flash of a thought, I had convinced myself that I'd already lived a long and full life, that it had been a great run and that if my time had run out, so be it.

But apparently, Louise didn't need my help to handle the situation.

"Oh, Jesus, Jesus!" she screamed, invoking the praise and power of the Lord she so fervently worshiped—and jumped in front of the guy with the gun.

"No, don't kill him, kill me!"

A heroine in a novel couldn't have done it better, and even at that pivotal moment, I was struck by, of all things, her agility. Despite back problems that limited her movement, she was as agile as a cat when she leaped in front of the gunman. I was never prouder of my loving wife, although I had no time then to dwell on it. The gunman was flabbergasted. Her action, emboldened through her many years as a devoted Christian, momentarily stopped him in his tracks. Louise implored the robbers to think about the senseless murders they were about to commit, and how it would devastate our children and grandchildren.

After the gunman shoved Louise aside, I thought maybe I'd gained a little leverage.

"Fellas," I said, "the cops are gonna be here any minute. Are y'all crazy? You gotta get out of here."

Those clever words dropped on deaf ears. Neither indicated a trace of panic. And they sure as hell didn't leave. They just continued about their business in a military manner. I was convinced they had to be pros; they didn't even curse.

But then the short, sullen one accidentally pulled his mask up. He was Asian, and he knew I saw him. And I knew at once that his slip might cost me my life. But when he didn't shoot me immediately after I saw his face, my poker instincts kicked in again. I felt reasonably certain he wasn't going to kill us. Not certain, mind you, just *reasonably* certain.

They placed the barrels of the pistols against our heads and the menacing one said with a note of icy finality, "Enough of this. We're gonna kill you both if you don't tell me where the safe is."

"I told you I don't have a safe," I said. "I've never had a safe in my life. But if it's just money you want, I've got some money in my pocket."

The short one grunted something indecipherable and leaned forward. I told him I had seven or eight thousand dollars, and that seemed to get his attention.

"Where?"

"It's in my front pocket."

He reached in my pocket and came out with those $500 chips left over from the poker game. He hurled the chips on the floor and said angrily, "You call that money?"

"No, it must be in my other pocket," I said. He reached in the pocket and jerked out the cash and the leather pouch.

"This don't look like $8,000," he said.

"Well, I think it is."

He jammed it in his pocket, along with the little leather pouch containing $90,000-plus in chips. If I had told him the pouch was full of chips, he might not have taken it. He obviously had no use for the $500 chips he scattered all over the floor. But I didn't tell him anything because I had forgotten I even had the $90,000!

"We'd better go," he told his tall, threatening partner.

They snapped handcuffs on both of us, then used a third set to handcuff us together. We could hardly move, the cuffs were so tight and painful. The guy with all my money, the shorter one, removed my billfold and started to leave.

"Buddy," I said, "leave that billfold. There's not any money in it, just credit cards and my driver's license. It'll be a lot of trouble replacing them, and they're not gonna do you any good. They'll just get you caught if you use them."

He stopped and looked down at me. I must have been an awful sight with blood splattered all over me, my glasses broken, and my eye cut. He just stood there silently for perhaps forty-five seconds, as if he had fallen into some kind of hypnotic trance. I didn't know what to think as we stared at one another.

Had I pushed my luck too far?

Without a word, he turned and tossed the billfold over his shoulder and walked out with his partner, closing the door behind him.

I'm lying there handcuffed, barely able to move, bleeding all over everything and Louise still thinks I'm having a heart attack. She's trying her best to calm and comfort me. I told her I had been faking the heart attack, and was okay. She was visibly relieved.

"After thirty-five years of marriage, did you ever think we'd wind up like this?" she asked, forcing a faint smile.

"No, I didn't," I mumbled, trying to see through the blood.

Then we looked at one another, shook our heads, and burst out laughing. With the danger passed, we struggled around for a while trying to figure out what to do next.

"What's that flashing in your pocket?" she asked as we tumbled around on the floor.

I glanced down as best I could. "It's my cell phone."

"We'll call the police on it."

After more struggling, I managed to dial the operator, who put us on hold! Then she told us to dial 911.

I hung up, redialed, and angrily told the operator, "Get me the police!"

She said, "For what?"

I told her, "My God, woman, I've been robbed, I've been pistol-whipped, I'm handcuffed to my wife, I'm lying on the floor and I don't want to answer a bunch of questions. Just get me the police."

Eventually, she did.

"We're on our way," an officer responded, trying to reassure us.

We crawled over to the door and, with great difficulty and no small amount of pain, got it open. Next, I dialed a neighbor. "Hang on," he said. "I'll be right there!"

The next thing we heard were security officers from the Las Vegas Country Club, apparently notified by the security operator who had nearly gotten us killed.

"Is everything all right?" one of them hollered.

"Yeah!" I screamed, "everything is all right now. Come on in here. We've got the door open."

They walked in with their guns drawn.

"The robbers have left," I said. "Have you got a hacksaw or something to take these cuffs off?"

One guard pulled out a key and unlocked the handcuffs, explaining that most handcuff keys fit all cuffs. My neighbor came running in at about the same time, arriving just ahead of the police. It was over.

Almost.

The ordeal had a bizarre twist that, to this day, I cannot fathom. Throughout the entire invasion, neither of my two dogs had made a sound. I own a shy little Bichon named Cutie and a toy poodle named Casper, among the most spoiled dogs in history. To this day, Casper thinks he's a pit bull. He barks at everything he sees, and attacks everything that moves. He's a lovable little rascal, but very territorial, and he'd already bitten several people while defending his turf. By actual count, the number hit forty in mid-2008 when he bit a workman during a visit to Montana and was approaching fifty in the summer of 2009. Even our friends who frequently drop by know to be wary of him because he's liable to jump up and bite them.

At the time of the robbery, Casper was four years old and never once had failed to meet me at the door when I returned home. Not once. If people walked in with me, I had to restrain him from charging and biting them.

The dogs were upstairs with Louise when I got home that night. It was nothing short of a miracle that they didn't come bounding downstairs and attack the invaders. I was certain that if Casper had gone after the gunmen like he did everybody else, they would have harmed him in some way; in fact, they probably would've shot him. Then they would've wound up having to shoot me, too. And probably Louise. I loved my dogs very much, and if the intruders had hurt them, I would have taken some kind of crazy, uncontrollable action.

And it probably would have been fatal.

So, we were extremely lucky. I couldn't explain why the dogs didn't come down the steps. We talked about it afterward, and some people said that animals sense fear or danger. I don't know what the reason was, but I don't believe that was the case in this instance. Maybe it was divine intervention. My Christian beliefs, precipitated by the heartbreaking event of my daughter's death many years before, certainly didn't rule out the possibility of God's presence in our home that dreadful night.

Whatever it was, it didn't save the cops. When the police arrived, Casper came charging down the steps, barking and creating a big fuss.

And he bit a policeman.

Chapter 31

Some gamblers are like zircon: They may lack certain
properties considered genuine and endearing, but that
doesn't mean they are without sparkle.

B etween the gamblers and the gangsters, I've met a lot of colorful
people through the years, characters whose stories I'd have a hard
time believing if I didn't know about them personally. Many I
considered friends, or least acquaintances that shared a good time, even
those who might have stumbled into a felony conviction or two. I wouldn't
suggest that everyone I met along the way became my friend, but if you
looked hard enough you could find something to appreciate in each
individual.

How else could I have enjoyed the company of a ruthless killer
like Tony Spilotro or the moral infractions of my gambling group down
on Exchange? Gamblers, at least the guys that I played with, kept life
interesting—and that's what I loved about Las Vegas. The town was just
full of characters.

For instance, there was Stu Ungar, a troubled soul if I ever met one.
Stuey was the only person to actually win the World Series of Poker three
times. The only other three-time title holder, Johnny Moss, was voted the
championship one year—the very first year the event was held in 1970—
and won the tournament the other two times. They made a movie about
Stuey called *High Roller: The Stu Ungar Story*, and it was a pretty good
depiction of him.

While Stuey was a good friend, I had a love-hate relationship with
him. It just depended on the setting. In a gambling environment, Stuey was
the most arrogant and offensive person I've ever known. I believe he was
the only guy I nearly slugged at the poker table. I only outweighed him
3 to 1—330 pounds to 110. And I wanted to slug him on more than one
occasion. He was absolutely insufferable at the poker table. I saw Stuey
throw cards at the dealers and curse at them like a shore-leave sailor. I saw

him spit on a dealer for giving him losing cards. At the Golden Nugget one time, I saw him curse a woman dealer until she called the floorperson over, took her badge off and said, "I quit."

Then she turned to Stuey and said, "You S.O.B., come outside, and I'm going to kick your ass." This was a big athletic-looking lady.

Stuey wisely declined.

Stuey was the best winning poker player I ever saw, and he was one of the worst losing poker players I ever saw.

But away from the table, I loved him. The girls all loved him. He was smart and witty, a lot of fun, and he had a tremendous sense of humor.

I don't know what Stuey's IQ was, but I'm sure he was a genius. He had all the innate abilities of what it takes to make a great poker player, except one—discipline. And that's the reason he wasn't one of the great players of all time. If he had learned self-discipline, he would have been the very best.

Stuey was not oblivious to his shortcomings. I thought his quote in *One of a Kind,* his biography, was particularly revealing: "There's an old saying in poker that at the table your worst enemy is yourself. I'll tell you one thing. In my case, truer words were never spoken." He was among the most degenerate gamblers I've ever known—and that's saying something. After winning his second title in 1981, Stuey was asked what he did in his spare time. He told the reporter that the only time he wasn't gambling was when he was sleeping or eating.

And when asked what he would do with his winnings: "Lose it," he said.

That was Stuey. He bet on horses, ball games, golf, anything. He beat me out of $800,000 playing golf one time. Later, we went to Nashville to play some guys, and I played him again. I won my $800,000 back, plus another half million or so. When we got back to Vegas, he had the money to pay me, but before the weekend was over, he had lost it all betting on horses and sports.

I never got paid.

He earned his reputation as one of the best poker players by winning back-to-back World Series championships in 1980 and 1981. But then he got on drugs. He sank even deeper into drugs after getting divorced by his wife, Madeline, in 1986, but the big blow might have been when his stepson Richie committed suicide not long after. The young man hanged himself with a VCR cord in the garage at the Las Vegas Hilton. Some speculated that the boy suffered from an inferiority complex because Stuey was so vocal and high profile. Madeline told me that Richie had assured her that he would "be successful in the next life."

It was all very sad.

Stuey borrowed money from me for Richie's funeral. And he paid me back.

Drugs ruined Stuey's life. He snorted so much cocaine that it actually ate his nose off. Doctors performed reconstructive surgery on it, but it didn't turn out very well. And he was a vain fellow to boot.

Stuey returned to the poker table in mid-1997, making one of the most remarkable comebacks I've ever seen. His first WSOP championship in 1980 was the result of being a young man who played aggressively, gained confidence as the tournament wore on, and benefited from a healthy dose of luck. But his third championship, in 1997, demonstrated his true brilliance. It came after more than a decade in a drug haze, after the death of his stepson, after rehab, after reconstructive surgery on his nose.

I was at the last two tables with him in '97. He was playing poker like I imagined Stradivarius played the violin. I was sitting there in the Horseshoe watching him, drinking coffee with my leg propped up on a chair and my ears ringing with the sounds of roulette wheels and slot machines in the background. And I was dumbfounded. I knew the physical, mental and emotional strain he was under, and I was thinking, "What a testimony to his real ability. Nobody will ever know how great he would have been were it not for the drugs." His heads-up performance that day against John Strzemp, an executive at the Mirage, demonstrated his true brilliance.

Stuey was undoubtedly the best tournament player ever. His poker style was perfect for tournament competition. He won a third of the major events he played when one out of forty would be excellent. However, in cash games, Stuey wasn't even among the best. He could have been, but his volatile temperament was his Achilles Heel and he couldn't overcome his personal demons. He'd just steam off his money. Sometimes he got so mad after losing a hand it looked like he really didn't care if he put all his money in bad and went broke.

The sad truth was—as he showed so many times at the poker table, the dog and horse races, and all his other compulsive gambling habits—that he didn't.

Stuey had a lot of gamble in him. I was playing no-limit hold'em with him at the Horseshoe the year before he died, and we played a pot that will tell you a lot about him. I had K♥ Q♥ and raised the pot. Stuey reraised me trying to steal the pot right there. I knew the way he thought, so I called him. The flop came A♥ 10♥ 3♠. He bet and I raised him with my royal flush draw. Stuey had a pair and a flush draw. Stuey's hand couldn't be dead no matter what I had, so he moved in a monster bet. Obviously, I had to call him. I turned my hand up and showed him I was drawing at a royal flush. The pot was so huge I was prepared to lay table insurance to save some money if our hands were close. Then Stuey turned over his hand, the 8♥ 3♥. Knowing this was a close hand, I offered to split the pot or at least take part of our money back. I knew Stuey was in desperate financial shape, so it seemed like something he might reasonably consider.

"No, let's gamble," he said.

That was just Stuey's mindset.

The turn and the river were blanks and Stuey won the pot.

Stuey was found dead in a room at the Oasis Motel in Las Vegas on November 22, 1998, the thirty-fifth anniversary of the assassination of President John F. Kennedy. Stuey was forty-five. Small amounts of cocaine, methadone, and Percodan were found in his system, but were not considered the cause of death. The Clark County coroner attributed his death to a heart attack: "The cause is accidental death by coronary arteriosclerosis. The heart condition developed over a period of time. The death was brought on by his lifestyle."

During the funeral, we took up a collection to pay for the ceremony and burial, and most all of us contributed. By some accounts, Stuey had won $30 million in his lifetime, but was penniless when he died. His death occurred a year and a half after he had won $1 million and his third WSOP championship. I couldn't get over the tragedy of this young mind gone to waste. He was a rare talent.

Stuey was posthumously inducted into the Poker Hall of Fame on May 14, 2001. Two hundred of the world's biggest poker luminaries, plus his ex-wife and daughter, attended the celebration at the Horseshoe.

✪✪✪✪✪

Jack Straus, one of poker's great raconteurs and characters, was a piece of work. In August of 1998, at age fifty-eight, Jack died in an environment I reckon he would have chosen to breathe his last breath—the poker table. He suffered a heart attack during a high-stakes poker game at the Bicycle Club in California, the same year he was enshrined in the Poker Hall of Fame. I don't know if he won that last hand or not, but I suppose, knowing

Straus, that he might have gone out broke, figuring he had some other kind of play on the next hand.

Jack was an excellent poker player, an action guy. In a two- or three-handed game, he was dynamite. An aggressive player has an edge in a short-handed game because, if he's got any kind of hand at all, you can't force him out with a raise. A guy's tendency to call too many bets in a regular game is a weakness that actually turns into a strength in a short-handed game. Jack played more like I described in my book *Super/System* than anybody I've ever seen.

His 1982 victory in the World Series was a story they still talk about today. Straus had pushed all his chips into the middle on a bluff, got called and lost the pot. As Straus was leaving the table, the dealer called out to him and pointed to the spot beneath the newspaper he had been reading. There was a chip wedged between the table and the rail that belonged to Jack. Since he hadn't announced all-in, that chip was live—it wasn't considered part of the pot. So Jack sat back down, won several hands in a row, and parlayed that single chip all the way to the championship. That incident gave birth to the poker saying, "A chip and a chair," inspiring poker players for generations to come. Meaning, you always have a chance if you've got any chips at all and are still in the tournament.

I can't believe somebody didn't write a book about Straus—or he didn't write a book. It's almost a shame. He had a vivid imagination and, like Benny Binion, he was a great storyteller who could keep you enthralled for hours. He got involved in the most outrageous schemes and bets, something that never ceased to amaze me. I beat Jack out of a lot of money on the golf course, but I had to keep an eye on him. He was always up to something, and usually that something gave him a dubious edge. His idea of gambling was to get the best possible odds, one way or another, so you always had to be on your toes around Straus when gambling was involved.

Jack was a good-time guy, sometimes too much so, as Louise and I discovered when we went on a Caribbean gambling junket with him to Curacao, an island where gambling was legal. On the plane down there, Jack and his buddies got to passing out brownies laced with marijuana.

"Boy, these are good," she said. "Could I have another one?"

Naturally, Louise conked out after a couple of brownies. When told later about the pot, she wasn't impressed at all with Jack and his friends' idea of fun—that's to put it mildly. That was the only illegal dope she ever tangled with in her entire life, and she didn't soon let up on Jack for that transgression—or my ears either. I thought it was kind of funny, but I wasn't about to tell Louise that.

We headed home after three or four days and had to go through customs. Now, Straus had a bunch of outlaws with him—most anybody Jack knew had a checkered history—and the immigration authorities were taking extra special interest in this motley group. They were examining everybody very closely for drugs and all varieties of contraband. Some were ordered to remove their clothes for strip searches.

Louise, not pleased to be lumped in with Jack's cronies and not about to be strip-searched by anyone, marched up to customs.

"I'm Louise Brunson," she said defiantly. "No drugs, no alcohol, no tobacco."

The official looked at the headstrong young woman with the fire in her eyes and right away pegged her as a total square. He couldn't have realized either that just days earlier, she'd been higher than a kite on pot brownies, though it was no fault of hers.

"Well then, lady," he said, "just go right on through."

And she did.

I don't know that Louise ever forgave Jack for the brownie escapade. I think she did get a kick out of it, though, when they strip-searched me.

As addictive and degenerate a gambler as Stuey and Straus were, there was one guy who showed up in town that even outdid them, which wasn't easy. That man's name was Archie Karas. In 1993, Archie had the most phenomenal run in gambling history. He took a single $100 bill and won thirty-something million dollars with it—then lost it all back. It was one of the most incredible things I had ever seen.

Archie started out playing pool with a local executive in a pool hall located near the Liberace Museum, and parlayed that into high-stakes games where he grew his bankroll to about a million dollars. That's pretty amazing right there, but Archie was just warming up. He started shooting craps and won, won, won. He played some poker with that money too. I played him a couple of times, but we never played for long because he wanted to make a crapshoot out of it. He liked having antes so high that you had to play almost every hand to just stay even. He was hard to beat, too, because he played each deal so aggressively, it would cost you a bundle to see the cards through to the end. You simply had to have the best hand to beat him.

I'll never forget one hand. We were playing $10,000/$20,000 seven-card stud—boy, that's high! I had a jack showing and a jack in the hole, and he had been raising every pot. He brought it in with a 6, I raised him, he reraised me, I reraised him, and he reraised me. Finally, I just called. Remember, each raise was for $10,000! At that time, you could buy a house for that kind of money, so it was like the two of us were betting houses back and forth. By the time a hand got to seventh street, it was like we had a whole row of houses lined up in the pot. It felt like we were playing Monopoly.

Next card Archie caught a deuce and I caught a third jack. I bet and he called me. The fifth card was a blank for each of us, and I bet and he just called. It went like that all the way to the river, seventh street. On that last card, I made a full house and bet again.

He turned his hand over and said, "Well, I can't call you now because I can't beat those two jacks. I know that's all you got!"

All he had was just two sixes! No sane player would have seen that kind of action all the way through with those cards. That's the kind of player he was. If he won, he just beat you. There wasn't anything anybody could do. Archie was going to keep pushing those chips in the middle. If he had the best hand, he'd win every time because he never threw his hand away. You couldn't bluff him off the pot no matter what you bet. He played Chip more often than he played me; I took a piece of Chip and he took a piece of me because we couldn't afford to play as high as Archie wanted. The man was on a mission and he just kept gambling higher and higher.

But Archie loved playing craps more than anything else. He did most of his craps playing at the Horseshoe, the only casino that would take bets as high as Archie wanted to play. Consequently, he won most of the money there. At one point, he got so hot that he owned *every* $5,000 chip the Horseshoe had. It was unbelievable. Becky Behnen, who ran the Horseshoe at the time, had to buy back the chips from him. What some people suspected, and he got pretty damn close, was that Archie wasn't just trying to win a lot of money—he wanted to win the Horseshoe itself!

While Archie had the most amazing run I'd ever seen—maybe the greatest one ever—it was bound to end sooner or later. He kept hitting those craps tables, and the tide started turning against him. He played harder and harder, until finally, inevitably, all the money was gone. Every penny of it. Archie had managed to gamble it all away—all $30 million of it! You couldn't even cram that much money into a pickup truck.

I saw Archie afterward and he didn't complain about his reversal of fortune. Losing the money didn't seem to bother him.

"I set a record nobody will ever break," he said—that seemed to be what he was interested in.

○○○○○

Chuck Sharp, a good friend and former neighbor of mine at the Las Vegas Country Club, was a small-limit stud player, but one of the most successful sports gamblers in the history of Las Vegas. After he made a bunch of money, he decided to retire to Thailand. He was kind of a thrifty guy and things were pretty cheap over there. Besides being a gambler, he was also a womanizer who was seldom without a new girlfriend.

On his visits back to the States, he'd tell me how plentiful the girls were in Thailand and update me on his conquests. He came in one night and said, "You know, Doyle, I think I've found my soul mate. We really get along good."

"That's great, Chuck," I said. "Tell me about her."

"She's eighteen years old and she's beautiful."

"Sounds nice, Chuck, but that's a lot of age difference."

"Yeah, but I think I'm gonna marry her."

"Well, certainly I wish you all the happiness, but what does a sixty-three-year old guy find to talk about with an eighteen year old?"

"Oh," he laughed, "she can't speak English."

Who knows? Maybe he had found the perfect mate.

Another odd friend was named James "Doc" Ramsey, an old gambler who played the Texas Circuit and was a very good poker player. I often wondered why he never came to Las Vegas. When I finally asked him, he said he had tried to drive out several times, but when he'd make it to the hill by Boulder City and see the lights of Las Vegas, he'd suddenly get short of breath, like he was going to have a heart attack.

"So I'd just have to turn around and go back home," he explained.

I think he died without ever making it to Vegas.

○○○○○

Poker players are always looking for more action, whether it takes the form of crazy bets or just practical jokes. I always chuckled over this one. One night, a friend of mine who was usually a pretty quiet guy when sober, got a little tipsy. After the game ended at midnight, he called a mutual friend of ours, the great tournament poker player T.J. Cloutier.

When T.J. answered the phone, my friend said to him, "This is Jack. Could I speak to Tommy?"

"No, you've got the wrong number," T.J. said.

"Oh, I'm sorry," my friend allowed, and hung up.

About thirty minutes later he called T.J. again and said, "This is Chris. Is Tommy there?"

"No, you've got the wrong number," T.J. said again.

My friend would hang up, wait thirty minutes and then call back using a different name, but always asking, "Is Tommy there?"

Pretty soon, T.J. got furious and started screaming into the phone. Finally, about three in the morning, my friend called T.J. one last time.

"This is Tommy," he said. "Have I had any calls?"

Chapter 32

Poker is a war—people only pretend it's a game.

I t's been said that all is fair in love and war. Well, you might say the same thing about gambling. Non-gamblers no doubt wondered how I could play cutthroat, no-holds-barred poker and golf—and how I could fraternize with known killers, gangsters, underworld figures, and thugs—and yet remain close friends with my opponents.

First off, there's nothing personal in a poker game. The object is to win your opponents' money. Afterward, all is forgiven, if not forgotten. Sailor Roberts and I were the best of friends but remained fierce competitors at the poker table. There was a time when Sailor and I played harder against each other than anyone else. I loved to beat him, and he loved to beat me. I would forever cherish the memory of winning his dog Flirty on the golf course in San Angelo. It might take another professional gambler to understand how we were so intensely competitive with our friends, yet walked away from the golf course or the poker table with no hard feelings, regardless of the outcome. It was just a way of life and, usually, we held no grudges.

Second, relationships that are formed over the poker table become a common ground for friendship. When you spend a lot of time with somebody at the poker table, you tend to develop a certain camaraderie. What that person does outside the cardroom in his private life is not something you necessarily know about or judge if you do. And in my younger days before I was married, we sometimes went out socially chasing women. These relationships formed at the poker table or on the golf course certainly did not include an endorsement, approval, or personal involvement in whatever other activities, nefarious or wholesome, a person may engage in in the outside world.

The common ground is that we enjoy a challenge, and like just about everyone else, we love to gamble—though to different degrees. My game happens to be poker, and some golf too. Other people may like sports betting, bingo, slots, the lottery, or whatever catches their fancy. I do a lot of my gambling in a cardroom; some people choose business, or real estate, or whatever they do. Everyone has his own preferences. That's why they make chocolate and vanilla.

I don't choose who sits down to play with me. I'm just there to play and I'm happy to accommodate anyone willing to risk his or her money at poker, my game of choice. Fact is, I like action. It's a common trait among many people. It just happens that some folks like action more than others. You usually find these kinds of people at the poker table. They've got a name for this, too: compulsive gamblers. I'm convinced that most all the top professional poker players are compulsive gamblers, including me. The good ones, well, we just figure out how to win.

Gamblers are renowned for making crazy bets. Now, you might think that if anyone would know better, it would be the professionals themselves. But we just can't help ourselves.

I once played a poker tournament in Australia while making side bets on Wimbledon tennis on TV. I bet on a loser. Come to find out, we were watching a delayed telecast of the tournament, which was being played halfway around the world and had been over for hours. I don't know if the people I was betting with knew that or not, but I sure didn't. And I lost.

Telling that story brings a smile to my face. You see, I'm a gambler—now and then, you just end up in situations like that; it goes with the territory.

It's like Puggy Pearson used to say about Jack Straus: "Ol' Straus would bet on a cockroach race!"

And I might be the person betting against him!

Poker players are an eclectic group of oddballs that also tend to be eccentric. I suppose there is no more accurate way to describe this particular fraternity of individuals. Take this guy I know, Brian Zembic. Zembic was a character unlike any I'd seen. Gamblers will do just about anything to win a bet and Brian proved that with one of the craziest bets I'd ever heard of. One guy bet him $100,000 that he wouldn't get breast implants and leave them in for an entire year. Brian accepted the bet and won it. If that's not odd enough, consider this: Zembic chose to keep the 38C breast implants in place at the end of the bet because, he said, the girls loved the implants and he was having the time of his life.

Sounded kind of sick to me.

One friend bet him $14,000 that he couldn't remain holed up in a bathroom for thirty straight days. Zembic could have his meals brought in and was permitted to have a pillow and a blanket for sleeping. As soon as the bet was finalized, Brian entered the bathroom only to discover that his buddy had arranged for his friends to use that bathroom for *all* their daily functions. Still, Brian stuck it out for the thirty days and won the bet.

That also sounded sick.

Zembic had been carrying on about what a great ping-pong player he was, but I knew a dealer down at the Bellagio who I liked for this bet. I bet Zembic $25,000 on the match. My man had been the national champion some years before, and you would think he could beat just about anyone. At least I did. But he didn't beat Zembic. Seems that Brian was the Canadian champion and was in better form. They were both great players, and it was really something to watch.

Brian told me later that he should have received odds on our ping-pong wager because he was handicapped. "The breasts got in the way of my swing!" he said.

One of the guys I liked to bet with was Huckleberry Seed, the 1996 World Series of Poker champion. One of Huck's siblings is named Cotton, another is Caraway. Huck is a professional poker player from Montana, and he loves proposition bets, especially oddball ones. I figure Huck must have died and gone to heaven when he moved to Vegas and found the rest of us ready and willing partners for all his craziness.

Like Zembic, he is a little "different."

Huck was a pretty good runner, so we had a lot in common besides gambling. We made a series of athletic bets, including one in which he claimed he could run a 4:40 mile. Being an ex-miler and knowing how difficult that was to do without proper training, I jumped at the bet. To his credit, Huck came close, running a 4:47 mile.

I was up about $100,000 on various bets against Huck when he proposed a $25,000 wager that his brother could run a 4:15 mile. I snapped that one up, too. So Huck brings his brother from Montana into Vegas and I meet them at a high school track on the south side of town. Word had gotten around on this bet and the track was packed with half the gambling community; they had gathered to watch and bet on the proceedings. My friend Ted Forrest showed up and wanted to bet me $5,000 on Huck's brother, claiming he just wanted some action. That got me suspicious, so I told him if he just wanted some action he could have $5,000 of my bet with Huck. Ted didn't buy into that.

I looked across the track and saw why. There's Huck's brother warming up, and he looked like a deer. I mean he had a beautiful stride. And he had brought a good miler with him as a pacer. Sure enough, the guy ran an outstanding 4:12.

Another time, Huck bet a poker player named John Hennigan, an action junky, that Hennigan couldn't spend six weeks in casino-free Des Moines, Iowa, without leaving the city limits. I knew John was too antsy to last and I would have taken a piece of that bet if I had known about it. Well, Hennigan figured he could work on his golf game during that time, but after two days, he was going batty and couldn't stand another minute. He paid off the bet and fled Iowa as fast as he could.

Huck once made a big bet that he could play four rounds of golf in one day, shoot under 100 on each round and do it on one of the hottest days of the year without benefit of a cart. He would do all this using only three clubs, a 5-iron, a sand wedge, and a putter. The kicker was that because he shot a 100 on one of the first rounds, he had to play an extra eighteen holes. He won the bet.

Huck made a bet against Phil Hellmuth Jr. that he could stand submerged up to his shoulders in the Pacific Ocean for eighteen straight hours. He didn't realize how cold the ocean was, and even with a wetsuit on, Huck didn't last more than three hours.

I've always loved golf as a gambling sport, a game that even today I can't resist playing when there's big money on the line—even though I'm not too mobile nowadays. But golf wasn't the only sport I'd play: I'd gamble on most everything, regardless of any physical limitations. One of the sports I always liked was tennis. I won't say I was very good at it, but when there's money on the line, I feel like I've got an edge. Especially when it's big money.

One of the more unusual characters I ran across at the poker table, Eduardo Sabol, was a Peruvian obsessed with gambling on tennis. Eduardo owned a big manufacturing company in Peru and he loved to gamble. Loved the action. He played baccarat and craps around Las Vegas and started playing in our poker games. What was unusual, at least among poker players, was that he also wanted to gamble on tennis. As luck would have it, Jack Binion and I had started playing tennis. Neither one of us looked capable of pinging the ball back and forth—no one was going to accuse me of being slim and Jack wasn't the most athletic-looking person I'd ever met—but in our usual excessive manner, we'd go play nonstop for hours on end and gamble for thousands of dollars. And we finally got a little better.

I was still pretty amateurish when I played Eduardo, but he wasn't very good either. Like me, he just loved to gamble. He was a lot younger and very fast on his feet, but I could serve pretty well. Because of my bum leg I was somewhat limited in movement so I'd rush to the net immediately and either win or lose the point right away. We bantered back and forth for a while, set up our wagers, and finally decided to hit the courts.

Eduardo and I squared off in something of an historic tennis match. We played $10,000 a game and $50,000 per set. But because of my leg, it turned out that I couldn't play singles for very long, so we played just one set. I beat him 6 to 3. And I won $80,000, a pretty good amount in those days. It was a great match and I was pretty proud of my win.

I think this match occurred early in January, which likely made me, at that time, the leading money winner for the year in tennis, a claim I could probably also make in golf, given all the gambling I did on the greens as well. I always laughed about this one: If someone came to meet the great and versatile athlete who was the leading money winner on *both* the tennis courts and golf greens, they might be a touch surprised to find a somewhat immobile three-hundred-plus pound man with a bum leg.

Eduardo returned to Peru, where his life took an unexpected turn for the worse. He went from being very rich and one of the highest gamblers in Vegas, to being very poor. I heard that he lost his factory in Peru during a time of government instability.

I also heard that what money he had left he lost gambling.

✪✪✪✪✪

One year during the World Series of Poker I made an outrageous golf bet with Howard Lederer and Huck Seed, but the wager itself wasn't as crazy as the circumstances. My good friend, Mike Sexton, a commentator on the World Poker Tour, would be my partner against them. I hadn't played golf in years because of my bum leg and knee surgery, and I couldn't walk without crutches. Well, Howard and Huck had been playing a lot of golf, and they'd been trying to lure me into a bet.

As everybody in the poker world knows, that wouldn't be too hard to do.

"Okay," I told them. "I'll take Sexton as my partner in a scramble, but you'll have to let us play from the red tees, the ladies' tees."

In a scramble, both players hit a shot and then play the best one. We agreed to a $20,000 Nassau at the TPC Summerlin golf course. With an automatic two-down press on both nines, we'd be playing for potentially $100,000. They figured they had the "nuts," a cinch bet, and they were chiding me the next day for accepting the wager. But I knew that the tee-box advantage would be difficult for them to overcome.

"If you think you've got the nuts, double the bet to $40,000," I said. They doubled.

When I got to thinking, I told Mike we'd better go out and see what we could shoot. Like me, Mike hadn't played in years. The next day, we shot a 76, which is a wretched scramble score, especially from the red tees.

"I can't believe we're this bad," I told Mike. "We're gonna get killed. I've got to get us out of this bet."

Back at the poker table the next day, I hinted at offing the match. "What do you guys want to do with this bet?"

Howard and Huck were indignant, insisting the bet was on.

"I'll tell you what," I said. "You can either double the bet or cancel it."

They doubled it to $80,000.

Mike seemed a mite worried, but he assured me he could improve with practice.

"I'll go to Florida and train with Harold Henning," he said, Henning being a friend of his on the Senior PGA Tour.

I flipped him a couple of $5,000 chips for expenses.

When Mike returned two weeks later, a friend of mine watched him play and told me, "Doyle, you've got the nuts."

The next day, I told Howard and Huck my knee hurt and offered again to cancel the match or double the bet. They doubled it to $160,000; we could now win or lose as much as $800,000. Actually, I had given Mike a freeroll, so I could win $800,000 or lose $1.6 million on a single round of golf!

Game day rolled around after the WSOP, and you'd have thought this was a championship match. All the gamblers turned out, following the game in carts while wagering millions of dollars among themselves.

And half that action was on a guy that could barely walk!

Mike and I jumped out to an early lead, but we were down one stroke after our bogey at the fifteenth hole. On the sixteenth, it got worse. They had an easy six-footer for birdie and we were fifty feet out. Mike went first and missed.

I remember it getting real quiet as I gripped my putter and put it in motion. As soon as I hit the ball, I knew I had hit it good. The ball disappeared in the hole and everybody just went crazy, like a scene from a movie. I think that shot demoralized Howard and Huck. We won the final two holes and $320,000 for the day.

But I paid a steep price for the victory. The game temporarily wrecked what was left of my knee, and I couldn't play golf again for years.

○○○○○

During my old Exchange Avenue days, a pal named J.J. Donahue and I bet a local businessman named Slim that he couldn't walk the twenty-five or so miles from downtown Fort Worth to the Dallas city limits without stopping. The requirement was that he had to make the trek carrying a one hundred-pound sack of cement. Slim was a big man, about six-foot-two and 230 pounds. Most mornings, he devoured a pound of bacon, six eggs, and a loaf of whole wheat toast for breakfast.

Slim won the bet, but he died of a heart attack at age fifty.

I've seen, participated in, and heard about a lot of crazy bets in my lifetime, but I think the one Johnny Moss took on in his earlier years, has to be craziest one of all—even more so than Zembic and his breast implants—because this one nearly cost Moss his life. I remember hearing about Moss getting into a fight in San Diego against a huge guy who was heard bragging in a bar that he had never lost a fight. This tough bar fighter had supposedly won one hundred fights and lost none. I'd say that's a pretty outstanding record, but apparently, Moss wasn't impressed.

Moss was with some friends and, of course, they were always looking for some kind of bet. They offered Moss $15,000 to $1,000 that he couldn't knock the man out. The bar fighter, of course, didn't know about the bet. Moss got in close to the bar fighter and sucker-punched him, but unfortunately, the man was as tough as advertised. He also didn't appreciate the surprise punch and when he got over the shock of the sudden attack, he beat the living daylights out of his assailant. Johnny ended up a bloody mess with multiple broken bones. He was rushed to the hospital in critical condition.

Puggy Pearson, who loved prop bets and once lost a four hundred-yard race for $500 with my eight-year-old son Todd, was stupefied.

"You're crazy!" he told Moss. "Why'd you make that bet?"

"Fifteen to one was too good to pass up," Moss said.

Chapter 33

*Be who you are and say what you feel—because those that matter
don't mind and those that mind don't matter.*

Memories have a way of catching up with you. They sure did for
me in 2000, when I ran into my old college girlfriend, Ann Falls,
the only woman I was ever serious about other than Louise. Our
paths crossed quite unexpectedly at Hardin-Simmons when my childhood
and college friend Riley Cross was inducted into the university's Hall of
Fame. Ann looked great, like she was in her forties, and we talked about
those glorious college days.

While it was real nice to see Ann and know that she was doing good, it
brought back bittersweet memories of my sporting achievements at HSU.
I was real proud of Riley for getting inducted into the Hall of Fame, but at
the same time, it kindled some of my anger at the hypocrisy of the school.
Here I was, one of the most accomplished athletes at HSU, and I was being
completely shunned because of my gambling background. Meanwhile, my
two college buddies Riley and D.C. were now enshrined.

Of course, my hometown and my university were in the middle of
the Bible Belt and everyone had strict moral values. HSU wasn't very
appreciative of my poker playing, but they tolerated it because of my
sports accomplishments. But that didn't seem to matter—or at least their
memories got short—when it came to getting into their Hall of Fame.

Later on when I received some publicity for my World Series of Poker
wins, rather than gaining respect from people I knew back home or from
HSU, I got shunned. People I went to school with actually walked across
the street to keep from speaking to me. It bothered me plenty back then;
having people look down on me was a bitter pill to swallow. They seemed
to think I was a gangster and had done something disgraceful.

I never really understood the widespread stigma attached to poker
players, especially by Texans, even after I moved to Las Vegas. They
didn't call us "poker players." They called us "gamblers." Most people

assumed that if we were gamblers or poker players, we also had to be underworld figures, or at least involved in some kind of illegal activities such as drugs or prostitution. My sister Lavada sort of looked on poker players that way.

"You spend too much time watching reruns of all those TV gangsters in *The Untouchables*," I told her.

Like other poker players, I often encountered the stigma issue. It was ironic that some of the same people who wanted nothing to do with me in my Texas Circuit days would call me when they came to Las Vegas. They said they'd love to see me and go to dinner and all that stuff. I generally brushed them off. I was courteous, but I couldn't erase the memories of their blackballing me, looking down the tips of their noses at me.

On the flip side, I appreciated even more my true friends, the guys and gals in Sweetwater like Gary Austin, Van Baucum, Jerry Lawrence, Clyde Hollingsworth, Doris Welch, and of course Riley Cross. Their attitude was simple. "Playing poker is just what Doyle does. So what?" I was thankful for their support; it meant a great deal to me.

I learned that coping with the stigma was part of being a professional poker player. When I moved to Las Vegas, I realized what a wonderful atmosphere the city had. We didn't have to worry about the adversity and dangers of the Texas Circuit, about getting robbed or arrested, or collecting the money when we won. For those of us who had gone through the hijackings and the police busts, the rip-offs by cops, sheriffs, and bail bondsmen, Vegas was poker paradise, Tony Spilotro characters aside.

I never saw anything wrong with gambling. The only time I felt a tinge of guilt was when we played with the working class, the guys that pumped gas in the service stations or sold shoes at the local store. They didn't make much money, and they didn't have any business gambling for sizeable stakes. But then again, that was their decision to make. I didn't force or encourage them to gamble, they made the decision to come to the games and play—I just happened to be a better player and won their money. Even so, I thought our poker games were nowhere as bad or corruptive as the slot machines and lotteries. At least in poker, players have a fair shot at winning, and the playing field was level.

Though it was a real blast seeing all my old schoolmates at my college reunion and reliving the great times we had together—and I was real proud of Riley—still, my exclusion from the HSU Hall of Fame kind of stung and reopened some old wounds.

✪✪✪✪✪

Three years later, I invited my whole basketball team to a fifty-year reunion at my home in Las Vegas. Surprisingly, all but two of the twenty-five players were still alive. Given our ages, that was pretty amazing. Twenty-two showed up at my home; this was *fifty* years after we'd had our championship season in the Border Conference. We were among the elite sixteen teams that comprised the NCAA basketball tournament at that time. My old teammates had become educators and preachers and businessmen. None of them played poker, and that's what you'd expect. Hardin-Simmons has deep Baptist roots, and I'm betting I was the only one who turned out to be a professional gambler in the history of the school. I was the black sheep of the university.

But the reunion made up for just about everything else. It turned out to be one of the fondest experiences of my life, and we scheduled a return engagement in late 2008. I remember thinking at our first reunion that the feeling of power I get at the poker table is like the feeling I got when I was playing basketball with these guys. It was crunch time. I had to perform, to accomplish, to make something happen. We all reminisced about that championship season, and time stood still.

The winning basket, the winning game—it all came back to us.

Book IV
Further Adventures

★

Chapter 34

*Poker language is funny. Fat chance and slim chance
mean the same thing.*

It seems that when I stop playing poker for any length of time, I have
actual physical withdrawals—I get weak, dizzy, fatigued, depressed,
and it makes me wonder about my health—but when I start playing
again, the symptoms disappear. It's something about this need for constant
action me and my fellow gamblers have, and outsiders are often surprised
at the lengths and risks we'll take to get our fill. Take me, for example. I
always need a bet in play, and usually, it's got to be multiple bets or I feel
unfulfilled.

One time I was in Reno at the Amarillo Slim Super Bowl of Poker
actually trying to lose my dwindling chips in a tournament so that I could
fully concentrate on an unbelievable deuce-to-seven side game with easy
players and slots of cash. With at least several hours more before the
tournament would finish, I couldn't pass up this opportunity and sat down
to play. Meanwhile, I was forfeiting blinds and antes in the tournament.
Every once in a while, I would come running over to the tournament game
and bet all my money in the dark. But every time I did that, I won. Then I'd
leave and go back to play in the side game for fifteen or twenty minutes.
Then back to the tournament game, where I'd play a few hands. I'd catch
some kind of a hand, move in with it and, incredibly, win another pot. To
an outsider, I probably looked like a country chicken with its head cut off,
but I kept winning in both games.

Finally, we got down to just three tables in the tournament and I had
accumulated quite a large amount of chips. I was well positioned to go all
the way. Looking at that big pile of first-place money, $265,000 in large
bills, really caught my attention and I withdrew from the cash game and
concentrated on the tournament. I made it to the final table, got heads up
with the final opponent, and eliminated him, winning the $265,000 and a

matching pair of silver-plated shotguns. I also won a Chevrolet Blazer that I drove back home.

Another time, at the World Series, I was running back and forth between a preliminary tournament game and a huge live game. I won that tournament too. That time, however, I didn't get a Blazer, just the cash.

And if you think some minor health ailments will slow a gambler down, think again. It seems only death will stop us from getting our bets in play. A gambler might do any crazy thing to either win a bet or stay in action. It's just part of how we're made up.

One of my favorite stories of how serious a gambler takes his action concerns Johnny Moss. Moss played for several days with us and I could see he wasn't feeling too good. He was a bit sluggish and his color wasn't right. I was keeping an eye on him when suddenly, in the middle of a hand, he just keeled over. We got an ambulance right away and didn't know what would become of him.

Like the poker players we were, we got back to the game.

Later that evening, the game was still going and we were shocked when Moss showed up and took an empty seat.

"It was only a *mild* heart attack," he explained.

Knowing Moss, it didn't overly surprise me to see him back in the game.

Another of my favorite stories illustrating a gambler's commitment to a bet involved Joe Bernstein and, surprisingly, it had nothing to do with cheating. Joe suffered a heart attack one night during a blackjack game at the Horseshoe, slumped in his chair, and fell on the floor. He was just lying there and moaning. The people at the table continued playing the hand, as if nothing had happened.

One of his friends at the table finally leaned over, showed Joe his cards and said, "What do you want to do with your hand?"

"What's the dealer got up?" Joe asked in a croaky voice.

"He's got a king up," said his friend.

"Hit me," Joe said.

When it came to the ability to ignore distraction, perhaps no one rivals my good friend Dewey Tomko. Dewey is an unusual fellow; at least I've never met anyone quite like him, which is saying something given the crowd I've hung out with. A one-time kindergarten teacher in Florida, Dewey never ate anything except toast and eggs, cheeseburgers, and pizzas until he was forty years old.

"Well, haven't you ever tasted a baked potato?" I asked him once.

"No, not one," he said.

"Ever eaten a steak?"

"No."

"Fish?"

"I wouldn't eat one of those things," he said.

We were at a Chinese buffet one night at the Horseshoe. I filled my plate up with sweet and sour pork and then sat down with Dewey and Jack Binion.

Dewey studied my plate, and said, "What's that?"

"Sweet and sour pork," I said.

"Man, that does look good," he said. "What's in it—chicken?"

Dewey's got a heart of gold and would help anybody, but he lives in his own world. If he's not interested in something, he figures it's a waste of time studying it, especially when it might intrude on his poker focus.

He had another rather unusual habit, which I often thought contributed to his occasional naiveté. Dewey wouldn't watch television, wouldn't watch the news, and wouldn't read newspapers.

One time I asked him why.

"Because there's nothing but bad news on those things."

Dewey might have been naïve, but then again, he might have been more perceptive than the rest of us. Whatever Dewey's real or perceived shortcomings, golf wasn't among them. He was close to being a scratch golfer, even though he said he wasn't.

Dewey reminded me of Corky McCorquodale, one of the rounders I played with on the Texas Circuit. Corky was so intensely focused on poker to the exclusion of everything else that he sometimes forgot what month it was or who the sitting president might be. In other words, he was not unlike a lot of poker players, then and today. Corky had a rather attractive wife who had many fetching attributes, but an appreciation of gambling economics wasn't among them. One night she burst into our poker game and headed straight toward her startled husband.

"Damn you, Felton McCorquodale," she screamed, "there you go getting drunk and losing all our money again!"

She then proceeded to whack him in the head with her purse as we scrambled back from the table. We watched from a safe distance as she flailed away at poor Corky, who had beat a hasty retreat under the table. We didn't dare laugh or say a word, and of course, we didn't lift a hand to help poor Corky, who was curled up in a ball trying to protect his head. But it was pretty funny, at least for us. After his wife scooped up a fistful of cash and stormed off, he crawled out from under the table with his hair sticking up like a couple of birds had run through it, and sat down like nothing had happened.

"Gentlemen," he said nonchalantly, "deal me in."

I suspected Corky's pride was hurting, though not quite as much as his head.

The incredible commitment and exceptional ability to focus on a game that some poker players possess is both extraordinary and, sometimes, outright bizarre. Some guys just live in a bubble, insulated from the world around them—be it family, where they parked their car, or when they last ate. One friend of mine was so focused on his game that he had no idea what was going on in the world. He asked me one day, "Doyle, who is this Saddam Hussein?" This was during the Desert Storm war with Iraq in the early nineties. This friend is the same one who asked, "What's the difference between Sweden and Switzerland?" and, "Is the Isle of Man close to the water?"

He was serious.

These poker players are smart people, but they just live exclusively in a poker world. They can calculate pot odds computer-fast in their heads without even consciously thinking about it, but grasping the nuances of geography or current events can befuddle them. A guy I knew couldn't always remember the names of all his kids, especially after a couple of beers.

I told him he might want to focus on his family a little more.

Chapter 35

There are three rules for success:
First, keep going; second, keep going; third, keep going.

From 1999 to 2001, the World Series of Poker events came and went without my participation. I hated not playing, but I felt like I had no choice. When Jack Binion, who took over as principal owner of the Horseshoe after Benny died in 1989, got into a dispute over control of the Horseshoe with his sister, Becky Binion Behnen, I got dragged into things. Not directly, but being Jack was my best friend, it had a big effect on my feelings about playing in the WSOP. Jack had continued to run things more or less the way it had been for years. I'd go down there to visit him, and of course, I'd play every spring when the Series was running. Every time I entered the Horseshoe, I couldn't help but glance at the booth where Benny used to hold court. I'd get this empty feeling looking over there and not finding him.

To settle their differences, Jack unhappily ended up selling his interest, and Becky was left in charge of the Horseshoe. Naturally, I sided with Jack and refused to play in the WSOP for three years. I didn't feel right playing with Jack no longer being a part of the casino. So many memories over so many years had happened at Binion's—it just wasn't the same for me without Benny, and now without Jack.

It was a hard decision to make, because I'd played in every one since its inception in 1970, about thirty years. I had won my eighth bracelet in the $1,500 Seven-Card Razz event in 1998, my first one since 1991, and was the current all-time money winner, which made it extra hard to not play.

There was also another consideration in my tough decision to boycott the WSOP during the dispute with Becky: Jack's wife Phyllis, a wonderful friend who helped my family through some of our darkest moments. She is a great cook, a perfect hostess, a world traveler, and wealthy in her own right. I liked that Phyllis said exactly what she thought, which is a trait

I've always admired in people. I realized she was someone I could ask a question and know I'd get an honest answer. She also had issues with the Behnen family. We became good friends right away and we really cemented that friendship when she and I conspired against Jack to get a swimming pool built at her house.

During the intervening years of the dispute, it was hard to sit back and watch while the World Series was being played, but I consoled myself by engaging heavily in the side games.

In early 2002 I asked Jack if he thought I should participate in the World Series, as I knew he'd made some kind of peace with Becky. Jack said, "Sure, go ahead." I had badly missed playing the tournament that had become such an important part of my life for all those years, twenty-nine in a row by 1998.

I was the only one who'd played the WSOP every year.

I didn't get very far in the Main Event, but I know that a lot of players were both surprised and pleased to see me back. After all that time, playing every year, I suppose I had become a fixture at Binion's come springtime. It just wasn't right without me—I certainly felt that way, and more than a few players told me that's how they felt too.

In 2003, feeling that new poker players were passing me by in the bracelet count, I surprised a bunch of folks by entering the preliminary events as well, something I hadn't done the previous year. I did well, winning the $2,500 H.O.R.S.E event and my ninth gold bracelet. The $84,080 prize money was nice, too, but the side bets were even more profitable. Chip had given me 10 to 1 against winning a bracelet on a $25,000 bet. People that saw me smiling when I picked up the prize money were only about 25 percent correct on the money end if they thought the winnings were satisfying; 75 percent of that smile was reserved for the $250,000 I had won from Chip.

Despite my happiness at picking up another bracelet, one disturbing trend was apparent in poker; it looked like the game was dying out in cardrooms in Vegas and around the country. As 2002 rolled around into 2003, fewer games were being spread and cardrooms were being phased out to give extra space to more profitable casino games, particularly slots and video poker machines. Entries in the Main Event of the WSOP in 2002 had inched up slightly from the year before, from 613 players to 621 players, but one cardroom after another in Vegas was closing down. People just weren't playing that much. It seemed like the people in the mainstream had reverted to perceiving poker as an old man's game played in smoky backrooms.

The future of public poker wasn't looking too good.

But in 2003, three remarkable events changed the landscape of poker—and my life along with it.

The first occurred during the 2003 World Series when an unknown accountant from Tennessee named Chris Moneymaker won the Main Event. I thought it was a pretty interesting story given that his name was so unusual. The cheap qualifying events that the Internet poker sites sponsored had fed truckloads of players into the tournaments. That's how Moneymaker got there—he turned a $40 satellite entry into $2.5 million. Moneymaker's win was a big story, one that inspired millions of poker players, throwing kindling into a raging fire. Every amateur looked at Moneymaker and said to himself: "That could be me."

And indeed, they were right.

Winning the Main Event was not just a pipe dream, because *anyone* could win it and, like Moneymaker, ride a dream into stardom and riches.

The second event that greatly increased the popularity of the game was the precipitous growth in Internet poker. Players anywhere and everywhere in the world could log on to their favorite poker site and play from home. The technology had advanced such that it was easy for people to gamble in their pajamas. Hundreds of thousands of players, and soon millions, began to do just that. The jolt provided by Moneymaker, a player who qualified for the Main Event online and went all the way to win the championship, was enormous.

The third event that changed everything was the launch of the World Poker Tour on the Travel Channel. Though the first WPT tournament was played in late May 2002 at the Bellagio, less than a week after the 2002 World Series of Poker Main Event had concluded, the actual premiere of the TV show debuted almost a year later, on March 31, 2003. I didn't think much of the idea when Lyle Berman approached me and Chip when he was looking for investors in this new proposition—staging poker tournaments and televising them in the United States and around the world. Lyle and WPT co-founder Steve Lipscomb thought we'd be the perfect guys to approach for this idea. I couldn't find fault with that logic, but the other part of the logic was what eluded me: "Who would want to watch us play poker on TV?"

We listened to their novel presentation, but I was so gun shy from failed investments that I turned it down. Chip did too.

How ironic. There I was, all my life taking shots at shaky investments having nothing to do with poker, many of them doomed from the get-go. Finally one comes my way with the right people behind it, with the right vision, at the right time, involving the right game—my game—and I turn it down! Life's strange and so are the choices that people make. You never know what the next deal brings. Sometimes you play hands and wish you hadn't. And sometimes you throw away hands, only to see a perfect flop, and you wished you'd stuck around to enjoy it.

That's one flop I sure wish I'd stuck around for.

The World Poker Tour became a raging success. This new breed of televised poker transformed the game into a national obsession. Even viewers who didn't know how to play began watching the WPT poker shows on the Travel Channel. Everyone was transfixed by the odd characters that participated, the massive amounts of money they were winning, and the excitement generated by the innovative lipstick cam—a camera built into the table that revealed the players' hole cards to the viewers. Now the viewers knew something the players didn't. This made for great reality TV.

At first, the pros weren't too keen on revealing their cards to the cameras and letting people know how they played their hands. But we all got used to it, and with the massive upside brought on by television, it was a small sacrifice to make for all the notoriety and money it brought into the game—and directly into our pockets as well.

Chris Moneymaker's victory, Internet poker, and the launch of the WPT had come together in some sort of perfect storm that catapulted poker to unprecedented heights. Poker began enjoying a popularity it had never before seen.

Our game entered a new era, and we just had to evolve along with it. What I didn't see then, but came to realize soon enough, was how this explosion in popularity would affect not only my life but also the entire game. Main Event participation had been growing steadily—in 2003 there were 831 players in it, up from 639 the year before—and now it began to skyrocket. The 2004 Main Event tripled to 2,576 and then doubled again in 2005 to 5,619 players. What had happened to poker was mind-boggling. Interest in the game was springing up everywhere. I could hardly believe what was going on.

After seeing the WPT's success, ESPN jumped on the bandwagon and expanded its coverage of the WSOP and, before anyone knew what had hit them, poker became a national obsession. Magazines sprung up all over the place, instructional poker books were being published by the thousands, and tournaments were being run every day of the week in Las Vegas. But it wasn't just Las Vegas where legal action could be found. The Internet had become a hotbed of poker with millions of players competing all over the world.

All these sunglass-wearing oddballs and eccentrics I had been playing poker with for years, guys that no one would take a second look at—except to check that their wallet was still where it belonged—suddenly became celebrities on national television.

Coinciding with all this interest in poker was the re-release of *Super/System*. Mike Caro introduced me to Cardoza Publishing, the biggest gaming publisher in the world. Cardoza was based in New York and seemed to have a pretty good handle on the business, so I went along with Caro's advice. The company had a lot of good gambling and poker titles and also published the Mad Genius' books so I decided to give it a try. I figured a few more sales with the better distribution they promised wouldn't hurt. We struck a deal to get *Super/System* into paperback for the first time and distribute it into mainstream bookstores around the country with a $29.95 price tag. It was the first time the book had ever been sold for less than $50.

I didn't think much would happen, but brother, did I underestimate the forces at work and the power of national distribution. The timing was perfect. The first printing sold out in weeks and the second printing wasn't even off the press before the third printing was ordered. As the poker boom exploded in 2003, sales really took off and we were moving twelve thousand books a week, with some weeks reaching fifteen thousand copies or more. The book reached #1 on Amazon worldwide and shot up to #1 on the *New York Times* best-seller list for how-to books.

I'd always thought of myself as a poker player, and now I was a best-selling author as well!

The original edition of *Super/System*, which I had titled *How I Made Over $1,000,000 Playing Poker,* became a collector's item, selling for $500 and $600 on Ebay. I even saw an original signed copy going for $2,500!

It was amazing how much had changed in such a short time, but all this activity was only the tip of the iceberg. Prior to the 2003 poker boom, my gambling life had revolved around the cash games mostly, and in the spring, the World Series of Poker tournaments, plus lots of high-stakes golf. Of course, I found plenty of occasions for sports betting and prop bets. Mostly though, I was Doyle Brunson, poker player. But when the boom hit, I was pulled in so many directions at the same time—between cash games, all the new tournaments that were springing up everywhere, and business propositions that kept coming in from every direction—sometimes I could hardly think straight. With all this activity, life as I knew it really changed.

I became Doyle Brunson, businessman—not that plenty of gambling wasn't also involved.

★ Chapter 36

There is never a wrong time to do the right thing.

I've been very heavy most of my adult life, but being overweight didn't really strike home with me because I was able to move about swiftly enough, golf with a low handicap, and stay active. But when I turned seventy, I realized my legs weren't carrying me well. In fact, my bad leg was giving me extra trouble with all the extra pounds I was carrying and it hurt to walk, let along play golf. Along with my age, or at least in combination with it, all that weight was becoming an increasingly difficult burden, so I started considering my options for removing pounds from my frame. Of course, trying to shake up some big bets as an incentive was one of them—I could always find takers. But as I thought more about it, maybe that wasn't the best idea. My weight loss bets were legendary in the poker world and I seemed to lose most of them. Word around the cardrooms was that they were among the easiest props to win. And I suppose they were. I just loved to eat; and while I had a powerful willpower for many things, dieting wasn't one of them.

Most everyone I was around knew that.

Some years back, Chip, who was also heavy at the time, and I made a serious decision to lose some weight. There's a health spa a few miles outside St. George, Utah, and Chip and I decided to visit there a while and improve our dietary habits. We were determined to lose big pounds during our stay and return to Las Vegas as new, lighter, healthier men. It was an expensive spa, and we paid a month in advance, about $6,000 each. It was baseball season and we were betting a lot of games so we installed a $4,000 satellite system in our rooms where we could sweat the games. We felt it was well worth it. Just because we were in gastronomic jail didn't mean we couldn't enjoy our other earthly pleasures and do some betting on the side.

The next day we went to all their exercise classes, even the swimming classes. We ate all our meals at the cafeteria where the diet food they served was reasonably good.

That second night, Chip asked me if I had noticed the Sizzler Restaurant where we turned off the highway. When I said yes, he suggested that we go eat our last meal there before we really got into this diet. Naturally, I said okay and almost beat him out the door to get there. We got to Sizzler and knocked a hole in their salad bar. We also ordered two or three entrees each. I mean, we gorged ourselves. I don't think that restaurant had ever seen anything like it, at least judging by the looks on the employees' faces. When we finished, Chip looked at me, and I looked at him. Without a word being said, we got in his new BMW and drove 120 miles per hour back to Las Vegas.

We laughed about that many times afterward because we never attempted to recover any of our money from the spa or that $4,000 satellite system.

One of my many weight-loss bets was against Chip. We often tried to get the better of one another while improving our health habits at the same time. We once bet $50,000 on who could lose the most weight over a certain number of months, and somehow the newspapers got hold of that story. Chip promptly gained about seventeen pounds and some reporter at the *Washington Post* thought that was a pretty interesting insight into the lives of gamblers. I suppose it was. The newspaper said it proved how little $50,000 means in Las Vegas.

While eating was a temptation I could hardly resist, and I lost bet after bet over the years, I didn't lose *all* my bets concerning weight, or concerning my limited physical abilities because of those extra pounds. I did win a few of them here and there.

When I was forty-five years old and weighed three hundred pounds, I was playing poker one night at Caesar's Palace when the conversation turned to doing sit-ups.

"I bet I could do five," I said.

"Doyle, you couldn't do one," said Roger Moore, a future Poker Hall of Famer. It was true I hadn't done sit-ups in years, but I had done as many as three hundred sit-ups at a time back in college. Roger had noticed that between my excessive weight and bum knee, I had a great deal of trouble walking.

However, I reckoned I still had a bunch of sit-ups left in me, my excess weight notwithstanding.

"How much you want to bet?" I asked.

Roger had $64,000 in front of him and pushed it across the table. I was afraid if I pounced on that big a bet, he would back off.

"No," I said, "not that much. How about $20,000?"

"Done!"

I got down on the floor and acted like it was killing me to do five, but I did it. Before the night was over, I had bet Roger another $20,000 I could do twenty sit-ups. Laughing, he seized on that in a second. At a $1,000 per sit-up, it was about the quickest $20,000 I ever made.

But this next bet, which occurred some years later, was the wildest of my weight bets—and for a significantly greater sum of money. And it wasn't quite so easy as doing just a few sit-ups, which I had no problem with; in fact, I damn near starved myself to death trying to win this one.

One night, a bunch of high rollers were in town playing with some of the regulars at the Regency. I got up to go to the restroom, and I was having more trouble than usual walking on my bum leg. When I got back to the table, they were all laughing at me lumbering awkwardly around the poker room.

"I think I'm going to shed a hundred pounds," I announced defiantly, which triggered a new round of laughter.

Their laughter might have been because I'd made countless weight bets and only rarely won one. My credibility in that regard was worse than suspect. It was known that I'd lost hundreds of thousands of dollars on weight bets.

"Well," I said, even before the laughter subsided, "what will you lay me that I don't do it?"

"What do you want?" asked Lyle Berman.

Lyle not only was a cofounder of the World Poker Tour, he was the entrepreneur behind many other successful ventures, including several Indian casinos and the Rainforest Café. We were often making big bets against one another, not just at the table, but with propositions that had nothing to do with cards. That was just as true with my good friends Bobby Baldwin and Chip, as well as many other poker players. We were all gamblers with an insatiable appetite, actually an obsession, for action.

"I don't know," I replied coyly. "I'll take a hundred to one."

"Nope, but we'll lay you ten to one," Chip said

"How long I got to lose it?"

"Two years," Bobby declared.

"Okay, y'all got a bet."

I wagered about $40,000 on the spot, but it was a big, big game, and every time I won a pot, I tossed another $10,000 at one of those guys. With my track record in such bets, they snapped them up without hesitation. In fact, they'd laugh, pick up the money, blow on it and stick it in their pockets. By the end of the game, I'd wagered $100,000 to win $1 million. There were other bettors, but the main three were Bobby, Chip, and Lyle.

The first year I didn't lose an ounce. Oh, I'd drop a few pounds on the Atkins Diet here and there, but I'd quickly gain it back. And every time we met, they'd ride me unmercifully. They took extra pleasure in ordering fattening foods and desserts at the table and slowly devouring them in front of me. They weren't just counting their money, I think they'd already spent it! I finally decided to give dieting a serious shot, and I lost thirty pounds on the Atkins in about a month.

"You know, it might still be possible to win this bet," I told myself.

Then I went on an extreme Atkins diet. Instead of eating beef and cheese and stuff, I ate a lot of fish. I mean, *a lot* of fish. Louise said if I ever got off that diet, seafood restaurants all over Vegas would be closing down. She also came up with some good fish recipes herself, and suddenly my diet was both healthy and tasty—and I'd lost nearly seventy pounds with four or five months to go.

Now the guys weren't laughing so much. In fact, they got a little worried. The doorbell would ring, I'd open the door and there would be a deliveryman with candy from Chip or pizza from Lyle. Anytime I got near the Bellagio, Bobby ordered me exotic meals and made sure they delivered lots of desserts to my table.

But I handled it pretty well, and I kept exercising. I couldn't walk much because of my leg, but I did a lot of swimming. When I got to within ten pounds of the target weight, they knew I had them. I did go to my doctor to make sure my blood levels and general health were okay.

"Yeah, you're doing fine," he assured me.

So for an added incentive, I laid another guy 100 to 1 odds—$100,000 to $1,000—that I'd win my original bet. Two weeks before the deadline, I was two pounds over the target. A week later, I was still two pounds short. I didn't want to do the drastic stuff, like diuretics and starvation. We got in a big game at Sam's Town, and the main three participants of the bet were all there. They knew to the ounce my weight status.

"Tell you what, guys," I proposed magnanimously, "I'll give you a two percent rebate if you'll go ahead and agree to pay the ninety-eight percent and let me start eating right here, right now."

They huddled for a few moments and accepted my offer. It cost me $20,000, but it was worth it! I mean, I was hungry and I ate a bunch. My poker game had been deteriorating, and I blamed it on the diet because I was hungry all the time and couldn't concentrate on the game. And then at the next WPT tournament, the guys piled up my million dollars on the table, brought out a gigantic dessert tray and alerted the television folks. That's how my fat bet made national television.

A little known clause of that bet will give you an insight into gamblers. Had I chosen to have any body part surgically removed, it would have been weighed and counted against any weight that I lost. That sounded crazy, but some gamblers would do anything to win a bet. My high-rolling buddies didn't think I was that crazy, but they weren't taking chances either. I was always threatening to have my bad leg amputated, and they fretted that for a million dollars, I just might do it.

One of my spectacularly awful food bets occurred in 1969 at the Texas Gambler's Convention in Reno hosted by Tom Moore, who owned the Holiday Casino there. Tom had a standing $20,000 challenge that no one could eat a quail a day for thirty consecutive days. I'd heard about this bet, and being more than slightly proficient at eating, I decided I could do it. Well, each day that bird looked bigger and bigger. Pretty soon, it resembled a buzzard. After three weeks, I surrendered and conceded the bet. I knew I couldn't force down another quail without becoming deathly ill—and Tom's wager stipulated that throwing up was not allowed.

Then the famous pool hustler Minnesota Fats showed up at the casino and offered to make the same quail bet. Fats boasted that for $20,000, Tom could get a turkey, stuff it with quail and he would eat *that* for thirty straight days. Wary of Fats' well-earned reputation for winning food wagers, Tom declined. A wise move on Tom's part, because I had seen Fats in action back in Texas in the 1950s when he had demolished those turkeys on the Jacksboro Highway.

Food and weight bets were popular props in the poker room, where players sit around all day and night, and typically don't get much chance to exercise or take care of themselves physically. Money can make people do some strange things, especially gamblers. For $10,000, some of the guys I know would eat a diseased yak.

One comical wager involved two friends of mine. One night at the Mirage, some of the high rollers were talking about dares. Howard Lederer, a vegetarian, allowed as to how he might eat meat for $10,000. His friend David Grey shoved $10,000 in chips across the table and dared him to eat a hamburger. Howard promptly ordered a cheeseburger—loaded with onions, pickles, lettuce, and tomatoes. I guess he figured enough vegetables might help mask the fact that a bunch of meat, which he was unaccustomed to and liable to get sick from, would be entering his system.

It worked. Howard got the salad burger down, adding insult to injury by not getting sick.

Aware that David hated olives with a passion, Howard offered him a chance to get his $10,000 back. All he had to do was eat two olives. The last I heard, the olives remained uneaten, the dare unaccepted. Word has it that they were at a party later and David spotted a relish tray loaded with olives.

David nudged Howard and said, "There must be a million dollars worth of olives on that tray!"

I thought about all these crazy wagers, and my weight, and thought I had to get serious if I really wanted to lose weight. I wasn't convinced that a sizable bet would be incentive enough to drop the number of pounds I felt were necessary to lose and to keep them off. Even though I'd had a few successes through the years, there were far too many failures to count, so in late 2003, I decided to have gastric bypass surgery. This time, no bets were involved. I'd heard a lot about the procedure—I knew a bunch of poker players who had good results with it—and I decided it might be a good idea for me to try it too. A San Diego specialist, Dr. Alan Wittgrove, performed the surgery, and it worked well. I lost a lot of weight, although not a single person afterward accused me of being svelte.

I started thinking about playing and betting on golf again—and was able to walk around much better too.

Chapter 37

Don't be afraid of pressure.
Pressure is what turns a lump of coal into a diamond.

There's something about professional gamblers I can't quite explain and you kind of have to be around us to even begin to understand. We need that adrenaline rush, the tension of a big bet, and the thrill as it plays out to stay alive. Maybe we're like drug users who need that next big fix—only our fix is the action. Without the pressure of big money at risk, the bets don't hold our attention. I mean, the bets we make have to be substantial enough to where it hurts to lose or feels good to win. It's got to make our hearts pump hard; it's part of what makes our blood flow.

I thrive on the pressure, always have. Whether it was back at Hardin-Simmons taking a big shot, at the poker table bluffing with all my chips at stake, or on the greens, where a pressure putt is needed to win a bet, I play my best when the game is on the line. When big money is on the line, guys tighten up; they freeze and start playing conservatively, not loose and easy like they normally would. The pressure gets to them. I can't tell you how many times I've seen a good golfer miss shots he normally hits—all because of the money involved. They pull their swings, and their shots go wide. And then they have to shoot out of the rough.

In poker, I see the choke factor all the time. Really good players move up to stakes they're not used to and get off their game. And that's when he really gets in trouble, because he's playing where he's not comfortable.

Thing is, you have to separate yourself from the money; it can't mean anything at the time because if it does, you're going to have that in the back of your mind, weighing on you. All the top gamblers have one thing in common, a complete disregard for money. It's not that we don't respect money—I suppose we just respect it in a *different* way than everybody else. It all comes back to playing in a comfort zone that's good for you, but not so good for your opponent.

There was a time where it seemed like I'd bet everything I had, day after day. It wasn't uncommon for me to bet my whole bankroll and get broke. I've been broke so many times, and have gambled with all my money at risk so often, it didn't mean anything to me to go broke one more time. I'd always make more money somehow and get back in action. But regular guys, they don't know that feeling of having it all on the line. They're not used to it and, because of that, it affects their game.

In the early days, like today, I had a lot of gamble in me. I'd bet on just about everything if I liked the situation, and the more I had, the bigger I'd bet—whether it was poker, golf, tennis, sports betting, or anything else. I once played nine holes of golf, lost all my cash, and couldn't play the back nine because I was out of money. I had to go home. I was used to losing all my money, so it wasn't anything special when I had larger amounts at risk. I always chuckled when I heard Jack Straus explain his philosophy on gambling: "If you were supposed to hold on to money, it would have handles on it."

A lot of folks don't understand the gambler's world, and I suppose I can't blame them. We make bets beyond a normal person's comprehension. A man might work hard all year to take home $20,000, $40,000, or $100,000. I bet those kinds of sums all the time without thinking.

I used to have more money riding on a round of golf than most of the top golfing pros would make in an entire year. If you take some of those pros and put them in my game and give them the right handicap, I'll take their bets. The kind of pressure they play under in their professional lives is an entirely different type of pressure than when they've got serious money riding on the outcome. When I was in my golfing prime, I played with a lot of the top golfers, including Lee Trevino, which was always fun. I admired Lee because he was a money player. He started out as a golf hustler, and he was a great one.

I also liked what he said about pressure. He pointed out that the professional golfers talk about the pressure of sinking a ten-foot putt to win $100,000. But they're still going to win $50,000 even if they miss the putt.

"That's not pressure," Trevino said. "Pressure is when you've got a four-footer to win or lose $10 and you've only got $5 in your pocket. That's *real* pressure."

He was right.

Lee showed up and watched one year at the PGI in Vegas and he seemed genuinely impressed with the caliber of play. At least the caliber of our short game. He was amazed at the stakes we played for. "I never saw so many chip-ins and long putts made in one day in my life," he said.

I often wondered how those top pros would do in some of our high-money games. I would have played Jack Nicklaus in a heartbeat if a fair handicap could've been set. Obviously, he was much better than I was, in a different category altogether. For that matter, with a fair spot, I would've played anybody for any amount. Because of that, I developed a nationwide reputation in the golf world and got lots of high action.

A gambler will check the price of a car before buying it with personal money, but will bet $100,000 without flinching because his gut tells him to make the play. He'll toss off a $10,000 chip betting whether the flop will be all black, but might drive an extra mile to save a few cents on a gallon of gas.

That's the way it is with gamblers.

I've met plenty of poker players who thought the same way I did, but never quite like a billionaire Dallas banker and entrepreneur who showed up in Las Vegas one day and made such a stir with his craving for high-stakes action that he became the subject of countless magazine articles, national headlines, and even a book, *The Professor, The Banker, and the Suicide King* by Michael Craig. He also became the center of attention for every high-stakes player in Las Vegas, including me.

Chapter 38

Poker is not a game where the meek shall inherit the earth.

Dallas billionaire Andy Beal was the inspiration and driving force behind the biggest poker game ever played. Beal liked action. High-stakes action. That was fine with me, except that Beal had an angle—he liked to play for sums of money that would take players out of their comfort zone. I could understand a thing or two about that. But Andy turned the tables on something that was usually my strength: His limits were so high, he took me and my fellow Big Game players out of *our* comfort zone.

Which wasn't an easy thing to do.

Andy was the owner of a private bank in Big D, the Beal Bank, and also had built a spaceship—not everybody you meet can say they've built a vehicle for outer space. On a business trip to Las Vegas in February 2001, Andy wandered into the Bellagio poker room one evening because he got bored at the blackjack tables. When he decided to try his hand at poker, instead of starting at the bottom and working his way up, he chose to start at high limits. And work his way up even higher.

Here's how this whole game played out. Andy, then forty-eight years old, sat in on an $80/$160 game. He wasn't there long before a colorful, hard-drinking poker pro named Mike Laing took a seat. Laing had become part of Vegas lore during a seven-card lowball game in which he was running bad and angrily vowed to eat the next hand-killing high card the dealer dropped on him. Sure enough, up popped a king on the very next card. Mike grabbed the card, crumpled it up in his hand, and tried to swallow it!

He recovered at a hospital, but the card didn't.

Mike waved a handful of cash in Beal's direction and challenged him to flip a coin for a rack of chips worth $2,000. Andy obliged and won the toss. Mike pushed in another rack, then a third, losing twice more. He had just lost $6,000 in three quick coin flips. He challenged Beal to one more flip, double or nothing. This time he won and got back to even. Finally, they got down to the business of playing poker, only the second time Andy had ever played in a Vegas cardroom.

Beal enjoyed it and returned the next day and moved up to a $400/$800 game. He played late, until there were just two opponents left: a poker pro we called Irish and my son Todd. Andy went on a run, cleaning out Irish, who left, and continued playing Todd heads-up into the morning.

Todd and Beal agreed to meet up and play the next afternoon. Todd didn't exactly believe Beal's story about playing for much higher stakes, possibly even $10,000/$20,000—about twenty-five times higher than what they'd just played. You hear a lot of talk around a poker table and when that talk stretches a bit far, you tend to ignore it.

As Todd would soon find out, Beal wasn't stretching.

Soon, word got around about this Dallas banker. And poker players being poker players, we were all itching to get a piece of that action. I was one of them. Todd and Chip were there, along with Jennifer Harman and a bunch of other high-stakes players. The game had started at $400/$800. But at Andy's insistence, it quickly grew in limits to $1,000/$2,000, $2,000/$4,000, $3,000/$6,000, and then $4,000/$8,000. Beal then wanted to play $10,000/$20,000, which is huge.

It was higher than any of us could afford by ourselves. I gave Chip $500,000 and took 50 percent of him. He sat down with a million dollars—you needed that much to play in a game that size. Most of the other players partnered up to afford the stakes and we put together an eight-handed game. Andy won; I don't remember how much, but I do know Chip lost $850,000. I remember that distinctly, because I had to pay half of it. I have pictures of Andy sitting behind racks and racks of $5,000 chips, and he made all of us get into the picture with him. We were bleeding inside and we had to look happy for him, smiling and everything. But brother, we had just taken a beating and it hurt.

Beal returned to Dallas to attend to his affairs. When he talked again about coming back to Vegas and upping the stakes, this time Todd believed him. We did too and couldn't wait for another shot at him.

I always liked to play as high as I could get my opponent to go, but even I had my limits. And Andy quickly reached them. He proposed raising the stakes to $20,000/$40,000. Now, that was higher than any of the professionals wanted to play, including me, but Beal had one condition: he would take on only one player at a time. There were always people buzzing around in his ear saying, "You know you can't play because those guys are playing the same money and you don't have a chance." It was total bull; every one of us was playing to win. Andy had played just one time in the real big game, and several times in the smaller games, but now he wanted to play heads-up because he was afraid of collusion.

"We don't do that," I told him. "If that happens, we weed it out." But he said he felt more comfortable playing two-handed, so I said, "Okay, let's get it on."

A bunch of us pooled our money and we played on and off against Andy, one player at a time. He played us real tough, getting up as much as $5.5 million in a series of marathon poker sessions over the next days, weeks and months. Only a late run by Howard Lederer got us even. By then, near the end of 2001, Andy had had enough. He told us that he was through with poker and wouldn't play again.

But we'd been around gamblers long enough to know better, so we weren't surprised when Andy showed up in Vegas in 2003 to challenge us again. We knew he had a lot more gamble in him. The first trip he was a winner but the next couple of times Andy lost millions of dollars. That didn't faze him at all. He was determined to beat us. He went home, bought a bunch of books, studied and practiced. Then he came back for more. He was getting tougher and tougher and wanted to play higher and higher.

We settled on a $50,000/$100,000 game, a $10 million freezeout, winner keep all. These were enormous stakes, well beyond anything anyone had ever played. Losing the entire $10 million wouldn't be all that hard to do; just a small swing of luck and a few million dollars could easily change hands. After much discussion, some twenty of us pooled our money, about $500,000 each, and formed a syndicate to spread the risk. Andy was talking a lot of money, and none of us wanted to get blindsided by one bad run of cards and lose everything. We told Andy what we were doing and he agreed to it. We designated one player to play him heads-up. When that player got tired, we replaced him with another player in our syndicate.

A lot of egos were involved with all the poker players in the syndicate: I mean, everybody wanted to play, but I didn't have too many problems. I felt like I knew who the best heads-up players were, and they left it to my judgment, directing who would play, when they would play, and for how long.

Meanwhile, Andy was playing his advantage beautifully. The high stakes he demanded and that we ultimately agreed to after much negotiation put us out of our comfort zone. No one had ever played that high—or anywhere near that high. A single pot could reach $1 million, a staggering sum for a poker hand. Andy tried to push us further by insisting on early-morning games, knowing that poker players rarely stir before noon.

I suppose he didn't get to be a billionaire by accident.

When Beal got ahead $5 million, mostly against Jennifer and Todd, the group started to get nervous. For some of the players, the money invested in this game was about all the money they had. If Andy broke us, we knew he'd come back for another round and, naturally, we'd have to accept that challenge. Some of us could come up with the money, but others would be wiped out.

Andy was very aggressive. He would just bet and bet and bet and never throw his cards away, so you had to show him the best hand at the showdown—you couldn't bluff him out of the pot. Anybody that doesn't lay down his hand is liable to beat you, and that's what happened. Andy beat one player after another. I played him a little bit, but he didn't really much want to play me because of my reputation. I don't like to play heads-up anyway, so I didn't care. The other players wanted to play, and I was happy just being the captain. When a player was off his game, I'd pull him out and put another one in. It was a huge advantage for us.

The second day I chose Todd again to take on Andy. I felt he was the right guy for that round and it was the right choice: Todd won $7 million for the syndicate before Andy called it quits. The next day Todd won another $6.5 million. It was a remarkable performance that momentarily broke Andy and sent him back to Dallas a $10 million loser. We all breathed a huge sigh of relief; if we had lost, many of our syndicate members would have gone broke.

In mid-May of 2004, right in the middle of the preliminary events at the 35th World Series of Poker, Andy came back. He wanted to play heads-up $100,000/$200,000 limit hold'em—in other words, the largest stakes for a poker game in history. To put these stakes in perspective, just the opening bets on the first two rounds of betting, the preflop and flop, would be $100,000 *each*—and they would be higher if there were any raises. The latter two rounds of betting, the turn and river, would cost $200,000 per bet. If there were raises, a single round of bets could add up to $800,000—the price of a luxury home in most parts of the country. This is in a *single* betting round, not even an entire hand. Each pot could be in the millions! There was danger to the stakes Andy wanted to play. He could win $20 to $40 million and severely damage the high-stakes poker economy. Eventually, after some bickering back and forth, we agreed.

The game began the afternoon of May 12, broke for the night, resumed early the next morning, and ended the evening of the 13th. I was still feeling the effects of recent surgery and didn't play, but during the course of action Andy went heads-up against Todd, Chip, Hamid Dastmalchi, Gus Hansen, and Jennifer Harman, a murderer's row of poker pros. When the dust settled, Andy had nearly $22 million in chips in front of him, and was a $10.6 million winner. In one span, he had beaten Chip out of roughly $8 million.

It was a remarkable accomplishment and a blow to the egos and bankrolls of the syndicate pros. None of us had ever played for that kind of money. It was also no coincidence that Andy chose the time of year when all the pros were focused on the World Series events.

But like most gambling escapades, there was a sequel and it occurred just two weeks later. Andy timed his visit during the Main Event, this time for a $30,000/$60,000 game that escalated the second day to $50,000/$100,000. Todd got us ahead by $5 million the first day, and Howard Lederer won us what had to be a world-record, single-session $9.3 million the second day.

Andy said he had enjoyed the challenge immensely but probably wouldn't be playing again because of the time and travel required to keep his game at the highest level.

That's what he said.

Chapter 39

*Accept the fact that some days you are the pigeon and
some days you are the statue.*

I t's really hard nowadays, with the huge fields of players, to get to a
Main Event final table at the World Series of Poker. Even though I
have an advantage in the tournaments, against three hundred players
or even thousands, I don't figure to win. No pro does. There are just too
many pitfalls you have to avoid to even get to the final table. You always
think you have a chance to go deep in the big one, of course, and sometimes
you really believe you can win it. But at the same time, the stark reality is
that it's just not likely to happen. You have to catch a lot of breaks to get
through that many players. When you can't reach back for more chips like
you can in a cash game, the best player won't necessarily win.

But you always have that dream.

In the Main Event of the 2004 World Series of Poker, when I was
seventy years old, that dream was very much alive. There were 2,576
starting players, a huge field, making the odds of winning the whole thing
awfully long. At the time, it was the biggest tournament ever played. And
with only fifty-three players remaining, I was still in it. I was playing great
poker, and it seemed that destiny might just take me to the finish line.

A lot of people were watching, and a big part of me was thinking, "I
may do it again."

But I got knocked out on a technicality. It was at a point where I said,
"I bet. I move in."

I had put a tough decision on my opponent. He had to match a bet for
my entire stack, about $400,000, or muck his cards and forfeit all the chips
already in the middle. There was about $60,000 in antes and blinds in the
pot and I wanted to win it without a contest. I was figuring he would get
out of my way and give me the pot.

I was right—almost.

Turned out the kid didn't hear me—it was actually Bradley Berman, Lyle's son—because there was a lot of noise in the room. Spectators crowded around our table and reporters were everywhere, everyone hoping to catch a piece of history. Bradley thought I had only made a normal-sized bet, because I had only pushed a few chips out in front of me, indicating that a bet was in play.

"I'm gonna raise it," Bradley said.

"No, Doyle's already moved in," the dealer told Bradley. "You can't raise here."

"Oh, then, I'm out," Bradley said, pulling back the stack of chips he had started to push to the middle.

But there was an irregularity here, so the dealer called the floor supervisor over for a decision. You see, once you announce a bet, you have to put those chips into the pot. But with all my chips committed, no raise was possible.

"No, you said you raised. You must go ahead and call Doyle's bet," the floorperson ruled.

So, he was required to put all his money into the pot. We turned over our cards to determine the winner. I had two tens and Bradley had an A-7, a hand he wouldn't even consider playing against me. I was in the lead, more than a 2 to 1 favorite to win the hand. It appeared that I'd gotten a lucky break, not a bad break.

Then Bradley caught an ace on the flop, putting me in bad shape. The turn and the river didn't help, and since he had more chips than me, all my chips were gone—I was eliminated on a fluke. If I had won that pot, I would have been among the chip leaders and possibly gone on to win the tournament. That would have been something. But the rules were the rules and my tournament was over. I was terribly disappointed.

I got up slowly, suddenly exhausted after all those hours of play. When you get knocked out of a big tournament, especially *the* big tournament, it's a long way up from the chair to your feet, and a long way out of the tournament playing area. It's a terrible feeling to know you're no longer in it. But as bad as I felt, and I felt awful bad, one of the most gratifying moments I've ever had in a poker room occurred right then and there, and I had to do everything I could to stop tears from coming to my eyes. Spontaneously, as I got out of my chair, the players at my table stood up and began applauding. Pretty soon, all the players in the tournament got up as well and joined in.

I'd never seen anything like it. The entire room suddenly exploded in noise. Over a rousing ovation, an official grabbed the mike and announced, "Doyle Brunson has been eliminated." Tournament officials even stopped the game clock.

I tipped my hat at the crowd and, supported by my crutch, slowly walked out of the room, every eye upon me. I guess the players and the fans were giving me something back for all the years I've put in, the bullets I've dodged, and all those flops I've seen through the years.

Out in the hallway, the applause faded away as the players sat back down and continued playing the game I had first played some fifty years before.

Chapter 40

Winners never quit and quitters never win.

After the 2004 Main Event and all the activity with Andy Beal, I settled into a lull, one of the few I'd ever experienced. I was feeling the effects of my gastric bypass surgery and wasn't eager to play much poker. Mostly, I was just tired and couldn't play for as many hours as I was accustomed to. I ended up having lots of extra time on my hands. And that's when I decided to write a sequel to *Super/System*. My publisher had been on my back to think about a sequel, so one day I just got started on it. I guess I had forgotten how much work the first book had been, maybe I'd gotten light in the head, or maybe it was the constant need for action that drove me to do *Super System 2*, I don't know. I do know that it wasn't easy getting this massive project together.

Like the original book, I called in the best of the modern-day players to contribute: I brought in two of my original contributors, Bobby Baldwin and Mike Caro, plus a new all-star team: Daniel Negreanu, one of the finest young players in the game; Jennifer Harman; my son, Todd; Lyle Berman, and Crandell Addington. Two-time world champion and fellow high-stakes player Johnny Chan wrote the preface.

Meanwhile, I entered the late summer of 2004 in the throes of an extended run of bad luck, one of my worst ever. It looked like I was going to have my first losing year in five decades. Even though I'd done well in the World Series of Poker, finishing fifty-third in a field of 2,576 players, I was disappointed because I didn't win. With the poker craze sweeping the country, I was concerned that my abilities might be eroding at a most inopportune time. The cash games were better than they had been in years, and I was playing in them instead of the tournaments. Problem was, I wasn't playing well and was also playing very unlucky.

I started losing and the losses kept coming. It seemed like I couldn't win no matter what I did. If I was drawing at cards, they wouldn't come; and when they did come, someone made a bigger draw. I found sets hard to come by, but when they did, I'd be facing a straight, and if I got that straight, I'd be looking at a bigger straight or a flush. My aces would lose to kings and my kings would lose to aces. Nothing was working. Instead of taking a break like I usually do when I go on an extended losing streak, I kept playing and the losses kept coming. After several months, the carnage wasn't pretty: I had lost about $6 million.

I kept asking myself, "Have I really lost it? Should I retire?" I actually started thinking about quitting.

Those thoughts were on my mind as I retreated to my second home in Montana to rest and decide what to do. It was a critical time for me. Poker had been my life for some fifty years and, for the first time, my confidence had eroded. I felt vulnerable and seriously considered hanging it up. I couldn't sustain losses like that, financially or mentally. Never had doubt sat upon me so heavily. I stayed in Montana for a month doing a lot of soul-searching and pondering my life. At the same time, I was giving my body the proper time to recuperate from the gastric bypass surgery I'd had some six months earlier.

In hindsight, the effects of my gastric bypass surgery probably took a bigger toll than I realized. For the first time in my life, I couldn't eat very much. I wanted to eat, but I got so full so fast that I couldn't force any more food into my stomach. The doctors actually reduce the stomach during surgery so there was physically no place to put the food, and I think my energy suffered because of it.

I also thought age might finally be catching up to me. At seventy-one years old, I started to wonder, "How long can I go on at this level?" I'd never gone loser for more than a month in my career, and here I was struggling mightily in a game I'd always dominated. I started wondering if my days as a top player were over. I'd always felt that a poker player goes downhill at fifty. He ages out of his top skills and can't compete the way he used to. Not many guys over fifty can play high-stakes poker and even fewer over the age of sixty. In fact, I only know of two or three. But I'd played my hand more than twenty years past that age. Maybe those five decades of playing were all I had in me?

After staying away from live poker for so long, I started to feel better physically. And although some self-doubts had crept up on my emotions, I decided to go play the World Poker Tour event at the Bicycle Club in the Los Angeles area. I was going to avoid the cash games—I felt that I couldn't handle another big losing session—and concentrate on the tournament. I told Louise my concerns and she supported my decision.

She knew I just wasn't right, me moping around the house, and agreed that I needed to get back on my feet.

I felt like I had something to prove when I arrived at the Bicycle Casino in late August of 2004. The largest field ever assembled for a WPT tournament had showed up. Among the 667 contestants were the best poker players in the world, the usual tough opponents who played the major events.

When the tournament started, I felt uncharacteristically nervous. I hadn't felt like that playing poker since maybe the first time I sat down with Johnny Moss so many decades before. Except this time, unlike when I played Moss, I didn't have the brash confidence to balance out my nervousness. This tournament was important to me and I was afraid that a bad result would change how I felt about the game and, ultimately, my life. But as soon as the game got going, I lost myself in the cards.

Turned out, I was at the top of my game. I made the right decisions all week, which is almost essential in winning a tournament of this magnitude—that and being lucky with the hands you select to play, and avoiding the hands that are impossible to get away from. I was fortunate in that regard, but I also knew that I was playing as well as I'd ever played.

As each hour went by, then each day, I got that old feeling back again. I advanced right on through the first, second and third days and into the final table of six players. Lee Watkinson had a huge lead over the five of us with several million in chips, about two-thirds of the chips in play. It's pretty hard to overcome that kind of advantage and it looked like he was going to win the tournament. While I had over a million in chips, none of the other players except Lee had more than a few hundred thousand.

For the first time in my career, I adopted a more patient, less aggressive strategy because I could see that I could probably finish at least second playing that way. This was a big tournament with second place paying about $575,000, and third place paying about $275,000. It was also the first time in my life I had ever played *not* to win a tournament, where I actually sat back and waited to try to finish up second or third. My aggressive style compels me to play to win, not to worry about where or when I might get knocked out. But I played conservatively, keeping an eye on the second and third place money, playing just to last as long as possible. I sat back, waited, and watched without attempting to improve my position on the leader, which is what I routinely try to do. Watkinson had made a huge splash on the tournament scene in 2004 with some big finishes, and was the toughest opponent at the table. I felt it would come down to the two of us.

They started going out—one, two, then three of them were gone in less than an hour, all at the hands of Watkinson. I hardly played a hand at the final table, letting him reduce the field for me.

Finally, Lee broke everyone—except me.

It was money time, the place where I've always felt that I have an advantage over any opponent. I was vastly outchipped, at least 3 to 1—Lee had a mountain of over $5 million in chips—but I knew I had an advantage over him because he didn't have my years of experience. I started dominating our heads-up play, chipping away at Lee's stack. I could feel where things were heading, I just knew. I picked up a few more hands and looked at Lee's pile of chips and then at mine; we were about even. Then I won a few more small pots, and slowly stole the chip lead away from him.

I knew I was wearing him down, that he was beginning to feel anxious when the key hand came up. I had the Q♥ 9♥. The flop came with Q♦ J♠ 4♣. I knew that if Lee had any kind of a draw, he was going to bet. So I checked. He bet $400,000 and I raised him $2.5 million, a substantial overbet.

My large raise convinced Watkinson that I was on a bluff and was trying to take the pot away from him. He was already steaming from some earlier pots I bet him off.

He looked at me awhile, trying to get some kind of read, some kind of fix, while I watched him weigh his options. He was examining my body language, my expression, how I rested my hands, searching for anything that would give him a clue as to the right decision he should make. I sat silently, waiting on him, my mind kind of taking in the scene, analyzing what he must be thinking. I'd been in this situation a million times, maybe two million times—no way of accounting for how many times over the past fifty years—while my opponent sized me up. Watkinson's tournament was on the line and he had a crucial decision to make.

I watched and waited.

"I call," he finally said. I'd been running over Lee and he thought he had the right hand to take a stand.

He was wrong.

Lee turned over the Q♣ 3♣, exactly the hand I wanted to see. I was a huge favorite. We both had queens, but my kicker would play if he didn't get lucky and spike a 3 for a two-pair hand or get runner-runner clubs for a flush. But neither situation materialized for him on the turn or the river.

I won my first WPT championship!

It was my most satisfying win in a long time, probably since my World Series Main Event victories several decades earlier. It was even more important to me than the $1.2 million first prize, though I didn't mind that part at all, because it replenished my bankroll and shored up my formerly sagging confidence. If I hadn't done well in that tournament I might have quit right then and there. But at this crossroads in my life, whatever doubts I had disappeared like the whirling dust devils that blew through my old West Texas prairie.

I felt great about my win not only because I became the first WSOP champion to ever win a World Poker Tour event but also because I started winning again in the cash games, which were more important to me. At age seventy-one, I was back—if in fact, I was ever gone.

The victory certainly validated an honor the WPT bestowed upon me some months earlier. In February, I was one of three players to be inducted into the WPT's new Poker Walk of Fame, along with actor James Garner, the poker-playing Maverick on the popular TV series, and Gus Hansen, who won three WPT tournaments in its inaugural year. The ceremony took place outside the Commerce Casino, where we put our handprints into wet cement to mark the occasion.

✪✪✪✪✪

Interest in poker continued to grow like wildfire, and with that growth came opportunity. The biggest one ever to land in front of me—and the most time consuming—came in the form of the Internet. A couple of investors approached me about endorsing and being the spokesperson for a new online poker site using my name and likeness, so I made a deal with them in 2004 and they opened the site for customers later that year. They called it Doylesroom and they launched it with plenty of fanfare and publicity.

Doylesroom wasn't the first time I had been involved with online poker. Back in the early 2000s, I was part of one of the first poker sites, Highlands Poker. These were the early days of Internet poker and only two other sites, Party Poker, and Planet Poker, which Mike Caro was involved with, were in operation. When Highlands went broke, I had to personally pay all the people that had deposits there, because my face was on the site, and my reputation was involved, even though I only owned about 15 percent of the business.

Promoting Doylesroom involved a whole lot of work—appearances, book signings, tournaments, and strategizing. As I got older and had more responsibilities because of Doylesroom, I needed help, so I called my nephew Ken Hale from Texas to work with me. He's been indispensable to me, like my right arm. But that didn't stop me from doing what I loved best: finding plenty of opportunities for new betting action.

One of them took the form of betting how long a man would live.

This wager was about the sniper who was shooting people up in Washington, D.C., and the surrounding areas. When police finally caught the guy, they decided to extradite him to Virginia because they thought justice could be served as quickly as possible there. They were just looking to execute this guy, and I believed he wasn't going to be alive in five years. I figured he was going to be killed immediately. So, I laid 10 to 1 with David Grey, $100,000 to $10,000, that the sniper wouldn't be alive in five years. Howard Lederer heard about the bet and said there was no chance they'd get through all the appeals and everything that soon. I told Howard the system was going to fry him right away, and that if they didn't, somebody else would kill him. I talked to my friend, David Chesnoff, the criminal lawyer, and he agreed with me, so I bet Howard $50,000 even money on that same bet.

Of course, the sniper was put in maximum security and guards watched him twenty-four hours a day. When the appeals process came some years later, it became pretty obvious that he wasn't going to be executed, and I settled the bet off at a discount.

I also had a $100,000 bet with David on who was going to break the home run record. He had Ken Griffey; I liked Alex Rodriguez. Well, Griffey got hurt and it became clear he had no chance to break the record. It looked like A-Rod was probably going to do it, so I had to off that bet to balance out the sniper bet. I got a discount and paid David a reduced amount.

That's often what happens with the big bets we make. We'll take insurance and pay a discount to get off a bet when we're on its short side.

When I returned to Las Vegas from my WPT victory at the Bike, I continued working on *Super System 2*, and turned to the only guy I could trust to help me finish this project, my good friend and frequent collaborator, Mike Caro, the Mad Genius of Poker. He was a heck of a writer and indispensable in getting out the original book, and I knew that I couldn't get this one written without his help. Caro had written many books himself, including his landmark work, *Caro's Book of Poker Tells*, and was the perfect guy for this project. Except for one problem: Caro is the world's biggest procrastinator. I mean, this guy would announce books and twenty years later, he'd still be talking about them and still not getting them done. Or even started.

Remembering all the trouble I had getting him motivated for the first project almost thirty years before, I had to come up with an answer to solve this problem.

First, I tried to work with the Mad Genius by phone and e-mail, but didn't get good results. He was living out in the Ozarks somewhere, fishing or something, and I couldn't seem to get him motivated. Not that I expected anything different. So I went to Plan B, which was really Plan A all along. And that was to get Mike to Las Vegas where I could keep an eye on him. In particular, both my eyes.

I flew the Mad Genius out and we got the book going over his kicking and screaming—well, I did feed him—and it started to take shape. Mike was the key guy, the glue that would hold this all together. He was gifted, but a Jekyll and Hyde for me. Great stories and horror stories. Mike has always helped me. He edits what I write and writes things that I edit. We work good together. But as always, it was hard to motivate him, even with him living in my house. We'd work two or three hours, then he'd go somewhere, be gone all day. When he came back, he'd say, "Well, I'm gonna have to go home in a few days, Doyle."

"Well then, we're gonna have to get some work done," I'd tell him.

And he'd be gone the next day. Clearly, plan B wasn't working. I needed a better solution. So I locked the doors and wouldn't let him leave. I told him how it was going to be.

"We're gonna get up in the morning," I said, "we're gonna eat breakfast, and then we're gonna work; we're gonna have lunch, and then we're going back to work. We're gonna work until we go to bed, and that's how we're gonna get this done."

Boy, he didn't like that. He just stared at me like I was talking in some kind of Martian language. Mike is absolutely the most brilliant guy when he gets up in the morning, but by the end of the day, his concentration level is not very high and he can hardly speak. But I kept him motivated and working as long as I could every day.

The project took a lot of time, but then one day after a whole lot of hard work, we were done with it. I sent *Super/System 2* off to the publisher— and then I did one more thing.

I let the Mad Genius go back home.

Chapter 41

Life is one sweet song. Enjoy the music.

W hen I walked into the opening event of the World Series of Poker on June 3, 2005, I was mesmerized by what I saw. For the first time since it all began, the Series had moved from the downtown Horseshoe Casino to the Rio All-Suite Hotel and Casino just off the Las Vegas Strip. What a change! While the Horseshoe was dingy, smoke-filled, and cramped, the Rio was massive and wide open. The tournament area at the Rio was sixty-thousand square feet, bigger than several football fields, and equipped with two hundred poker tables.

And they needed every one of 'em.

Some 2,200 players and 500 alternates swarmed the place. I had never seen anything close to the sheer magnitude of it all. In the Horseshoe, you could easily toss a football from one end of the room to the other. But in the Rio, you'd need an NFL quarterback to reach the far wall, and I'm not even sure the best could make that distance. I think you'd need the kicker; the playing area was that enormous.

Players had been waiting all year for the WSOP to roll around, and finally here it was. During its six-week run, more than thirty-two thousand players would compete in the forty-five events for a prize pool that exceeded $100 million, more than double the record set in 2004. It dwarfed the Indy 500 and the Kentucky Derby. The Main Event itself drew more than 5,500 players and had to be spread out over two starting days. It was almost unbelievable to me, but all nine players at the final table would walk away millionaires. That was a far cry from the early days, when the total prize pool for the Main Event would barely tip the scale by today's standards. These developments were something I never could have predicted. I don't think anyone could have.

I couldn't help but recall the humble beginning of the first World Series elimination tournament in 1971 when six of us sat down to play, and Johnny Moss walked away with $30,000.

Nostalgia washed over me. I missed my old friends, the old games at the Horseshoe, and those marvelous years. I could see that old gang of road gamblers fighting it out at that first final table. There were also people like Bill and Ken Smith, Sid Wyman, Benny Binion, and all the old-time poker players who are now gone. I wondered what they would say if they could see what I was looking at now. It was a strange feeling, kind of overwhelming. I felt grateful to be one of the privileged old-timers who got to witness the remarkable evolution of our game.

Standing there in that big room, I felt tears come to my eyes as I looked across the sea of players. It was the first time I had cried since I lost my daughter.

Every World Series is a special time of the year for poker players, but little did I anticipate just how extraordinary this one would be. I had won nine gold bracelets, each one for a victory at the World Series of Poker, but one thing that created a big hole in my life was not seeing my son Todd win his first bracelet. Todd was a great cash player, I thought one of the very best, and a great tournament player as well, but he hadn't yet made his mark in the one venue all poker players live for: The World Series of Poker.

He had a shot at it, though. Todd was playing the $2,500 Omaha High-Low 8-or-Better event and doing real good, down to the last two tables. I was playing in some side games, and following the progress of the tournament he was in. Players kept on getting eliminated, and when it got down to three-handed, I left the side game and sat down to watch the rest of the tournament. I was really excited and thought Todd might win a bracelet. One more player busted out, and Todd was down to heads-up. I tensely watched the action on every hand. After awhile, the two of them got it all-in and I could tell by Todd's demeanor that he felt real good about his hand.

And then he won!

Todd had secured the first-place prize of $255,945 and his first gold bracelet! I walked over to him with a grin on my face that no one could have wiped off, bowed to him, and shook his hand. I wanted to hug him I was so proud, but I restrained myself and settled for whispering my congratulations.

There was more excitement to come. For years I had been the Series' bracelet leader, and when the 2005 events began at the Rio, I was tied with Johnny Chan and Phil Hellmuth Jr. with nine each. But Johnny had taken the lead outright by winning one of the early events, and though I knew it was a long shot, I wanted to regain a share of the bracelet leadership. Badly. People were making such a big deal out of the bracelet count, and it seemed like everybody was saying I was too old to compete in these tournaments. Naturally, winning another one started taking on more importance to me.

And I did! I won the $5,000 Short-Handed No-Limit Hold'em event with a first-place prize of $367,800. That prize money was more than I had won at either of my Main Event world championships in the seventies. Still, the money was secondary, just the icing on the cake. Not only did I tie Johnny and maintain my bracelet lead at ten, but even more special, Todd and I had achieved something never before done: we became the only father/son winning team in World Series history. And that made a proud father even prouder. I know Louise was real proud of Todd too.

✪✪✪✪✪

An ironic thing happened when I won the tournament. I had captured both my world championships with 10-2 hole cards, a most unlikely winning hand that had become known in poker circles as the "Doyle Brunson." People still ask me about those 10-2 hands in poker, if I played them much after my two World Series wins. It's funny, I did get kind of partial to those starting cards and played them many times after that. They're not the best cards, and for a reason—let's just say, I don't play them anymore.

In the key hand this time, I had caught a 10 and a trey as down cards. I bet my opponent, Minh Ly, all the chips he had, about $200,000.

I was bluffing, and he called.

"What you got?" Minh asked, turning up K-Q.

"I got Doyle Brunson's big brother," I said, showing Minh my 10-3, an awful hand. The flop came J-4-3, giving me a pair of threes and the lead. The turn and river were blanks, helping neither one of us, and that was it.

I won my tenth bracelet.

Catching up to Johnny and winning my tenth was a thrill, a huge victory for me, and my World Series just kept getting better. I was honored and proud to give the introductory speech for Jack Binion and Crandell Addington, who both got inducted into the Poker Hall of Fame. The ceremony was conducted in the big Amazon room at the Rio, the very room where the World Series events were taking place. The audience was filled with poker players, poker professionals, and fans. I felt every bit as honored as the two inductees themselves, who are two of my best friends. Jack was the heart and soul of the World Series of Poker for years and along with Benny, responsible for its existence in the first place. Crandell was one of the groundbreaking Texas gamblers and the author of "The History of No-Limit Texas Hold'em" chapter in *Super System 2*.

I'd only played in five of the forty-five events in the 2005 World Series because of the big side games, but mostly because shortly after the first event, I flew to Texas to attend my 55th Sweetwater High School reunion. I wasn't overly keen on leaving Las Vegas during the most prestigious poker event of the year, but given that this might be the last chance I'd have to see some of my old friends, I couldn't pass up the opportunity. I was really looking forward to reliving some of the old times from my childhood, and I just had to go.

Seeing all my old classmates was as special as I had imagined. I couldn't believe how the years had aged some of them, while others, exactly the same age as I was, still looked great, vibrant and healthy—like Riley Cross, one-third of Longworth's Three Musketeers of yesteryear. In a class that graduated 136 students in 1950, we knew of ninety-four living members. More than fifty of them had come from near and far to attend the reunion, including our class president, Jack Scott, who became a California state senator, and had skipped a dinner where he was to receive an honorary doctorate from a major university. That was a testament to the camaraderie we shared so many years ago, and the special time it was in our lives.

As we relived the old times, the years rolled away and we laughed and talked about our youthful escapades. Riley and I shared memories of our childhood compatriot, D.C. Andrews, the Musketeer turned school superintendent who had laid down his sword for good in 1999. We reminisced about the time we were coming back from a baseball game— my father, D.C., Riley, and me. Daddy was driving round a curve, and when he spit out the window, the car shot off the highway and out into a cotton field. It happened to be one of our cotton fields. He wheeled around, pulled back on the highway, and drove on down the road like nothing had happened. Daddy never said a word. I always laughed about it with D.C. and Riley. I can still see that old car ripping through our cotton field with all those specks of white flying onto the hood and windshield.

D.C.'s death closed an enduring chapter of lifelong friendship among three West Texas boys who played and fought and chased girls in earnest collaboration in the forties and fifties. His death was particularly troubling to me at the time. "How could this strong, healthy mountain of a man—he was only sixty-five—be stricken down by a deadly malady?" I pondered. "How could he die before me?"

I should have understood. It was cancer. At his funeral, which was open casket, I put my hand on his and thought, *Rest in peace, my friend, my buddy, my brother.* The Three Musketeers of Longworth, Texas, their swashbuckling days a fading memory, were no more.

Riley wasn't as close to me as D.C., who was my first best friend, because D.C. and I had double-dated with two girls that were close friends. D.C. would get his dad's car on Friday nights, and I'd get my dad's car on Saturday nights. Riley usually stayed in town with the girls he was dating, hanging out with the other football players. D.C. was even closer to me than my brother Lloyd, we spent so much time together. He was like a second brother to me.

But time has got a way of separating people. When I started gambling, I didn't fit in with the turns his life had taken, so we grew apart for some years. But when D.C. started teaching in the school district where Louise and I were living in the greater Fort Worth area, a little town called Everman, we started getting close again. Our daughter, Cheryl, went to school there and D.C. was one of her teachers. We had a lot of good times playing golf, and we'd reminisce about the old days and all the mischief we got into and the adventures we experienced together.

The reunion was great, but I was really looking forward to getting back to Las Vegas and playing the Main Event. I had done well the year before with my impressive yet disappointing fifty-third place finish, so I felt like I could give it another country ride. Before the Main Event started, Doylesroom hosted an appreciation party at the magnificent Miranda Ballroom at the Rio. Some 1,500 people poured into the ballroom, including many of my poker buddies. I just couldn't get over how many people were there and how big poker had grown. Louise was shocked by what some of the young girls were wearing. Or not wearing. She worried that several of them might spill out of their tops when they leaned over to snuggle up for the photographers. I overheard her reaction when she was conversing with her friend.

"I thought I'd seen it all," she said, more in awe than anything else. "They're cute little girls, but I've never seen anything like this, at least not out in public. Doyle thinks I've lost my mind, but some of these uniforms reflect every mother's nightmare. I bet their mommas would have fainted."

It was Mike Sexton who introduced me at midnight as the "Godfather of Poker." Earlier a new poker magazine, *All In*, had made its debut with a cover story that was headlined: "An Exclusive Interview With The Living Legend."

Well, the "Legendary Godfather" got himself shot down in flames less than twenty-four hours after the party. I was ousted from the Main Event in a matter of hours, yet still got a standing ovation from the players when I rose to leave. I regretted going out so early, but if I had to go out, I'd rather go out quickly. It's not as painful that way. I'd had a heck of a run in the Main Event the year before, but I guess a second run was not meant to be.

The next year, I came close to winning the tournament that bears my name, the Doyle Brunson Five Diamond Poker Classic, which was played at the Bellagio. It's the second biggest tournament on the World Poker Tour, with a top prize of nearly $2 million. I made a third-place finish worth more than $500,000. It would have been pretty ironic if I'd won the tournament, and though it was disappointing not to win, it was gratifying to have such a high finish.

But it was another Brunson that really made a mark at the poker table in 2006.

Chapter 42

Insanity is hereditary—you get it from your children.

There's something different in the Brunson blood, maybe a poker gene or poker DNA, because the game has figured prominently in the lives of three generations of Brunsons. For all I know, that poker DNA may go even deeper. I didn't know much about the lineage of my grandfather or great-grandfather on my father's side, but I was really curious about them. I wondered if those Brunsons had gambling in their blood. Were they great risk takers? Researching my family roots, I eventually went back even farther, tracing my lineage to the Brownsons and Bronsons of Essex, England, in the 1500s. Those early surnames weren't quite Brunson, but they all meant "son of Braun," and they were all from the same family tree. I learned that the first historically recorded Brunson in America was Roger Brunson, who could be traced to Connecticut in 1625. Except for Native Americans, no families could trace their roots to this continent further back than the Brunsons.

Which brings me back to the present day.

I'd never talked much poker with my son Todd—in college, he was actually preparing to be a lawyer—and I even discouraged the game, but he ended up playing poker professionally anyway, despite my weak objections. When he quit his fourth year of college to play poker, Louise came storming into my office kicking up a bunch of dust. She was furious. I truthfully said to her, "Louise, I didn't even know he knew how to play!"

I was as surprised as she was. We had never once played poker in the Brunson household, not even for fun.

And Todd got pretty good at it too. Thinking about my son and my father, I suppose that lineage just keeps getting passed down. First it was me playing poker without my father's knowledge—and Dad playing poker without me knowing about it—and now Todd burning his own path at the poker table. I'm sure if Todd has any children, they'll be poker players too, regardless of what their father or grandfather says. It just might be in the blood.

But I never thought my daughter Pam would become another serious poker-playing Brunson. I knew she enjoyed playing low stakes for fun—she had started playing in Oceanside, California, in 1990—and usually with Todd, but soon after Doylesroom opened in 2004, she began putting long hours in online. I put up $1,000 for her to play in the cheap limit games and get her feet wet. One day I looked on the cashier's page and saw where she had a couple of thousand dollars or more and was drawing money out. I was proud of her modest success, but really didn't pay much attention to it. In fact, for many years, I discouraged her from playing and even cringed at the thought of her dating a poker player.

She started playing our bounty tournaments as Queen Kitty, her online name, $25 buy-in events where the goal was to knock out the bounty players in addition to trying to win the tournament itself. We had hundreds of players each week.

I've played in the tournament for several years, and I've made it all the way to the final table a time or two. But it's difficult to get good results with a bull's-eye on my forehead. Everybody's gunning for me and they know if they knock me out they're gonna win at least $500 and have a shot at $25,000. So there's a lot of incentive for players to alter their strategy just to take me out.

Pam began having such good results we made her a bounty also. And in a 2006 tournament with more than seven hundred players, she won the whole thing! And I thought, "How amazing is that? I've never won it. Neither have Todd or Mike Caro. And then here comes my daughter and she does it." After some time, she'd won several tournaments at Doylesroom, which is really hard to do. Now I really started paying attention. Maybe there was something to those Brunson poker genes. Pam got more serious about poker and started playing the big live events at the World Series of Poker.

She approached me about wanting some extra help for the tournaments, but it wasn't my help she wanted—she wanted Casper's help, I mean Casper the Friendly Ghost!

You see, a while back I used a card protector at the poker table that was a likeness of Casper the Friendly Ghost. A card protector is an inexpensive little weight that poker players put on top of their cards to keep their hands from being *fouled*, mistakenly taken away from them by the dealer when their hand is still in play.

I got so lucky whenever I used my Casper protector that my gambling friend Howard Lederer offered me $3,500 to leave it to him in my will. I wasn't sure he was serious until he plunked down his money. So, I bequeathed Casper to him. Casper was already gaining fame because poker players had gotten wind of our deal. ESPN even picked up on the story.

You may not believe in ghosts, but a bunch of poker players sure did. Casper started taking on a life of his own, and top players started clamoring for his services. I started renting Casper to other players. Charging them $500 every thirty minutes seems ridiculous, but when you're playing very high-stakes poker, it is an insignificant amount if a player feels it brings him luck. Poker players were lining up for Casper and as the demand grew, so did the price. Casper reached the pinnacle of his career when he started renting for $5,000 an hour to a poker player from Greece.

I figure I rented him out for over $25,000 in a one-year period. Not bad for a $5 piece of black rock!

Pam borrowed Casper for the World Series of Poker in 2006 and outlasted Todd and me. That, of course, caught our attention because we never heard the end of it.

Meanwhile, without Casper, I didn't do anything special at the Series and busted out without any significant results. However, my fondest memory occurred right before the Main Event that year when Doylesroom hosted a roast for me at the Bellagio. The prime rib and lobster were delicious, but the best part was the entertainment. Brad Garrett from *Seinfeld* was really a hoot as MC. I had one of the best laughs I'd had in a long time, though Brad was too hard and crude with Pamela Anderson, one of the roasters. She didn't like that too much, so she stormed out early. Truthfully, I didn't like it either, and it made me wonder if there was some kind of history between the two. Otherwise, it was one of the funniest and most entertaining nights I could remember. The other roasters included Chip Reese, along with Phil Hellmuth Jr., Barry Greenstein, Mike Sexton, Gabe Kaplan, Jennifer Tilly, Todd, and Willy Johnson, a comic pretending to be a childhood friend. They all told inglorious and embarrassing stories from my past, some of which I'd conveniently forgotten. All the top players and many of my friends packed the tables.

Unfortunately for Todd and me, Pam had Casper again the next year at the 2007 WSOP, and outlasted us for the second year in a row, finishing 364th out of 5,700 players in the Main Event. She picked up $35,000 for the finish. Poker players started calling her, "The last Brunson standing." I thought it was kind of funny, but it got under Todd's skin a little bit, especially when Pam proceeded to outlast him (and me) at three straight World Poker Tour events. Hardly a month after her 2007 World Series performance, Pam entered a WPT ladies' tournament in Los Angeles and won the darned thing. Later in the year, Pam played in the inaugural poker tournament in the Hard Rock Casino poker room, and won again. This time, her grand prize was a custom Harley chopper.

Norm Chad, a World Series announcer on ESPN, told Pam he couldn't believe she and Todd were related. "You're like Bambi," he said, "and Todd's like Godzilla."

Pam explained why she liked playing poker against Todd so much. "He used to criticize me at the table in front of other players. That's why I like to beat him so much now. I love Todd dearly, but nothing gives me more joy than kicking his butt at the poker table."

She sounded just a whole lot like me talking about Sailor or Chip when she discussed Todd. Yep, that's my girl.

The legend of Casper continued to grow with Pam's successes, especially after Pam pleaded on national television for the right to the Casper card protector.

"Howard," she said in a TV appeal to Lederer, "please let my dad have Casper back. I know that he sold him to you, but he means so much to me, and he needs to stay in the family."

The next time I saw Howard, I pressed him on the subject.

"You know, he's now an historical part of poker," I maintained. "You've gotta let me have him back."

Howard thought about it for a little while, and after some serious negotiating, he surrendered that little $5 piece of rock for $7,500. That's right—more than twice what I had sold it to him for!

I had decided not to finance Pam in 2007 because these big tournaments are such a crapshoot. But Todd had bought half of her for $5,000 and shared the $35,000 she won. I got to reconsidering. It takes a lot of luck to win even one of the preliminary events, but Pam is a competent player and she can do it. I would be awfully proud if she could win a bracelet at the WSOP like Todd did in 2005. It would be the crowning achievement in the Brunson poker trilogy, especially if Casper went right along the way with her.

And if that happens, they'd surely induct Casper the Friendly Ghost into the Poker Hall of Fame.

Chapter 43

Be wary of a man who urges you to take action in which
he himself incurs no risk.

A t midnight, on September 30, 2006, as their last piece of business before adjournment for the election, Congress passed the Unlawful Internet Gambling Enforcement Act (UIGEA). This act, tacked onto a home-security bill (SAFE Port Act), prohibited the transfer of funds from financial institutions to Internet gambling sites.

The repercussions were substantial across the entire industry. The biggest site for players, Party Poker, where more than half of all online poker play occurred, lost the majority of its value the following day on the London Stock Exchange—billions of dollars of lost value within twenty-four hours. Party, along with other publicly traded sites, announced that they were going to pull completely out of the U.S. market. Suddenly, hundreds of thousands of online players had no site on which to play, a void that was immediately filled by other Internet poker sites.

The UIGEA hit Doylesroom like a hard slap in the face. Actually, more like a roundhouse right that knocked us nearly senseless. Our online software provider reacted to the new legislation by blocking our access to the U.S. market, a devastating blow that wiped out the majority of our player base. It sent us desperately scurrying to pick up another provider. It also killed a deal we had been negotiating that was worth hundreds of millions of dollars. I stood to get a good piece of that, but that deal disappeared like a wisp of smoke in the prairie wind.

To say I was disappointed would be an understatement the size of the great state of Texas. It was a blow, but there was more bad news. The effects of the UIGEA were far-reaching and they had hit home elsewhere. In particular, one of the most exciting ventures I'd ever gotten involved in, the Professional Poker League, was among its victims. The league had eight teams, each one led by two co-captains. We signed sixty-four of the top poker players in the world to exclusive contracts and appointed the co-captains.

On October 7, the inaugural draft of the PPL was held at the Venetian, the host casino and our main sponsor. Todd and I were co-captains of one team, with the other seven teams co-captained by stars such as T.J. Cloutier, Dewey Tomko, Chip Reese, Erik Seidel, Cyndy Violette, Jennifer Harman, Phil Ivey, and Daniel Negreanu. The captains then had a draft, in turn picking their team from a pool we selected until all sixty-four players had been selected. In the end, each team had a total of eight members. I was chosen as a spokesman for the project, what they called the "captain of the captains," along with Chip Reese, who was intricately involved in the formation of the league, and Dr. Michael Minor, the PPL founder.

I believed the PPL would take poker to the level where it really belonged, not involving just the relatively small poker community, but the general public as well. It was going to be huge—I know the public would have loved it. The major TV networks were ready to be players in the project, and I was convinced that poker would have become more entertaining than ever. The producers intended to showcase the players quite a bit, which would be a home run for all of us. The Venetian even built a showplace facility for the poker players, and everything was first class: the top production people in the country, the top marketing people, the top publicity people, and about best of all, Jack Binion, who had sold all of his properties to Harrah's Entertainment, would be the league commissioner.

The PPL was going to require a great deal of money, and most of it could come from only one place: Internet poker sites. The major ones were ready to back the project. Then that damned UIGEA torpedoed the advertising aspect, and the Internet sites had to pull their support. That killed the proposed league, which was an awful shame.

I'm not prone to getting on the soapbox very often, but I have some strong opinions on this subject. If the politicians had legalized gambling, regulated and taxed it like they do in Las Vegas—I'm talking about offshore bookmaking and the Internet poker sites and casinos—the national debt would be substantially less. It would have raised billions and billions in tax dollars. And most every major site would be delighted to have the government as a partner, which would legitimize the while industry and allow them to grow without artificial restrictions.

But nobody had the foresight to do it. Instead of legalizing, regulating, and taxing gambling, the government has wasted billions of dollars fighting it.

Of course, the Bible Belt is still dead-set against gambling. Texas has all sorts of money problems, but certain influential Texans remain staunchly opposed to gambling. It's largely a handful of self-righteous, hypocritical Texas politicians who put the knock on gambling. It's not only hypocritical, it's stupid. Tens of thousands of Texans routinely cross state lines to gamble in neighboring Louisiana, Oklahoma, and New Mexico, or make frequent pilgrimages to Vegas. If people want to gamble, they're going to gamble. The government and law enforcement and the churches aren't going to stop it.

While the Professional Poker League was stillborn, someone figured out that the marriage of golf and gambling would play well to TV audiences and be able to survive in the new UIGEA climate. Poker players love gambling on golf—we play high-stakes games all the time—so why not broadcast those games on national television? You have to understand that, if nothing else, gamblers are resourceful. If there is a way to make something work, we always find it. Actually, it was Dewey Tomko who broached the idea to the right group of guys. A former New York television executive, Joe Kreder, had read about Dewey's high-stakes gambling exploits in *Who's Your Caddy?*, a best-selling book about golfers, and contacted him. Dewey told Kreder and his two partners, Mark Braman and Nathan Frank, about the Professional Gamblers Invitational golf tournaments we used to have and suggested resurrecting a contemporary event for gambling golfers.

"Why not kind of update that thing and have a tournament?" Joe wondered, feeling out the idea.

I didn't think much about the chances of this project coming to fruition, but Joe and his partners moved ahead, forming a company called High Stakes Entertainment and gathering commitments from several networks interested in televising the event. They offered Dewey and me a piece of the company and titles as executive producers of the show, which we called *High Stakes Entertainment Presents Dewey Tomko and Doyle Brunson's Golf*. Maybe it wasn't the shortest of titles, but I began to take notice: It looked like this show might get going. We got ESPN interested in the broadcast rights and the Venetian Hotel and Casino agreed to host the tournament, providing rooms, prizes and a place to hold our banquet.

We were on!

This modern version of the PGI would only be vaguely similar to the historic golf tournament that Jack Binion and I had kicked off some thirty years earlier, but the underlying concept would be the same: high-stakes gambling on the golf course. We agreed on two events, first a three-man team scramble and then a two-man best ball. For the first event, nine gambling golfers would ante up $1 million apiece. With ESPN cameras taping the action at the Bali Hi Golf Club, three three-man scramble teams would play nine holes for $1 million a hole, which sounds much higher than it actually was. It's true that $9 million was at stake, but we weren't playing carry-overs, so when holes were tied there would be no payout. Still, for advertising purposes, $1 million a hole was plenty alluring and, even without carry-overs, we were playing real high.

Under the format, the teams would be handicapped by distance instead of the standard strokes; different tee boxes would be the equalizer. The low handicap golfers hit from the back tees, the high handicappers from the front tees, and the others from the two middle tees. I was skeptical at first, but Dewey had run such tournaments previously and was adamant that it would work.

"Just wait and see," he said. "We're going to get everybody where they can break eighty from whichever of the four tee boxes they hit their drives."

With the rousing words, "Let's tee it up and get it on!" by announcer Mike Sexton, we started the tournament. It was amazing how well the structure worked, especially for me with my bad leg and shoulder. The three scramble teams were evenly matched. They included Phil Hellmuth Jr., Russ Hamilton, and Billy Walters, owner of the Bali Hai club; Daniel Negreanu, Josh Arieh, and Erick Lindgren; and Dewey, me and Vince Van Patten, co-host of WPT poker and son of Dick Van Patten of TV's *Eight is Enough.*

It was a cutthroat, competitive game with lots of action and we came down to the final hole all even. With $1 million up for grabs, the stage was set for some eleventh-hour dramatics. This was sports television at its best! The difference in the game came down to an eighteen-foot putt on the last hole. It was my shot. I got lucky and sank it!

Dewey, Vince and I won the $1 million, but $333,000 of that was money we had put up, so we actually won $666,000 split three ways. Not bad for nine holes of golf.

ESPN got good ratings even though we were competing against NFL games. And the reruns also fared well, so we had another tournament, again with ESPN. This time we changed it up a little, making it an eighteen-hole challenge with nine two-man teams, each putting up $250,000. We handicapped it the same way, with tee-box distance rather than strokes, and with the low team winning a little over $1 million. Second place would get slightly more than $500,000 and third about $280,000.

Dewey and I never got into a rhythm on the front nine and shot four over par. Although Dewey missed a two-foot birdie putt at the second hole, he and I each birdied two of the first five holes, and suddenly we were back to even par. The leaders were probably three or four under at that point, but we knew anything could happen on the home stretch. Unfortunately, Dewey and I never sank another putt. Phil Ivey and David Oppenheim won it with two under par. New Yorkers Mickey Appleman and John Hanson finished second. Dewey and I took third, which got us back a little more than our $250,000 entrance fee. Seven of the nine teams were in contention until the very end, so our concept and pairings worked out well.

Further tournaments didn't come off right away as we had hoped, but we're all still willing to play when they do. As long as there can be high gambling action and lots of money to be won, we're ready to go.

What do you think? We're gamblers.

✪✪✪✪✪

I can't blame the UIGEA for this one. On Halloween night, 2007, after attending a party at son Todd's home, I slipped climbing out of my car and fell on the driveway. I assured myself that the bottle of wine I drank earlier at the party had nothing to do with it. Two days later, I was trying on a new pair of shoes when I slipped on the marble floor at my home and came crashing down on my shoulder. I couldn't blame this one on wine because I was drinking coffee, but I did toss out those shoes. I was afraid I had broken or dislocated my shoulder. The bad news was that I couldn't get to the doctor for several days because I was busy shooting instructional videos with Caro. After four or five long days working with Mike, a master at teaching strategy, I think we produced the best poker videos ever Mike surpassed even my wildest expectations of putting this thing together.

When I finally did get to the doctor for my shoulder, a series of tests and X-rays revealed nothing broken, just bad bruises.

But my little shoulder mishap was an injury quickly forgotten compared to what would broadside me just a few days later.

✪
Chapter 44

You will never find a better sparring partner than adversity.

O n December 4, 2007, I was awakened in the early morning darkness by the harsh sound of a ringing phone. I glanced at the clock, realized it was 5:30, and irritably answered the call. I recognized the voice of my nephew, Ken Hale, who works as my assistant.

"What's going on, Ken?"

"I think Chip just died."

I stared at the phone for a few seconds, my brain not quite taking it in. I was in shock. How could my best friend, age fifty-six and apparently in good health, be gone?

"Chip?"

"Sorry, Doyle."

"No," I told myself. "*No-no-no!*" I jumped out of bed, tossed on some clothes, and drove to Chip's house as quickly as I could. As I entered the house, the sobering reality of what had happened really began to hit me. The distraught faces of his children—daughters Brittany and Taylor and son Casey—brought terrible grief to me and I cried along with them. I learned that Chip had actually gone to the doctor the day before and a chest X-ray had revealed a shadow on his lung. The doctor told him he was coming down with pneumonia, gave him a shot, and sent him home. That night, the doctor, who had been taking poker lessons from Chip, called his patient to see how he was feeling. Chip said he felt fine, and when he learned the doctor was playing poker at the Red Rock Casino, he even volunteered to come watch him play.

"No thanks," the doctor quipped. "If they saw you sitting behind me, they wouldn't play with me anymore!"

They laughed and hung up.

Chip spoke by phone with his girlfriend for half an hour or so, told the kids goodnight, and went to bed. Casey, then nineteen, checked on his father about 4 a.m. and discovered him lying in bed in a fetal position.

Top: Left to right, Pam, Todd, Louise, and Doyla.

Right: A great shot of Louise and Cheryl; this was before we met.

Bottom Left: Left to right in the mirror, Doyla and Pam.

Bottom Right: Pam, Doyla, and Todd.

Top: Doyla and I celebrating her birthday with a homemade cake.

Right: Doyla posing for a portrait. I love this shot of her.

Bottom: Doyla as a teen with her proud father.

Top: Todd's first and last haircut.

Left: Todd's getting some ideas in his head; turns out they were pretty good ones.

Bottom: Todd's first championship win.

Top: Todd and Pam join me at a book signing appearance at the WSOP.

Left: Todd's first World Series of Poker bracelet. I'm not sure who was more proud of that achievement, Todd or me.

Bottom: Pam at a televised WPT final table

Top: Pam won the tournament at the Hard Rock poker lounge and this custom Harley-Davidson chopper too.

Right: Cheryl, me, and Louise in front of the $1 million display at the Horseshoe.

Bottom: Pam showing the Brunson genes with a win in the World Poker Tour ladies tournament.

Left: My sister Lavada with husband Jackie Hale, and their children, Ken and Cindy.

Below Left: Lauren, Jeff, Angi, and Christan at the beach.

Right: Four generations of the family: In the back, Cheryl, Jeff, and Louise. Christan and Lauren are in the front.

Bottom: At my wedding. Going left to right, Jackie Hale (Lavada's husband), my sister Lavada, Louise, me, and Mom. In the front, Jackie and Lavada's children, Ken and Cindy.

Left: On a family poker crusie. Left to right in the rear. Todd's wife Anjela, Todd, Pam, and Cheryl. In the front, Louise.

Below: My grandson Jeff, his wife Angi, Jeff's two daughters, Lauren and Christan, Louise, Cheryl, and Todd.

Todd's wife Anjela, Pam, Louise, me, Cheryl, friend Elizabeth, and Jeff's wife, Angi.

In August 2004, with World Poker Tour announcer Mike Sexton at the Bicycle Club in the Los Angeles area, posing with the first-place money of $1.2 million.

Three-time WSOP Champion, Stu Ungar. I had a love-hate relationship with him. It just depended upon the setting.

DOYLE BRUNSON

Cowboy Wolford (left), Jack Binion (center) and 1978 World Champion, Bobby Baldwin (right).

Steve Wynn looks on as Bob Hooks, an old-time road gambler, prepares to make a bet, circa 1976.

One of the guys I liked to bet with, Huck Seed, 1996 World Champion.

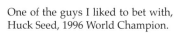

Tony Spilotro (left) with his attorney, Oscar Goodman, the future mayor of Las Vegas.

My all-star contributors from the two original *Super/System* books. From top row, left to right, Lyle Berman, Chip Reese, Bobby Baldwin, Todd Brunson, Crandell Addington, and Daniel Negreanu. In the front row, Jennifer Harman, me, and Mike Caro. Missing are Joey Hawthorne and David Sklansky from *Super/System* and Johnny Chan and Steve Zolotow from *Super System 2*.

Welcome Back, Kotter actor, comedian and poker player Gabe Kaplan.

From left to right, Todd, me, country music singer Dierks Bentley, Ken Hale, and Hoyt Corkins.

Top: Socialite Paris Hilton.

Bottom: Actress and media sensation Pamela Anderson. No, this wasn't my wedding—Louise and I are doing just fine.

Top: Actor Leonardo DiCaprio.
Bottom: Actor Robert Duvall, from the set of *Lucky You.*

Top: That's Dewey Tomko on the left and Chip Reese on the right posing for a publicity photo for Line Movers, our short-lived tout service that offered sports advice and bets over a 900 number.

Bottom: Boxer Lennox Lewis.

Left: Golf has always been my passion.

Below: The ESPN announcer is interviewing Phil Ivey for *High Stakes Entertainment Presents Dewey Tomko and Doyle Brunson's Golf.* To his right is his teammate, David Oppenheim. I'm with Dewey Tomko.

Our house in Montana at Flathead Lake, which is the biggest natural lake west of the Mississippi. This serene environment is my home away from home and puts me back in touch with nature.

Middle: The side benefits of a long life; my great-grandson Evan.

Bottom Left: My two dogs, Cutie and Casper.

Death apparently was instantaneous, with no indication that he suffered. We later learned that death most likely occurred as a combination of the faulty heart and his brush with pneumonia.

It came as a shock because nobody was aware that he had any physical problems. He did have rheumatic fever as a child, which probably left his heart in a weakened state. While he'd been somewhat withdrawn the last six months, and hadn't played in the Big Game at the Bellagio in some time, he seemed healthy. We hadn't talked as much as we normally do, but I think he may have been preoccupied with family pressures.

I know that the third chapter of Ecclesiastes says there is a time to be born and a time to die. I guess it was just Chip's time to die. But I had a terrible time accepting that. We were about as close as two people could be—fierce competitors at the table and business partners away from it. Chip and I invested in some really far out business ventures and not a one of them was successful, so we always came back to poker. As a friend, he was always there when I needed him and I always tried to be there when he needed me.

Our friendship was no secret so I just kept getting e-mails, letters and phone calls from reporters wanting comments and stories. But there was no story to tell other than Chip had died unexpectedly and left a big void—in my life, in the poker world, and in the lives of all of us who knew him well. He was a personable guy, a man with a huge heart, generous to a fault. He was also a kind man with no enemies. Chip was just a winner in life, a total class act.

Everyone in the poker world knew how great a poker player he was. He played all the games well and just refused to lose. Chip proved his versatility and mettle at the 2006 World Series, when a new event, the $50,000 buy-in H.O.R.S.E tournament, was added to determine the world's best all-around poker player. The event consisted of five games: hold'em, Omaha eight-or-better, razz, seven-card stud and seven-card stud eight-or-better. Generally, only the veteran players were familiar with the strategies of that mix, and the huge $50,000 buy-in was designed not just to frighten off the amateurs, who were typically specialists only in hold'em, but to attract the top players.

The $50,000 buy-in H.O.R.S.E event was made up of the cream of the crop in the poker world, a who's who of the greatest and most famous poker players on the planet. Very few if any of the 143 players in the starting field were what poker players considered dead money, amateurs with no real shot at winning. You had to be good to get through this tough field. I mean, you had to be real good. I figure that the last nine players comprised what may be the greatest final table of all time. They included myself, Chip, T.J. Cloutier, Dewey Tomko, Phil Ivey, 1993 World Champion Jim Bechtel, and three young established pros with big reputations—Andy Bloch, David Singer and Patrik Antonius. We all fought pretty hard to get heads-up for the championship, but when the dust settled, it came down to Chip and Andy. When they got done playing, Chip took down the $1.7 million top prize, establishing what all the pros already knew: Chip Reese was the best all-around poker player in the world.

Besides the H.O.R.S.E championship, Chip, who didn't play many tournaments, was the owner of two other WSOP bracelets, and was a great gin and backgammon player.

The poker magazine, *Card Player*, used to run a poll where people could vote for the best player. For twenty years they ran it, and every time they published the results, Chip would call me on the phone. It was a ritual we had.

"Congratulations!" he'd tell me.

I'd ask him why.

"You were voted the second-best poker player in the world!"

"Oh yeah? Who was first?"

"Guess?" he'd answer, then hang up the phone.

I didn't have to.

After the funeral, Chip's remains were cremated, and some of his ashes were placed in a gold alloy that was melted and fashioned into crosses to wear on chains around the neck. Each member of his family received one. I did too. I wore my cross for a couple of days, and while it gave me a warm feeling, I couldn't handle the memories it brought. They were so strong, I had to put it away.

For two months after Chip's death, I rarely left home. For the first time since my bypass surgery in December 2003, I began gaining weight. I'd sit at my desk all day long every day, thinking, answering e-mails, doing a little writing.

Or I'd just be staring blankly at my computer screen.

It seemed like it was too cold to swim so I turned the heat off in my swimming pool. I was too fatigued to play golf or even play much poker so I didn't do those either. My energy and health just didn't feel right. For the first time in my life, I started having heart palpitations. I went to a cardiologist, and she gave me a machine to wear when I thought I was having some kind of event with my heart. My blood pressure was high, which it had never been before, so I got a heart scan.

I thought I was accustomed to stress and I could handle just about anything, but the loss of Chip was affecting me more than I realized.

Losing my best friend in the world took a lot out of me. Chip and I had been through so many adventures together—trying to raise the *Titanic*, that disastrous Christian TV station, the deadly face-off with Spilotro, and of course, decades of epic battles across the poker table. He was like a brother to me, a best friend who had been with me through many of the highs and lows in my life. Somewhere in my unconsciousness, Chip's death brought back some of the grief I still felt from my daughter Doyla, who had died over twenty years ago. I guess the emotions were the same, and one thing kind of touched off the other. Chip had helped me through that very tough time in my life, bonding a strong friendship even closer.

And now with Chip gone, I was just lost.

Grief is like a disease, a worm that eats on you from the inside out. It's something you can feel, but can't quite see. You're just not the same as you were before that worm started in on you. Losing Chip had affected everything: I had stopped playing golf, a game like poker in that it had wrapped itself around a lot of highs and lows in my life and untold millions of dollars. I would find myself staring vacantly at things. Like a piece of driftwood in the ocean, I was awash and just couldn't find myself. Food had lost its flavor, life its gusto. I just didn't know what to do.

Then one day I told myself, "I've mourned Chip for months, and I know he wouldn't want me to go on like this. Life's short enough for all of us, and I'll be seeing him before too much longer."

As much as I loved Chip and knew that my life would never be the same, I didn't need any clippings or photos or phone calls to remind me about our relationship. I put away all Chip's pictures and things, quit taking phone calls from reporters, and stopped talking about him. After I did that, I stopped having the events with my heart, and my blood pressure returned to normal.

Still, my mourning continued. On Valentine's Day, barely two months after Chip's passing, I thought of my father because February 14 was his birthday. Even though this occasion should have been joyous, it was a long day for me as grief built on grief. Dad had been gone for fifty years, and would have been one hundred and twenty-five years old. Fifty years! I could hardly believe that five decades, half a century, had passed.

My, was it that long ago?

It certainly didn't seem like it. I thought about how I still missed him. Then I thought about my mom. And Doyla. And then my pal Chip. All those memories kind of got thrown in that same pot. My birthday would be coming up August 10, making me seventy-five years old, the same age Dad was when he died.

While my physical health got better, emotionally, it wasn't so easy to move on. Poker, the game my life had revolved around for more than fifty years, just didn't have the same appeal and I didn't play that often. And it would also be a full year after Chip's death before I got back out on the golf course again.

It's one thing to want to let go; it's another thing to be able to do so. I thought of something Chip once told me: "I'll stop playing poker when they have my funeral. Then only God will know what I'll be doing." Well, I suppose he's not playing poker anymore, but who knows?

I'm sure God has a special place for a special guy like Chip.

Chapter 45

Reputation is made in a moment. Character is built on a lifetime.

Because of the great notoriety brought on by all the media, especially television, more people got to notice and know me wherever I went. Suddenly, I became a celebrity. It got so that I couldn't go anywhere without being recognized. I'd get mobbed at the Bellagio, where we usually played the Big Game. Just going from the poker room to the valet would take an extra ten or twenty minutes because I was besieged with fans who wanted to talk and pose for pictures with me. And of course, I was obliged to take a few minutes to accommodate them. Around the World Series was even worse. Everyone wanted my time. While all this was flattering, it got to be tiring. I could barely make it to the bathroom between the quick breaks in tournament play and get back in time when they started dealing again; I'd just get mobbed by all the fans. People would stop and speak to me in airports, restaurants and casinos, and always in a friendly way.

On one hand, I liked the attention, but for the most part, I just wanted to be left alone to play poker and go about my business. I always try to remember who I really am and where I came from. I missed the days when I was just a poker player.

I could barely get my thoughts around all the proposals that poured in, let alone handle them. They offered me video game deals and they wanted to make Doyle Brunson slot machines. I figured it would be good publicity for all my activities, so when you go into casinos now, you'll see slot machines with my picture on them. I'd go on the Internet and see Doyle Brunson beer—which I knew nothing about. I'd see Doyle Brunson T-shirts, Doyle Brunson caps, Doyle Brunson plaques, Doyle Brunson playing cards. I didn't know anything about a lot of those either. I certainly wasn't getting royalties on everything.

In one proposal, I was supposed to go to New York and play cards in the display window of a department store in a replica of a Doylesroom set using special Doyle Brunson chips. We got out of that one. There were a number of TV deals in the works and a major film company produced a movie on gambling and hired me as a consultant. I worked with the great actor Robert Duvall and even appeared in the movie, *Lucky You,* in a cameo role. I got involved with more TV and film productions than I could count. Over the next few years, TV shows with all sorts of concepts sprung up like prairie weed. It seemed like every one of them wanted me as a part of them. There was that great Professional Poker League, which never saw fruition because the UIGEA legislation killed the advertising possibilities, and ultimately, the whole show.

But the UIGEA couldn't kill everything. Not by a long shot. Poker was still a big draw and all sorts of entrepreneurs and TV people were looking to capitalize on it.

The great facility built by the Venetian for the ill-fated Professional Poker League was not wasted. They moved forward with another project I was working on called *The Real Deal*, the brainchild of Merv Adelson and some of Hollywood's heavy hitters who had access to the best directors and producers in the business. It was an audience participation kind of thing with people playing for prizes. There were some flaws in the concept and the show wound up getting canceled before it got into TV production, but for a while it looked like an interesting bonding of poker and TV.

Then someone came up with the idea of broadcasting live high-stakes cash games. Mostly what had been shown were tournaments, and they thought that cash games would make for good TV. They were right about that one.

High Stakes Poker was my kind of show, featuring a game where players could pull out as much money as they want, quit when they want, and add more money when they want. In other words, real poker. It was carried by GSN-TV, the Game Show Network. It wasn't that hard to convince me to play these games. A lot of the players on the show were better tournament players than cash game players, so it was easy pickings for me. I played fifteen times on the show and won fifteen times. I sometimes wonder how I came off a cotton farm in Texas and made it as a high-stakes professional poker player. After playing on that show, I began to wonder less about it.

I played the biggest pot ever on *High Stakes Poker*. It was against Cirque du Soleil billionaire, Guy LaLiberte. There was enough money in that pot, $818,100, to buy a luxury house with a custom pool. It was certainly an exciting hand. We both had a pair of aces, but I had the best kicker, so I won. I suspect that the smile they showed on TV while I was raking in that pot was genuine.

LaLiberte, a Canadian, visited the Bellagio one day and I noticed his car parked there. It looked like it had an airplane engine in it. I'd never seen a car like that before, so I asked Guy about it when I got to the poker room.

"There's only fifty of them," he said.

"How much did it cost?"

"$1.4 million," he said flatly.

"My gosh," I said. "I know they don't have any garages to fix that car. What do you do if something happens to it?"

"Oh," he said, "I keep another one for a spare out in my garage."

Things got to the point where you could turn on your TV anytime in the evening, any night of the week, and see poker tournaments, poker shows, poker players being interviewed, or poker being talked about. And not just in the United States. Tournaments were springing up in countries I had barely heard of. Everywhere, it seemed, people embraced our game with a passion. England, Sweden, France, Australia, Denmark, and a host of other countries jumped into the game with players flocking to online sites, live tournaments, and cash games wherever they could find them. Everyone had a chance to live the dream and every year more and more players proved it could be done. I was getting all-expenses paid invites to play tournaments around the country and all over the world. I took up some of these invitations, playing in Ireland and the Philippines and England, but all those hours in the air and different time zones were tiring and took a toll on me.

The power of television really struck home: People in Manila would point and shout my name, "There's the poker player!" I couldn't believe it. A casino had a poker tournament while I was there, and I was the star attraction.

The first European World Series of Poker tournament was held in London in 2007, and despite my resolve to travel less, Harrah's persuaded me to go. I had played in the first WSOP event in the United States back in 1970, and they said it was only fitting that I go to the first one in Europe. I didn't get very far in the tournament, but it did feel special to play in the inaugural European event. I was the only player there from the original six—heck, I was about the only one of them still alive.

Poker had become such a status symbol, or at least a cultural phenomenon, that movie stars, musicians, models, and all sorts of celebrities wanted to get into the game. You'd see them playing tournaments, getting involved in celebrity-related events, and just being part of all that was going on. They were making poker movies, looking at poker scripts, and just wanting to be a part of it all. Besides *Lucky You*, I also got a small part in *The Grand*, with Woody Harrelson.

Movie star Tobey McGuire, of *Spiderman* fame, got hooked on poker—he started playing in some World Series events and became an excellent poker player—and we almost went into business together. I met Tobey at the poker tournaments and became good friends with him. He came up with the idea of a $50,000 buy-in tournament and he wanted to use my name. His *Spiderman* movies gave him a lot of cachet in the production industry, and he was able to open the door to production people and get it on TV. Tobey thought it would get really big. I think we even formed a company. Tobey knew a lot of the rich poker players in Los Angeles that would put up $50,000, and that would bring in all the pros. They'd all come to play with these guys. It would be like waving a beefsteak at an alligator.

I know I sure like beefsteak.

Unfortunately, the timing was bad. When Doylesroom decided to come back into the United States, it made the idea unfeasible for McGuire's people. When that happened, Tobey's agent advised him not to move forward because it might be perceived in a bad light, so the idea never reached fruition.

Leonardo DiCaprio was making a documentary, *The 11th Hour*, about the environmental situation and the problems we faced. He was looking for sponsors and we decided to do it because he had done us some favors by wearing a Doylesroom cap, which got nationally publicized and really helped us out. We went down to Leo's suite and heard his presentation about the environment and why we should do it.

He talked to us for about fifteen or twenty minutes, and then I said, "Okay, we're in."

Later, Leo was laughing about it.

"I've been in a lot of meetings," he said, "but I've never seen anything like this one—where a guy I was presenting a project to would reach into his pocket, pull out this little billfold, and write me a check for $350,000."

Leo just wasn't used to how gamblers did things.

We took a percentage of Leo's documentary and thought it would be a bigger hit than it was, but we did recoup some of our money. I think we owned about 27 percent of the film. I'm a loser on the deal, but we still get a little dividend once in a while. It was worth it because Leo became a good friend of mine; he's a nice kid, and his film hopefully will have some positive influence on things.

Much of my time was spent promoting Doylesroom in one way or another, and we were able to bring some interesting celebrities on board to play. We got Paris Hilton to play on Doylesroom for a bit; and while she backed out because of the legal ramifications, her sister Nicky is an avid poker player and plays on the site. She's a really sweet girl. Pamela Anderson also got involved for a while; in fact, we gave Pam her own poker room, Pamandersonpoker.com. She was doing quite well with it until they passed that stupid Internet law, UIGEA, that scared everybody. Her advisors suggested she pull out, too. She was another surprise, a very personable lady. I had heard so many Pam Anderson stories, I was surprised to find out how nice she actually is. The trouble with meeting all the gorgeous gals is they tell me the same thing. "You remind me of my grandfather."

Ouch!

I'm not even thinking of retirement, but someday I will have to pass the torch. Doylesroom is in the process of signing a group of young Internet poker players who will be known as the Brunson 10. I've met a few of the early selections, and they are great kids. They will be the future of the site, along with our existing representatives.

Times had really changed from the early days when I played poker. Once, I was in New York for a news conference and an autograph-photo party at ESPN's bar and restaurant in Times Square, where people lined up to be photographed with me. Three decades earlier, having all those photographers crowding around me would have meant only one thing: the police hauling me off to jail with my arms pulled back and my wrists handcuffed.

More recently, I pounced on an interesting opportunity with a guy from France, David Benyamine. I bet him $150,000 that he couldn't break 90 from the back tees at Shadowcreek, a local golf course. He had a year to do it. He could barely get the club on the ball when we made the bet, so I thought it was the biggest lock I'd ever had on a bet. It's a tough course, and I just knew he didn't have much of a shot at improving enough to win the bet. An ex-tennis player, David, practiced golf for a year. By the time the year rolled around, he had gotten so good I could hardly believe it. I won the bet by one shot, but it was a miracle; I sweated it out right down to the last hole.

I pocketed that money—but only for a while. The time had come for the next bet, the next high-stakes wager that would get my heart pumping yet again.

I always like to keep my money in play.

★

Chapter 46

The best thing about the future is that it comes one day at a time.

Different doctors have told me that my body, as badly as I've treated it, must be programmed to last a hundred years or more. One said 125, another said 100, so I settled on 120, which was a fair compromise. But my heart was healthy, like a hard-working and tireless carburetor. That's probably because of the cleansing, rapid flow of blood through my veins during pressure situations at the poker table or on the golf course.

Well, okay, maybe not. But it sounds good to me.

So it was kind of ironic when, in January 2009, I got on a list of the "100 Most Likely People to Die" during that year. Mack Rawden, writing for the CinemaBlend.com website, listed me at sixteenth and gave me a 10 percent chance of expiring that year at seventy-five years old.

Apparently, he didn't know my doctors had me pegged in at 120.

He also didn't consider my good genes either. All ten family members on my mom's side lived into their nineties, with three of them passing 100. I think I take after that side; at least that's where my family tells me I got this bald head.

At first, I was a little upset with this ranking, even though the site was meant in jest, but then I got a phone call from Mack, and we made a $10,000 to $1,000 bet about my demise. Naturally, I took the over, and to Mack's credit, he said he hoped he loses. That made two of us. We decided to donate the winnings to the American Cancer Society. If I don't make it to 120, I'm planning on going out at the age of 102 in honor of the 10-2 poker hand that is named after me, so I think Mack made a bad bet.

But that wasn't the only list I got on. As I approached my seventy-fifth birthday, I landed on the most unexpected and least likely list of all, the Jenny Woo "Top 10 Sexiest Poker Players."

"He may be older than dirt," Jenny said, noting that "the hottest old man on the planet" is also the oldest man to ever appear on her Top 10.

Then Jenny added that "way over the hill is much better than being six feet under it!"

Who was I to argue?

While my heart was still beating soundly and I was still going strong, life and death always have a way of making their own decisions.

On April 6, 2009, I received a phone call from my nephew, Ken, and I could tell right away it wasn't good.

"Doyle, I've got some bad news. You might want to sit down."

As Ken hesitated, trying to find the right words, my mind raced through the possibilities. I didn't think it was anything about Doylesroom, which had been an ongoing difficulty, or anyone in the immediate family. I probably would have been the first to hear that kind of news. After I ruled out those possibilities, my mind immediately raced to the phone call I'd received from Ken some eighteen months before, when he told me that Chip was gone. He had that same tone of voice and I was pretty sure someone close to me had died.

But who?

"Go ahead, Ken, might as well get to it," I said, dreading the next words out of his mouth. There was some noise on the phone connection, interference I guess, and it kind of magnified the stillness on the other end of the line.

"It's Chip's son, Casey. He died a few hours ago. Looks like it might be some kind of drug overdose."

I was in shock. Drugs again, with another person close to me getting the worst of it. I was angry and upset, knowing that nobody ever wins when drugs are involved. This time, my dear friend Chip's son was the victim. I was overwhelmed and just sat there, not knowing what to think. It was a tough blow to me. Casey was a bona fide major league baseball prospect and had a bright future ahead of him. When Chip died, Casey's drug problems really got out of hand. He couldn't handle his father's death and started taking more and more drugs. I think he was in and out of rehab about three different times. I wish I could have done something, but you just can't help people when they're not ready to be helped. I saw Casey two or three nights before he died when I was driving home from a poker game. Casey saw my Escalade with the Doylesroom sticker on it and he yelled at me at a stoplight. We pulled over and he gave me a big hug. It was just a few days later that he died.

I felt guilty, like I'd let Chip down, but I don't know what I could have done. I remember Casey got in some trouble, and David Chesnoff, his attorney, got him off. I thought it would have been better for him to spend some time in jail instead, but it's hard to make that kind of choice for other people. It makes me sick just to think about all the people that have been lost to drugs. Must have been fifteen or twenty people I was close to that died from drugs. What a waste.

Everyone should have the privilege to grow old—gray hair, wrinkles, the marks and grooves on your face. Life experiences are what put those lines and marks on a person's face.

I know with mine, I've earned every one of them.

Chapter 47

The best vitamin for making friends....B1.

C asey's death got me to thinking how fragile life is. I remember not so long ago, when we'd be in the car and pass those wind towers in West Texas. They were maybe two hundred feet high and produced lots of electricity. The landscape was dotted with them. I'd watch all those big blades turn round and round and wonder how much electricity each one of them produced. Somehow, they just fascinated me, and it seemed like I could watch them forever. They became a part of the fabric of my memories and their familiarity gave me comfort.

Now, every time one of my friends died, I feel like one of those wind towers had stopped forever. That image would just sit there in my mind, a dead wind tower among a field of live ones, its tall structure reduced to a piece of empty steel. And a piece of me would just feel hollow inside.

With the passing of each friend, I started reflecting on things. The longer you live, the more friends you're going to lose. I guess that's just the way it is, but it's disheartening that these losses have escalated so much in the last few years. The death of Jamie Thompson at age sixty was reminiscent of Chip's passing. In fact, it was Chip who called me and said, "Can you believe Jamie Thompson died last night?" He'd gone to the hospital emergency room for a kidney stone problem, but it was a heart problem that killed him. Jamie was a very close friend, a former All-American basketball player at Wichita State, and still a scratch golfer at the time of his death in 2007. At six-foot-three and big but not overweight, he was a mountain of a man who played golf almost every day. Soon after I first met him on the golf course, I discovered Jamie didn't have one ounce of choke in him, so I took him as a golfing partner when I could. I found out later that he had refused money from my opponents to deliberately lose. It's hard to find a loyal and honest friend like that.

I have trouble believing so many big, strong, healthy guys have heart problems. I wonder if the medications they give these men have something to do with their dying, but death—and life itself—is a strange and difficult thing to comprehend in the first place.

I try not to dwell too much on the people who have passed—but on the gifts that life has given me. I've been blessed with a wonderful family, and more interesting people, good and great friends than any man could ask for. I think there were a half a dozen or so guys in my life that I would distinguish as my best friends.

D.C. Andrews was probably my best friend when I was growing up, with Riley Cross a close second. That was right up through high school. Then I met Raymond Hibler in college, and he was my best friend for a period of time. We were roommates in college and have stayed in touch, still talking on the phone several times a year. When I first started gambling, Wayne Hamilton was a guy I ran with for four or five years, until he died. I didn't feel as close to him as the rest of my best friends, but we spent a lot of time together.

When I came to Vegas, there was Jack Binion, my longest running best friend. We met back in 1969 at the Texas Gamblers Reunion in Reno. I can always depend on Jack if I need help and he knows I would do anything to help him. Jack has been extra special in my life. He is, without question, the best friend a guy could ever have. He's always been there for me, financially as well as spiritually, through thick and thin, triumph and tragedy. He loaned me $2 million when I was in that television station fiasco and never even mentioned a note or collateral. And contrary to my near-perfect losing investment record, I successfully invested with Jack in his company that operated riverboat casinos in several states. It was the best investment I ever made, and maybe the only one that ever made me money.

My other really close friend was Chip Reese. Chip was in the everyday mix of gambling. He was always at the poker game and when the games broke up we would go places. In 1991 he became the youngest member enshrined in the Poker Hall of Fame. But as a real pal, he was already in *my* Hall of Fame. He was there for me when my daughter died. He saw how distraught I was, and he was part of my religious support group, even joining me in reading the Bible, Christian literature and the prophecies. In my very darkest moments—including those times when I briefly contemplated suicide, which he may well have sensed—Chip put aside everything to help me. I believed with all my heart that he would be with me the rest of my life.

I was wrong.

There was also Sailor for so many, many memorable years, and Mike Caro, both of whom enriched me in countless ways. My traveling partner Slim would have to be mentioned also, along with Dewey Tomko and Doug Dalton. Doug, the cardroom manager at the Bellagio, is a longtime friend—we spend many New Year's together—and he was always there when I needed him. Back in the eighties, I owned a cardroom in Oceanside, California, with Chip and a fellow named Len Miller, and Doug came out from Vegas to run it for us.

They say if you can count your good friends on both hands, you're lucky. Well, I've been very lucky by that definition, or really, any definition. I've been fortunate to have hundreds. I've played poker with countless people, and I've become good friends with many of them.

While most of the interesting characters I knew were gamblers, Harry Claiborne, a friend of mine for years, was a notable exception. A flamboyant defense lawyer, prosecutor, federal judge and longtime friend, Harry was the assistant district attorney who tried and convicted Benny Binion—then went to work for him when Benny got out of jail!

After Benny hired him to be his personal attorney, Harry could usually be found in the Binion Booth at the Horseshoe telling stories. We had a roast once for Jack Binion in Louisiana, and Harry flew a private plane down there with Chip and me. All three of us spoke at the roast, but Harry was in a class by himself when it came to public speaking. He was an amazing storyteller and orator, eloquent and engaging. It was simply a joy to listen to his stories.

At one time, Harry was among the great high-profile defense lawyers in Nevada. He represented Rat-Packers Dean Martin and Frank Sinatra when they applied for gaming licenses in Vegas. One of my favorite Harry stories occurred when he was a seventy-five-year-old federal judge. A sixty-five-year-old drug dealer appeared before him for sentencing and appealed for mercy, claiming poor health. Harry was not remotely sympathetic, sentencing him to twenty-five years in prison with no possibility of parole.

"That's too long," the dealer whined. "I can't make it that long. I'll die before I get out."

"I know, son," Harry replied. "Just do what you can."

Harry was convicted of tax evasion and impeached in 1986 by the U.S. House of Representatives. The first federal judge to be sent to prison, he served seventeen months of a two-year sentence. About a decade later, battling cancer and Alzheimer's, Harry killed himself at age eighty-six.

I've also been extra privileged to have Louise, my very special wife who has put up with me for all these years and has been the most wonderful wife a man could possibly have. She's given me four fine children, she's been a terrific companion for almost half a century, and has been by my side through the best and worst of times. She's one in a zillion. I'm in cardrooms all the time and see these guys get calls from their wives and girlfriends. But in forty-something years, Louise never called me while I was playing poker unless it was an emergency.

She did have difficulty grasping how focused I became during a month-long tournament or an extended, high-stakes poker game. I concentrated so hard that I would actually feel as though a heavy weight lay between my eyes, and I tended to block everything from my mind except the game. She would talk to me and I wouldn't hear her. And even afterward, it took me a few days to wind down. She didn't cope with that very well, but that's understandable. She could have burdened me with guilt and regrets for my absences and preoccupation, for shirking family responsibilities in ways little and big, but she never did. It takes a special woman to be with a poker player, not just the time apart, which could be as long as three or four weeks at a time, but the mood swings that inevitably occur in this profession.

I think my dad and my brother would have been proud and pleased that I've had a successful gambling career. My sister Lavada would never be labeled a gambling fan, but I think she's proud of my accomplishments. I don't think my mother would have cared much either way because worldly things, monetary things, never meant much to her.

Understand that for more than fifty years, pretty much all I have done is look for a good poker game or a new golf course—or at least it seems that way.

I've had three remarkable children, daughters Doyla and Pam, and son Todd, and a lovely and very special stepdaughter, Cheryl. Cheryl is the spitting image of her mother: drop-dead gorgeous and a little Southern belle, an extrovert who, as we say in Texas, never meets a stranger. She has used her friendly and outgoing personality in public relations and marketing. For a few years she even dabbled in the poker world, running satellite tournaments at the World Series. When Louise was having her health problems and the kids were growing up, her daughter Cheryl quit her job in Texas and moved to Las Vegas to lend a hand with her younger siblings. It was one of the nicest things imaginable. She showed up expecting three kids but found five. Two friends of Todd and Pam were staying with us at the time because of problems at their homes. Our house was always the kid-friendly place with neighborhood children in and out all the time. I remember it being tough to sleep with all that noise. I don't know what we would have done without Cheryl.

Like her mother, Cheryl has a passion for investments and has been quite successful in real estate ventures. She married young and blessed me with a grandson, Jeff, who is close in age to Todd and is like another son to me. Jeff married a lovely girl named Angi, and has two daughters, Lauren and Christan, and one son, Evan, all of whom reside in Montana. Jeff takes care of the family properties there and is a big help to me.

Doyla was my firstborn and, as most firstborns are to their parents, she was very special to me. She inherited my father's disposition, meaning she seldom got angry. She was just a joy to be around. She was probably a little spoiled, as are all my children. Both she and Pam had their own horses and loved to go riding.

Like her mother, she was a devout Christian.

Pam, my second daughter, was born just fourteen months after Doyla. A bit of a rebel at times, she takes after me more than my other daughters. She's hard-headed, determined, and competitive, like me, and she inherited my sense of humor. Fortunately for Pam, she did inherit many positive traits from her mother—a heart of gold, and a caring, friendly, and compassionate nature.

Pam enjoyed playing low-limit poker, which might have been a clue for the series of events that would occur years later. She also had a love for animals and an affinity for the elderly. She went into the retirement industry after graduating from the University of Texas-San Antonio. She was the executive director at an assisted living retirement community in California and moved back to Las Vegas in 2000.

Todd was my only boy and my last born. He possesses many of my traits, good and bad. Todd's smart, stubborn, and loves to argue a point; in fact he's never lost an argument in his life—at least not that I've seen! Like Pam and I, he is grumpy in the morning and could be a very private person in some areas of his life. He attended Southwest Texas State at San Marcos and Texas Tech at Lubbock with the goal of becoming an attorney. Todd, an excellent debater in high school, would have been a natural and successful lawyer. But, alas, he flirted with poker in college, got hooked, and decided to follow in my footsteps. I pretended to be outraged, but secretly I was very pleased.

Todd established himself almost overnight as a world-class poker player, having won the first of his eleven major tournaments at the renowned Bicycle Club in California at the tender age of twenty-one. He continued to play and win in the biggest tournaments and side games, and quickly became a really good player. I don't think it's just a proud daddy talking through his hat, but if Todd had my killer instinct, he would possibly be the best player in the world. Todd married a wonderful young woman from Russia named Anjela, and they also settled in Las Vegas.

I don't have many regrets in life, nothing that would change my way of thinking and living, but I do wish I'd spent more time with my family when the kids were young. I do have priceless memories of our holidays together, our motor-home adventures, the summers in Hawaii, and our vacations in Montana. And I'm still collecting those memories. When I had a few days away from the poker table, we would load everyone up in our Pace Arrow motor home and take off. Sometimes we hit the road with no specific destination; we'd start driving and make split-second decisions as we rolled along. My mother always went with us, and we had lots of laughs and memorable experiences as we crisscrossed the United States.

Because Louise had life-threatening allergies and asthma, we frequently boarded planes and headed for the favorable atmosphere of ocean locations. She and the kids spent many a summer in Hawaii and I joined them whenever I could break free. Not surprisingly, Louise started buying condos and real estate in the islands and eventually made quite a bit of money—while the kids had the time of their lives.

I'm most proud that we formed a close-knit, loving family and remain so even as we grow older. Like most everybody, we have occasional skirmishes, yet we never fail to support one another. Some families tend to drift apart as they age, but the Brunsons have only grown closer and closer.

Even when I was extremely busy, I never missed a Thanksgiving, Christmas or New Year's Eve with my family. I still don't. Our entire family continues to gather at our home for holiday meals. Louise is a terrific cook, and our doors have always been open to relatives and friends for these special occasions. These were fun times. To this day, there is nothing like a Brunson Christmas.

It is funny, though, that Todd and I—not being nearly as open and outgoing as the girls—usually find ourselves on the outside looking in when the Brunson women get together. They sound like a bunch of teenagers at a slumber party, whooping it up and cackling like hens deep into the night. Just the same, it's a blast for Todd and me just being around them.

Seeing Puggy at family dinners would sometimes make me recall an incident from years earlier, when he invited me out to his hometown of Nashville for some high-stakes golf matches. No sooner had I arrived in Tennessee when Pug told me he'd arranged a special dinner that night in an exclusive downtown restaurant.

That was fine, but then he proceeded to inform me he'd fixed me up with a gorgeous brunette for the evening.

"No, Puggy," I interrupted. "I can't do that and you know it."

"Hell, Doyle, she's a livin' doll and lotsa fun."

"I'm sure she is, but—"

"Oh, don't give me that crap, Doyle..."

Puggy being Puggy, he wouldn't take no for an answer, and we finally struck a compromise of sorts. His brunette beauty would join us for dinner, but she would not be my companion.

Turned out, she really was a looker. Ironically, her name was Louise, which was a bit of a jolt. I was pondering this when our waitress appeared at the table to take our drink order. Her name: Pam. I figured the valet's name had to be Todd.

"Louise" and "Pam" torpedoed any romantic notions that might have developed that night. Puggy was kind of put out with me, but even he conceded the Louise-Pam episode was a hoot.

I still have a sense of guilt about the death of my daughter Doyla. I worry that I might have neglected her in some way. Certainly, her mother never did. But I've wondered if she would have lived had I chosen a different profession. I don't know and I'll never know, at least not in this life.

I've tried to compensate for the stereotype that gamblers don't normally contribute much to society through my charitable activities and contributions. I'm not a soft touch for panhandlers because I figure they're going to go buy drugs or booze. But I am inclined to help a guy who's destitute and trying to feed his family. I still send money to M.D. Anderson, the cancer center in Houston. If they hadn't helped me, where would I be?

I'm not a Bible scholar, but Romans 8:28 explains everything better than I can. It says, in effect, that we know that everything that happens to us is working for our good if we love God and are fitting into His plans.

Some years ago, I decided I needed a nice, quiet place to rest and recuperate when I got worn down. I bought a place by Flathead Lake in Montana, which is the biggest natural lake west of the Mississippi. I was visiting Chip, whose ex-wife is from the western part of the state, and I immediately fell in love with the area. Flathead Lake is spectacularly beautiful and I can boat or fish or hunt if I want to. It puts me back in touch with nature—the gorgeous pine trees and fruit trees, the lakes and rivers, and the animals, deer, elk, bear, everything. It's just so different from the gambling atmosphere—possibly because I've spotted no wolves and only an occasional snake. A sign over the entrance to our lake home reads, "Longway From Longworth," and is framed on either side by pictures of 10-2, the winning hands in my two World Series championships. I don't get to the lake home as often as I'd like, and when I do, I find myself working on various projects.

But it's not all relaxation; at least it wasn't on a particular evening when one of my all-time scariest episodes occurred in one of the most unexpected places—at a party. Chip Reese had bought a new house about eight miles from my home at Flathead Lake and was throwing a housewarming bash. Some of the partygoers were staying at my place, and we decided to take my pontoon boat to the party. Eight of us, including Louise, Todd, and his wife Anjela, boarded the boat and headed out across the lake.

We were having a grand time at Chip's house when we got word that a storm was brewing. Several of the revelers who were familiar with the area warned us not to attempt a return trip home via the boat. It was after dark and Flathead Lake is fifty-five miles long and twelve miles wide—a virtual ocean. But the waters were calm and, with Todd at the controls, we ignored the warnings and started back.

Twenty minutes later the summer squall caught us in the middle of the lake. I had heard about these Flathead storms, but I never imagined how treacherous they could become. The waves were five- to ten-feet high and smashed into our boat with shuddering power. I shouted at Todd to head for shore at once, but he refused, declaring over the sound of the crashing waves that it would be best to plunge headfirst into the storm to keep from capsizing. I was terrified that at any moment the giant waves were going to dump us into the chilly, turbulent water.

I was convinced that all of us would die.

I lost track of time while we were caught up in that stormy saga, but Todd not only got us safely to shore, he guided the boat right up to the front of our lake house. It might have been divine intervention again, but I could mutter only one word:

Whew!

Despite all its charms, my Montana getaway didn't slow me down as much as I hoped. It seems like I have only one gear and that's fast-forward. But if I ever do retire, that will be the place. It's my escape from the Las Vegas heat, where I can relax and renew my body and spirit. But most of all, my sanctuary at Flathead Lake gives me a place and time to reflect.

That is, once I *get* there.

The highway between Las Vegas and Montana can indeed be long when Louise has me trapped in the car. I like my dogs more than most anything, and the best way to get them to Flathead Lake is to drive. I remember a trip we took up there in the summer of 2008, Louise had me captive in an automobile for two long days and she talked my ears off. My eardrums felt like Sitting Bull's tom-toms sending out messages to all his tribes, and I was the messenger.

But bless her heart, Louise is the heart and soul of the Brunson family. And I cherish our Montana retreat as an opportunity to recoup some of the family time I missed while traveling the Texas Circuit.

Every minute of that time is a gift.

Book V
Royal Flush

Chapter 48

It isn't the destination, it's the journey.

I've been credited with playing a major role in the growth of poker. I've even heard it said that all poker waters flow through Doyle Brunson. But I'm not the only one who has promoted poker by any means. A lot of credit is due all those poker players who persevered many years ago—on the Texas Circuit and then during the early Vegas years—when times were tough and poker was a dangerous profession to practice. We all kept playing even when the money wasn't near what it is today, when we had to scrape to make a living, and sometimes scrape to stay alive. We persisted and kept the games going.

Of course, these accolades wouldn't be complete without giving credit to Amarillo Slim. He did a lot for poker in the old days because he was the first one who really worked the talk shows. In 1972, when he won the championship, Slim tirelessly made media appearances and opened the door for the future success of the World Series of Poker. Slim had some troubles in 2004, being charged with child molestation, and got a pretty bad rap in the poker community because of it, which I thought was a shame. I knew Slim really well from all the years we spent together and the many rooms we shared. He had his faults, but I never saw one thing over all the years that we traveled together that would make me think Slim was capable of doing what he was accused of. After all those troubles, which I believe stemmed from some falsely stated situations, Slim got back together with his formerly estranged family, which I think points to his innocence. I just want to set the record straight on my feelings about Slim.

Because of my standing in the poker community, I've received many accolades for my contributions over the years. *Bluff* magazine, which came out in early 2006, listed the most influential movers and shakers in poker. The group included Chip Reese, Johnny Chan, some of the top tournament players, a few major online poker rooms, and the co-founders of the World

Poker Tour, Berman and Lipscomb. No. 2 on the influential list was ESPN, which has broadcast the WSOP since 1994. The magazine placed me on top of the "Poker's Power 20.

While all that is flattering, with such recognition comes responsibility and I try to use whatever influence I have for the betterment and promotion of the poker industry.

It peeves me no end to see top players reap the benefits and pleasure of the game, yet feel no obligation to contribute much to its ongoing health. Poker must have people who promote and start the games, keep them going. It's ironic that I've gained a lot of publicity from spending so much time promoting the game because I never wanted the spotlight. At one time, I was quite uncomfortable being around television cameras and doing interviews with broadcasters and writers. But I've since accepted that I have become one of the most influential players and have an obligation to do promotions on behalf of the game.

Most everything has its upsides and downsides, I suppose. On one hand, I'm heartened to see poker becoming so popular with both women and men. It's gratifying to see the public look favorably on the game after what I had to endure for most of my life.

Many people are not aware that a lot of the "top" players on the poker tour are really marginal players who can't make a living in the live games. In my world, they're not *real* poker players, just tournament players that have ridden a good streak of luck to a big televised win.

I've long felt that Internet poker and tournaments have hurt live cash games. The big cash games need a nucleus of financially secure players, but many high-profile players don't have any money. Assessing the situation midway through 2009, I'd say that the poker-playing economy is very bad because so many players have spent all their money on tournaments and Internet poker.

Just about everybody knows that I like to play high. But I also want to play at a level that generates players—that's where the soft money is. When the stakes get too high, amateurs who want to see if they can compete with the top pros get shut out. They just don't have the kind of money they need to give the Big Game a try.

The Big Game is the highest regular stakes poker game anywhere, and it has a long history in Las Vegas, going back to the seventies when it was played at the Dunes. It moved to the Mirage in the eighties, then to the Bellagio in the nineties, and briefly, to the Golden Nugget in the '00s before returning to the Bellagio. Somebody jokingly called me the Cal

Ripken of poker since I've been a regular in that game longer than anyone. I suppose it's true. Some of the original players in the Big Game back in the sixties, like Puggy and Slim, have long since stopped playing.

It will be interesting to see how the future of the World Series of Poker and the big cash games progress, but one thing's for sure—as long as I'm able to hold my wits about me, I'll be putting my cash on the table, ready to wager it against the best players they can throw at me.

★

Chapter 49

If longevity doesn't improve your game, you're not paying attention.

If I created my own Mt. Rushmore of great poker players, in no particular order, I'd choose four players: Johnny Moss, Walter "Puggy" Pearson, David "Chip" Reese and Bryan "Sailor" Roberts. Johnny Moss has to be one of the faces because he contributed so much. Poker would have died out down in Texas without him. If that had occurred, poker as we know it would never have gotten to Vegas and proliferated into the giant tournaments we have today. Walter "Puggy" Pearson was the catalyst for all the action in Vegas for thirty years, from the sixties on up into the eighties. Puggy kept poker going until the WSOP finally got poker recognized, so he definitely has to be up there. Of course, David "Chip" Reese has to be one of the faces. He was simply the best all-around player I've ever known. He would play anybody, anytime. A lot of folks won't agree with my last choice, Bryan "Sailor" Roberts. He played all the games, but was particularly adept at no-limit. I actually think he could have been the greatest player of all time if he had the dedication, but he succumbed to the temptations of the world and never got the accolades he deserved.

With the exception of Chip, who was in his prime when he died, today's players remember these guys when they were old and past their prime. But believe me, they were tigers. I left out the youngsters, but they can make their own list in twenty or thirty years.

A lot of people are curious as to how today's young players compare with the old guard, those of us who came up through the tough cash games on the Texas Circuit and elsewhere. It's not as simple to compare the two as you might think. Many of the younger players are known less for their skills than for their success in tournaments, which generate the media hoopla and television coverage. And while there are some great players in the tournaments, a vast majority of them are unproven.

People talk about who the best players are, wondering how all these kids who are winning tournaments stack up, but no one can convince me that the best players aren't the ones who play for the big money. That is the true proving ground where you discover if you have what it takes or not.

I get ticked off when I hear tournament know-it-all players start talking about the old-time poker players not being any good. I'd like to see any of the self-proclaimed "greats" go back in time and play Johnny Moss, Pat Renfro, Sailor Roberts, James Roy, Bobby Hoff or a host of other guys that made their living playing no-limit hold'em. Naturally, that can't happen, but I've played against both generations and I feel that those old guys would chew up these young guns.

Playing poker in the places I did was a high-risk profession, especially back in Fort Worth in my formative years. None of the thirty-five or forty guys about my age that hung out together on Exchange Avenue made it into their thirties without getting hauled off or killed. That is, except for me and Corky Slagger. Corky kind of disappeared from the picture. I heard later that he broke his back riding bulls in the rodeo. Two out of forty are lousy odds, so I feel fortunate I survived those tough times.

During an early Las Vegas adventure, I was at the Horseshoe and noticed a guy bird-dogging me. I pretended I didn't see him and just ambled outside and stood around, then walked over to the Golden Nugget. The guy followed me but made no overt move. I strolled over to the Fremont and quickly ducked behind a row of slot machines. He came in too and started looking around for me. I slipped right up behind him and stood there like a totem pole until he turned around. My stalker was so startled he nearly jumped out of his skin. He took off without a word.

Another difference between the old guard and the new school of players has to do with integrity. In the old days, we developed long-lasting friendships by necessity. Our word was our bond. When we borrowed or lost money gambling with one another, we set a date to repay the money and we met the deadline whatever the costs. It was imperative to keep our word in financial matters. We had an appreciation for our profession that most of the young guys don't have today.

Why was I thinking about this?

Because when Chip died, only Phil Ivey called to say he owed him a big sum of money and asked where he could drop it off. Chip was always such a generous and caring guy that he regularly loaned money to a lot of players. Other than Phil, no players that I know of came forward to pay the debts they owed.

I don't know what I'd tell a young person who wanted to become a professional poker player today, because the business is so unpredictable. For every person who succeeds, a hundred fail. Other vocations are decidedly more acceptable and dependable.

When it comes to poker players, Benny Binion said it best, "If you've got talent, it's the land of milk and honey. If you don't, it's the elephant burial ground."

To make it today, to be a great player, you've got to play and play and play. There's no substitute for experience. If you're good, you'll soon know it. The cream does rise to the top in the poker world.

What does it really take to be a great player? First off, it takes *desire*, and maybe the need or the *obsession* to win money. Winning at poker requires a killer instinct. It's pretty difficult for a great player to emerge from a well-to-do environment. If a player has plenty of money, he probably has a tendency to approach the game as a sport. Additionally, you must be able to implement your skills at the poker table. Implementation is probably the biggest difference between good poker players and great poker players.

You must also have the temperament to play poker full time and learn to handle the days where you're stuck and nothing seems to go right. Poker, especially at the upper levels, requires extreme concentration. Take some time to set your priorities straight before you sit down to play any serious poker. If you have any major problems, wait until you solve them before you play. I learned that lesson the hard way. I've only had four major losing streaks in my life and each one followed something bad that happened and severely impacted my game focus.

The first time was right after I married Louise in 1962. She wanted me to quit poker and get a job coaching and teaching at a local school. I wouldn't do it and continued to play, but it seemed as though I couldn't win a pot until we got our difficulties resolved.

Then, twenty years later when our first-born daughter died unexpectedly, I attempted to play too soon, and had to quit because I couldn't concentrate. I lost a lot of money when I should have been home mourning my daughter with my family. I didn't play again for a year.

In fifty years, right up to 2004, I'd never had a losing year in poker. That's when I tried to play right on the heels of having gastric bypass surgery. I lost $6 million in the side games at the WSOP. That was by far the worst performance of my career. I finally turned my play around, but all that money was gone. With the Series in progress, the right crowd was in town and I was just playing unlucky. But even then, I staged a knockdown, drag-out comeback right up until the end of the year.

My fourth losing streak was precipitated by Chip's death. I tried to play after his funeral because the WPT tournament that has my name on it, The Doyle Brunson Five Diamond World Poker Classic, was going on and I felt obligated to participate. Everything I did was wrong and now I realize I shouldn't have tried to play.

In all four instances, I was mightily distracted and paid the price at the poker tables. When you have too much going on inside your head, it seems like there isn't enough room for poker and, consequently, you're not prepared to play your best game. And you lose. Most people don't seem to understand that much more than talent and knowledge are required to become a great poker player. You have to be able to handle adversity without going off the deep end. When I lose, I might feel a little bad, but that feeling goes away the next day. If you don't know how to handle losses, you're in the wrong game.

"What really separates top pros from good poker players is when things are going bad," Chip used to say. "It's like life. It's a long road that doesn't turn. It's how you handle the adversity in a poker game that matters."

Calculate your results by the year, not the day, week or month. At the end of the year, add it all up and see how you've done. Over the years, the truly great players will stand the test of time.

One of the questions I get asked a lot is which one of the young players is the best. There are a lot of good players out there but my answer is always the same: "Come back in twenty years and see who is still here." I have seen many, many talented young guys put up good results for a year or two. Then something happens and they vanish. Or at least, their chips do. Hometown champions are the juicy tidbits the top pros are lying in wait for. You see, playing poker for a living is a lot harder than people think, even though so many big tournaments make it more likely that an average player can be successful—at least for a while.

There are many talented young players and I've got my opinions on which ones I think are the most promising. I think my son Todd is as good or maybe better than any of the new generation of players. He has proven himself in the cash games and the tournaments. Time will tell.

An argument surely could be made for Phil Ivey to be at the top of the list of today's young players. He's the kid from New Jersey who has been burning up the tables. Phil has a lot of gamble in him, and he's played well in both the tournaments and the cash games. It's a bit too early to tell for sure, but he may be the future king of the poker world. He's got the potential, which he demonstrates daily in the highest stakes poker games in the world. He's also won six gold bracelets at the WSOP, plus a major WPT tournament in Los Angeles in 2008 for $1.6 million in prize money. As this book goes to press, Phil is at the final table of the 2009 WSOP. That is a great accomplishment, and I hope he wins it.

Gus Hansen is another good young player. His aggressive style reminds me of an exceptional player from the past, Jack Straus. Gus plays more like I described in my book *Super/System* than anybody I've ever seen except Jack. Gus won three major televised tournaments in 2003, one of the most extraordinary feats since Johnny Chan's incredible run in 1987–88, when Johnny won two World Series Main Events back-to-back. Gus hasn't been as successful in the side games as he's been in tournaments, but I think he will get there someday because he's very smart—he just needs some seasoning.

Daniel Negreanu is also one of the most successful young tournament players out there. His domination of so many major tournaments in 2004, and continued great play since then, validated my selection of him as a contributor to *Super System 2*. He is richly talented although, like Gus, he hasn't totally proven himself in the real big money games.

A few other up-and-comers I should mention are Ted Forrest, David Chiu, David Benyamine, a Frenchman, and a richly talented newcomer from Finland, Patrik Antonius.

If I had to pick just two young players that would stand the test of time, Antonius and Negreanu are my favorites to still be playing at a high level thirty years from now. Someday we will see how accurate my predictions are.

There haven't been many great women poker players in the past, but I know a dozen or more women whose skills rival the good male players today and their numbers are increasing. I believe that Jennifer Harman, Kathy Liebert, Cyndy Violette and Annie Duke have paved the way for female players. In my experience, most women are not as competitive as men at the poker table, but Jennifer Harman is. Jennifer plays in our big games, higher than any woman has ever played before.

She's gutsy, too. Jennifer was playing poker with us just before the 2007 World Series started when who should walk into the cardroom but Jimmy Chagra. I hadn't seen him since he had gone to prison almost thirty years earlier, but I've always been good at recognizing people from years past. He was standing right by our table when I spotted him.

"Chag!"

"That's me," he said, smiling.

I went over and gave him a big hug and we visited for a few minutes. Well, Jennifer has always been a notorious steamer when she's losing, which she was doing right about then, and became increasingly impatient with this stranger in the room. I could see what was coming. She turned around and told Jimmy to move. He did. Then she lost another pot and summoned the floor manager over.

"Get this blankety-blank out of here!" she demanded.

I butted in and said, "Jennifer, do you know who this is?"

"No, I don't care if he's Al Capone, get him out of here."

She was determined to get rid of this nuisance, merely a convicted drug dealer accused of complicity in the murder of a federal judge, the same murder that actor Woody Harrelson's father went to prison for. Thirty years earlier, given Chagra's volatile nature, this story might have had a different ending.

As Jimmy turned to leave, he looked at Jennifer and said, "I used to tip more money than you've got in front of you."

He might have been exaggerating a little bit because he was upset, but I suspect he wasn't. In the seventies, I saw Chagra tip a cocktail waitress $10,000 for bringing him a water. I'd also heard of times when he tipped a lot more than that. Jimmy had even less regard for money than some poker players I've known. Rumor had it that when he was having a good night—and that could mean he was winning in excess of a million dollars—cocktail waitresses could make more in tips than they would the entire year. One night he asked a cocktail waitress what her yearly income from the job was.

"With tips, about forty-five thousand dollars," she said.

"So, why don't you just quit?" Chagra said, flipping her that much in chips.

She did.

Supposedly, he once tipped more than half a million dollars after a huge night playing craps. He would play as high as anybody in those days and, if he was winning big, he could single-handedly change the profit line of a casino—and an employee's life if he was in a big tipping mood.

Later, after the '07 World Series got started, Chagra showed up and sent word that he'd like to meet with me. He laid a sad story on me and said he needed to borrow $15,000. He explained something about a book and a movie being in the works and that he'd pay me back when the movie came out. I gave him the money, never expecting to see it again.

Sure enough, I didn't.

Chagra died in July of 2008 at the age of sixty-three. Given all the money I'd won off him, I suppose I can't complain too much.

Chapter 50

In order to see the rainbow, you have to endure the rain.

M y old pal Dewey Tomko was inducted into the Poker Hall of Fame in 2008 and I was the keynote speaker. Naturally, I was real happy for Dewey and welcomed the opportunity to tell everyone about him, especially since young players never saw him at his best. In the eighties, Dewey won more money in tournaments than anybody. He was also a tough cash game player even though he didn't play in some of the ultra-high-stakes games. Of course, Dewey was one of my "Magnificent Seven" golfers who seldom if ever choked when big money was on the line.

Introducing Dewey brought back memories of a roast that was held for me at the Bicycle Club Casino in the Los Angeles area in 1992. It was the first time I'd heard of any poker player getting roasted, so it was pretty special to me; elaborate, too, with ice sculptures and all the trimmings. A lot of people were there, including D.C. Andrews, my best friend from childhood, and Bill Scott, my basketball coach at Hardin-Simmons. My longtime friends Jack Binion and Sailor Roberts showed up, as well as almost all the old-time gamblers, and people like Bobby Baldwin, Lyle Berman, Chip Reese, and Mike Caro. Seven or eight people spoke, and I was really moved.

I remember Dewey relating old stories about our golfing exploits together. One time we were in Nashville playing a couple of high rollers named Willie and Sam, and they were killing us. They beat Dewey and me five days in a row and we were several hundred thousand dollars down. Dewey kept wanting to quit, go home and regroup, but I wouldn't let him.

"We're losing a lot of money and we can't beat them," he whined. "Let's get out of here."

"Nope, we're staying and getting our money back," I told him.

We just kept playing for ten more days, and finally we won our money back and then some. Dewey paid me one of gambling's supreme compliments. "Doyle," he said, "you've got the heart of a lion. I've never seen anything like it." Coming from one of my Magnificent Seven, that meant a lot.

Dewey also told about coming to Vegas years ago to test his golfing skills. He said he lost $15,000 to me, went home to Florida, worked on his game for a year, returned, and lost $96,000 more.

"Two times he broke me and sent me home to teach school," Dewey told the group. "But I got my bankroll up again and came back. We've had a lot of successful matches on golfing trips around the country." He recalled the time he won me more than a quarter-million dollars on six holes. "It's an exciting life," he laughed, "but nobody understands it because it's not real. They think we're nuts."

Louise was at the roast and she talked about her life with me and my gambler buddies: "It's been like riding the biggest Ferris wheel in the world," she said. "No, make that a roller coaster. There have been a few dips along the way."

One particular dip occurred almost ten years after the roast, and was really an eye-opener. In 2001, temporarily, my marriage took a hit. And as things often do, it was over something stupid. At least that was my opinion of the situation. It all started when I came in one night after a poker session, and Louise was still up.

"Honey, can you loan me $50,000 for a couple of weeks."

"Yes, sure," I told her.

It was an unusual request from Louise, but I didn't think too much about it and gave her the money. She was going to use it for a couple of weeks, then give it back to me when her rental checks came in. Louise always had her money separate from mine.

Two weeks pass, three weeks pass, four weeks pass—I hear nothing.

"Louise, did you forget about my $50,000?" I finally asked.

"No," she said, looking square at me.

"Well, are you going to give it back to me?"

"When hell freezes over!" She just stared at me with those cold, icy blue eyes of hers.

"What are you talking about?" I said, taken aback.

"You know what I mean," she said with an edge to her voice. Like all women, I could sense this was just total nonsense and I told her I had no idea what she was talking about.

"That girl called," she said, finally getting to the point.

"What girl?"

"That girl you've been having an affair with. The one that's carrying your baby. She called up here, and was crying and bawling, and told me she was pregnant by you."

I was more than a little stunned by this and reminded Louise of a little fact she had forgotten.

"Honey, you know it couldn't be so because you were right there when I had that vasectomy. Louise, someone's trying to blackmail us or something."

"Well, I know the baby's not yours, but she thinks it is."

This went on for two or three weeks and obviously I kept denying it. The girl even called back, but instead of getting an irate wife on the phone, Louise prayed for her. But she was still upset with me. It got to the point where my daughter Pam got involved as a mediator. I was sitting on the edge of the bed one evening reading a book when Pam came in the room with her mother.

There were a couple of long seconds of silence and a whole lot of tension in the room as they stood around. Finally, I looked up from my book to find out what they were up to.

"What is it, Pam?" I asked.

"Well, I think mom should forgive you," she said, "and I think you should promise not to do it anymore."

Boy, I jumped off that bed and said something I've never said before or since: "I swear on Doyla's grave that I'm innocent!"

My face must have been as red as a boiled lobster. That convinced them because they knew I would never make that kind of oath unless I was telling the absolute truth.

Louise never did give me back that $50,000.

★
Chapter 51

We don't stop playing because we get old; we get old because we stop playing.

In August of 2008, we had another basketball reunion, this time at my home in Montana. Seventeen of my teammates from 1950 to 1954 made it this time; of the other five that had come in 2004, three had died and two were having health problems. They came from as far away as Florida but most were from Texas. The youngest was seventy-one and the oldest, an army vet when he entered school, was eighty-two.

We spent three days together. The years rolled back and, except for a couple of earlier reunions, it was as though we hadn't been apart for over fifty years. The guys brought their wives and we had a terrific time. What a great group of people! We had a cookout on the lake each night and shared a lot of laughs and memories. We took rides on my pontoon boat that seats fifteen people. A couple of us rode my jet skis and I called the rest a bunch of wimps because they wouldn't get on them. Those things go sixty miles an hour and really give you a rush when you hit a few bumps in the water.

The reunion showed us how old we're getting. You realize you're as old as your classmates are, but some of them looked really old to me. Still being close after fifty-five years shows the special camaraderie about our team. Amazingly, only one of us has had a divorce, quite a record.

As I told Louise, "When we Texans make a commitment, we mean it."

The reunion also brought back other college memories. I'm often portrayed as a cowboy and the reality is not that far from the truth. Growing up, I used to ride horses and do some roping, an activity that intensified when I was in college. My basketball team lived in the same building as our two-time college national champion rodeo team and we got to hanging out with them. Dick Barrett, who won all kinds of national rodeo awards, was a good friend of mine, and we spent lots of time doing cowboy stuff.

We had a dummy calf named Buford set up for roping and I got pretty good at it. We stayed in touch, Dick and me, and he played in several WSOP tournaments.

Even today, I get reminded of basketball, my first true sports love, when I come home after a poker game. I felt it was kind of ironic when LeBron James bought a house two homes down from me. I've never run into him but, interestingly, the house between us is owned by Harold Miner who was known as "Baby Jordan" when he played in the NBA. Harold won the slam dunk contest at the NBA all-star game twice. Of course, LeBron is one of the game's top stars so there's lots of basketball history between our three houses. I understand LeBron is also an avid poker player.

⋄⋄⋄⋄⋄

In January of 2009, Hardin-Simmons University sent a letter informing me that I had at last been voted into the Athletic Hall of Fame. My name had been brought up to the selection committee twenty times previously and each time it was rejected. I knew that my credentials as an athlete during my college years certainly qualified me, but I was in a dilemma if I should accept. After all those years of being shunned because of my profession, I was torn between my pride in *finally* being accepted and my hurt at not being accepted a lot sooner.

Being overlooked for all those years had bothered me for a long time.

After some soul searching, the truth was that getting this nod of recognition was important to me, an honor that I'd always wanted. My induction completed the Longworth triangle of three kids from a little farming community in West Texas who grew up as friends from two or three years old, went through grade school, grammar school, high school and then college together, and ended up together in the Athletic Hall of Fame of a major university.

As 2009 came around, my life hadn't slowed down a bit. In the World Series of Poker Todd and I were quick exits and, once again, Pam was the last Brunson standing—much to her delight. But the tournament action wasn't the big story. Nothing could compare with the high-stakes side games at the end of the '09 series—they were in the outer stratosphere. Three players from Finland and two from France joined our local pros in the biggest games imaginable. Pots over a million dollars were common. The main game was pot-limit Omaha and all these guys were among the best players in the world. That game lasted about a month. I won't go into the specifics of winning and losing, but I can verify that Finland is much richer than it used to be.

The Chinese poker games were also huge, the biggest in history. We played as high as $20,000 a point. At one time, I had a $2.1 million swing in about one hour. That's gambling!

Actually, I yearn for those earlier, simpler days. Well, maybe not those days back on Exchange Avenue or dealing with psychopaths like Tincy Eggleston or Tony Spilotro—I could live without those dangers—but I couldn't live without the excitement. Yet the simplicity of those days sounds appealing to me, especially since the poker boom has caught me up right in the middle of all the hullabaloo. I'm busy all the time.

I almost wish I wasn't involved in all these ventures, even though I've made a lot of money and have truly enjoyed certain aspects of it. It's just that I've come to wonder if it's been worth it. You can only sleep in one bed; you can only drive one car. You only need one house, and I've got two, counting my lake home in Montana. When I look back at what my life was like twenty years ago, and then look at what it is now, I get sick. No life is as good as being a pro poker player with no other concerns!

So why am I doing all these things?

If I couldn't compete anymore and get those juices flowing, I think I'd just dry up and die.

There's another question I sometimes ponder: What if I lose my edge and can't win anymore? Then I'll know my opponents are too good for me, and I would realize it's time to move down to whatever level I can compete and win. It's a hard thing to drop in levels, but winning is very important to me. And if I can't win, I'm going to quit.

I reflect sometimes on Johnny Moss. He had as great a love for poker as anyone who ever lived. Poker was his life—and except for women maybe, he had no outside interests. You know, Moss lost everything playing poker. He played past his prime and gave it all back, everything he ever won.

Playing too long happens to most poker players. I've seen it happen a thousand times. Players get too old and they lose their edge. Like boxers, they stay in the game past their prime, and the next generation takes its thunder from the guys who were once champions. I know the reality of going out broke is a possibility, but I try to protect against it by self-examination. After every poker game, I go home at night and replay the hands in my mind. I remember all of them and give myself an appraisal of how I did, especially after a losing session.

Did I play badly? Did I make the right decisions? I evaluate my play constantly.

Still, there's always the possibility that I might go broke and never be able to come back. Most poker players do go broke a time or two during their careers. Personally, I must have gone broke one hundred times in my life, maybe more—but not since 1977, four years after I arrived in Vegas. I won't ever be destitute though, because of Louise. She's wealthy in her own right. I've also got opportunities those other guys didn't have— endorsements, public appearances, and I can write books.

People wonder sometimes if I ever ask God to let me win a bet. Never, but after a loss, I do find solace in the Christian teachings. I'm able to remind myself that this loss is unimportant in the grand scheme of life. I do not set as good an example as I would like, but I'm better than I was.

I'm often asked about the difficulty of someone in my profession being a Christian. I avoid those kinds of discussions. I only talk with people I feel are genuinely interested in what I have to say about my Christian experience, and what I did to get to the point where I am now. Everyone's entitled to his own beliefs, and I personally don't think I'm doing anything wrong by gambling. Some of the finest and most honorable people I've ever known have been in the upper echelon of the gambling world. Their word is their bond.

I've been fortunate to go longer than most; in fact, I think a major claim to my fame is my longevity and I'd like to be remembered as a player who played high-stakes poker longer than any player ever has. Even today, at seventy-six years old, long past when most people retire, I'm proud to say I still compete in the highest games I can find. I suppose it's possible that I'm not quite as sharp as I once was—and some days I might feel my age and don't care to play as long as I used to—but there's still plenty left in my tank, plenty of good years ahead of me. I suppose one day that will all change, but I don't know when that day might come.

I can't make that same longevity claim in golf, but it's a sport I've loved ever since I first got on the course back in the sixties. I use a crutch to walk, but I can still match up with these young gamblers on the greens, and I hope I can play until I die. And what better place to draw your last breath than on a good golf course!

The similarity between athletics and gambling has always been striking to me. They both trigger the same exciting rush, which I'm sure is what has lured me to the poker table day after day. Even after I broke my leg, I still craved competition. A big poker game provided a euphoric jolt similar to my big basketball games, and I think that might have contributed to my good health.

It may sound strange, but to some degree I attribute my overall good health to poker, and my poker longevity to my health.

I believe that my competitive spirit keeps me going physically as well as mentally. Until the age of sixty, I could remember every basketball game I played in college, plus the names of everyone I played with and the starters on the opposing team. I remembered how many points I scored and most of the baskets I made. That is how vivid some things are to me. Such recollections have begun to fade, but I can still remember the names of most of the players I played against in the big games in high school and college.

Some people have a photographic memory; I don't, but I'm close. Pretty much all the top poker players have terrific *recall*, a poker term that describes the ability to remember hands, situations, or players from the past. It makes the difference between good players and great ones.

How long can I keep playing at a high level? When will I lose my edge? I don't rightly know, but today, as I write these words, there is no slowing down for me. I'm still hungry for that win every time I play, and I still love playing in the Big Game. Sometimes, my poker-playing friends would tease me about my age, saying I had lost 10 percent of my game. Well, maybe that was true, but I like to tell them that I was 30 percent ahead of everybody else to start with.

Taking it careful, going slow, being conservative—that's not my mentality—nor is it the mentality of a real poker player. Risk is a part of my life and it's always been that way. At heart, I'm a gambler and I can't help myself.

Everything I have is ready to play.

Chapter 52

Be yourself. Who else is better qualified?

I 've come to realize that life's experiences are ours to keep and cherish. Permanent gifts, like diamonds that sparkle in your head. When I journey back to my college years at Hardin-Simmons, it's as if I can remember it all, the games, the glory, the shots I made, the shots I missed. It all plays out again, brand new, on a basketball court in my mind. Everyone's there, my friends, my teammates, the crowds. Those vivid memories have been with me for years. So real, so cherished.

I feel you own your experiences. They are yours to keep. What you do now will become a permanent part of you. The good things and the bad things. Think about that as you go through life. I can't tell you that the cards you're dealt will be the ones you want, but whatever they turn out to be, play them wisely, and honestly, and with passion and pleasure. That's the secret.

I believe we're given the freedom to live our lives pretty much as we choose. Looking back, I couldn't seem to get certain things quite right. An injury cut short my athletic career, my one and only job out of college was a joke, and a bad one to boot. My ill-fated investments speak for themselves.

Maybe poker *was* my path to greater awareness after all and it was intended for me to be a poker player.

As I grow older, I've found that time tends to gild those problems that might not have been so special in the making. For instance, the blurred days and sleepless nights and surviving the battles in North Fort Worth, the ever-present mix of vulgarity and violence—even those times are sprinkled with fond and unforgettable memories.

It's hard to believe it's been a half of a century since Louise and I started our life together in Texas. It seems like yesterday that Todd, Pam, and Cheryl were children. Now they are grown and I'm blessed that they have turned out so well. It has been a real adventure and all the experiences, good and bad, blend into incredible remembrances.

I think back on why I embraced poker in the first place. It was always challenging, exciting, and rewarding, an ongoing educational and emotional adventure that continues to this day. And I am thankful that I chose my own path or at least followed the path chosen for me and embraced the opportunities that came my way. I still play poker because it energizes me and keeps me thinking young. Sure, the money is part of my motivation, but there's also the adrenaline rush you get when that last card is turned over, that slight hesitation while your brain takes in all the information, and the thrill of victory if the pot is pushed your way.

But I chose the profession of poker for another reason. I play poker because of the freedom. I am my own boss, set my own hours, choose my own friends, and select my own adversaries. I feel as free as a fluffy white cloud floating in a bright blue sky. That's the most beautiful part of being a gambler, the freedom....

And the memories.

Epilogue

Skating on thin ice is better than skating on no ice at all.

Gamblers are supposed to be unemotional and calculating people capable of handling any situation. I suppose I fit in there pretty well, with one exception. When I start talking about losing my friends and family I can't help getting tears in my eyes. That was one of the concerns I had about writing this book, along with all the criticism I'm bound to get. But after careful thought I decided to bury my feelings and do it.

A lingering mystery in my life is linked to that spring night in 1998 when the two masked intruders invaded our home and threatened to kill Louise and me. To my knowledge, they were never caught. But I'm less interested in their identity than I am just curious to know if they ever cashed the $90,000 in $5,000 chips they took from me. When the change of ownership at the Horseshoe occurred a few years ago, lots of people exchanged chips for cash. I imagine that's what the robbers did.

But it's just something I've always wondered about, since they spurned the $500 chips they found in my pocket.

I know this will also sound strange, but I'm thankful the robbers were professionals. They didn't harm Louise, and while they did bang me up pretty good, they did no real, lasting physical harm. From their perspective, I probably deserved to be beaten because I refused to give them the code to disengage the alarm. It prevented them from looting the house or doing whatever they intended to do. There's not a lot of good that can be said about that horrible night, but at least the robbers were not a couple of cheap sadistic thugs. How many times have we read about home invaders who torture or kill their victims?

The person I'd really like to get my hands on is the scurvy bastard who sent them out to our home in the first place.

A magazine writer later wrote about the robbery and posed a funny question: "How do you play against a gambler who's not afraid to bluff with his own life?"

In all honesty, what I did was more dangerous than brave. For the most part, I was simply responding to my gambler's instincts. I had forgotten about the $90,000, so I thought I had no real money to give them. I just decided to face the consequences early by not giving them the code.

On the other hand, Louise deserved the press she got for her bravery. I'm still thunderstruck by her performance. I've always known she was courageous and caring and a very special person, and no doubt her faith in the Lord played a substantial role in her actions that night. Her jumping in front of that gun and telling the guy to kill her instead of me was amazing.

The robber was stunned.

And so was I—maybe the wrong Brunson was playing for high stakes at the poker tables. Louise said afterward she *thought* they might kill both of us but she *knew* they intended to kill me.

The bottom line was that we survived, that we didn't get seriously hurt. But it was a defining moment in our lives. We moved out of that house the next night. We were already in the process of building a new home and we simply moved in before it was completed. The security system is topnotch. An armed officer routinely follows me home whenever I pass through the security gate. He remains outside until I enter the house and wave.

I also carry a gun now.

I don't intend for my home or my family to be subjected to a nightmare like that again. God forbid that a similar incident should occur, but if it does it will be like an Exchange Avenue shootout if I've got even a fifty-fifty chance of getting them before they get me.

One of the worst things about that night was the action, or inaction, of the security alarm company. We took them to court and got a hefty settlement, and we would have gotten even more if we'd gone on to trial. But the events of that evening traumatized Louise to a certain extent and we just wanted to get it behind us. I think the memories upset her more than the actual robbery. She is hesitant about going outside at night. She wears a device around her neck when I'm not at home and she can trigger an alarm if anything happens.

I'm not minimizing what occurred, but it didn't affect me as traumatically because I'd been exposed to violence on many occasions—just not quite so personally. And if that was my day to meet my Maker, so be it.

I could look back even then and say, "Wow, what a ride!"

TEXAS DOLLY

My Father is a gambler,
a legend in his time.
Born in the west Texas Bible Belt,
he grew up strong and fine.

He was a star athlete in college,
majoring in business, basketball, and track,
until a freak construction accident
put him flat on his back.

Two years on crutches
brought his athletic dreams to an end.
The magnitude of his injury meant
his leg may never properly mend.

Disappointed and frustrated
with this turn of events,
he focused on his studies,
and played poker to pay the rent.

In spite of this heartbreaking tragedy,
he adjusted just fine,
becoming the youngest to earn a master's degree
from Hardin-Simmons at the time.

There were several job offers after graduation,
but none paid nearly as well
as those night time marathon poker games
that some said would lead him straight to hell.

At six foot four, weighing in at two hundred and twenty pounds,
this bachelor was quite a ladies man.
That is, until a blue eyed, southern belle, pharmacist
was dealt into his hand.

He was so in love wild horses
couldn't have kept him from marrying Lou,
even though she came with a large package,
Grandma, puppy, and darling daughter, me, too.

Some said he was kind hearted
to take on such a clan,
but I think he was darn lucky
to find so much love waiting for one man.

He told Louise he was a Bookmaker,
and she was ever so proud,
confident that he could plan a secure future
with this accounting background.

Our family was so happy
that a baby was on the way.
It seemed life couldn't get much better,
until that awful day.

Dad discovered a small mole
growing on his neck.
Diagnosed as malignant melanoma,
our lives were suddenly a wreck.

The doctors wasted no time before operating
in an effort to save his life.
They took what they could, sewed him up,
and broke the bad news to his wife.

They said he would not live
to see his first child born.
Mom should take care of business,
and the family should prepare to mourn.

Instead she started prayer groups,
refusing to give up hope.
She flew him to M.D. Anderson Hospital
where they put him through the ropes.

They agreed to operate again.
We would not give up without a fight,
but when they opened him up
the cancer was nowhere in sight.

Everyone declared it a miracle
that God had saved this man.
He would live to see his daughter Doyla born,
and he would get to play out his hand.

It's no wonder that his career took off,
nothing could hold him back.
He had stared death in the face and won,
against all odds, in fact.

Two more children were born into our home,
and life was never the same.
A daughter, Pam, to add much joy and love,
and a son, Todd, to carry on the Brunson name.

They called Dad Texas Dolly,
and the name seemed to stick.
When it came to choosing favorites,
he was everybody's pick.

II

He moved the family to Vegas,
and set about his game.
Two World Championship Poker winnings,
and eight additional gold bracelets,
brought him much notoriety and fame.

Once more our family was devastated
when our darling Doyla died.
They say if grief doesn't kill you,
it will make you stronger inside.

Commentators often refer to him as
"The Godfather of Poker", rightly named
due to his longevity, popularity
and his genuine love of the game.

He has seen poker evolve
from a seedy back room game,
into an International Sport played by millions
seeking money, notoriety, and fame.

Texas Dolly is an Icon.
He has won, and lost with the best.
His books will give you some insight,
and teach you strategies that you can test.

If you know anything about gamblers,
you know that their word is their bond.
If you find one that doesn't have honor
he won't be around very long.

Texas Dolly sits down at the poker table
with honor, and class every time.
My father is a gambler,
A Legend For All Time!

Written for my Dad with Love,
by Cheryl

★
About the Authors

Avery Cardoza is the author of *Lost in Las Vegas*, a fast-paced comedy-thriller about two hapless Las Vegas vacationers who find themselves broke, homeless, and hunted by vicious killers as their lives spiral out of control. He is a million-selling author of twenty-one books and the former editor-in-chief of *Player*, a national men's lifestyle magazine.

Mike Cochran spent most of his four decades with the Associated Press roving Texas, particularly West Texas, and reporting on many of the nation's top stories. They included the JFK assassination, the Oswald slaying and funeral, the Ruby trial, and the U.S. Space Program, including the Apollo 11 moon-landing mission and the Challenger and Columbia Shuttle explosions. Selected ten times as the Texas AP Staffer of the Year, he has won six Headliner awards, two Stanley Walker journalism awards, the AP's international feature writing award and was a three-time nominee for the Pulitzer Prize. He entered the Texas Intercollegiate Press Association Hall of Fame in 2004. In 2008, he was honored by the Texas Associated Press Managing Editors for distinguished service and contributions to Texas journalism. And then in 2009 he was invited to join the state's most prestigious literary organization, the Texas Institute of Letters.

He's the author of *Texas vs. Davis*, the definitive book on the murder case of millionaire T. Cullen Davis, and *Deliver Us From Evil*, a trilogy of true-crime stories, which was the inspiration for a CBS Television movie, *Fugitive Among Us*, starring Eric Roberts and Peter Strauss. With an AP colleague, John Lumpkin, he co-authored the book *West Texas*. As a senior writer for the *Fort Worth Star-Telegram*, he wrote the text for the newspaper's book on the Fort Worth tornadoes, *Shattered*, which won a Katie award in 2000. Cochran's most recent book was *Claytie,* the biography of millionaire Texas rancher-wildcatter-politico Clayton Williams Jr., published in 2007.

Cochran, a 1958 graduate of the University of North Texas, grew up in the small West Texas town of Stamford and is married to his high school sweetheart, Sondra. The couple lives in Fort Worth.

Mike Blackman, an editor-researcher on this book, is the Fred Hartman Professor of Journalism at Baylor University. A retired editor and vice president of the Fort Worth Star-Telegram, Blackman edited Mike Cochran's biography of Clayton Williams. He grew up in the oil fields of West Texas near Doyle Brunson's hometown of Longworth and remembers the basketball exploits of Brunson's Hardin-Simmons Cowboys in the early fifties. He holds degrees from Baylor and Ohio State..

PHOTO CREDITS

In addition to photos from the family albums, we would like to acknowledge and thank the following:

Photo of Tincy Eggleston, Courtesy, Fort Worth Star-Telegram Collection, Special Collections, The University of Texas at Arlington Library, Arlington, Texas.

Photo of Amarillo Slim–Johnny Moss–Benny Binion, and Tony Spilotro–Oscar Goodman, courtesy, University of Nevada, Las Vegas—Special Collections.

Hall of Fame Honors
& Bracelets

HALL OF FAME HONORS

World Series of Poker Hall of Fame
Texas Poker Hall of Fame
Seniors Poker Hall of Fame
Commerce Walk of Fame
Tropicana Vegas Legends Hall of Fame
Hardin-Simmons University Hall of Fame

WORLD SERIES OF POKER GOLD BRACELETS

1976	$5,000 Deuce-to-Seven Draw
1976	$10,000 No-Limit Hold'em Main Event Championship
1977	$1,000 Seven-Card Stud Split
1977	$10,000 No-Limit Hold'em Main Event Championship
1978	$5,000 Seven-Card Stud
1979	$600 Mixed Doubles (with Starla Brodie)
1991	$2,500 No-Limit Hold'em
1998	$1,500 Razz
2003	$2,000 H.O.R.S.E.
2005	$5,000 No-Limit Shorthanded Texas Hold'em

INDEX

INDEX

INDEX

INDEX